READING THE TWO BOOKS OF GOD

"*Reading the Two Books of God* is a delightful companion through the times of the year: both calendar and liturgical. . . . Mann invites the reader into deeper consideration of aspects of nature and Christian Scripture that may have been skimmed as familiar or rudimentary. The reader is likely to experience both nature and Scripture differently after reading this offering."

—Anne Herndon, retired counseling psychologist

"Understanding his sermons in terms of Scripture and nature, Tom has gracefully woven his theology through them. In his sermons, you hear and see his love of nature and his profound understanding of the biblical Scriptures. . . . The ideas he gleans from the Bible, his garden, and his hikes are fresh and redemptive. This book makes the Bible meaningful and the earth integral to each day of our lives."

—Lucy A. Austin, retired pastoral counselor

"An extraordinary collection of sermons that engages the reader's imagination and intellect, *Reading the Two Books of God* integrates a spiritual sensuality of experience with a reverence for Scripture and theology (with a dash of gentle humor). . . . Mann challenges readers to a deep listening and a deep looking at time. Highly recommended—a superb and rare blend of scholarship, theological humility, and commitment to the goodness of the created world."

—Linda Browne, chaplain, Salemtowne Retirement Community

"*Reading the Two Books of God* is an extraordinary gift to religious leaders and others who seek to hear God through the words of ancient poets and prophets and through the whispers, thunders, and 'wow'-inducing ordinariness of canyons, deserts, oceans, mountains, and neighborhood backyards. Each sermon invites readers to proclaim 'glory' and then head outdoors to experience that 'glory' with Scripture in their hearts and minds and the sacred dirt of God's good earth under their feet."

—Jill Y. Crainshaw, Wake Forest University School of Divinity

"*Reading the Two Books of God* is a compelling argument for not reading Scripture and nature as though they had nothing to do with one another but understanding each in light of the wisdom offered by the other. . . . This beautifully written book will enrich both readers' faith and their commitment to social justice for God's good but imperiled earth."

—George W. Stroup, Columbia Theological Seminary, emeritus

Reading the Two Books of God

Sacred Time and Place in Nature and History

Thomas W. Mann

CASCADE *Books* • Eugene, Oregon

READING THE TWO BOOKS OF GOD
Sacred Time and Place in Nature and History

Copyright © 2022 Thomas W. Mann. All rights reserved. Except for brief quotations in critical publications or reviews, no part of this book may be reproduced in any manner without prior written permission from the publisher. Write: Permissions, Wipf and Stock Publishers, 199 W. 8th Ave., Suite 3, Eugene, OR 97401.

Cascade Books
An Imprint of Wipf and Stock Publishers
199 W. 8th Ave., Suite 3
Eugene, OR 97401

www.wipfandstock.com

PAPERBACK ISBN: 978-1-6667-1985-7
HARDCOVER ISBN: 978-1-6667-1986-4
EBOOK ISBN: 978-1-6667-1987-1

Cataloguing-in-Publication data:

Names: Mann, Thomas W., author.

Title: Reading the two books of God : sacred time and place in nature and history / Thomas W. Mann.

Description: Eugene, OR: Cascade Books, 2022. | Includes bibliographical references.

Identifiers: ISBN 978-1-6667-1985-7 (paperback). | ISBN 978-1-6667-1986-4 (hardcover). | ISBN 978-1-6667-1987-1 (ebook).

Subjects: LSCH: Nature—Religious aspects—Christianity. | Nature—Biblical teaching. | Sermons, American—21st Century.

Classification: BV4253 M34 2022 (print). | BV4253 (ebook).

Unless otherwise noted, Scripture quotations come from the New Revised Standard Version Bible, copyright © 1989, Division of Christian Education of the National Council of the Churches of Christ in the United States of America. Used by permission. All rights reserved.

Scripture quotations marked (JPS) are from *The Jewish Study Bible*, © 2004, Oxford University Press, including the Jewish Publication Society *Tanakh: The New JPS Translation According to the Traditional Hebrew Text*. Copyright © 1985, 1999 by The Jewish Publication Society with the permission of the publisher.

Figure 1a: Steeple photo courtesy of i.Stock.com/rickschroeppel.

Figure 1b: Kiva, © 1940, Bandelier National Monument, photo courtesy of National Park Service. Used by permission.

Figure 2: Replica of the Mesad Hashavyahu Ostracon Photo courtesy of GU-theolog (Wikimedia Commons: https://commons.wikimedia.org/w/index.php?curid=9711232/.)

Figure 3: Plumb line photo courtesy of iStock.com/ezza116.

Figure 4: A stained glass window depicting the biblical Tree of Life, courtesy of the Reverend Craig Schaub.

In memory of Constance Weigle Mann
1947–2014

Contents

Preface | xiii
Acknowledgments | xix

PART 1: THE CIRCUIT OF THE SUN

Introduction: Jacob's Pillow | 3
Beach Time | 11
The Woods in Winter | 15
Seedtime and Harvest | 19
Spiritual Phenomena: Making Sense | 26
Rivers in the Desert | 37

Constructing Sacred Space

Tent or Temple? | 43
The Steeple and the *Sipapu* | 53
Tree House Sanctuary | 59

In the Backcountry

Sierra Nevada: Ant Assaults Mount Everest | 65
Message from Taboose Pass: Wilderness Pedagogy | 72
Huntfish Falls: Vagabond Stew | 81
Wind River: Beef Stick and Grace | 88
Wind River: Follow the Leader | 93

PART 2: THE CIRCUIT OF THE YEAR

Introduction: Jacob's Promise | 103

Advent

"Keep Awake!" | 109
"Here I Am" | 115

Getting Close to Home | 120
Getting Ready for Christmas | 128

Christmas Eve
The Stable Animals' Reunion | 133

Epiphany
A Kingdom of Kudzu and Crud | 141
Baptism of Christ: The Uncongealed Word | 147

Lent
Ash Wednesday: The Sting of Death | 155
Eat Less, Chew More | 162

Holy Week
Palm Sunday: Two Parades, Two Kings, Two Crowds | 167
Maundy Thursday / Passover: The Man with the Tattooed Arm | 176
Good Friday: The Passion of God | 188
Easter Laughter | 194

All Saints' Day
Watching Over One Who Grieves | 203
A Meeting in the Air | 207

Holidays
New Year's Day: A Time of Janus | 215
Martin Luther King Jr. Day: The View from the Mountaintop | 221
Excursus: Prophecy | 226
Earth Day: The Fungus among Us | 257
Independence Day / Thanksgiving Day: The Heart of a Pilgrim, the Mind of a Prophet | 265
Labor Day: Laboring on Labor Day | 273
Indigenous Peoples' Day / Columbus Day:
  How the Gibeonites Became Israelites | 278

EPILOGUE: The Two Books of God, Autobiographically | 287

Bibliography | 291

Preface

How do you "tell time"? Children (long ago) used to learn how to do that by observing the hands on a clock. Now, of course, there are all sorts of digital devices that show the time of day, as well as the date, and a lot more. But the time that is told by the hands (or digital face) of a watch is only one dimension of time. When someone says, "I had the time of my life," it often has nothing to do with minutes and hours but a joyous emotional experience. The time was existentially "momentous," a moment not so much to be calibrated as celebrated—in a sense, timeless.

This book will focus on the time of our lives as it is shaped by two forms of scripture—the Bible and creation, the latter being the "other book of God." You may ask, since when are there *two* books of God? Most people can probably understand why the Bible could be called the book of God—indeed, the Good Book. Judaism can claim original authorship of the Bible, tracing it back to the book of the Torah attributed to Moses. Fittingly, Muslims named the Jewish people "the people of the book." Of course, Muslims have their own sacred book, the Qur'an, and adherents of other religions hold other books sacred (e.g., Hindus have the Upanishads). All these texts fit the common understanding of what a book is—a collection of writings on paper between a front cover and a back cover (contemporary electronic versions aside).

To be inclusive, we could refer to all of these nonbiblical texts as books of God, but they are not the subject of *this* book. Rather, the second book of God in what follows is nature (or, to use its theological counterpart, the creation), traditionally called the Other Book of God. In the third century of our era Saint Anthony the Great (251–356), one of the desert fathers, was asked by a visiting philosopher how such a learned man as he got along in the desert without books. Anthony replied, "My book is the nature of created things, and as often as I have a mind to read the words of God, they are at my hand." Not long after that, Saint Augustine (354–430) also identified nature as an alternative scripture: "Some people, in order to discover God, read books. But there is a great book: the very appearance of created things. Look above you! Look below you! Note it. Read it. God, whom you want to discover, never wrote that book with ink. Instead, He set before your eyes the things that He had made. Can you ask for a louder voice than that? What, heaven and earth shout to you, 'God made me!'"[1]

So, the two books of God in what follows are the Bible and nature. Identifying nature as a book of God has by no means been limited to ancient writers like Augustine. For example, as one scholar notes, John Wesley, the founder of Methodism, "affirms that God's Word is revealed in two books—the Book of Scripture and the Book of Nature." He continues, "Nature, or creation, is revelatory of important aspects of truth about God."[2] What Wesley called "natural philosophy" included our knowledge of the world as gleaned by the science of his day. Moreover, readers of the book of nature are not limited to ecclesiastical figures. Some of the most articulate readers are naturalist writers and poets. Gerard Manley Hopkins was a reader: "The world is charged with the grandeur of God."[3] John Muir, one of the most eloquent—one could even say evangelistic—writers about nature called it "the divine manuscript."[4] Ken Burns's PBS series on the US national parks opened with the episode titled "The Scripture of Nature," and much of that episode appropriately recited the writings of Muir.[5]

Wendell Berry's classic poem "The Peace of Wild Things" provides an eloquent example of someone reading the "other book of God." Berry describes how in "despair for the world" he goes to a body of "still water," where "the wood drake / rests in his beauty on the water." There his "despair *for* the world" is relieved by "the grace *of* the world," and he is "free."[6] This place and time are spiritually significant because Berry experienced there a moment of healing, grace, and peace. When he sees the wood

---

1. Sermon 126.6, https://www.orth-transfiguration.org/st-augustine-354-430/. See also https://www.interfaithsustain.com/opening-the-book-of-nature-creation-ecology-and-economy/.

2. Mann, "Wesley," 30, 11.

3. Hopkins, "God's Grandeur."

4. Muir, *Nature Writings*, 228.

5. Burns, dir., *National Parks: America's Best Idea* (3-episode miniseries).

6. Berry, *Collected Poems*, 69 (italics added).

drake resting on the water, it brings *him* rest. No particularly religious language is used, nor is it needed, but many of his other poems would support the conclusion that the grace of *God* is mediated by the "grace of the world" which God has created, the peace of God mediated by the "peace of wild things"—as he says elsewhere, "the holy Spirit in the air."[7]

Beauty is at the center of this poem—the natural beauty of a bird floating on a pond. As one theologian suggests, "Beauty is the core of the experience that opens people to God."[8] I think that is because the beauty of nature intimates the artist who created it. Nature is "creation." Such experiences often are the subject of the book of nature, not only for theologians, artists, and poets, but scientists. As Paul Davies suggests, "all great scientists are inspired by the subtlety and beauty of the natural world . . . the universe is intrinsically beautiful."[9]

What follows will focus on the ways in which our sense of time and place is shaped by the two books of God. Part 1 will focus on ways in which experiences in natural places stimulate theological reflections. In some cases, the place itself (geography) is integral to the experience (e.g., "Sierra Nevada"); in others, the place is incidental, simply the location where the experience took place (e.g., "Beef Stick and Grace"). Part 2 will focus on the book of Scripture as it is employed by the Revised Common Lectionary of the Church, supplemented by secular holidays.

The Bible shapes our sense of time partly because historical events reported there undergird the annual lectionary of liturgical readings, from Advent through Pentecost, largely focused on the life of Jesus and the beginnings of the Church; nature shapes our sense of time with its cyclical seasons from winter to spring, summer, and fall, or (agriculturally) from seedtime to harvest. Corresponding to the temporal milieu there is also the spatial: the Bible and the lectionary emphasize places of historical (and sometimes political) interest—Egypt, Canaan, Mt. Sinai, Jerusalem, Babylon, Corinth, Rome. Nature's places are ahistorical—mountain, desert, forest, wilderness.

The different notions of time and place render different evaluations of holiness, of what is sacred. Consider a river. In the Biblical tradition, the Jordan River is prominent. Its significance lies in that it is the

---

7. Berry, *Timbered Choir*, 91. The title of the book (repeated in a line on page 83) suggests that trees sing in praise of the Spirit, just as the psalmists say they do (Ps 96:12; 148:9). The trees are "Apostles of the living light." See also n. 12 (below).

8. Austin, *Beauty of the Lord*, 35.

9. Davies, *God and the New Physics*, 220.

boundary of the land of Canaan (the "Holy Land"), which the Israelites crossed after their exodus from Egypt; or it is significant because it is where John the Baptist baptized Jesus (tour guides will show you the spot). Of course, the Jordan River can assume more ethereal significance, as in the old hymn "On Jordan's Stormy Banks," where Canaan's "fair and happy land" is no longer a geographical territory but heaven. So, the Jordan River can be a political boundary in ordinary space and time, or it can be a spiritual boundary, referring to a reality that is beyond space and time. What we might call our biblical "river spirituality" lives within the tension represented by Canaan as geographical territory and Canaan as spiritual realm, and it is unwise to break the tension and live only on one side. Fixating on Canaan as heaven can lead us to abandon "geopolitics," in which freedom is the foundation for justice; fixating on Canaan as political territory can lead to a militant and exclusive nationalism.

But "river spirituality" also includes our reading of the book of nature. In nature's realm, a river is significant for any number of reasons having nothing to do with historic events, but because it is the source of water and food, making life itself possible, or simply because it is beautiful, and can generate an awesome waterfall (Niagara, Yosemite). The spiritual significance may apply to other bodies of water, such as a lake or the ocean, or just a local pond, as in Berry's poem. Historic places are sacred because of events that happened there; natural places are sacred because of what *is* there, which is to say that something about the place itself *mediates* the sacred.

Just so, a river may become sacred not because of an event in history, but simply because of its intrinsic qualities *as* river. People don't raft down the Colorado River, through the Grand Canyon, because John Wesley Powell did (although they may be inspired by his story); they do so because such rafting is an exciting adventure, especially when there are class-4 rapids involved, and because the canyon is visually an incredibly beautiful, awe-inspiring place. Many visitors to the Grand Canyon find it to be a *spiritual* experience. Even Richard Dawkins, the self-proclaimed atheist, has said that when he looks at the Grand Canyon, "'I am overwhelmingly filled with a sense of *almost worship*.'"[10] Much the same could be said of most national parks. Although many people may not articulate it this way, when we say that the experience is awe-inspiring it evokes theological interpretation in two ways: awe, and an encounter with the

---

10. Quoted in Fideler, *Breakfast with Seneca*, 202 (transcribed from a video clip; italics Fideler's).

sublime, are at the heart of an experience of the holy (see the Introduction that follows), and the primary meaning of the word *inspire* is "To affect . . . by divine influence."[11] Inspiration implies Spirit. Almost any land may be valued as "holy land" when one experiences there the spiritual presence of the One who created it in all its wild beauty, from the vastness of a canyon to the wood drake on that small, still pond. The 18th century theologian Jonathan Edwards was acutely attuned to such aesthetics, and could even extend his reflections christologically: "'the beauties of nature are really emanations or shadows of the excellencies of the Son of God.'"[12]

So-called nature poets like Berry are some of the most eloquent expositors of creation spirituality. In one of her poems, Mary Oliver encounters a fawn in the midst of the woods, and she asks the question, "what is holiness?"[13] Clearly, for her the encounter itself is holy, a sacred time, and thereby the woods become sacred place. As she says elsewhere, "The door to the woods is the door to the temple."[14] Her question is key to exploring the "books of God." Like the Bible, creation's scripture may deserve the adjective "holy" as well, not as an intrinsic quality, but as a mediatorial function that points to the One who is beyond the text. Experiences like Berry's at the water or Oliver's in the woods are sacramental, conveying through nature the reality of spiritual healing.

I do not intend to oppose one dimension of time and place over against another, much less the books of God. They can be complementary. Indeed, in what follows, they are *always* in conversation. For example, "Beach Time" is informed by Sabbath time, "Beef Stick and Grace" by manna from heaven. Psalm 19 provides a good model of how both nature and Scripture work together: the heavens fill us with awe by "telling the glory of God." The time frame here is structured by the "circuit of the sun." And the Torah enriches our life, "reviving the soul." The time frame here is primarily rooted in the *narrative* of the Torah, providing the basis for the liturgical circuit of the year in both the Jewish and Christian communities. The phrase "time frame" is suggestive here in that the circuit of

---

11. *American Heritage College Dictionary* 4th ed. (2002), s.v. "inspire."

12. Quoted in Austin, *Baptized into Wilderness*, 12. Similarly, for Muir, the majestic trees of the Sierras proclaimed "the gospel of beauty," and, as with Berry, they are "apostles" (Austin, *Baptized into Wilderness*, 67; see n. 7, above).

13. Oliver, "The Fawn," in *Twelve Moons*, 13. I have explored Oliver's reading of the other book of God in Mann, *God of Dirt*.

14. Oliver, *Upstream*, 154.

the sun and the circuit of the liturgical year frame our spiritual experience. The time of our lives is both; we live by two spiritual calendars.

What follows is a collection of sermons. If you are now reading this second sentence in the paragraph, perhaps you have not succumbed to our culture's disparagement of the genre of sermon or of preaching or lectures. All three words—*sermon, preaching,* and *lecture*—can be used pejoratively—as in, "Don't preach to me!" (or, worse, "*at* me!"); and, "I don't need to be lectured by you." I once read a film review that grew increasingly critical until the reviewer finally lamented that the substance of the film had fully degenerated into a "sermon." John Muir held no such prejudice. He was one of those who could hear nature's voices, and he enjoyed listening to "grasshopper sermons" and "plant people preaching."[15] I do not like being referred to as a preacher, because the word narrowly defines what ministers do, but preaching is still at the heart of much worship, and, I argue, good preaching is rooted in the two books of God.

---

15. Muir, *Nature Writings*, 161, 233.

Acknowledgments

I am grateful to the congregation of Parkway United Church of Christ who provided a community of liberal-minded people more interested in asking provocative questions about faith than following dogmatic answers. Two from Parkway are my unofficial archivists whose preserving and even rereading old sermons encouraged me to put together this collection, Janice Huesman and Genie Carter. Genie even provided star ratings! I also thank Jan Sawyer, who assembled a kind of focus group who provided helpful comments about the manuscript. Also, Jan's piano skills (along with those of Genie) always ensured that a service would be inspiring no matter what I said. Another parishioner, Dr. Anne Herndon, has been supportive in numerous ways since my first visit to Winston-Salem. She has read the entire manuscript, and brought to it her experience as a psychotherapist, as well as her extensive knowledge of spirituality. Finally, The Rev. Dr. George Stroup has been a colleague and friend for over fifty years. George is a systematic theologian whose wisdom has helped enormously. His extensive comments and questions about the manuscript have sharpened my argument, especially when he challenged my interpretations. Moreover, the friendship between his family and my family has been a blessing for many years.

    I have dedicated this book in memory of my wife, Connie, partly because she not only had to listen to most of the contents of this book, but especially because she was always my best editor. She would often acquiesce to my request to read a manuscript before Sunday, and give me her thoughts. Her reading was informed by her liberal arts education at St. Johns College (Santa Fe), and a year at Yale Divinity School, but more so by her intelligence, common sense, and compassion. Her favorite criticism was to say, "That's one of those Yale words," by which she did not mean any disparagement of that university, where she had deep family connections, but a recognition that a word like, say, *ontology*, would be nonsensical to anyone without a divinity school degree. It was a reminder that I was not lecturing to graduate students in a PhD class on Hebrew Bible. I once heard a parishioner say, "Thank God for Connie Mann." But he didn't say that because he knew that she had spared him from words like *ontology*; he said it because, like many others, he knew her as an embodiment of that spiritual quality that the prophet Micah told us God most wants from human beings—kindness.

PART 1

The Circuit of the Sun

Introduction: Jacob's Pillow

"We Are Climbing Jacob's Ladder" is one of my favorite spirituals. In my church we used to sing it while celebrating communion, accompanied by an autoharp or just a cappella. The spiritual is based on the story of Jacob, who, fleeing from his vengeful brother, spends the night in a place where he dreams of a ladder going up to heaven (Gen 28:10–22). The lyrics of the spiritual focus on the imagery of climbing the ladder, implicitly assuming that we, the singers, are doing that as well. "Every round goes higher, higher." Much as I love singing the spiritual, there is a problem with how it appropriates the story. In his dream Jacob doesn't climb the ladder; it's the "angels" who are climbing (and descending) on the ladder. Actually, the traditional translation of "ladder" itself is questionable. So, the NRSV provides a footnote that says "*stairway* or *ramp*." But I wouldn't suggest changing the words of the spiritual. Can you imagine singing "We are climbing Jacob's stairway"?

However, I would suggest that we shift our focus from the ladder to the object that plays a much more crucial role in the story—Jacob's pillow. Before falling asleep, Jacob takes a stone and puts it under his head. Getting the meter right is awkward, but we would sing, "Resting now on Jacob's pillow." This change would literally bring us down to earth, lying down on the ground rather than rising up to heaven. While we can appreciate why the composers of the spiritual—presumably slaves—would aspire to heaven (which could mean the North as well as the metaphysical reality), that is not the focus of the story. Instead, from the outset, the story focuses on the earthly site where Jacob encounters God.

The location in Hebrew is "the place," which the NRSV renders as "a certain place." The use of the definite article in Hebrew here is oddly premature, easily prompting us to inquire, "Wait, *what* place?" It would make more sense at the end of the story, when Jacob leaves. Standing at the outset, the description of the location alerts us to its centrality: *where the story "takes place" is the heart of the story*. In fact, the designation "the place," or "that place" or "this place," occurs three times in v. 11 and again in vv. 16–17. It's as if the author is a contemporary real estate agent advising us on the chief criterion for buying (and selling) a house: "location, location, location."

The Hebrew would be better rendered by "The Place." The definite article and capital letters suggest that this is *sacred* space. Place with a capital *P* signifies space that is charged with sacred significance because of a sacred Presence. The holiness of the place is represented by the stairway connecting heaven and earth. Trees and mountains can function the same way—rooted in the ground, but stretching into the sky. Such a connection is the *axis mundi* of folk stories, the center of the world. When Jacob awakes, he says, "Surely Yahweh is in this place—and I did not know it!" (my translation).[1] "And he was afraid, and said, 'How awesome is this place! This is none other than the house of God, and this is the gate of heaven'" (vv. 16–17). He sets up a "pillar" (i.e., a stele) and pours oil on it, not, of course, petroleum, but a scented vegetable oil used in anointing, thereby sanctifying the place. Then he names the place *beth-el*, meaning "house of God" (vv. 18, 22). Moreover, at the conclusion of the narrative, Jacob says that the stone which he has erected "shall be God's house" (v. 22). The story is a typical etiology, a narrative explanation of the origin of a sacred place and its sanctuary, well known from comparative religion.

"He was afraid, and said, 'How awesome is this place.'" Jacob's experience is a prime example of *religious* experience (or, for those disaffected by organized religion, of spirituality). The classic philosophical study here is Rudolf Otto's *The Idea of the Holy* (1923), in which he showed how the feeling of awe is a combination of both fear and fascination prompted by an encounter with the numinous, i.e., with a mysterious divine presence. It is important to acknowledge the fearsome dimension of encountering the holy; there is something ominous about the numinous. As one commentator on the Jacob story has noted, "What is meant originally is the power dwelling in the stone, its dynamic energy such as

---

1. Yahweh is the personal name of God that the NRSV renders as "the Lord," following Jewish tradition, which uses Adonai (literally "my lord"). The Hebrew consonants are *yhwh*. Traditional avoidance of writing or speaking the proper name derives from respect and reverence, much as one would not address a queen or president by their given names but instead as "Your Majesty" or "Madam President." I will occasionally use the name, with the recognition that, as the Tao Te Ching says, "The name that can be named is not the eternal Name."

can kill a person."[2] A similar distinction differentiates the beautiful from the sublime, for the latter involves the element of fear. As one author says, the "awesome splendor and magnetic power . . . [and] the radiance and glory of God are revealed in nature as well as in the greatest works of art, and neither are necessarily comforting or pretty."[3] We will see examples of the numinous throughout, e.g., in the natural phenomenon of a thunderstorm. But the positive side of fear is awe. Theologian Abraham Heschel's classic, *God in Search of Man: A Philosophy of Judaism*, has an entire chapter on awe. "*The beginning of awe is wonder,*" he writes, "*and the beginning of wisdom is awe . . . Awe is a sense for the transcendence, for the reference everywhere to Him who is beyond all things.*"[4] The fearsome dimension of the holy is a way of recognizing those key words, *transcendence* and *beyond*. We tend to think that wisdom is a rational faculty, but Heschel suggests that it starts with the *feeling* of awe. Just so, Jacob says, "how awesome is this place."

But note what has happened in the history of tradition, which will require a brief foray into biblical criticism. By "criticism" I do not mean criticizing; I mean analysis. Biblical criticism rightly observes that there are often multiple authors at work in texts, sometimes with different, conflicting, or even contradictory messages that they want to convey. Here the consensus of biblical critics is that a second author has inserted within the pillow story an *audition* story (vv. 13–14). God *speaks* to Jacob and promises to protect him on his journey and to give him the land of Palestine. A place in nature is supplanted by a place in history. Indeed, one could say that the spiritual significance of the natural space is repressed in deference to a geographical *territory*. In terms of time, the shift is from Jacob's personal experience with the awesome, numinous presence in nature to a theology of "God's acts in history," with all of its political complexity. The promise of land, previously announced to Jacob's father and grandfather, is a structural anchor for the ancestral narratives of Genesis, reappearing at numerous points (12:7; 26:1–5; 50:24). The horizon of the promise extends far beyond the context of the personal experiences of the characters to include the historical experience of the people of Israel and their claim to the land of Canaan, and the promise continues in the New Testament. The place of the stone pillow is natural;

---

2. Westermann, *Genesis 12–36*, 457.
3. Jensen, *Substance of Things Seen*, 81.
4. Heschel, *God in Search of Man*, 74–75 (italics original).

the land of the promise is territorial, including a range of connotations. Needless to say, the controversial political ramifications of the promise still haunt the land of Palestine.

It is remarkable (and fortunate) that the redactor who put together the dream story with the promise story retained the former. The retention is surprising in that erecting such pillars and suggesting that a stone can signify God's dwelling place are highly questionable in later biblical theology. "You shall not set up a stone pillar," God commands in Deuteronomy, something which "the LORD your God hates" (16:22; cf. 12:3–4). Jeremiah shames those who venerate a stone, thereby "committing adultery" (Jer 2:27; 3:9). Underlying these strictures is the fear of paganism—to coin a word, *lithophobia*.

The history of tradition in the Bethel story points to a fundamental problem that confounds the Christian community's relationship to nature. By and large we have heeded the warnings about paganism rather than identifying with Jacob's dream experience. The significance of the promise, and of historical time, has dominated Christian spirituality, sometimes to the extent of demeaning creational time. The linear time of history is deemed superior to the cyclical time of nature. Historical time is moving forward (the argument goes), not just circling around in an endless repetition. Historical time allows for progress, whereas creational time is paralyzed in the present, if not stuck in the past. The liturgical calendar—and the lectionary—focus exclusively on the trajectory of the promise (a point that we shall pursue more positively in Part 2).

In fact, sometimes the lectionary takes a text that could speak to us of the awesomeness of God's presence in nature and twists it to apply to an historical event. For example, one of the Old Testament readings for every Sunday celebrating Jesus' baptism (the Sunday after Epiphany) is Psalm 29, a magnificent evocation of God's "glory" in a thunderstorm. God doesn't say anything here in words; revelation is not linguistic, it is phenomenal, couched in the sound of thunder, which is nonetheless God's "voice." The lectionary apparently has appropriated the psalm by connecting the imagery of water to baptism and the life of Jesus, but as a result has literally watered it down, stolen its thunder. The shift would, I think, disappoint the eighteenth-century theologian Jonathan Edwards, attuned as he was to the "sweetness" of God experienced in nature, who wrote how he felt the presence of God in the "appearance of a thunderstorm," in which he heard "the majestic and awful voice of

God's thunder."[5] Edwards uses the word "awful" here not in the sense of something that is bad but something that is awe-full, precisely as Jacob says; the awe-full is terrible, but in the sense of terrifying. In his book on the spirituality induced by frightening places in nature, Belden Lane argues that such places render people speechless and thereby open them to experience a reality beyond words: "If we cannot know God's essence, we can stand in God's place . . . where terror gives way to wonder."[6] I think Otto and Heschel would agree, not to mention Jacob.

The devaluation of creational time by historical time expressed in the liturgical year is ironic, involving a kind of contradiction. On the one hand, the lectionary follows the trajectory of the promise and the linear time from Advent through Pentecost. On the other hand, the liturgical year itself is cyclical, repeating the same seasons year in and year out (albeit in three lectionary formats). Every year the same things happen over and over. Amusingly, some Christians ridicule so-called pagan religion with its celebrations of, say, the annual winter solstice, even while they celebrate the annual birth of Christ.

Our reading of the story of Jacob has revealed a fundamental theological tension. On the one hand, creation spirituality would affirm Jacob's experience of the numinous presence of God and his desire to commemorate his experience with a natural object: "this stone shall be God's house." Note that he does not say the stone is God, but that the stone is the place where God might be at home. Nevertheless, much of Christian tradition has taught us to beware of such veneration as idolatry, often subsumed under the epithet of *pantheism*. We have restricted what "house of God" refers to (church buildings), thereby ignoring the "stone" where God's presence may, by grace, be revealed to us (see "Constructing Sacred Space," below). And an all-too-easy consequence can follow—disinterest not only in honoring that stone but in protecting it. I once heard of someone who, while driving through the magnificent White Mountains of New Hampshire, looked out the window and said, "Someday they're going to find a use for all these rocks."

---

5. Edwards, *Personal Narrative*, para. 7. Seventeenth-century New England theologian Cotton Mather preached on *Brontologia sacra*, literally the sacred interpretation of the study of thunder and storms, or 'the voice of the glorious God in the thunder'" (Jenkins, *Climate, Catastrophe, and Faith*, 129). For the phenomenology of thunder, see "Spiritual Phenomena" (below).

6. Lane, *Solace of Fierce Landscapes*, 65.

By contrast, consider how a naturalist such as John Muir could talk about "stone sermons." Indeed, the collection of his essays called *Nature Writings* announces in its title that Muir is fascinated by natural place, most especially in the landscape of Yosemite Valley and what became Yosemite National Park. Muir often described the natural wonders of Yosemite as "cathedrals." Indeed, Muir judged the soaring mountains and creeping glaciers, Sequoia groves and flowery meadows, singing streams and thunderous waterfalls, frolicking Douglas squirrels and soaring eagles, as more revealing of God's glory and love than any human-made structure—"a window opening into heaven, a mirror reflecting the Creator."[7] He was an evangelist for nature: "Climb the mountains and get their good tidings. Nature's peace will flow into you as sunshine flows into trees."[8] This is a "gospel" ("good tidings") rooted in the natural world.[9]

Muir was gifted with acute attention—a deep looking and listening, shared by many poets—that allowed him truly to see and hear the beauty around him, which for him was "the beauty of the LORD" (Ps 27:4). What he saw and heard was a gospel of ecological interrelatedness that rejected traditional religious notions of human mastery. When Muir describes the landscape of Yosemite as "opening into heaven," he is in company with Jacob, for whom the place of Bethel is the "gateway to heaven." When Muir wonders at Yosemite "reflecting" the Creator, he sees with Heschel's eyes the wondrous "reference everywhere" to God.

There is much to be gained in reading the book of nature alongside the book of Scripture.[10] Our scientific reading of nature's book is indispensable for our knowledge of the world. Take cosmology, for example. Our understanding of the universe, and our place in it, is radically different from the biblical "three-story" version, with earth in the center, and water above the sky ("firmament") and beneath the earth, as described in Genesis 1. How the earth came to be influences our understanding of God as creator. Similarly, our knowledge of botany and the process of photosynthesis supplements and, indeed, enhances the biblical story of the origin of flora and fauna—including humans. In the biblical story,

---

7. Muir, *Nature Writings*, 243.

8. Muir, *Nature Writings*, 55.

9. For extended interpretations of Muir's writings, see Austin, *Baptized into Wilderness*; and Cohen, *Pathless Way*.

10. Following tradition, I will use the word *Scripture* to refer to the Bible, although one could use the term also for the book of nature, in the same way that Muir refers to nature as a "manuscript."

God creates all plants and creatures "out of the ground," so we are all physically related (Gen 2:7, 9, 19). Moreover, some texts suggest that humans and animals "all have the same breath" (Eccl 3:19; cf. Gen 7:2). Science adds something that the biblical authors could not know, that the plants breathe in carbon dioxide and breathe out oxygen, which we breathe in. As one writer suggests, "this exchange of gas is what the word 'Spirit' means."[11] The scientific observation reinforces biblical pictures of creation as an interrelated and interdependent *community*. In terms of respiration, flora and fauna—the trees and we—are one organism (see below, "The Fungus among Us").

In turn, our reading of the natural world helps to correct *mis*-readings of Scripture. In the first biblical creation account, God grants "dominion" over all creatures and commands them to "fill the earth and subdue it" (Gen 1:26–28). This lofty view of humans as the "image of God" easily leads to a confusion about our place in nature, that we are somehow its "lord" rather than God's majordomo, and has resulted in the exploitation and destruction of nature rather than careful conservation. (To employ an analogy from the PBS series *Downton Abbey*, it would be like Carson acting like he *owned* the place, as if *he* were Lord Grantham.) In contrast, Muir saw our place in nature as much more humble: "Why should man value himself as more than a small part of the one great unit of creation? And what creature of all that the Lord has taken the pains to make is not essential to the completeness of that unit—the cosmos? The universe would be incomplete without man; but it would also be incomplete without the smallest transmicroscopic creature that dwells beyond our conceitful eyes and knowledge."[12] Mary Oliver puts it this way: "I would not be the overlord of a single blade of grass, that I might be its sister."[13]

There is also a curious irony in our reading the book of nature: it is a book without words. Except for the sound of ocean waves or a waterfall, a bird's song or wolf's howl, if nature speaks to us, it is in silence. It is not verbal. Indeed, this silence is another feature of Jacob's pillow,

---

11. Margulis, "Talking on the Water." The same Hebrew word can be translated with "wind," "breath," or "spirit," but the primary meaning is the natural.

12. Muir, *Nature Writings*, 826, where he also alludes to our "common elementary fund," "the dust of the earth." Buddhists share a similar perspective: "We need to drop the assumption that the way we look at things [as a species] is inherently more valued than the way other animals look at things" (Wright, *Why Buddhism Is True*, 237).

13. Oliver, *Blue Pastures*, 93.

as distinguished from Jacob's promise. In one the numinous presence is silent; in the other, God makes a long speech (28:13–15). If we worship the creator in nature, we do so wordlessly, except, perhaps, for our own ecstatic "Wow!" Nature writers may talk about a voice that they hear, but it is not audible in any normal sense. As one scholar says, "Even boulders and rocks seem to speak their own uncanny language."[14] Again, Psalm 19 provides a biblical model when it seems to refer to the irony of wordlessness. The heavens "tell," the firmament "proclaims," the day utters "speech," and night "declares," but, "there is no speech, nor are there words; their voice is not heard" (vv. 1–4). Psalm 19 points us to the glory of God; systematic theologian David Kelsey argues that "The primary appropriate response to God's intrinsic glory is silence."[15]

How different is worship as practiced in the average Sunday morning service! Most worship services, especially but not only Protestant, suffer from a tyranny of words. Foremost, of course, is the sermon, but also there's the call to worship, the reading of Scripture, spoken prayers, announcements, even hymns, which at least have the merit of being words set to music. Such worship is altogether wordy. One of my childhood memories is of riding home in the car from a Sunday morning service when the preacher had held forth for an unduly long time, and my mother sighing and saying, "Sometime I'd like to go to a Quaker service and just sit in silence for a while." As mystic Meister Eckhart puts it, "Silence is the language that God speaks, and everything else is a bad translation." Reading the book of nature is predominantly sensual, employing all of the senses in addition to the auditory sense, and especially the visual sense. We are inspired by the place that we see, and time is quiet time.

---

14. Abram, *Spell of the Sensuous*, 63. Abram's book is an eloquent exploration of the ways so-called primitive cultures relate to their natural settings.

15. Kelsey, *Human Anguish*, 28.

Beach Time

Many years ago, I and my beach buddies decided for our annual beach week to rent an oceanfront cottage, instead of one a couple blocks away. It had been a year of various troubles for some of us—including cancer surgery, and an ambiguous prognosis—so we splurged. There's nothing like the reminder of mortality to encourage one to live more exuberantly.

I had hardly arrived when I noticed a plaque hanging next to the cottage door that opened to the beach: "Once each year, like migrating salmon, all humans should force their way to the sea and walk humbly into the water. They should let the waves splash them, and the sand suck from under their feet. They should do it, young or old, hale or frail, for it will more greatly improve the mind than any treatment devised by any branch of modern medicine." I took this as a favorable omen, since I am always looking for homiletic material.

Going to the beach fulfills a kind of animalistic instinct, and the ocean may well be the place out of which all of life came. Going to the beach is going home.

Maybe that is what we are really yearning for, finding again the lost parts of ourselves. Maybe that's what a vacation is supposed to be, a kind of spiritual rejuvenation. The word "vacation" (like "vacuum") comes from the Latin *vacare* meaning "to be empty." To create a vacuum, you empty out a space and replace it with—nothing. Traditions of all sorts, from Saint Paul to Lao-Tzu, recognize emptying oneself as the most basic of spiritual disciplines.

At the beach, I subtracted hours of watching the nightly news, instead spending several evenings playing Canasta (losing miserably). I subtracted reading the newspaper every morning; instead, I read novels by Nevada Barr and Wendell Berry. I subtracted the traffic noise from the parkway near my home (motorcycles that sound like five-hundred-pound bumblebees). Instead, I listened to the ocean, lulled to sleep by the rhythm of the waves, the rhythm of rest. There was beer before lunch, hour-long naps after lunch, and margaritas before dinner.

On vacation, of course, the main thing you're supposed to subtract is work, right up there with the hectic schedules that most of us of all ages seem to keep. But increasingly all of our electronic communication capabilities make cessation almost impossible. When cell phones first became widely available, a magazine ad showed a man standing in a mountain stream while fly-fishing. In the foreground of the picture, on the bank of the stream, there was a picnic basket, and on top of it was that cell phone. The marketing message said, "Now you never have to miss a call." Barring emergencies, wouldn't one *want* to miss a call—especially work related—while fly-fishing? Now your beach time could easily be disturbed by work-related emails and texts (the electronic kind), FaceTime talks, or a Zoom conference. To cease from all such busyness (and business) is to observe Sabbath, in one spiritual tradition. (Of course, that should include making notes for sermons.) As one author says, "'The Sabbath dissolves the artificial urgency of our days.'"[1] That's a wonderful phrase—"artificial urgency"—for it describes all those things that we think we *have* to do that we really *don't* have to do.

Abraham Heschel called the Sabbath "holiness in time," one of Judaism's temporal "cathedrals," that fuses time and place.[2] Heschel refers to the cyclical time of nature, not the linear time of history. Sabbath time is uneventful, when nothing "happens." The beach is one of the most impressive demonstrations of cyclical time. The tide comes in and goes out, every six hours, controlled by forces beyond our control—the moon's gravity pulling the ocean now one way, now another. We cannot change this time, much less stop it. Tides are inexorable. As the old saying goes, "the tide waits for no man" (and it isn't any more patient with women). Nature's time is relentless and unsparing. If you plop down in your beach chair at low tide and doze off, the ocean will move right over you. Nature exhibits a kind of impersonal brutality, as well as beauty (another reminder of Otto's fear and fascination). The relentless advance of the waves can lull you, but also intimidate you. After all, the ocean or sea is the Deep, invoking ancient notions of sea monsters and chaos.[3] The

---

1. Wayne Muller, quoted in Bernstein, *Splendor of Creation*, 127.
2. Heschel, *Sabbath*, 8.
3. Gen 1:2; 7:11 (one source of the flood); Job 38:8–11; Ps 77:16; Isa 51:9–10. The film *Jaws* evoked such ancient associations with dangerous monsters, as do a more

beach is not all sand castles and snow cones; it is also rip tides that carry people to their death, and sharks that do the same more violently. Fortunately, none of us was attacked by a shark, although some of us swore we saw their fins (most likely porpoises). But even without such dangers, the sheer vastness of the ocean, and its endless cycles, reminds us of infinity, and thus of fragility and, yes, our mortality. As one theologian says, "whatever mediates the infinite is holy," and the holy "repels with its greatness."[4]

The beach is also the landscape where the meeting of heaven and earth is most pronounced (like Jacob's ladder or stairway). The state of Montana bills itself as Big Sky Country, but at the beach the sky is bigger, at least when you're looking out to sea. The horizon is sharp. Everything is reduced to two panels, uninterrupted by the jagged line of mountains (which otherwise I love). It's like looking at a split-screen display of infinity. But the really big sky appears when you're looking up. On one of those rare days when the ocean surface is as calm as a lake, you can venture out and float on your back (or cheat and use an inflated device). Then all you can see is sky. You feel the water beneath you, supporting you, but you see only sky. You are looking into infinity, in the *place* of sky, into heaven. You are *in* heaven.

To be sure, although infinity impresses on us our finitude, we do not head for the beach intent on pondering death! But part of the beauty of the beach is the sense of poignancy it instills in us by making us think of what the metaphor of returning to the sea means ultimately. Saint Augustine seemed to have the same spiritual journey in mind when he prayed at the start of his *Confessions*, "Our hearts are restless until they rest in Thee."

Restlessness is all too much with us, but not in the spiritual way that Augustine had in mind. This is why the Sabbath made it into God's top-ten list of rules. Rule number 4: "Remember the Sabbath day, and keep it holy" (Exod 20:8). The Sabbath is primarily a *day*, but it also is a quality of time—restful time. It is a time for simply being, not doing, for enjoying the gift of life, not for making a living. But we have a long history of looking on rest with suspicion. As Catharine Albanese suggests, the Puritans inherited from Calvinism "a new consecration of time."[5]

---

recent book and film titled *The Deep*.

4. Olson, *Depths of Life*, 88–89.

5. The quotations in this paragraph come from Albanese, *America*, 109.

Time became the medium for getting things done, and thus, ironically, the way to make one's salvation visibly manifest (the latest version of this is the so-called success gospel). Thus, the Puritans banned the numerous religious holidays (numbering close to 200) "which interrupted the daily work schedule" and "invited onslaughts from the devil." The word *holiday*, of course, derives from "holy day," but now *work* days assumed the stature of holiness. "Thrift, sobriety, industry, and prudence—all were to be cultivated instead of the moral looseness that for them the holy-day calendar engendered."

In the opening biblical story of creation, God blesses and sanctifies only one day, the Sabbath day, as holy. God works for six days, enjoying the work, repeatedly calls it good, and in the end, all of it *very* good, but the day when God does *not* work is the day that is holy. God rests. Otherwise, even God would be restless! The Bible uses an interesting word to describe God's Sabbath rest. It says that on the seventh day of creation, God "rested and was refreshed" (Exod 31:17). A more literal translation of the NRSV's "refreshed" (*nephesh*) would be "resouled." *Nephesh* can mean "soul" or "spirit" or "being," and is closely associated with wind or breath. On the seventh day God "takes a breather." God replenishes God's soul. The ancient rabbis would say, "as it were," because one doesn't think of God as needing replenishment, but such is the importance of Sabbath time that even God needs to take a break. Even God needs beach time.

Fortunately, where I live, I don't have to decide whether I prefer the mountains or the sea, for I live in Piedmont, North Carolina, which is equidistant from both (so I live in the "Variety Vacationland," as promotional brochures like to say). I prefer the mountains for the vistas and the physical activity of hiking and backpacking, but I prefer the beach for sheer relaxation. It's the only place where I can sit sluggishly and not feel like a slug, not get bored or restless, even when not reading a "beach book." It's something both visual and audible, sensual: the constant, mesmerizing motion and sound of the waves crashing on the surf, best experienced while sitting in a ground-level beach chair right where the little waves are rolling gently into your lap. There, to repeat a phrase from Wendell Berry, I experience the "grace of the world, and am free."[6]

"Once each year, like migrating salmon, all humans should force their way to the sea and walk humbly into the water."

---

6. Berry, *Collected Poems*, 69.

The Woods in Winter

Not long after I came to Winston-Salem, someone told me about the woods behind Reynolda House—the grand estate bequeathed to the town by the family of tobacco magnate R. J. Reynolds, which has since become a museum. A trail meanders through the woods, around a field, and down along a stream that becomes Silas Creek. Since then, I have walked there many times, and in all seasons of the year. There is something in our culture's symbolic landscape that prefers such places in spring or summer, or perhaps in the fall—but not in winter. Certainly, you will see more walkers there in May (or July or October) than in February. We seem naturally more inclined to the lush greenness of spring and summer, and the brilliant colors of fall, than to the bleak drabness of winter, perhaps all the more so in our climate where we so seldom have the beautiful cover of snow. Here, the woods are not whitewashed, as it were, but drained of color, the forest floor covered with dead, gray leaves. No wonder that we do not welcome this season with the greeting, "Ah! Winter!" the way we welcome spring.

Our predilection for the warmer months has its spiritual counterpart. Much religious symbolism derives from the imagery of spring and summer. Consider these familiar lines from the Song of Songs: "Arise, my love, my fair one, / and come away; / for now the winter is past, / the rain is over and gone. The flowers appear on the earth" (2:10–12). Of course, the spirituality here is that of two lovers, but many of the same images are used for the divine. Consider Isaiah's equally familiar lines about Israel's spiritual rejuvenation: "the desert shall rejoice and blossom; / like the crocus, it shall blossom abundantly" (35:1–2). In fact, this prophet's favorite word seems to be "spring up"—God is "doing a new thing, now it is springing up" (43:19, my translation). No wonder that the liturgical color for the longest season of the church year (Pentecost) is green, symbolizing the growth of the church (Epiphany, for many of us, in winter, is white). Spiritually, it would seem, winter has only a negative connotation, as my dictionary suggests when it cites "a period of time characterized by coldness, misery, barrenness, or death."[1]

Now, I do not want to do away with spring, or with the springtime dimension of spirituality. Probably both the natural and the spiritual preference for spring are ineradicable, and should be. But to keep winter completely outside of our spiritual lexicon seems a bit unfair, something (I suspect) like the prejudice our culture holds for being young over being old.

What lessons, then, do we find in the woods in winter? What do we *sense*? For one thing, we hear very little. The woods are strangely silent. . The stillness is all the more apparent if the ground is covered in snow, nature's great muffler. Moreover, the frigid air is pure and clear, unburdened by the heaviness of summer's humidity. We breathe more freely, as if we we're suddenly relieved of asthma. The lightness of winter's air instills in us a levity of being. The stillness is part of what makes the woods a sanctuary.

What do we see there? Surprisingly, we see much more then than we do in summer. In summer, we seem to be immersed in a world of color—everything around us is green. Green leaves, millions and millions of them, form a canopy over our heads and all around us, and green plants cover the forest floor. Not so in winter, when all is dark and bleak. It is almost like walking out of a color and into a black-and-white photograph. There is a stark beauty here that summer obscures. Imagine one of Ansel Adams's magnificent black-and-white photographs converted into color and you will begin to see what I mean. In color, those photographs would seem baroque, florid, almost tacky. Just so, the woods in winter offer something that colorful summer lacks: chiseled edges, a sharpness of images, deep contrasts between light and dark.

The woods in summer are almost one-dimensional. The Eastern woods are so pervasively dense that hikers have named the Appalachian Trail the green tunnel. Often you can scarcely see a hundred feet beyond where you are standing. Not so in winter. In winter, the woods are three-dimensional. With the trees stripped of their foliage, you can see deep into the forest. You see the *depth* of the woods. You discover that the earth has contours, little ridges and gullies, small rivulets that you had

---

1. American Heritage College Dictionary 4th ed (2002), "winter."

not noticed in summer; over there is a dead, fallen tree, covered with moss, slowly disintegrating, something the lush vines had obscured in August; here is a rock outcropping that leafy shrubs had hidden. Now you see the essential *shape* of things. It is almost as if you can say, "So *this* is the way the woods really are." But you can also see *through* the woods. If you are walking on a ridge in the mountains, you can see distant vistas that would be completely obscured in summer. In summer you see only what is in front of you; in winter, you see *into* the woods and out, and—perhaps most remarkably—up.

In the woods in winter, we no longer see the forest, but the trees. As with the ground, so with the trees—we see their elemental shape, their skeletal structure, unadorned by leaves. We see the different textures of bark, the massive trunks, the intricate lacework of limbs and twigs. I had walked through the woods behind Reynolda House many times and not really noticed the effect of this . . . well, this vision, this structural vision. Until one winter day something about the trees drew my eyes up and up to their tops and beyond. There was something about the sublime grandeur of these trees, their stark, naked simplicity, the way their branches seemed to reach for the sky like thousands of fingers, as if in praise to God—and something welled up inside me and I found myself saying, "Glory!" And I said it out loud.

I quickly looked around and, thank God, there was no one there to hear me. Probably would have thought I was some kind of religious fanatic. But uttering "glory" in such a setting is perfectly appropriate. One could even say that *not* to utter it, or at least think it, would be spiritually obtuse. The psalmist who wrote about the heavens declaring the glory of God certainly thought so (Psalm 19). So do poets like Mary Oliver, who, as we have seen, thought that going to the woods was going to "church," where one might experience holiness. Indeed, she says elsewhere "Glory is my work."[2]

John Muir certainly felt the same way when he immersed himself in California's Sierra Nevada mountains, where, he said, "Never before had I seen so glorious a landscape."[3] Indeed, he embarrassed two steely-eyed visiting scientists when he danced around "shouting 'Look at the glory! Look at the glory!'"[4]

---

2. Oliver, *Leaf and the Cloud*, 10.
3. Muir, *Nature Writings*, 219.
4. Worster, *Passion for Nature*, 205.

Unfortunately, the word *glorious* easily *is* used for subjects less worthy of the word. It's like that most egregiously misused word *awesome*, which has become so trivialized that it can refer to something like a new brand of designer underwear.

"The heavens declare the glory of God," says the psalmist, and so do the woods in winter. Of course, I hasten to admit that I do not have such an experience every time I go there. In fact, I have had such an experience in that particular place only once. Most of the time, I just see trees. But then I do not experience the sublime every time I go to Scripture either. Much of the time, I just see words. But I return to those words, as I return to those woods, because at *one* time they led me to praise, because they led me to a Presence that is beyond the words and beyond the woods.

Here is perhaps the greatest irony, the paradox, of the woods in winter. Yes, they do speak to us of decay and dying. That is why we use the phrase "in the dead of winter," but not "in the dead of summer." The wintry woods symbolize for us dreariness and adversity. They are bleak, cold, frozen, numb. And yet, though winter is the darkest time of the year, there is more light in the woods then than on the longest day of summer, and we can see this light because winter's adversity has opened a window into heaven. Winter has ripped off the leaves, torn down the arboreal canopy. In the woods in winter, you can see the sky.

Seedtime and Harvest

Numbers 28:11–15

When was the last time you celebrated the feast of the new moon? How about the equinox (vernal or autumnal) or the winter or summer solstice? For many ancient peoples, the new year really began at the winter solstice, which, in our hemisphere, usually falls on December 21 or 22. That's the shortest day and the longest night of the year. After that, each day gets longer and longer, until the summer solstice reverses the cycle. The winter solstice was a time of great celebration, for it represented each year the victory of light over darkness. Imagine, after all, if the days continued to get dark and you, too, would celebrate the coming of the light. Just ask people who suffer from SAD—seasonal affective disorder.

The early Christians saw an opportunity to capitalize, as it were, on the solstice celebration. According to the old Julian calendar, the solstice fell on December 25, so Christians claimed that date as Jesus' birthday. Call it a sort of spiritual annexation of time. Nowadays, caught up in our preparations for Christmas, both material and spiritual, few of us even notice the solstice. The sun rises victoriously, but only a few neopagans notice, much less celebrate (although some Christian communities are reviving the observance). Our neglect of the winter solstice once again shows how much history has triumphed over the cycles of nature in our sense of time. Again, this is surprising, because the winter solstice is really the beginning of spring in that each day brings more and more sunshine, which is what makes spring happen, after all.

Ancient people, of course, were as attentive to the lunar cycles as the solar. In biblical Hebrew, the word translated "month" literally means "new (moon)." In the ancient Israelite calendar, the feast of the new moon played a prominent role, lasting for several days, and requiring the sacrifice of no less than two bulls, a ram, and seven lambs, along with grain offerings (Num 28:11–15). The feast was culturally—indeed, politically—important as well, officiated by the king from his throne, at which attendance was *de rigueur* (1 Sam 20:5, 18, 24).

Neither the new moon nor other cycles of nature ever appear in the standard Christian liturgical calendars. The Jewish liturgical year, on the other hand, has preserved the new moon tradition with a liturgical "blessing the moon" ceremony.[1] Maybe Christians need to revise their calendrical celebrations, with an eye to the farmer's almanac, and the annual appearance of the harvest moon might be a good time to do so. Usually, it appears in September or October, and is just one of numerous others (full corn moon, full hunter's moon). Observing the harvest moon would be an exercise in refamiliarizing ourselves with nature, countering what I discovered in my first web search for that phrase, which referred me to a video game by that name!

One worthy text to include for a new moon observance would be the lines from the conclusion of the flood story: "Seedtime and harvest, cold and heat, summer and winter, day and night, shall not cease" (Gen 8:22). After the disaster, God promises a return to order, to the rhythms of nature, the seasons of the year. In a sense, the flood story represents the disintegration of creation, a reversion back to the state of chaos, in which the world is totally covered by water. But after the flood, the waters dry up, and the land reappears—it is a new creation. The world returns to the order of its beginning, when God set the sun in the sky to give light by day and the moon to give light by night. The regular rising and setting of the sun, the rising and setting of the moon—and its varying shapes from crescent to full—are "for signs and for seasons" (Gen 1:14).

The biblical thanksgiving for the full moon is surprising in that, elsewhere in Hebrew Scripture, we find all sorts of warnings against worshiping the moon, along with the sun and stars. After all, these astral bodies were deities for other peoples. The sun was Shamash, and the moon Sin (pronounced "seen"). But Israel was forbidden to worship the moon and the sun; that was roundly condemned as idolatry. So, it is surprising that Israel still retained a feast of the new moon, despite its potential for leading the people astray into spiritual lunacy (so to speak).

---

1. Interestingly, the NRSV translates the key words of Num 28:11 with "the beginnings of your months," whereas the JPS uses "your new moons," thereby retaining more literally the natural object.

Why this lunar calendar? Why have a feast of the new moon? Surely, after a while it would be difficult to get all excited about another new moon—every month. A full moon is often beautiful, but it's not as if we don't expect it. We may say wow! at its beauty (especially at a harvest moon), but not wow! that it's simply there predictably every thirty days. Perhaps that familiarity is precisely our problem.

The feast of the new moon celebrates the created order marked by seasons of nature rather than events of history. As we saw in "Jacob's Pillow," Western spirituality and worship have largely ignored the seasons and emphasized the events, primarily Passover and Hanukkah in the Jewish tradition and Christmas and Easter in the Christian. The shift from the natural to the historical is rooted in interpretations of the Hebrew Bible, where the originally agricultural festivals (Exod 23:16–17) were subsumed within the exodus traditions. So, the month ("new moon") of Abib, literally "new ears of grain," becomes the new *year* month (Exod 12:2). Agrarian time merges with historical time. Eating unleavened bread, probably originally "expressing anxiety about the success of the coming harvest," now evokes the memory of having to leave Egypt in a hurry, before one could add yeast to bread.[2] Biblical scholars have often praised the transformation as a process of "demythologization." In fact, these historical associations have shaped our very notion of time, as is evident in the abbreviation AD, "year of the Lord," i.e., Christ.[3] Just as ancient Israel altered the liturgical calendar to begin with the exodus, so Christians altered the calendar to begin with the birth of Jesus. Theologian Karl Barth reflected the notion of demythologization in claiming that "Everything depends on whether time has a different center from the constantly disappearing and never coming 'now' of the pagan concept of time." Indeed, for Barth "true time-consciousness depends on a consciousness of this middle point," which is "faith in Jesus Christ."[4]

Ancient Israel's prophets especially nurtured the so-called linear conception of historical time. For them, God is always doing something new. An oracular line that we have already repeated from Isaiah puts it succinctly: "I am doing a new thing" (43:19). But if there is a dimension of time in which God is always doing something new, there is also a

2. See study note here and throughout Exodus by Jeffrey H. Tigay in Berlin and Brettler, eds., *Jewish Study Bible*, 159.

3 Or, for Muslims, A. H. ("after hegira"). The Jewish calendar goes all the way back to creation. To be inclusive, we now use CE (Common Era).

4. Barth, *Church Dogmatics*, 2/1, *Doctrine of God, Part 1*, 629.

dimension of time in which absolutely nothing new happens. As Ecclesiastes says, there is "nothing new under the sun" (1:9) Just so, Psalm 19 revels in the daily circuit of the sun as a manifestation of God's glory (vv. 4b–6), and, after all, the solstice marks the *biannual* circuit of the sun. And here's the significance of that ordinariness: it's comforting to realize that there *is* an order to the world that continues, *despite* what happens in history. It gives us a sense of security to recognize that God has given us natural time as well as historical times. The reliability of seedtime and harvest is a seasonal reassurance that all things will be well. As Wendell Berry suggests, "To live, to survive on the earth, to care for the soil, and to worship, all are bound at the root to the idea of a cycle."[5] The cycle of days and weeks and months is nature's dull, plodding way of reminding us of the faithfulness of God, the blessing inherent in the quotidian.

Every year where I used to live, the arrival of autumn was loudly announced by a flock of Canada Geese that would fly over my house headed for a nearby pond. As they flew overhead in their perfect V-formation, I imagined them looking down at me and honking, "Fall is here." In some mysterious way, they, and many other migratory birds, and monarch butterflies, know the annual cycles of nature. It is another reminder that nature has its seasons, its rhythmic patterns. Despite all the turmoil of human history, despite all the hassles and frustrations of our everyday lives, all of our hectic schedules created by *our* scheme of time and measured by our precise digital watches, there is another scheme and another time—creation's scheme, creation's time. The geese are honking their assurance of nature's reliability.

But, of course, the regularity of seasons is not just spiritually uplifting; it is physically essential. The feast of the new moon may be *relatively* minor compared to the grand historical festivals. But the historical relativity should not obscure its *existential* significance, for life itself depends on the cyclical regularity of natural time. Without seedtime and harvest, there would be no agriculture, and therefore no food. Seedtime and harvest are essential to the continuation of life itself. Without seedtime and harvest, we would die. Maybe it is lunacy that we do *not* have a feast of the new moon.

In fact, maybe a feast of the new moon would alert us to what happens when our ecological irresponsibility threatens the very order that God has promised. In response to the international meeting on climate

---

5. Berry, *Art of the Commonplace*, 285.

change taking place in 2014, a Peruvian farmer described his predicament: "We used to have regular seasons, summer and winter, during which we planted our seeds, but now with the climate changing we work the land but sometimes we cannot plant seeds; there is no production."[6] It's as if he's just read the story from Genesis, and is saying, "But it's no longer true. Seedtime and harvest are *not* reliable anymore." For a long time now, we have realized that the timing of nature's cycles is changing. Spring now comes to parts of the world weeks sooner than it has for thousands of years, one of many signs that we are altering the climate of the planet, and thus distorting God's creation. Another sign appears in sea level rise. In the essay above, "Beach Time," I alluded to the cyclical reliability of the tides, but *where* the tide stops is no longer reliable. Where the beach will be in fifty or a hundred years is not at all certain. As the climate changes, the ocean warms, and warm water expands, so the beach is moving inexorably inland, already invading coastal towns like Miami and Pacific islands like Kiribati. Moreover, evidence is already appearing that the Gulf Stream that circulates water in the Atlantic Ocean, is slowing down. If this trend continues, it could catastrophically affect the climate of the Eastern United States coastline and Western England, Europe, and Africa.

In the context of the flood story in which God's promise is embedded, what we are doing is darkly ironic.[7] God brings on the flood by altering the very cosmic structures that God has created. At the beginning of creation, God made a "dome" called sky to separate the cosmic waters (the "great deep"), making space for the earth to appear in between. "Windows" in the sky let through some of the water in the form of rain, just as "fountains" allow water to come up through the earth (e.g., springs). God initiates the flood by opening the windows and the fountains and *leaving* them open for forty days. God ends the flood by closing the windows and fountains, so that the creation is restored to its primeval order (Gen 7:11–12; 8:2). The dome protects the earth from the danger of the cosmic waters—and, God promises, will do so forever. Scientifically, the dome is what we call the atmosphere, which, heretofore, has kept Earth in the "Goldilocks" state of not too hot and not too cold.

---

6. *PBS News Hour*, "Peru's Indigenous People."

7. I have presented this irony in my editorial introduction to an issue of *Interpretation* ("Creation Groaning") devoted to the crisis of climate change, "Guest Editorial," 339.

Now consider what we are doing. In burning fossil fuels, we are creating our own dome—greenhouse gases—that surrounds the earth, gradually overheating it to the extent that we are changing the pattern of seedtime and harvest, as the Peruvian farmer has observed. As I write these words in the summer of 2021, a newspaper article provides an update with the title "The Year Summer Came with Dread." "This is the summer that feels like the end of summer as we have known it."[8] Not only is the world struggling to rid itself of the deadly COVID-19 virus, but also suffering from drought, heat waves, torrential rain and floods, and massive wildfires—fires stretching even into regions like Siberia. The parallels become even more ironic when we compare the biblical flood story to the effects of climate change on living creatures. In that story, Noah takes representatives of all species aboard the ark and thus saves them from extinction, even "unclean" animals—snakes alive! (7:2; alas, no plants). But global warming is already threatening numerous species, from coral reefs to polar bears. Indeed, scientists warn of a sixth extinction, rivaling previous geologic extinctions. As many as half of all species could disappear by midcentury. But this new extinction, again, is not natural; it is human-made. As a biologist suggests, "'Humans have become as great an influence on the planet as the asteroid that wiped out the dinosaurs.'"[9] The result is the greatest example of hubris in history: *we* are creating a "new heaven and new earth" (Isa 65:17; Rev 21:1). Accordingly, scientists have suggested a name for our geologic era—the Anthropocene. *This* is lunacy!

On December 21, 2020, nearing the conclusion of surely one of our darkest years due to COVID-19, Margaret Renkl wrote an op-ed in the *New York Times* titled "Looking for Light on the Longest Night of the Year." She acknowledges how "modern pagans," like ancient peoples, celebrate the solstice, and how, each year, we may all share in the yearning for light: "Like steadfast friends who see us through everything a cold world can throw our way, the solstice reminds us, every year, that light is coming. It tells us that darkness is never here to stay."[10] Significantly, what Renkl deduces from the reliability of the natural cycle of the solstice—the biannual circuit of the sun, and what Barth calls "the pagan concept of time"—looks very much like what he deduces from the reliability of God

8. Hubler, "The Year Summer Came with Dread," A10.

9. Hubler, "The Year Summer Came With Dread," A10, quoting Anthony Barnosky of Stanford University.

10. Renkl, "Looking for Light," A19.

as revealed in Christ: "There is no such thing as a future that is dark ... what is to come is not a kingdom of darkness but the Kingdom of God."[11] Whether the optimism of both the naturalist and the theologian proves true depends on humanity having the will and the determination to alter how we are changing the climate so that seedtime and harvest do not fail.

Maybe it is time to recombine the circuit of the sun and the circuit of the liturgical year. No doubt we will not want to sacrifice two bulls, a ram, and seven lambs, but perhaps celebrating the feast of the new moon isn't such a bad idea after all.

---

11. Barth, *Church Dogmatics*, II/1, 629.

Spiritual Phenomena: Making Sense

Psalm 29

What does it mean to "make sense" of faith? Most people would probably respond to that question by saying, Well, making sense means thinking about your faith. It means using your reason to figure things out. Making sense is something that we do with our mind. If something makes sense it means that it is logical and rational. In contrast, something that doesn't make sense is something that is illogical, something that "doesn't follow," as we say. Something that doesn't make sense is nonsense. Of course, there is much to be said for this understanding. Most of us place a high value on reason as a source in reflecting on faith.

But there are other ways to "make sense." In a book called *The Spell of the Sensuous*, David Abram explores a branch of philosophy called phenomenology. That's a wonderfully long word, obviously derived from the word *phenomenon*. Phenomenology may sound abstract, but its intention is the opposite. Instead of thinking about abstract ideas and concepts as is often the case in philosophy, phenomenology invites us to turn "toward the world as it is experienced in its felt immediacy."[1] "The sensuous and sentient life of the body itself," he says, lies "at the heart of even our most abstract cogitations."[2] Instead of having our heads in the air, so to speak, phenomenology insists that we keep our eyes to the ground. Attend to the phenomena that are right here. Don't just think—feel, smell, listen, look, taste. "Making sense" must here be understood in its most direct meaning: to make sense is to enliven and enjoy the senses.

---

1. Abram, *Spell of the Sensuous*, 35. For a Buddhist perspective, see Wright, *Why Buddhism Is True*, 228.

2. Abram, *Spell of the Sensuous*, 45.

My favorite praise poem for Easter is E. E. Cummings's "i thank you god."[3] Abram's notion of making sense as enlivening the senses compelled me to visit Cummings again. In "i thank you god" Cummings appeals to the senses of taste, touch, audition, and vision, and suggests that it is through these senses that belief in God is possible. Abram has made me notice that Cummings leaves out mind, because thinking isn't a sense! And notice what is truly remarkable: it is the senses that lead us away from doubt and into a realm of spiritual conviction. Faith begins with something we hear and see, or something we touch and taste. Nature offers us the sights from a grain of sand to the stars in heaven, the sounds of the loon or the coyote or the katydid, the taste of wild blueberries, the smell of fir trees, the touch of a cool mountain stream or a warm, coral-blue sea.

Let's focus on hearing and seeing, and come back to touch and taste. Let's take a phenomenon from nature as an example—thunder, a phenomenon that we looked at briefly in the Introduction. How do we make sense of thunder? One way is to understand meteorology. A typical explanation of thunderstorms will include advice on how to protect yourself from being struck by lightning. The physics of lightning involves the transmission of electrical charges. You know how sometimes you can walk across a rug, touch something or someone else, and feel a sting of electricity? You sometimes even hear a little snap when you make contact. Well, that's how we make sense of thunder. When there is an *enormous* jolt of electricity jumping from one cloud to another, or from a cloud to the ground, there is an *enormous* snapping sound, and that's what thunder is. BOOM! This way of making sense, of course, is the scientific way, and we can't live without it. Knowing what causes thunder protects us from getting electrocuted.

But consider for a moment how limited this way of making sense is. When I was growing up, I heard the explanation that thunder was the sound of the angels bowling in heaven. That explanation is not far off from the ancient one. In the ancient world just about everybody thought that thunder was the voice of the gods, of Baal and Zeus and Thor. We consider that to be a primitive way of thinking. Of course, it is woefully inadequate for our knowledge of the world, but does the physics explanation adequately get at what we feel when we hear thunder? Isn't there still

---

3. Cummings, *100 Selected Poems*, 114.

within us a kind of wonder and awe at the sheer power of the sound, at how it seems to split the sky and shake the ground?

In our *experiencing* the *phenomenon* of thunder, we have another way to think about making sense of it. It is not *merely* to understand its physical cause; it is also our *physical reaction* of seeing and hearing, of fear and excitement. In fact, we would have to say that the *sensory* way of making sense is primary, even with our scientific knowledge. We feel the thunder before we think about it. Making sense of thunder is something that we do with our whole *bodies*, not just our minds.

We alluded to Psalm 29 in the Introduction, noting that its place in the church's lectionary locates it historically, in the life of Jesus, and not naturally, that is, in the book of nature. The poem has a framework composed of heavenly temple and earthly temple, and within the frame there is a picture of God, an image of God, if you will. The image is not anthropomorphic (God portrayed with human characteristics). It is an image of nature, an image of awesome power: a thunderstorm. "The God of glory thunders" (v. 3).

In Psalm 29, even the repeated phrase the "voice of Yahweh" is not anthropomorphic but meteorological. The Hebrew word for "voice" (*qol*) can also be translated as thunder, and could be here. It is the voice that speaks to Moses on Mount Sinai when God appears, but "appearance" is misleading in that it implies visibility: "there was thunder and lightning, as well as a thick cloud on the mountain" (Exod 19:16). God descends on the mountain "in fire," and the mountain shakes, as if in an earthquake. The cloud phenomenon of the thunderstorm is visible, but God is not.[4] Then, "Moses would speak and God would answer him in thunder" (*qol*; Exod 19:19). The same imagery appears in Psalm 18:7–15. Here anthropomorphism returns when God spews out fire and red-hot coals from his mouth; smoke comes out of his nose. Actually, it looks more dragon than human, but here still his voice sounds in thunder (*qol*), with flashes of lightning. The language that God speaks here cannot be represented by words, which is almost everywhere else the case. In Psalm 29, the thunderclaps punctuate the psalm seven times. Perhaps the only way it could be represented would be by the beating of a thousand base drums and the crash of a thousand cymbals, with flashing strobe lights for visual effects.[5] Boom! Boom! Boom!

---

4. The cloud is one symbol of divine inscrutability. See "Constructing Sacred Space: Tent or Temple?" (below).

5. The word *qol* is alternately translated with "thunder" and "voice." In the NRSV

Let's look at the picture of God as thunderstorm more closely. The storm is moving from west to east. It is as if we are watching the television weather report and the Doppler radar scan. Try visualizing and *hearing* it as you read a literal translation of Psalm 29: *[The storm is out over the ocean.] BOOM! Voice of Yahweh over the waters; the God of glory thunders: BOOM! Yahweh over mighty waters; voice of Yahweh in power: BOOM! Voice of Yahweh in majesty. [Now it is moving inland.] BOOM! Voice of Yahweh breaking cedars, making Lebanon skip like a calf. [Now it moves to the desert.] BOOM! Voice of Yahweh flashes forked flames of fire: BOOM! Voice of Yahweh makes the wilderness whirl. [Now it moves to the forest.] BOOM! Voice of Yahweh twirls around oaks, stripping the forest, and in his temple, all say, "Glory!"*

Can you see it? Can you hear it? To the ancient Palestinian, next to occasional earthquakes, thunderstorms were the most powerful occurrences in nature. The power of the storm was seen and felt in the dark clouds and wind, rain, or hail, booming thunder and flashing lightning. The storm's power is raw, elemental, untamed—frightening and exhilarating at the same time, precisely the phenomenon described by Rudolf Otto in the Introduction.[6] That's how we feel when we see lightning and hear thunder. The experience is sensual. The lightning triggers something primitive, something deeper than words or concepts. We sense the thunder through our ears and sense the lightning through our eyes. Few of us probably stop to *think*: electricity jumping from cloud to ground. Our immediate experience is not mental but sensual, and the feelings of fear and excitement are part of that experience. To ancient peoples, this power was more than meteorological; it was theological. The power of the storm was divine power. It was a power of ambivalent effects: it could cause destruction, and yet it was the source of the fertility of the land on which all living things depended. To borrow a phrase from Annie Dillard, the storm was "grace tangled in a rapture with violence."[7]

The picture of God as a storm deity was widespread throughout the ancient Near East. With this description, Yahweh could easily have been

---

and JPS of Ps 29, the English "voice" is used, but the JPS adds the explanatory note "claps of thunder." In the book of Exodus, the people are terrified by the theophany, and they ask Moses to intercede for them (Exod 20:18–19). The Ten Commandments are an editorial insertion within the storm theophany (20:1–17).

6. For a contemporary poet's view, see Oliver's poem "Lightning," in *American Primitive*, 7, and my discussion of it in Mann, *God of Dirt*, 41–42.

7. Dillard, *Pilgrim*, 8.

the twin brother (as it were) of the Canaanite deity Baal, or of Marduk of Babylon. Baal, for example, is referred to in extrabiblical texts as the "rider of the clouds," and he too is manifested by rain and thunder and lightning. Just so, Yahweh rides on the clouds and "the wings of the wind" (Ps 18:9–11). Precisely because the picture of the cloud rider was so thoroughly Canaanite, it is quite surprising that ancient Israelites employed it to describe their own God. After all, the Old Testament is full of stories in which Yahweh and Baal are chief rivals for the people's loyalty (and especially regarding rain and fertility, 1 Kings 18). From the perspective of the biblical authors, Baal was the epitome of a false God. Yet they did not hesitate to portray Yahweh in identical terms, risking confusion, if not even identification, between the two.

In taking such a risk, the biblical authors stood at the beginning of a long tradition that we call syncretism. *Syncretism* refers to the blending of sometimes-conflicting religious beliefs, usually as an attempt to reach consensus. In other words, if you want to convert those pagans to your beliefs, adopt some of theirs and make it look like you really believe the same things. When in conflict, don't resist—absorb. The Judeo-Christian tradition is a history of syncretism, ranging from philosophical concepts like "being" to cultural celebrations like Christmas. Indeed, the storm imagery even appears in the figure of Santa Claus, who rides through the heavens in a sleigh (read chariot) pulled by flying reindeer that include the names Donner and Blitzen, German for "thunder" and "lightning." Some myths just won't die.

Old Testament scholars used to dismiss the storm-riding, thunder-god syncretism as mere poetic ornamentation. The biblical writers, it was claimed, weren't really serious about this imagery the way those naive Canaanites were. The biblical God wasn't identified with thunder or lightning the way Baal was. To some extent, such claims are true. As the *Jewish Study Bible* notes to Exod 19:16 suggest, "In Israelite tradition, although the LORD is no mere storm god, these motifs were taken over to describe the overwhelming power and majesty of the direct experience of the divine."[8] Yet one wonders if the Canaanites were really as naive, or the Israelites as philosophically sophisticated, as such claims make out. In any event, we are still left with the question as to why the biblical writers employed such language, dangerous as it might have been, and I think the answer to that question goes back to nature and power. Perhaps the

---

8. The author of this note, and of study notes throughout Exodus in Berlin and Brettler, eds., *Jewish Study Bible*, is Jeffrey H. Tigay.

biblical authors could not avoid using the language of the God who thunders because it was an undeniable dimension of religious experience. A contemporary theologian puts it this way: "Where is overwhelming, vast, creative, and threatening power known? Through nature's power . . . the divine as the creative power that establishes all things is imaged or symbolized, that is, made available to our worship and reflection through the awesome grandeur of nature."[9] Note the implicit claim here: the religious response to the power of nature is not limited to so-called primitive peoples. The ancient language can yet enable "*our* worship and reflection."

One person who *literally* embraced the phenomenon of a thunderstorm was John Muir. As we've already noted, he listened to "storm sermons": "Storms are fine speakers [with] their voices of lightning, torrent, and rushing wind."[10] But he also enjoyed immersing himself in them. During one thunderstorm he climbed a hundred feet up to the top of a Douglas spruce and rode the tree, as its top "fairly flapped and swished in the passionate torrent," with both the tree and he "rocking and swirling in wild ecstasy," reminding us of the trees thrashing in Psalm 29.[11] Like the worshipers in Psalm 29, Muir no doubt could shout, "Glory!"

As I write these words, however, many people are still trying to recover from the devastating destruction from Hurricane Irma, not only where it made landfall in Louisiana, but on its path up to New England, when many people were killed, some drowned in their flooded basement apartments. Nature is not always beautiful rainbows and sunsets, and it bears reminding that the biblical rainbow signifies the end of the flood which drowned the entire earth and almost everyone on it. The victims of Irma were not shouting "Glory!" But Muir was thoroughly aware of the destruction that storms and floods could wreak on both nature and the human beings in their paths. In words that seem uncannily contemporary, Muir describes a flood in Yosemite Valley virtually identical to what we see on our television screens when destructive storms make landfall, and he acknowledges the enormous human loss. Yet it was precisely the uncontrolled power of these natural phenomena that instilled in Muir—as in the biblical authors—a spiritual sense of wonder and awe. It is the danger in the power that makes it terrifying. Furthermore, Muir enticed his readers to see a flood from the point of view of the water

---

9. Gilkey, *Nature*, 147.
10. Muir, *Nature Writings*, 612.
11. Muir, *Nature Writings*, 469.

itself—rushing, exulting, liberated from confinement. The thrashing of trees in the wind that others could see only as hurtful, Muir saw as a "'festival'" in which the trees whirled and danced "'with glad excitement.'"[12] He also realized that the rainfall from such storms and even floods were crucial to the ecological fertility of the land. His observation of the benefits of such so-called natural disasters on nature, aside from human concerns, mirrors God's enlightening of Job, "out of the whirlwind," about the "torrents of rain" that fall "on a land where no one lives . . . , to make the ground put forth grass" (Job 38:25–27). As I noted with regard to natural disasters before, however, many scientists increasingly blame in part *human-induced* climate change for otherwise natural phenomena like floods, hurricanes, and wildfires.

What is so strangely attractive about natural disasters, like hurricanes, earthquakes, tornados, and floods? Why are people so drawn to the pictures—especially televised pictures—of such events? Isn't it partly because they are awed by the enormous power of nature, and are reminded of how frail and powerless we humans can be, and that we are not in control? A gentle rain, with no thunder and lightning and no wind, does not instill fear. Storms present contemporary human beings with one of the forces of nature that is beyond our control, before which we must stand helpless, and from which we must flee (something like the tide at the beach). Although we can predict storms and therefore be forewarned, our inability to control them makes us little different from our ancient ancestors. Storms present us with the limitations within which we must live, and in the wake of their destruction, they point to a power that far transcends human beings. That is precisely why ancient people were drawn to thunderstorms, using them as signs pointing beyond the natural phenomena themselves to the mystery and power and majesty of God—in a word, to the awesomeness of God.

To reflect on the power of nature is to ask if we have become completely disenchanted with it. It is true, of course, that nature no longer holds the mysterious quality for most contemporary people that it held for ancient people. This disenchantment is a result of our scientific understanding. We know that thunder is not the voice of God but the sound of air expanding due to the heat of lightning. We know that wind is not the breath of God but the result of changing temperatures, and rainbows

---

12. Quoted in Austin, *Baptized into Wilderness*, 28.

are not God's disarmed weapon but merely the refraction of light though water vapor particles (cf. Gen 9:13).

At the extreme, nature becomes simply something for our utilitarian consumption. The chairman of the US House Resources Committee once described his environmental perspective this way: "If you can't eat it, can't sleep under it, can't wear it or make something from it, it's not worth anything." And when asked what he sees in trees, he said, "I see paper to blow your nose."[13] (Maybe we need a few Canaanites in Congress.)

For all the gains of a scientific worldview, there is something lost as well, because in the thunder, in the wind, in the rainbow, there is yet something primeval, something archetypal, something deeply spiritual. It is true that the answer to the old children's song "Oh who can make a rainbow?" is *I* can with a spray hose. But how many times have you seen a rainbow and thought about it as light refracted on water vapor? Haven't you, instead, stood transfixed and said at least "Wow!" if not "Glory!"? There is still something in the power of nature that can speak to us of God. We make sense with our senses—seeing and hearing—not just with our minds.

Judeo-Christian tradition, of course, is hardly ignorant of the sensuous in worship. That's why we have sacraments, like a Passover Seder or the Lord's Supper. Sacraments appeal to our senses—to touching, tasting, hearing, seeing, smelling. Sacraments provide another way, other than words, to "make sense" of our faith. In the Seder, eating bitter herbs evokes the bitterness of slavery in Egypt. At the Lord's Supper, the table is central to our worship because the table is the place where we "make sense" of the story of Jesus in eating and drinking. Baptism uses water and touch. But there are other ways our senses are engaged. Listening to music reaches something deeper in us than words can. Art and architecture appeal to our visual sense, communicating in symbols, colors, textures, and forms—something that words alone cannot do.

To return to E. E. Cummings, it is the senses that lead us away from doubt and into a realm of spiritual conviction. Faith begins with something we hear and see, or something we touch and taste. Let's look now at touching.

After I and a number of my parishioners participated in a retreat during which there were extended times of silence, we introduced Quiet Sundays, Sunday services in which there was no sermon but five to ten

---

13. Quoted in *Las Vegas Sun*, "Where I Stand."

minutes of silence, often preceded by a poem. Following the silence, we celebrated the sacrament of healing, in which people were invited to come forward for anointing with oil and a brief prayer. It's an ancient tradition called *unction*, but for us it was not limited to those who are sick or dying (last rites). *Healing* more broadly signifies restoration of spiritual wholeness: in a word, *shalom*.

The first time we had the liturgy of healing, I just knew it wasn't going to work. I guess I figured that a lot of people would be reminded of the excesses of hyperbolic televangelists and so be turned off. Or maybe they would see the anointing oil and think of snake oil. Most people, I was convinced, would just think the whole thing a little hokey, a word that comes from *hokum*, meaning "nonsense"! But having a little oil rubbed on your forehead is anything but non-sense. It is touch-sense. Anyway, I stood there at the front with the little bowl of oil in my hands for what seemed like an eternity, and no one came—confirming my doubts. But then one brave soul came forward, and when the rest saw that nothing harmful seemed to happen, half the church ended up there, some with tears in their eyes, for reasons I could not fathom. So, with the stubborn old rationalist in me kicking and screaming, my senses told me that this touching was healing indeed.

One traditional definition of a sacrament is that it is a visible sign of an invisible grace. Another would be that it employs physical substances to communicate a spiritual reality. Sacraments *are* sensual spirituality. One way to make sense of who we are spiritually is to come in touch with the earth out of which we are created. Biblical anthropology is earthy, quite literally. "Out of the ground" (*adamah*), God the sculptor shapes an "earthling" (*adam*; Gen 2:7). God places the earthling in a garden that God has planted and charges him to be the gardener, to work it and care for it. One could even translate "work it" in God's charge as "serve it" and care for it. This agrarian anthropology may seem different, even conflicting, with the relatively lofty picture in the opening chapter of Genesis, where humans are created "in the image of God," or, as Psalm 8 puts it, "a little lower than God" (v. 4). But that anthropology also may be interpreted ecologically: we are "that part of the rainforest recently emerged into thinking."[14]

Among various activities, gardening provides a primary opportunity to get in touch with earth. Mahatma Ghandi once said, "To forget how

---

14. Seed, *Thinking Like a Mountain*, 36.

to dig the earth and to tend the soil is to forget ourselves."[15] Contact with soil is a rarity in our culture, especially when it comes to growing vegetables. It would be easy for children to think that vegetables magically come in plastic packages or metal cans, from a grocery shelf or freezer. They do not have the sensory experience of digging in the dirt, planting seeds, watching the plant germinate and grow, watering the ground, and pulling competing weeds until the vegetables appear, ready for harvest. Of course, many people, especially in urban settings, simply do not have access to garden space, and some neighborhoods have earned the sad label "food desert." So, increasingly neighborhoods are converting vacant lots into community gardens. But, however limited it may be, one can dig and plant with a single indoor pot.

Gardening is one way to remember who we are, to make sense of our identity as earthlings, caring for the earth. It can be a deeply spiritual activity, whether it's growing vegetables or flowers. By "spiritual" I mean an activity (or inactivity!) that puts us in touch with the Creator. The spirituality of gardening is based in physical contact with the earth. Some gardeners refuse to wear gloves precisely so that their contact is unrestrictedly tactile. Cookbook author Genevieve Ko recommends a similar sensuality in preparing dough for baking: "Skipping the mixer and working by hand allows you to experience the tactile joys of the process . . . sensing when dough comes together by feeling and adjusting accordingly."[16] Just so, gardeners can enjoy "getting down and dirty"! I do not mean to equate earth with God but to suggest that touching the earth is a kind of sacrament—that is, a physical gesture involving a physical substance that re-presents our connection to (and dependence on) the divine. As Larry Rasmussen says, "To identify something earthly as holy and sacred is not to say it is God. Rather, it is of God; God is present in its presence."[17] And, of course, working in the ground evolves into another sensual experience in that the produce from gardening leads from touching to tasting. Wendell Berry puts it well: "Sowing the seed, / my hand is one with the earth / . . . / Hungry and trusting, / my mind is one with the earth. / Eating the fruit, / my body is one with the earth."[18]

---

15. Quoted in Sinclair, *Spirituality of Gardening*, 144.
16. Ko, "Baking," D2.
17. Rasmussen, *Earth Community*, 239.
18. Berry, *Collected Poems*, 130.

The work required for gardening can be a form of meditation, an exercise in mindfulness, which reminds me of the Zen saying, "When I eat, I eat; when I sleep, I sleep." I once showed a film to college students about a Buddhist monk who was practicing walking meditation. The monk was walking barefooted in a garden on a path of pebbles. There was no sound. The camera moved back and forth from his face to his feet. His face showed a look of intense concentration, but the most amazing thing was his feet. He was moving incredibly slowly, which, unfortunately, prompted one of my students to blurt out, "Why is he walking so slow?" Of course, he was walking slowly because that was all he was doing. He was not headed anywhere. His head was in his feet. In fact, the camera finally zoomed in on his toes, and you could see them feeling the pebbles, almost like individual fingers, exploring each pebble for its texture before moving on. Through his toes, he was being fully present in the moment. In a sense, he was reading the other book of God not with his eyes but his feet. Paying attention in this way is a form of prayer.

Just so, I have often found that I have been working for an hour or more focused completely on the task at hand, digging or planting, weeding or harvesting, and realized that I have thought of absolutely nothing else for the whole time. In particular, I have had no negative thoughts about the past (regrets), no worries about the future (anxieties). I have been fully present in the moment, sensing with my hands. I have been focusing my attention on the one activity. Such single-minded attention is countercultural in that it abstains from multitasking, a divided mental focus that many people prize. Simply watching a television news channel almost requires the ability to entertain several messages simultaneously—the news anchor talking, a subscript that presents the current topic, another subscript of "breaking news" continually streaming across the screen, then possibly an inset with stock market data and yet another inset box alerting you to an upcoming program.

Sometimes the way to "make sense" of faith is to taste, touch, hear, and see what's in the book of nature, the other book of God. It's what Augustine recommends in the passage about that book that I quoted in the Preface: *attende*—"attend to it." Grace is waiting there in the phenomenal provisions of nature, which are the gifts of the Spirit: the sensual sight of lightning, the sensual sound of thunder, and the sensual feel of dirt on your hands and of food in your mouth. As the psalmist says, "Taste and see that the LORD is good" (34:8).

Rivers in the Desert

Santa Fe, New Mexico, like much of the Southwest, is situated in a semi-desert area. Except up in the high country, there are few trees and no "woods" in the sense that anyone back east would use the term. Compared to the lush greenness of forests, Santa Fe seems dry and perhaps even desolate. Of course, it is the very absence of woods as you drive along almost anywhere that makes the place so majestically open. Unobstructed by trees, you can see for miles all around you. So, what may seem desolate at first becomes a kind of barren beauty, a beauty immortalized in paintings by Georgia O'Keefe.

The absence of woods, of course, is due both to the type of soil and to the small amount of rainfall, especially in the summer months (a problem increasingly exacerbated by climate change). One summer we arrived at what proved to be the end of a long drought. There were numerous bumper stickers saying "Visualize Rain." Little did the local residents know that my arrival with the intention of going backpacking guaranteed that there would be rain! But that happened near the end of our stay. For the first week or two, the drought lingered.

The dryness in that climate is so chronic that water rationing is sometimes imposed, and some residents have installed minimum-flush toilets and planted buffalo grass, which needs very little water. The air is so dry that the local United Church of Christ has no air conditioning. In fact, it has a reflecting pool inside the sanctuary to add humidity to the air, an architectural feature that would be insane in North Carolina.

One of the distinctive topographic features of this area is the hundreds of dry streambeds called arroyos. At least they are dry in the summer, unless there has been a thunderstorm in the mountains above. In the rainy season these arroyos can be flooded with water, but in July (when we were there) they are usually dry as a bone.

There was an arroyo near our house, and I used it as my path for daily walks that took me eventually up to the top of a little mountain. The streambed is a mixture of sand and rocks, without a hint of moisture. There is no red clay, no baked mud, as in the East. Except for an occasional cottonwood tree or desert wildflower, there is little vegetation along the arroyo, and the surrounding landscape is dotted only with scrub conifers (piñons), sagebrush, and cactus. In the dry heat of the sun everything bakes as if in a cosmic oven.

One day I was walking up this arroyo and all of a sudden just ahead I saw what looked like a dark streak in the middle. As I drew near, I realized that the streak was not simply dark-colored sand or rock but moisture. The arroyo was wet, and the moment I realized that it was a kind of shock, like being startled by an unexpected loud noise—or better, by the sudden movement in a ballet whose beauty takes your breath away. And immediately as I looked up and my eyes followed the wet stain ahead, I saw that it gradually grew from moist sand to an extremely shallow stream to a continuous flow of water that was several inches deep. I was standing at the place where this stream simply vanished into the sand. I was standing at the boundary between the dry and the wet, and it seemed like a miracle that there could be water here at all. On my way back, an hour later, I had the opposite experience. I followed the stream as it grew more and more shallow, until there was the barest film of water and then simply wet sand and then just moist sand and then the dryness again.

If we are honest, we will acknowledge that our spiritual life includes both of these images—the dry and the wet. Our spiritual life moves in both directions as a pendulum swings from one side to another. Sometimes our life is like that stream that first runs deep but then shallower and shallower and finally seems to vanish, leaving us all dried up; and sometimes when it seems that we will walk forever without water, there it is in front of us—suddenly, unexpectedly, miraculously—and we run ahead until we reach the point where the water is deep and we can dip our hands in it. This reading of the book of nature corresponds to the biblical book, where ancient Hebrew poets speak to us about what it is like to follow the stream until it runs dry, and what it is like to walk in the desert and suddenly see it turn wet. "O God, / . . . / my soul thirsts for you / . . . / as in a dry and weary land where there is no water" (Ps 63:1). "I will make / . . . rivers in the desert, / . . . / to give drink to my chosen people" (Isa 43:19–20).

In a novel by Ron Hansen called *Atticus*, the man by that name has a ne'er-do-well son named Scott. Scott is a poet who has never really produced much poetry, or much of anything else, unlike his older brother, who is a successful businessman. Scott spent several years in a mental institution for depression and now lives in Mexico, spending away a trust fund from his father. If you hear echoes of the parable of the prodigal son, your hearing is accurate, and at times the novel makes the comparison explicit, though never overbearing.

There is a flashback scene early in the novel in which Atticus and Scott are riding in a car, on the way to the airport, for Scott to fly back to the shambles of his life after a visit home. It is New Year's Eve, and Scott seems to be in a darkly pensive mood, drawing figures on the steamed-up windows. He senses his father peering at him, questioningly, and he begins to recite a poem by Gerard Manley Hopkins. "Thou art indeed just, Lord, if I contend / With thee; but, sir, so what I plead is just. / . . . why must / Disappointment all I endeavour end?"[1] In inferior prose, why does everything I try seem to get me nowhere? Both poets are complaining about their lack of fulfillment, and claiming that God has something to do with it. In its nineteenth-century language, Hopkins's poem seems even to claim the original of the saying, "With friends like this, who needs enemies?" "Wert thou my enemy, O thou my friend, / How wouldst thou [be] worse?" And then he says, "birds build—but not I build; no, but strain, / Time's eunuch, and not breed one work that wakes." The poet has gone dry and seems to be less productive than a bird building its nest. And then the final line: "Mine, O thou lord of life, send my roots rain."

Scott, the unproductive poet, then interprets his predecessor's poem in these words: "You've got this priest who's given up sex, money, honors, the works, and as a kind of compensation for that Hopkins hopes that God will at least help him out with spiritual consolations and poetry. Kind of a religious man's quid pro quo. And it doesn't pan out. All he feels is desert."[2]

Hopkins has followed the stream until it vanishes in the sand and all that's left is dryness—and so has Scott. All of our poets, ancient and modern, agree that this feeling of everything being desert is an inescapable part of what it means to be a human being. The desert is the spiritual state of estrangement—a feeling of being "out of place," perhaps with ourselves

1. Hansen, *Atticus*, 36.
2. Quoted in Hansen, *Atticus*, 36.

or with other people or our work, or simply with where we want to be. "All he feels is desert." All he feels is what the psalmist felt, thirsting "in a dry and weary land where there is no water." All that Hopkins can do is to pray and wait for rain.

If you are familiar with Hopkins's poetry, you know that his work had at least as much rain as desert, even though his achievement was scarcely recognized before his death. It is unfortunate that such poems as this one on disappointment are not as well-known or quoted as those from his "rainy" seasons. And, of course, it is ironic that the very poem that speaks of poetic dryness is itself a poetic gem, but that is the great power of poetry—that it can provide a shape and order to what is otherwise chaos and thus offer at least the semblance of endurance.

The poet who questions the justice of God, who entertains the image of God as enemy, is in good company with numerous poets of Scripture. The largest category of subjects in the Psalms is laments by people who find themselves in "the day of trouble" (e.g., 77:2). Virtually all of them plead with God to help them, and most express some conviction that such help will eventually arrive. But, like Hopkins and Scott, they can also accuse God of malice, of causing their pain, even of being their enemy. One poet who hopes for the redemption known from Israel's exodus story nevertheless says, "I am so troubled that I cannot speak." Worse, she cannot sleep either, and the reason is that God keeps her eyelids from closing (77:4). Here, God is the tormenter, a picture most graphically illustrated in the suffering of Job: "The arrows of the Almighty are in me; / my spirit drinks their poison; / the terrors of God are arrayed against me" (6:4). Then, with another allusion to God's "archers," he says, "He slashes open my kidneys, and shows no mercy" (16:13). Another lament psalm ends with no redemption, only "in darkness" (88:18). We do not have to adopt the theology of such laments to understand and affirm the psychology, that is, to acknowledge the reality of such spiritual pain, sometimes so deep that it ends "in darkness." An old proverb says "misery loves company," and many people who are miserable have found comfort in these scriptural expressions of conditions like grief or depression or despair. When they are so troubled they cannot speak, the psalmist speaks for them.

But, to return to our modern poets, the Hopkins who begs for rain is the same one who would at another time write this line: "The world is charged with the grandeur of God."³ And this: "Glory be to God for dappled things / . . . / Praise him."⁴ And as for Scott, at the outset of the novel, we already know how desolate he became, because Atticus is on his way to retrieve his body after he has (allegedly) committed suicide. In the end, Scott turns up alive, albeit chastened, and emerges with a new identity. So, all is not desert in the end, and the novel is set in the fictional Mexican city of Resurrección.

The exilic prophet Second Isaiah spoke to people in a spiritual desert very similar to that described by the psalmists and by Hopkins and by Scott. We hear their lament: "'My way is hidden from the LORD, / and my right disregarded by my God'" (40:27). But the role of the prophet now is to report a heavenly command issued to "comfort my people" (40:1). So, the prophet imagines a hydrologic transformation: "When the poor and needy seek water, / and there is none, / and their tongue is parched with thirst, / I the LORD will answer them. / I will make the wilderness a pool of water" (Isa 41:17–18).

When Jesus talked about the realm of God that he himself brought, he most frequently employed the device of narrative fiction. He told parables, stories about what that realm was like, because there is no direct way to talk about that great mystery which brings an end to estrangement and creates a new world. When Second Isaiah talked about the coming of that realm, he also used the language of fiction—not of prose, but of poetic imagination. He said that the coming of God's realm was like finding a river in the desert. It is like my experience of walking up a dry arroyo and suddenly coming upon a stream, so startling that I gasped for breath. In fact, Second Isaiah is so enamored of the natural image that he can equate it with the spiritual: "I will pour water on the thirsty land, / and streams on the dry ground; / I will pour my spirit upon your descendants, / and blessing on your offspring" (Isa 44:3).

One of my favorite writers, Nevada Barr, sets some of her novels in the Southwest. In one of her books the heroine, a park ranger, comes upon a scene in a dry canyon that Second Isaiah could have imagined: "a breeze sprung up, carrying with it . . . the fresh smell of water, unmistakable in the desert, always startling. One never grew accustomed to miracles . . . an emerald pool filled by a fall of purest water."⁵

3. Hopkins, "God's Grandeur."
4. Hopkins, "Pied Beauty."
5. Barr, *Track of the Cat*, 3–4.

For Second Isaiah water in the desert was not an accident of geography. Although it is fictive—part of his imaginative construal of God's coming realm—it is nonetheless real, and it is a symbol for the recreative power of God. "I will make the wilderness a pool of water / . . . / so that all may see and know, / all may consider and understand, / that the hand of the Lord has done this, / the Holy One of Israel has created it" (Isa 41:18–20). Creation is not only a past event of history. It is the process of God's ongoing redemption that is happening now, in the present. Water in the wilderness is a metaphor for the recreative power of God that can make all things new. That is why in the Twenty-Third Psalm the phrase "he leads me beside still waters" has its immediate parallel in the phrase "he restores my soul." Suddenly, we are back with Wendell Berry at the pond, where his "despair for the world" was relieved, and he was "free."[6]

The arroyo was dry as a bone, then damp, then wet, then a rivulet, if not a river, in the desert; then, downstream, it dried out again—the rhythm of our lives. In nature's book of God, in the words of Scripture, in the imagination of poets and novelists, we see the pattern of our own spiritual journey. We cannot truly appreciate Hopkins's praise for the "grandeur of God" unless we also attend to his lament for the "disappointment" of God. And yet, within the prophetic imagination there is a deep conviction that there always is (or will be) a final coming of the rain. In the end, there will be rivers in the desert, which is simply one way of expressing that hope rooted in the God who always re-creates.

---

6 Berry, *Collected Poems*, 69.

Constructing Sacred Space

Tent or Temple?

2 Samuel 7:1–13

Does God have a place? More pointedly, does God have a place on earth (leaving heaven aside for a moment)? Moreover, leaving aside *natural* places where we might experience divine presence, is it possible for us to *construct* sacred space that might convey that presence?

Jacob, we recall, supposed that the stone pillow on which he rested his head could be considered God's house, however controversial such a notion would be to other biblical authors.[1] But the Exodus story also drives to the establishment of a place for God. The book of Exodus as a whole has a trajectory. Most Christians seem to think that the book pretty much reaches its climax when the Israelite slaves escape from Egypt, but by then we're less than halfway through. Judaism, of course, has always appreciated that the story moves on to the appearance of God on Mount Sinai and to the giving of the Ten Commandments and other legal ordinances (i.e., Torah). But the trajectory continues, because, in addition to Torah, God gives Moses the plan for a sanctuary: "Have them make me a sanctuary," God says to Moses, "so that I may dwell among them" (25:8). So, the real climax of the book as a narrative comes where you might expect it, at the end, when the "glory of the LORD" fills the

---

1. As noted above, the story is the foundation legend for a sanctuary at Bethel ("house of God"). See below.

newly constructed sanctuary, thereby consecrating it (40:34–35). Taken as a whole, the exodus story is about liberation, law, and liturgy. It does not end with the liberation of the oppressed, however important that is; it does not end with the legal foundation for justice, even though that is of paramount significance (see the Excursus on prophecy, below). No, it all ends with the dedication of God's place, "the tabernacle of the tent of meeting" (40:2).

One of the later biblical stories that talks about a structural place for God relates to King David's desire to build a "house" for God, that is, a temple (2 Sam 7:1–13). David himself has constructed a house with fancy cedar paneling, truly fit for a king, and now he thinks that God ought to have such a house also. It doesn't seem right for God to have to stay in a tent, which heretofore has been God's dwelling. David has something much grander in mind, and God doesn't like the idea.

God says, "I've always gone around in a tent and tabernacle" (the two being different words for the same thing). "I've never dwelt in a house." Given the Israelites' location in the wilderness before entering Canaan, the sanctuary was necessarily portable; it could be packed up and moved to a different place, virtually anywhere. I once showed children in church how this works by erecting my backpacking tent, then taking it apart, putting it back in its stuff sack, and into a backpack—ready to go to the next campsite. The Hebrew words are theologically rich, employing the prefix letter *m* (*mem*), which signifies "place of." So "tabernacle" is *mishkan* (with *shakan*), "place of tenting" or "encampment"; and "sanctuary" is *miqdosh* (with *qadosh*), "place of holiness." God's "holy place" has been a transitory "campsite."[2]

The dedication story from Exodus (40:34–38) describes the movement of the tabernacle in accordance with the "cloud" of God's glory. This cloud is similar to the "pillar of cloud" that led the Israelites out of Egypt, then led them to Mount Sinai where God appeared to them "in a dense cloud" (19:9). The tent is a kind of movable Mount Sinai, the place where God will continue to meet with the people, wherever they go. The entire forty years of the wilderness journey is directed by the movement of the tabernacle, itself determined by the movement of the cloud that hovers over it. Whenever the cloud lifts up, the people move on; whenever the cloud stays over the tent, the camp stays where it is. As another text puts it, "At the command of God they would camp, and at the command of

---

2. The Gospel of John invokes the tenting metaphor in describing the incarnation as God's "tenting" in Christ (NRSV "lived," Greek *skenoō*: "to encamp").

God they would set out" (Num 9:23). The people's journey is literally guided by the movement of the cloud and tabernacle. It is the ultimate "spiritual direction."

David's idea of a temple has touched a raw nerve. God, in fact, seems quite satisfied with the tent. And in fact some kind of tent has served quite well until now (1 Sam 2:22; 6:17). God likes to move around. God doesn't want to be tied down to one place. A rolling stone gathers no moss, and God doesn't want to be mossy. God would rather live in a mobile home than a fixed house, even if a mobile home seems a bit shabby. That is the only way that God can be free. God sounds like a teenager who just got her driver's license and loves to drive the car, and whose parents have grounded her. But a profound theological principle is at stake. God cannot be restricted to a particular place; much less can God be contained in a building. That is the danger of a temple: the way people gradually come to think that God is somehow *limited* to this particular spot.

You can see the danger when David's son Solomon *does* build a temple. It is a magnificent structure of stone walls, complete with cedar paneling on the inside, and considerable gold. At the temple's dedication, just as at the completion of the tabernacle in Exodus, "a cloud ... [that is] the glory of the LORD filled the *house* of the LORD" (1 Kgs 8:10–11). Then Solomon gives a long prayer that concludes with these words: "God has said that he would dwell [*shakan*] in thick darkness" (that is, the cloud of glory); "*I* have built you an exalted house, a place for you to dwell in [*yashab*] forever" (1 Kgs 8:12–13). Gotcha! God—it would seem—is now contained, for the second word for "dwell" implies a fixed structure. Moreover, temple building is inextricably intertwined with empire building, and Solomon goes on to repeat the story of how God declined the temple plans of David but approved his own, as well as the perpetuation of his political dynasty forever. But Solomon's dedication speech turns into a prayer in which he acknowledges the theological problem with temple and divine presence: "Will God indeed dwell on the earth? Even heaven and the highest heaven cannot contain you, much less this house that I have built!" Here the conflicting theologies meet, no doubt with some help from the Deuteronomistic editors. In fact, the peculiar Deuteronomistic solution to the problem appears in the next verse, when Solomon relates God's promise regarding the temple, saying, "'My name shall be there'" (8:29). To use a technical term, the divine name is a *hypostasis*, that is, a "stand-in," for God. The name represents God, that is, re-presents the presence. The "name theology" is a way to affirm that God is present without threatening divine transcendence.[3]

So, the imagery of the cloud and "thick darkness" conveys a nagging theological reservation: God is essentially invisible, inscrutable, and therefore fundamentally unknowable. The danger in Solomon's phrase "a place for you to dwell in forever" is that it threatens to cheapen God's sovereign majesty. As theologian David Kelsey says, "God's intrinsic glory ... cannot be domesticated."[4] A classic book on mysticism expresses this inscrutability in its title: *The Cloud of Unknowing*.

In a more folksy way, a story about Moses conveys the same ambiguity. The story employs anthropomorphism, a word derived from two Greek words, *anthropos*, meaning "human," and *morphē*, meaning "form." Anthropomorphism is the use of a human analogy to talk metaphorically about something other than human. The biblical authors used it on almost every page to talk about God—indeed, even to say that God "talks" is an example of anthropomorphism. So are references to God as seeing, thinking, walking, going up, coming down, growing angry, growing tender. So are references to God's hands, mouth, and arms. Even though Hosea can have God say, "I am God and no human" (11:9), the biblical authors consistently think of God as relating to human beings in the same terms that humans relate to each other. But there are, of course, limits to the usefulness of anthropomorphism if we forget its analogical status. If understood literally, anthropic images of God can trivialize God, and God becomes a good buddy or the man upstairs.

The biblical authors were well aware of the limits of anthropomorphic descriptions of God, and in the story from Exodus one author has both stretched such descriptions to the limit while at the same time using them to affirm their nonliteral—that is symbolic—meaning. The author does this primarily by using the word "face."

The scene happens after God has appeared in the awesome phenomena of a storm, has delivered the Ten Commandments and assorted other legal pronouncements as well as instructions for building that tabernacle. More crucially, the story follows the disastrous incident of the golden calf, in which the Israelites almost succumb to the sin of idolatry. Now God has commanded Moses to leave Mount Sinai and resume their journey to

---

3. See Deut 12:5 and the editorial note there by S. Dean McBride Jr. in Meeks, gen. ed., *HarperCollins Study Bible*, 288. Other examples of hypostasis are the figure of Wisdom (e.g., Prov 8:22–31) and the Christian formulations of the persons of the Trinity.

4. Kelsey, *Human Anguish*, 29.

the land of promise, and the imminent departure makes Moses extremely anxious. Will God go with them or remain on the mountain? Perhaps this anxiety was amplified by the familiar ancient notion that some gods resided on a mountaintop and did not leave to go elsewhere.

God has told Moses that God will send an angel as a vanguard (33:2), but that isn't enough for Moses. So, God relents and says, "My presence will go with you" (33:14). Here the NRSV translation obscures the anthropomorphism, for the Hebrew says "my face." The face is closely associated with a person's anatomical identity, a phenomenon now employed by face-recognition technology on my iPhone. So, an alternative translation for v. 14 would be, "I myself will go with you." But Moses is still not satisfied with this promise. He has already asked for more. He has asked for God to "let him know" God's ways. Now he makes an even more bold request: "let me see your glory." The root meaning of the Hebrew word for "glory" is weightiness, substance, or essence.

When the glory of God appears to people, it is not really the glory that they are seeing, because it is hidden in the midst of meteorological phenomena like clouds, lightning, and smoke, as it was on the mountain of Sinai. In one story, Moses even enters the cloud that obscures the glory (Exod 24:15–18), and this is the glory that eventually fills the tabernacle and Solomon's temple. But Moses seems to want more. He seems to want an unhidden view of God. First, he wanted knowledge, and was given only the promise of presence; now he wants complete revelation, an "unveiling" of the deepest core of God's identity: transparency of the hidden, secret self of God. God, at least, interprets his request that way, for God responds by saying, "I will make my goodness pass before you, and I will say my name, but you may not *see* my face." God's goodness refers to God's activities, the effects of God, what God does, rather than God's essence, who God is. The name discloses God's identity, yet it is also ambiguous, as it was when first given to Moses: "I am who I am" (3:14). When God offers God's name instead of God's glory, it resembles the Deuteronomistic name theology.

Here is where the author stretches anthropomorphism to its limits, for God says to Moses, "I will put you in a crevice of the rock, and I will cover you with my hand, and I'll let you see my back, but not my face." God is an artful dodger. So, God puts Moses in the crevice, sneaks up to the opening, puts his hands over Moses's eyes, and quickly jumps across, lifting his hand only in the last split second so that Moses can see God's fleeting back. The glimpse that Moses gets is sort of like that given in the old gunslinger joke: "Do you want to see the fastest draw in the West?" "Yes," says the hapless addressee. "Want to see it again?"

Even Moses, who came closer to God than any other human being in the Old Testament, was not allowed to see God's face. Moses *talked* with God face-to-face (Num 12:8), but when it came to *seeing*, Moses was limited, like all humans, to an indirect relationship—Moses could only be face to back with God.[5] The author also explains why human beings may not see God's face: to do so will mean death (Exod 33:20). The idea is not punitive; it simply reflects the Hebrew understanding of the awesome majesty of God, despite anthropomorphism. We are again in the realm of the numinous as described by Rudolf Otto (see above, Introduction). If we think of God in contemporary terms as, say, energy, God would be like nuclear fission. You don't want to get too close to nuclear fission. Or we could think of God as like a star (say, our sun), the source of all life on this planet, but lethal to any object that comes too near.

A scene from the film *Raiders of the Lost Ark* grotesquely illustrates the danger of encroaching on holiness. When the Nazis find the biblical ark, they take it to a cave and attempt to open it. When they do, a kind of toxic vapor swirls around them, with appropriately spooky sounds, and we watch a scientist, who has looked into the ark, as he screams in horror and his face melts.[6] So, the prohibition of seeing God's face is an anthropomorphic way of talking about protecting human beings, but also the transcendence of God. The prohibition stands behind Israel's aniconic tradition, which is rooted in the story of the theophany on Mount Sinai, when the Israelites "heard the sound of words but saw no form" (Deut 4:12).

---

5. The author of this story, remarkably, seems to contradict what is said only a few verses before, that God "used to speak to Moses face to face" (33:11), although the point there may again be to emphasize Moses's unique communicative relationship. Cf. Num 12:8, where the Hebrew literally is "mouth to mouth," but the claim that Moses "beholds the form of the Lord" is unique. The concluding encomium about Moses in Deut 34:10 says that God "knew [him] face to face," but this does not necessarily mean that Moses sees God. These passages are straining to distinguish Moses's status of unparalleled prophetic intimacy with God (Deut 34:10). In a sense, Moses is the exception that proves the rule of divine inscrutability. Other examples of seeing God include Gen 32:31; Exod 24:10–11; Isa 6:5, and each of these allude to the danger therein.

6. The scene actually fits rather well with the biblical understanding of the ark, especially the story of one hapless fellow who grabs hold of it to prevent it from falling off a cart and is instantly struck dead by God (2 Sam 6:6–8).

To return to Solomon's liturgical oration:"I have built you an exalted house, a place for you to dwell in forever . . . But even heaven and the highest heaven cannot contain you, much less this house that I have built!" (1 Kgs 8: 13, 27). What, after all, is a more fitting architectural medium for communicating the presence of God, the tabernacle or the temple? Perhaps a contemporary illustration will help: a mobile home or a building? A mobile home or an RV suggests that God is free to move about rather than constricted by one space, and mobility seems to reflect the very mystery of God. Even the respective Hebrew verbs in the David story reflect the difference between mobility and place: God likes to "move about"; God doesn't want to "live" in one spot (2 Sam 7:6–7).

The metaphors of tent versus temple have their obvious theological and spiritual counterparts. Theologian Jürgen Moltmann wrote a book called *Theology of Hope*. He based his thinking in part on the Old Testament images of God's mobility. He suggested that the God of Israel was radically different from the gods of other peoples. Moltmann assumed that the early Israelites were nomads, people who were constantly on the move. Quoting another scholar, he wrote, "'The gods of the nations are locally bound. The transmigration God of the nomads, however, is not bound territorially and locally. He journeys along with them, is himself on the move.'" "'Nomadic' religion is a religion of promise" for which history is an ever-unfolding drama, a continuing adventure.[7] In contrast, the religion of agricultural peasants is tied to place, and the cycles of nature. The god of agricultural people simply goes around in circles; the God of Israel moves forward in history. Here is a restatement of the issue that we first saw in the story of Jacob's pillow versus Jacob's promise.[8]

When God says "I have always gone about in a tent or tabernacle; I don't need a house," God would seem to agree with Moltmann, which must be very reassuring for the theologian. But our story goes on to an apparent contradiction. God says that it will be okay for David's *son* to build God a house. It seems that God is having a hard time making up her mind. The story, like so many others in the Bible, is a composite reflecting

---

7. Moltmann, *Theology of Hope*, 96–97, quoting Victor Maag.

8. One could argue that constructing a sanctuary at the place Bethel involves a similar theological conundrum. Later, Jacob erects an altar there (Gen 35:1–3). Amos 5:4–5 criticizes those who equate a sanctuary with the presence of God when they live unjustly (referring specifically to Bethel). For a lengthy condemnation of hypocrisy in worship, see Jeremiah's famous temple sermon (Jer 7). See the Excursus on Prophecy, "The Plumb Line," below.

different opinions about theology and politics. The biblical text is often something like the minutes of a meeting in which various disagreements are discussed. The secretary (editor) tries to pull together the different voices without stifling any of them. So it is here. God says to David, "I don't need a house; a tent will do." God says of Solomon, "He will build me a house."

In fact, the editor has to compromise. The editor has to hold together a theology of God's presence symbolized by the mobile tent, along with a theology of God's presence symbolized by a temple, a fixed building. Or, to put it differently, the editor must come to terms with the historical reality that David did not build a temple for God, but Solomon did.

Does God have a place on earth? No, according to one view (or at least not a *fixed* place); yes, according to another. In his classic book *The Sacred and the Profane*, Mircea Eliade suggests that just as there are sacred times, there are sacred spaces. In traditional religion, he says, "sacred space makes it possible to obtain a fixed point and hence to acquire orientation in the chaos of homogeneity."[9] That's a wonderful phrase: "the chaos of homogeneity." Eliade suggests that if all places are the same, there is *no* place that can function for us as a fixed point. We have no reference point to use for orienting where we are, and the lack of such a point means that we live in chaos. Sacred spaces are like points on a map; they help us to know where we are. Eliade suggests that if there is no center point, there really is no world.

Eliade says that contemporary, secular people lack any sacred spaces. They may have some places that are special—the home in which we were born and grew up may, for some, be sacred—but otherwise we often lack a place that is truly sacred. The result is that we live in a sadly "shattered universe . . . consisting of an infinite number of more or less neutral places in which [we move,] governed . . . by the obligations of an . . . industrial society."[10]

If every place is the same (that is, "profane"), then no place is sacred (that is, "holy"). Our culture is nothing if not mobile. I can count at least a dozen places where I have lived, including four states and four cities. We move around, often because new employment requires it, what Eliade calls the "obligations" of "industrial society." Perpetual mobility has its negative connotation, after all—rootlessness. Ask people who call

9. Eliade, *Sacred and the Profane*, 23.
10. Eliade, *Sacred and the Profane*, 24.

themselves army brats or Methodist preacher's kids, who moved all the time, and you'll often hear a yearning for place. Moving is high on the list of stressful situations.

And what about God's presence? Maybe there's something to be said for God dwelling in a house as well as God always moving around. It is remarkable to contrast Moltmann's disdain for agricultural peoples with the agrarian spirituality of a writer such as Wendell Berry. In one of his novels, he describes a farm family called the Branches. "The Branches have led a sort of futureless life. They have planned and provided as much as they needed to, but they take little thought for the morrow. They aren't going any place, they aren't getting ready to become anything but what they are, and so their lives are not fretful and hankering."[11] The Branches are like so many others in the fictional town of Port William: they "aren't trying to 'get someplace.' They think they *are* someplace."[12]

It is the same with our experience of God's presence. There are particular places that are sacred because we have experienced God's presence there. It may be the One whom we encounter in nature, but it may also be the One whom we experience in a building. It's comforting to have a place where we can go repeatedly and hope to experience God's presence. A place *grounds* us, not in the sense of confining us (or God) but in the sense of providing us a connecting point to the one whom we call the "ground of our being." Author Scott Sanders says, "The likeliest path to the ultimate ground leads through my local ground . . . I cannot have a spiritual center without having a geographical one; I cannot live a grounded life without being grounded in a *place*."[13]

A place becomes sacred because from time to time we experience God's presence there. But there is a caveat embedded in those Hebrew words *mishkan* ("tabernacle") and *miqdosh* ("saced place," "temple"): the *presence* is ephemeral, not fixed, much less guaranteed, whether the place is a tent or a temple. Hundreds of years after the time of Solomon, the prophet Ezekiel would describe in fantastic detail how the glory of God *departed* the temple (Ezekiel chapters 1 and 10). The temple was "the place of [God's] holiness" (Ps 24:3, my translation), but holiness is transitory. I was reminded of the impermanence of sacred space when on a

---

11. Berry, *Hannah Coulter*, 52.
12. Berry, *Hannah Coulter*, 67.
13. Sanders, *Staying Put*, 111 (italics original). Sanders is speaking of natural landscapes. See below on steeple and *sipapu*.

second backpacking trip to a place where I had once felt the presence of the Great Spirit at a particular spot on the trail, I felt absolutely nothing.

Both early Judaism and Christianity developed worship places without a temple, a process accelerated for Judaism after the destruction of the second temple in 70 CE. We hear of household churches in the New Testament, which one scholar suggests resulted from "a meditation on the *location* of the holy presence of God."[14] Both Jewish and Christian communities adopted similar names, *synagogue* and *ecclesia*, both words referring to the congregation or assembly of worshiping people. Although most churches and synagogues would probably say that the community, not the building, *is* who they are, eventually they find that they need a building in order to do their congregating.

The sanctuary of the church that I served for many years was designed to look from the outside like a tent. The architect was deliberately using the biblical "tabernacle in the wilderness" as a model. But the "tent" is made of bricks and steel. The sanctuary is about as unmovable as any structure can be. It isn't going anywhere. So, in one architectural design, the sanctuary is both tent and temple. It combines the metaphor of a God who in his mystery cannot be pinned down, is always on the move, leading us into the future, with the metaphor of a God who dwells there, who makes the building her home, a place that is the people's fixed point of reference, a place that makes a world out of our chaos, a place where we can meet with Holy Spirit, where we can find rest for our souls.

---

14. Bovon, *Luke*, 345 (italics added).

The Steeple and the *Sipapu*

FIGURES 1A AND 1B

In distinction from natural spaces, like John Muir's Yosemite "cathedrals," the architecture of human-made sanctuaries reflects the spirituality of the builders, or at least of those who worship there. The variety is enormous, ranging from modest storefront house churches to massive cathedrals and mosques: Notre-Dame (before the 2019 fire), Chartres, Hagia Sophia.

As I said in the previous section, the architecture of my own church reflects the design of the biblical tabernacle with its tent-shaped roof (see below, "Tree House Sanctuary," for the interior). Prominently missing from the roof is a steeple. I assume the architect thought it incongruous with the imagery of a tent. Many churches of more standard design have steeples. In many ways it is what sets churches apart from other buildings. Steeples define the buildings above which they rise as sacred space. In the design of mosques, minarets serve the same purpose, and share the basic shape of a spire. That purpose extends to a theological statement: the steeple and the minaret point to heaven. They force our gaze to look up to the sky. Theologically they are architectural expressions of the transcendence of the divine, whether called God or Allah. In its most extreme version, that transcendence could suggest that God is wholly other than this world, than the creation.

I once did a children's sermon using a stepladder as a prop. (One adult commented to me that such sermons were the only ones that were easily comprehensible!) As I climbed the ladder, I asked if I would get closer to God the farther up I went. I then suggested that maybe God was to be found at the bottom of the ladder, and not at the top, that God could be experienced on the ground. Rather than (or at least in addition to) being up in the sky, God might be found down on the earth, in fact, that God *is* down-to-earth. This imagery again reminds us of the story of Jacob's dream, with the traditional "ladder" going up to heaven, but, as we saw, Jacob experienced the divine presence very much on the ground—so much so that his stone pillow could represent that presence.

Some Indigenous American sacred architecture suggests a very different symbolic world from the steeple. Particularly prominent in Pueblo culture, the *kiva* serves as a community center and place for religious ceremonies. The structure of the kiva is an exact opposite to the steeple. It is basically underground, although some have walls that protrude above the surface as well. It is usually a round structure, and, remarkably, it has a ladder through the roof, but the ladder does not take one up to heaven, it takes one down, down into the earth. Moreover, in the center of the earthen floor there is a hole that penetrates even deeper into the ground—the *sipapu*. This is the place where holiness *literally* reaches its greatest depth.

The *sipapu* represents the opening into the underworld from which the first beings emerged and became human. From there they spread out into the earth as different tribes. The *sipapu* represents the community's sacred story, their narrative identity, much as "Eden" might for Jews, Christians, and Muslims. In fact, in interesting ways, this mythology resembles the Genesis origin stories of "earthlings" created by God "out of the earth" (Gen 2:4b–7) and, later, of the spread of different ethnic groups throughout the world (Gen 11:1–9, the tower of Babel). But the kiva reflects a reverence for sacred land and for the earth in general—often affectionately called *Mother* Earth.

Some Native Americans were appalled at the farming practices of European settlers, whose plows seemed like knives slicing the skin of the maternal ground. Equally baffling was the claim that land could be privately owned and sold like a commodity (a nationalistic understanding of real estate that led to mass evictions and the Trail of Tears). Childbirth customs of some Native Americans still include the ritual of burying the newborn's umbilical cord and the mother's placenta in the earth, a physical acknowledgment of one's ontological connection to the ground and to the sanctity of a particular land. Indeed, the architecture of the kiva and the *sipapu* reflect a spirituality that is profoundly grounded, earth centered.

The steeple points up to heaven; the *sipapu* points down into earth.[1] The steeple's orientation reflects a major stream of Christian spirituality in which heaven is the home from which we came and to which we shall return (at least, those who are among the saved!). In some ways, the shift from the earthly to the heavenly reflects the trajectory of the promise that we saw in the Jacob story, where a future homeland as territory replaced the natural place of Jacob's dream. The development is quite pronounced in the New Testament book of Hebrews, where the biblical ancestors like Abraham and Sarah "died in faith without having received the promises," which means the *fulfillment* of the promise, especially "the *land* he had been promised" (11:8–16). Hebrews depicts the couple as "living in

---

1. The mounds and pyramids of other Indigenous American cultures, on the other hand, are more like steeples in that they point up, not down. As one Native American says, "the mounds were built so that we could be closer to the Creator" (Glassman et al., dirs., "Cities").

tents," looking forward to a city and a "homeland," but not a geographical one—rather "a better country, that is, a heavenly one." Indeed, they are "strangers and foreigners on the earth."[2] In this view, the territorial—indeed, terrestrial—notion of homeland is completely left behind. Earth is foreign land, not homeland. To repeat a point made in the Preface, the understanding of sacred land is spiritualized, a sentiment echoed in much hymnody, such as "On Jordan's Stormy Banks," in which the promised land—"Canaan's fair and happy land"—becomes, not geographical territory, but heaven. The goal of the Exodus story—life as free people in "a land flowing with milk and honey" (3:8)—has become life after death, beyond this world.

The geopolitical meaning of homeland is, to be sure, fraught with existential difficulties and conflicts, but abandoning that meaning for an otherworldly reality has its own problems, not the least of which is forgetting the prophetic summons to social justice. Illustrative of the problem is the role of heaven in Black spirituals, eloquently explained by theologian James Cone.[3] Cone notes that heaven was used by slave owners in discouraging any hope for freedom in *this* life, and that such hope could become "pie in the sky by and by."[4] However, he argues that the meaning of heaven for the slaves was multidimensional, including not only life after death but also freedom in a place outside of the slaveholding states. "When black slaves sang, 'I looked over Jordan and what did I see, coming for to carry me home,' they were looking over the Ohio River."[5] The goal of Underground Railroad conductors like Harriet Tubman was not a train station in heaven but geographical places like New England or Canada (and she packed a pistol to guarantee her passengers' protection). In discussing the role of eschatology, Cone suggests that the "message about the future of God" meant that slaves "were liberated *from* the bondage of the present."[6] In fact, Cone can cite the very chapter of Hebrews discussed above in arguing that the heavenly city motivated slaves

---

2. The NRSV translates the same Greek word as "foreigners" in Hebrews and as "exiles" in 1 Pet 1:1, 11.

3. Cone, *Spirituals*, chapter 5: "The Meaning of Heaven in the Black Spirituals."

4. Cone, *Spirituals*, 91. American slave masters defended their views by appealing to early Christian texts: Eph 6:5–9; Col 3:22; 1 Tim 6:1–2; Tit 2:9–10; 1 Pet 2:18–25.

5. Cone, *Spirituals*, 81.

6. Cone, *Spirituals*, 85 (italics original).

to engage in "revolution against the present order."⁷ An earthy, grounded understanding of homeland and sanctuary entails liberty for all.

"Ground" was a metaphor for theologian Paul Tillich's philosophical orientation. He argued that "We must abandon the external height images" of God and replace them with "internal depth images of a deity who is not apart from us, but who is the very core and ground of all that is."⁸ To be "grounded" in our culture often has pejorative connotations—just ask any teenager, or disappointed airplane travelers. But for Tillich, being grounded was a symbol for a deep connection to the one who is the "Ground of Being." As one Tillich scholar, Duane Olson, suggests, "The choice of the term 'ground' in 'ground of being' reverses the traditional biblical spatial imagery for God, since in the latter, God is considered up in heaven."⁹ In less philosophical, and more agrarian, language, Wendell Berry sees our connection to the soil as determinative of our spirituality: "It is impossible to contemplate the life of the soil for very long without seeing it as analogous to the life of the spirit . . . Without proper care for it we can have no community, because without proper care for it we can have no life."¹⁰

Increasingly, I find myself drawn to the theology called *panentheism* because it speaks of a unity of being in which heaven and earth are not opposites. Panentheism says that God is in all things and all things are in God. God is not a being "up there," in heaven, apart from the world. Although God is more than the world (pantheism *equates* God and the world), God is radically in the world—with us. In his study of Tillich, Olson puts it this way: "the infinite upholds, pervades, and transcends the finite."¹¹ Note the three crucial verbs: God, as being-itself, "upholds" everything, another way of saying that everything is grounded in the Ground of Being, which "pervades" all that is and yet "transcends" all that is.

---

7. Cone, *Spirituals*, 86. Another remarkable biblical irony: the same chapter of Leviticus that inspired the antislavery movement with the proclamation of a jubilee liberation (25:10–11), providing the words inscribed on our Liberty Bell, also gave slaveholders a defense of slavery as a God-given institution (25:45–46, "You may keep them as a possession for your children after you, for them to inherit as property").

8. Tillich, *Shaking*, 57.

9. Olson, *Depths of Life*, 46.

10. Berry, *Art of the Commonplace*, 283. See "Spiritual Phenomena" (above) on gardening.

11. Olson, *Depths of Life*, 64.

In the summer of 1969 millions of people watched the Apollo landing on the moon. The moon was the goal of the mission, but, after seeing its desolate surface—and even touching it—what struck the astronauts most deeply was looking back at the blue, cloud-streaked dome of Earth. They saw Earth as home in a way that no humans had ever seen it before, and the 1966 photograph of Earth above the barren landscape of the moon continues to inspire us. They were moved by a sense of our globe's vulnerable fragility, and the need to preserve it from harm. One could say that they rediscovered a protective, filial love for Mother Earth.

We do not need to tear down our steeples and dig holes in the ground, but perhaps, like the astronauts' vision, the kiva and *sipapu* can remind us of what the US Catholic bishops have said in referring to "A Sacramental Universe": "The whole universe is God's dwelling. Earth, a very small, uniquely blessed corner of that universe, gifted with unique natural blessings, is humanity's home, and humans are never so much at home as when God dwells with them."[12]

---

12. United States Conference of Catholic Bishops, "Renewing the Earth."

Tree House Sanctuary

A real estate agent told me once that there are two kinds of people who look at houses. One type looks around each room, examining each in detail. The other type goes immediately to a window and looks outside. When you come into my church building, the architecture seems to want it both ways, depending on what room you're in. If you wander straight ahead to the fellowship hall, you find yourself in a large room surrounded on three sides by huge glass windows, drawing your attention outside, where you are surrounded by trees.

I often hear comments about this room from first-time visitors who invariably say something about the woods outside, about how lovely and peaceful it is to be there and look out the windows. It is sort of like being in a tree house. No wonder that the Sierra Club at one time met there and advertised the location as the only remaining forest in the neighborhood. But all sorts of people like the room for the same reason. Sometimes when there is an overflow crowd for a memorial service, we seat people in the fellowship hall with remote sound. Some people tell me that they prefer to be there, because just sitting there looking out at the trees is a healing experience. Then the room becomes indeed a sanctuary.

If you enter the building and immediately go left into what is the sanctuary proper, your reaction may be mixed. At first you may notice another wall of windows, looking out to a garden and trees. Otherwise, the room is almost all natural wood and brick. But as you look around, you discover that you are once again in a kind of tree house. The back wall is a stained-glass window, but it does not depict the usual biblical scenes with various human characters. It depicts the biblical tree of life. You can see the main trunk and the branches extending from it. You can see the leaves in various colors representing the seasons of our lives. Apparently, when the architect showed his drawing for the window to church members, there was an immediate objection. "It doesn't have any fruit," they said. "The tree of life ought to have fruit." So, the architect put some fruit on the tree, represented by the red panes. Maybe they are apples. The tree motif continues on the right-side wall as well, in the form of simulated branches and leaves in wrought iron. As I mentioned above, the architect designed the roof of the sanctuary to simulate the shape of a tent, suggesting the biblical tabernacle. But inside, you are surrounded by trees. The biblical image of the tree of life says that the leaves are "for the healing of the nations" (Rev 22:2; cf. Ezek 47:12). Could there be any better symbol of our yearning for peace in the world?

Already we are reading the two books of God. Nature provides the trees, and Scripture provides the lexical context. If you look to the front of the sanctuary, not surprisingly, you will see a simple wooden cross, which Scripture can refer to as a "tree" (e.g., Acts 5:30; Gal 3:13). Also, you will see standard furnishings for a sanctuary—a lectern, from which Scripture is read, a pulpit, from which Scripture is preached, and a table, at which the story of the Last Supper is retold. Moreover, the architect incorporated triangles in the stained-glass leaves, in the shape of the table, and even in the front and back walls, representing the Trinity. (There is no baptismal font—we use a seashell!) The architecture embraces the congregants in the sacred space created by the two books of God.

The architecture of both the fellowship hall and the sanctuary invite reflection on trees themselves, and how they can be a blessing in our lives. I will not dwell on the fact that our very lives depend on the oxygen produced by trees and other plants, that the air we breathe in is the air they breathe out (see above, Introduction; below, "Earth Day: The Fungus among Us"). But the ancient world understood trees to be symbols of life itself, even though they knew nothing of the process of photosynthesis. The tree of life is a motif that appears all over the ancient world, from Sumer to Egypt, from Greece to Rome. The motif was associated with fertility, nourishment, and rejuvenation. As one author says, "the tree stands for the mystery or secret of life. With its leaves and blossoms and fruit, with its capacity to remain ever green or to bud anew each spring, it captures the essence of [our] most fundamental strivings for survival and sustenance in this world and in the hereafter."[1] Because trees have a "sacred quality" they "become imbued with divine power."[2]

Now, any time that you mention fertility and divine power in the same breath you run into trouble, at least in the Bible. After all, some cultures had drawings or statues of gods with leaves and flowers coming out of their bodies. The use of such symbols in worship easily became open to the charge of idolatry. Jeremiah, as we have seen, complains about those in Israel who say to a stone, "You gave me birth" (2:27), but also added, "who say to a tree, 'You are my father,'" and he ridicules other people who carve a tree into an idol (10:3–5; cf. Isa 40:18–20). Deuteronomy prohibits using such objects in worship, saying, "You shall not plant any tree as a sacred pole beside the altar that you make for the LORD your God" (16:21). The result of such prohibitions is a kind of arboriphobia that continues to this day. As one author claims, "For nearly two millennia Christian missionaries have been chopping down sacred groves, which are idolatrous because they assume spirit in nature."[3]

God forbid that there should be spirit in nature! But the biblical arboriphobia, it turns out, is only one voice. The Deuteronomistic legislation reflects the situation in the eighth through sixth centuries BCE. It is now clear that earlier the symbol of the tree played a significant role in legitimate Israelite worship. In fact, one controversial archaeological discovery is of an inscription that refers to "Yahweh [the God of Israel] and

---

1. Meyers, *Tabernacle Menorah*, 174.
2. Meyers, *Tabernacle Menorah*, 95.
3. Spring and Spring, eds., *Ecology*, 28.

his *asherah*." The word *asherah* is the word for "sacred pole" in the Deuteronomic text. It seems to have been a stylized representation of a tree. It stood alongside the altar in the sanctuary and symbolically mediated the presence of God. Since the tree also universally represented blessing and fertility, the *asherah* represented its numinous power. It seems that women in particular were fond of the *asherah* as a means of worship—not surprisingly, since women's self-esteem was closely associated with fertility (or the lack thereof). So, the *asherah* apparently was a way of incorporating "the feminine dimension of deity" within the regular worship of Israel's God.[4]

Why, then, did the tree get to be taboo? The primary reason apparently is that the word *asherah* is also the name of a goddess of ancient Canaan. So it was easy to confuse the symbol of the tree with the existence of the goddess, and for later, orthodox Israelites like the Deuteronomists, this danger was too much. The fear of trees then reflects the competition between the God of Israel and the gods of Canaan, not a negative valuation of trees themselves (cf. Deut 12:2; Jer 2:20). Nevertheless, the symbolic power of the tree of life persisted in various ways. The lampstand called the *menorah* is one example. (Jews light the candles of a menorah to mark the days of Hanukkah, much as Christians light Advent candles.)[5] As described in Exodus, it sounds very much like a stylized tree (Exod 25:31–46). It has a main trunk and six branches. The branches end in leaves and flower petals, explicitly likened to those of an almond tree. The menorah was a lampstand functionally, but it was also a representation of the tree of life. There in ancient Israel's sanctuary is precisely the very thing that later generations considered heretical.

Sometimes it is a good idea to be conservative, and the tree of life is a case in point. The earlier generations of Israelites, I think, were on to something that those self-proclaimed "neo-orthodox" folks could not see. The neo-orthodox fear of feminine deities (goddesses) could easily become an aversion to trees, which (again all too easily) could morph into an aversion to all things natural. The fear of making an idol out of a tree prevented the neo-orthodox from seeing the blessing of a tree. The fear of divinizing a tree prevented seeing how divinity can be mediated by a tree. Remnants of the latter survive in texts like Gen 12:6, which refers

---

4. Miller, *Religion of Ancient Israel*, 36. See also Rasmussen, *Earth Community*, 205–7.

5. Note that the primary referent now for the Menorah is a historical event in Jewish history.

to the "oak of Moreh." The name Moreh means "revelation" or "guidance" (related to the word *torah*). Originally the name Moreh probably indicated that the tree itself was oracular. The location is the town of Shechem, which, like Jacob's Bethel, "was already a sacred place before Abraham."[6] Originally, this tree could *talk*, or at least communicate in some way with humans. In a way, the tree was like Jacob's stone functioning as the "house of God."

The combination of tree and stone, so condemned by Jeremiah, appears in another medieval allusion to the other book of God from Saint Bernard: "Believe me, you will find more lessons in the woods than in books. Trees and stones will teach you what you cannot learn from masters."[7] As one biblical scholar puts it, here nature "is the realm through and within which God becomes present in the world."[8] Given the biblical precedents of the oak of Moreh and the menorah, both of my church's tree-house rooms are utterly conservative, indeed, primitive, structures, especially the sanctuary proper, with its tree of life taking up an entire wall and winding into the rest of the room. Both rooms would be considered contemporary in terms of architectural style, but in terms of symbolism, one, at least, is old as the hills.

What would happen if we were to free ourselves of any vestigial arboriphobia left over from our religious tradition? What would happen if in contrast to those missionaries who cut down sacred poles, we were to celebrate the presence of spirit in nature, and specifically in trees?[9] Poets and scientists alike encourage us to do so. Mary Oliver perceives "the sentient lives of trees," capable of "communicating" with her, in some sense.[10] Wendell Berry's "Sabbath Poems" are titled *A Timbered Choir*, referring to the way in which trees sing praise to the Creator. They are "Apostles of the living light," bestowing "a blessing on this place," a "benediction."[11] Similarly, for Muir, the majestic trees of the Sierras proclaim "the gospel

---

6. Westermann, *Genesis 12–36*, 154, who notes the embarrassment of later generations. Shechem also sported a renowned oak tree (Gen 35:4, 8). Curiously Gen 12:6 adds the unnecessary word "place" (*mĕqom*), reminiscent of Jacob's scene (28:11).

7. https://en.wikiquote.org/wiki/Bernard_of_Clairvaux#Quotes.

8. Hiebert, *Yahwist's Landscape*, 110.

9. Foundational here is Martin Buber's classic *I and Thou* (original German edition 1923), especially his discussion of a tree as a spiritual subject (not just object), 7–8. Buber's book is a counterpart to Otto's *Idea of the Holy*.

10. Oliver, *Winter Hours*, 15.

11. Berry, *Timbered Choir*, 83.

of beauty," and, as they are for Berry, so they are for Muir "apostles."[12] Indeed, Muir communes with the "sacrament" that they offer.[13] Scientists increasingly tell us something similar to the poets: how trees communicate and protect each other, forming an interdependent community, which includes us (see below, "Earth Day: The Fungus among Us"). Theologically, a study of Paul Tillich suggests that "trees with their deep roots" provide a distinctive representation of how everything is grounded in God.[14] Psalm 104, an ode to Creator and creation, describes how God sustains the entire ecosystem, grass for cattle, food for humans (including wine!), and water for "the trees of the LORD," which "he planted" (vv. 14–16). No wonder the trees join in Berry's choir and sing for joy and in praise (96:12; 148:9). Perhaps worshiping in a tree house will instill in us not only an appreciation for the blessing that trees bestow but also an appreciation of our responsibility to care for them. Such responsibility will range from protecting the old growth forests that provide habitat for wildlife like the spotted owl to using trees sustainably—all the way down to what brand of toilet paper we purchase.

The architect of our sanctuary did, indeed, construct sacred space—that is, a structural space that opens us to the presence of the sacred in our lives. The sanctuary represents the two books of God most strikingly in the two walls facing each other: the tree of life and the "tree" of the cross. It is as if nature's spirituality of creation is behind us, and history's spirituality of redemption in front of us. We would do well not to separate the two absolutely. Perhaps what we need to do is to pay attention to both tree and cross, realizing that each in its own way represents to us God's presence and blessing.

---

12 Austin, *Baptized into Wilderness*, 67.

13 Austin, *Baptized into Wilderness*, 4.

14. Olson, *Depths of Life*, 46. See above, "Steeple and *Sipapu*."

In the Backcountry

Sierra Nevada: Ant Assaults Mount Everest

Job 38–41

Some proverbs ostensibly rooted in the Bible are illustrations of biblical illiteracy, a prime example being "the patience of Job." Surely no character in all of spiritual literature is more impatient, and with good reason. Job has lost his children, his property, and his health, and he wants an answer for why. God offers no answers, no defense of God's own actions, much less any apology for Job's suffering. After all his ranting and raving, after all his demands for a trial to vindicate his innocence, all Job gets is a blustering, bombastic deity who brags about his creative power and says not one word about Job's complaints. God gives no solution to the problem of evil. Job demands justice; God instead takes him on a *National Geographic* tour of the cosmos.[1]

After remaining silent for thirty-six long chapters, God does finally speak. But the medium of God's speaking is itself overwhelming and awesome. God speaks out of the whirlwind, that is, out of the terrifying power of a storm. Such an appearance is an ancient way of talking about God's presence, as we just saw above, but there is nothing comforting about it. Nor is there anything comforting about God's opening words: "who is this that darkens counsel without knowledge?" Like the Queen of

---

1. Parts of this essay first appeared in Mann, "Job and *The Color Purple*."

Hearts to Alice, God says to Job, "And *who* are *you*?" In other words, who is this wiseacre, this know-it-all, this bighead? And then God launches into a series of rhetorical questions. Where were you when I laid the foundation of the earth? Who brings rain on a land where no one lives? Can you hunt the prey for the lion, or provide for the raven? Do you watch when the deer give birth?

Job wants answers; God asks rhetorical questions. To each question, Job can only say, "I don't know. I don't know." Job wants his day in court, with God as the defendant; God takes him outdoors and asks him who controls the sea, brings the dawn, understands the vastness of the earth, creates light, makes the snow, calls out the constellations, and makes the lightning flash. Job demands the attention due to him as a human being, created in God's image; instead, God ignores his demand and asks him what he knows about all sorts of wild creatures—lions and ravens, mountain goats and deer, the wild ass and ox, the ostrich, the hawk, and the vulture. Instead of a courtroom, Job gets a guided tour of God's zoo.

Yet, in the end, Job drops his lawsuit against God, stops complaining, stops venting his spleen, stops mourning his losses. "I am small," he says. "I will shut my mouth. I had heard about you, but now I see you, and I give up dust and ashes" (40:4–5, my translation): that is, he gives up the ritual of grieving. Job is ready to live again. How shall we understand his transformation? How does God's deliberate *avoidance* of his questions leave Job with a "satisfied mind"? And what does it mean when Job says, "now I *see* you"?

Let's take a closer look at the wild things in God's zoo.[2] There is the lion, the "king of beasts." To humans, the lion is a fierce predator, an object of both fear and hostility. To humans, the only good lion is a dead lion. It is one of those wild animals that humans hunt and kill to protect either themselves or their flocks, or simply for sport. Ancient kings especially liked to go on lion-hunting safaris. A stuffed lion's head makes a nice trophy on the wall. But that is not the way God sees lions. From God's perspective, the lion is a vulnerable creature, dependent on God's care for food. In fact, it is really God who hunts the prey *for* the lion. The same is true for the raven. It is God who provides the raven's prey "when its young ones cry to God" (38:41).

The rhetorical questions about the lion and the raven turn upside down Job's "knowledge" of the world. Wild animals that appear to be

---

2. For the following, see Brown, *Ethos of the Cosmos*, 360–68.

self-sufficient are, in fact, needy. A creature for which humans couldn't care less, or worse, a creature that humans fear, each strangely now deserves human *compassion* rather than indifference or hostility. Job has been crying to God endlessly. Now he is silenced, and God lets him hear the crying of the raven's chicks.

Next in God's menagerie come the mountain goat and the deer. Suddenly the question is not about food and sustenance but veterinary obstetrics. Does Job know when the goats give birth, or observe when the deer calve? Literally, the word "observe" means "keep watch." Does Job watch over the pregnant deer? No, of course not. Humans may watch over pregnant *domestic* animals, but not the wild deer. Yet God does. Suddenly God appears to be a kind of midwife—a midwife to wildlife. And then the rhetorical questions lead to a statement: the young deer becomes strong virtually overnight, unlike human babies. And the deer are not tied to the place of birth—they are free to roam. Unlike domestic animals, the goat and the deer are unrestrained by humans. They live forever wild and free.

What is the effect of these little wildlife lessons? They change Job's passion to *com*passion. Job has all along been fixated on his own problems, his own feelings. He has been wallowing in his misery, and sometimes that is all that one can do. Sometimes it is good for you to wallow. A good friend of mine told me that one day she went to work all wrapped up in personal problems and within an hour she had had it. Her supervisor wisely saw this, took her aside, and said, "I don't know what's going on with you, but I think you need to just go home and sit in your misery." But one cannot wallow for long.

Part of Job's problem is that he is operating with an exalted view of his place, as a human being, within the grand scheme of things. After all, one of the Psalms says that human beings were created to be "little lower than God," exercising royal dominion over all other creatures (Ps 8:5). While that noble anthropology has its truth, it is not the *whole* truth. Because, in the grand scheme of things, human beings are really quite small, which is precisely what Job says in his first response. "I am small." John Muir, inspired equally by the vast majesty of the Sierra mountains as by the exquisite beauty of a minute flower, was an eloquent critic of anthropocentric hubris. In his comments evoking the Genesis story of creation, he suggests, "Nature's object in making animals and plants might possibly be first of all the happiness of each one of them, not the creation of all for the happiness of one."[3] And here's the redemptive part of Job's immersion in wildness—the realization of his smallness in the grand ecology has a way of reducing what seemed to be the enormity of his pain. The experience of ecological smallness can lead to spiritual rejuvenation.

On one of my backpacking adventures with the Sierra Club, we spent a week in Kings Canyon National Park on a trip called Deadman's Walk, a title that reminds us of the warning, "fools rush in where angels fear to tread." But the title derived from the name of a canyon that we hiked through—Deadman's Canyon. We camped on the third night at the head of the canyon, with snowcapped peaks above and wildflowers all around. The next morning, we began our climb out of the canyon, up and over Kearsarge Pass, a climb of a couple thousand feet.

Now, there are some wilderness lessons that I never seem to retain for very long, and one of them is how easy it is to underestimate distances. As we started out on the trail, I looked up toward the pass, and calculated that we would probably get up there in an hour. An hour later we stopped for a rest and the leader informed us that we just might be one-third of the way up. As we were all looking up at the pass, someone noticed something moving, and then realized that it was other hikers close to the top. Each one of them looked like an ant on a surface so vast that they seemed *not* to be moving, and in that moment, I realized that *I* looked like just such an ant, and from somewhere in the recesses of my mind the words came: "ant assaults Mount Everest." That's precisely what it felt like at that moment. In the vast expanse of the Sierra mountains, stretching endlessly in every direction, we were merely tiny organisms, presumptuously pretending to "conquer" the mountain.

There is incredible arrogance in the words we tend to use for mountain climbing: *conquer, assault,* and—by far the worst—*peak bagging,* as if mountains are like birds that you can hunt and kill and stuff in a knapsack. But even standing, finally, at the top of the pass, I did not feel like Sir Edmund Hilary. I felt like Job, and I could say, also with great understatement, "I am small." I think my experience is similar to that reported by a guy who enjoys hang gliding over the Rocky Mountains: "I've always wanted to be in places that were bigger than me to show me how insignificant I am."[4] And here's the redemptive dimension—that hum-

---

3. Muir, *Nature Writings*, 826.

4. Lanchester and Wright, dirs., "Rockies." Fideler (*Breakfast with Seneca*, 51) reports a practice made famous by Marcus Aurelius called "'the view from above'": "it involves imagining yourself far above our planet and looking down on the Earth

bling experience is as spiritually uplifting as it is physically diminishing. Paradoxical as it may seem, the wilderness experience of being incredibly small is the catalyst for feeling incredibly alive.

I remember a field trip that I led many years ago for a group of residents at a halfway house, most of them recovering drug addicts recently released from incarceration. I took them up to Hanging Rock State Park, and we hiked up a trail that took us to a scenic overview called House Rock. Two comments by one guy struck me—one comment sad, the other joyful. The sad one came when we had barely gone a few hundred feet. He looked at all the rocks and boulders that usually are part of such a trail and asked, "How did they get all these rocks in here?" His question revealed how much he suffered from "nature-deficit disorder," that he had never had the opportunity to enjoy such a natural setting. But when we got to House Rock and he stood on the edge of the cliff, looking out over the Piedmont landscape, he suddenly spread out his arms and said, "I feel so free." It was precisely Wendell Berry's experience noted in the Preface.

Belden Lane provides the language with which to name the experience of smallness as a *liberating* experience in his book *The Solace of Fierce Landscapes*, with the subtitle *Exploring Mountain and Desert Spirituality*: "The austere, unaccommodating [wilderness] landscapes . . . [reveal] the smallness of self and the majesty of Being."[5] Lane has combined his exploration of nature with an exploration of his mother's death from cancer in a way that excludes any hint of sentimentality. "All theologizing," he says at one point, "must submit to the test of hospital gowns."[6] Yet much of Lane's book explores the ways in which being in nature, and especially in wilderness, can bring a strange kind of spiritual healing, already suggested in the juxtaposition of the words *solace* and *fierce*. One of his illustrations is the story of a man who in great spiritual turmoil went on a pilgrimage to Tibet, in search of some answer to his problems. One day he was walking to a remote monastery when he stopped to observe the scene around him—a stream surrounded by boulders and weathered trees. Soon he found that he could not leave, that something held him there, kept him from continuing his pilgrimage. Then he realized that "to walk by a stream, watching the pebbles darken in the running water, is enough." He stayed at the stream because his pilgrimage had brought him

---

below, to see how small we are, and realizing how tiny our personal troubles are in relation to the greater universe."

5. Lane, *Solace of Fierce Landscapes*, 53.
6. Lane, *Solace of Fierce Landscapes*, 35.

to one of nature's cathedrals. So, he came to this curious conclusion: "The things that ignore us save us in the end." Commenting on this story, Lane suggests that "in its very act of ignoring him, the landscape invited him out of his frantic quest for self-fulfillment."[7]

Theologically, the experience of being ignored, the experience of having one's turmoil met with indifference, is one dimension of the hiddenness of God, the technical name for which is *apatheia*. In this mode, God is apathetic, shows no feeling, no response.[8] Related to this theologically is the understanding of our knowledge of God as *apophatic*, referring to the great mystery of God that negates any of our names or metaphors or images, for God is beyond all such forms. The mystical tradition above all others has nurtured this aspect of spiritual experience, calling it the *via negativa*, the way of nothingness or emptiness. Meister Eckhart expresses the spiritual corollary of such emptying when he says, "God is not attained by a process of addition to anything in the soul, but by a process of subtraction." Lane puts the apathetic experience encountered in "fierce landscapes" quite bluntly when he says, "the desert doesn't give a damn."[9]

Isn't it strange that such an experience of apathy in the face of all our yearning for answers can provide a sense of spiritual rejuvenation that transcends all of our questions? In taking us out of ourselves, such an experience opens us to something far greater than all of our self-preoccupations—none other than the mysterious majesty of God. This is what Job means when he says, "now my eye sees you." He has heard lots of things about God (often *too* much from his friends!), but now he *sees*. And the result is liberation: "I will let go of dust and ashes." Here the *reason* for his suffering goes unexplained, but Job is empowered to abandon his questions and embrace life anew. Job does not repent *in* dust and ashes but repents *of* dust and ashes—that is, he resolves to turn away from his lament to another, radically different attitude, namely, that of praise.[10]

---

7. Lane, *Solace of Fierce Landscapes*, 54.

8. For the opposite, see the Excursus on prophecy and "Feeling Rachel's Pain," below.

9. Lane, *Solace of Fierce Landscapes*, 187. On Job, see Lane, *Solace of Fierce Landscapes*, 55–56. The apophatic understanding of God prevents its opposite, the "pathetic," from becoming mere sentimentality.

10. Job's seeing is more experiential than cognitive, prompted by having his vision directed to nature. Buddhist Robert Wright suggests a similar understanding of emptiness and the notion of not-self: "When I say 'see the truth,' I mean *see* the truth—actually apprehend the truth experientially" (*Why Buddhism Is True*, 228). See

In his famous essay "Walking," Henry David Thoreau wrote, "In wildness is the preservation of the world," and, for Job, God's instructions on wildness lead to his *spiritual* preservation. Like the wild ass, he can go free; like the ostrich, he can be careless; like the horse, he can laugh at fear; like the eagle, he can soar (39:5, 14, 22, 27). The title of Cheryl Strayed's account of her experiences on the Pacific Crest Trail, *Wild*, reflects Thoreau's axiom, and part of the subtitle captures the experience of Job: *From Lost to Found*. "Do you observe the calving of the deer?" God asks Job, diverting his attention to veterinary obstetrics (39:1). Imagining the birth of a fawn instead of venting his own bitterness is part of the redemptive process that leads to Job's experience of being "born again," wild and free.[11]

also "Spiritual Phenomena," above.

11. For a remarkable parallel to observing "the calving of the deer," and the spiritual transformation it effects in the observer, see my discussion of Oliver's poem "A Meeting" in Mann, *God of Dirt*, 36–37.

Message from Taboose Pass: Wilderness Pedagogy

Before leaving for a summer backpacking trip in California, I decided that I would devote a few sermons in the fall to the topic of wisdom. After some preliminary reading, I headed for Kings Canyon National Park, certain that I would there receive some inspiration. After all, there is considerable biblical precedent for divine revelations occurring on mountains, such as the Ten Commandments given to Moses (Exod 19–20) and the Sermon on the Mount given by Jesus (Matt 5–7). Moreover, part of our route was on the famous John Muir Trail, named for the legendary Sierra explorer. As reported in the Preface above, in Muir's eloquent (and rapturous) reports of experiences there, he talked about nature's "cathedrals," where there are "a thousand windows to show us God," and where he heard all sorts of sermons.[1] I arrived with ears and eyes wide open, ready to receive my sermonic inspiration. I waited patiently day in and day out, but nothing came—no thunderous voice, no burning bush, not even a "still small voice" in the wonderful silence of that wilderness. On our last night we camped just below the western side of Taboose Pass, and on the next day we headed over the pass and down the eastern side to civilization. It was unbearably hot and dry, and I had no revelation.

Now, we all agreed that the trail down from Taboose Pass was the worst trail any of us had ever hiked. Long stretches were little more than rock slides the size of football fields, and this made the trail both uncomfortable and difficult to follow. It was precisely in the middle of one such stretch that I received the message. Suddenly the heavens opened and an audible voice—well, no, that isn't what happened. What happened was that I realized I wasn't sure I was still on the trail, a situation that will surprise no one who has been backpacking with me. I looked around for a trail marker, and off to my right I saw what hikers call a "duck" (aka

---

1. Muir, *Nature Writings*, 60, 187, 268.

cairn). A duck is a little pile of rocks, usually three, with a large one on the bottom, a medium sized one in the middle, and a little one on top, often looking like a bird sitting on a boulder (hence the name). At that moment, the man who was right behind me (his name was Ben) caught up with me, and I suggested that he see if this was really a duck, and if it marked the trail.

As he drew near to the duck he called to me, "There's a note under it."

"Maybe it says something about the trail," I guessed, as he pulled it from under the rocks and opened it.

He came over to me with an amused grin on his face and said, "It has nothing to do with the trail. Read it yourself."

The note was written in lovely calligraphy in three colors of felt-tip pen, and here's what it said: "'Freedom is not freedom from others or freedom over others, but freedom from your own boundaries, limits, and the conditions into which you have thrown yourself,' Swami Amar Tyoti."

I have no idea, of course, who placed the note there, whether it was the Swami himself or (more likely), one of the Swami's followers. This I do know: unlike the tablets containing the Ten Commandments, this note was not written by the finger of God but by human hands. I was hoping for some sort of divine revelation; I received, instead, a human communication. Moreover, it was from a Hindu, given that Swami is a Hindu title roughly similar to Reverend or Rabbi, or perhaps to monastic titles such as Brother and Sister. And yet, when I read this note, I smiled even more broadly than my companion, because I realized that the message I had received at Taboose Pass was, in fact, a serendipitous confirmation of what wisdom is all about. And here is why: Wisdom is not something limited to the Judeo-Christian religion, but a universal store of knowledge, potentially meaningful and helpful to any human being who wants to learn how to live life to its fullest.

One of the most prominent books of wisdom in the Bible is the book of Proverbs, and a portion of that contains pedagogical instruction to a child by a parent. Etymologically, of course, that's what *pedagogy* means, derived from Greek words for "child" and "learning," and the core of such parental teaching says, "Happy are those who find wisdom" (Prov 3:13). We did not have children on our backpacking trip, but we had a young man, all of nineteen, who was just past the minimum age limit that permitted him to participate without a parent or guardian. His name was Adrian.

Over the course of four or five days, Adrian developed a very bad blister on one of his heels. By the time he attended to it, it had not only broken but become infected, requiring considerable first aid from the leader. This was my second trip with our leader (Roz), who was a wonderfully no-nonsense British expat. (On our first trip, in Yosemite, long before there were bear canisters for storing food, she had her husband sleep beside all the commissary at night to fend off bears.) When she discovered Adrian's blister, she gave him a stern lecture on foot care, not realizing that several others had told him what to do long before the blister had reached its serious state. On the first day of the trip, he had complained about what hikers call a "hot spot," a place where a blister will develop if not properly tended. But he ignored the advice offered him and pushed on. As a result, he was not a happy camper.

Now, Adrian had found out that I was a minister, and on the day after he had finally realized the seriousness of his blister and was hobbling along, now with it coated in ointment and bandaged, he and I were hiking together, and I asked him how his foot was. He said it was hurting, but he could manage. Then he asked me, "Do you have a blister?" I said, "No, I don't." Then he said, "Maybe that's because you're a minister of God." I looked for a smirk that would indicate he was joking, but saw none. "Absolutely not," I replied. "It's because I have learned how to take care of my feet." Even if Adrian's interpretation of my unblistered condition *was* in jest, it reflects a supernaturalist mentality, as if being close to God will protect you from life's pain and troubles. (The comment also assumes an unwarranted equation between being a minister and being close to God.) But the reason that I was happy and he was not was because I had benefited from the accumulated wisdom of many other people who have done more hiking and backpacking than I. It had nothing to do with theology; it had everything to do with hot spots. When I rejoined Ben on the trail later, the subject of Adrian's blister came up. Ben was the oldest member of the trip (at what seemed to me then like the ancient age of seventy-two!), so he was steeped in what we might call hikers' wisdom. As Ben put it, "If experience is the best teacher, Adrian has learned a lot from his feet this week." The wisdom writers of ancient Israel would have agreed with Ben. Experience is the best teacher—or at least one of the best. Wilderness pedagogy can teach us valuable lessons with our feet.

From the perspective of traditional religious teachings, wisdom is strange. Quantitatively, wisdom enjoys considerable space within the Hebrew Bible—the books of Proverbs, Ecclesiastes, and Job, even though the latter two are in some ways antiwisdom books (that's part of the strangeness; see below). Many people would even include the Song of Songs—that wonderful collection of erotic poems—within the wisdom materials. These books are part of the section called within Judaism simply the Writings, functioning as something like an appendix to the other two major sections of the canon—the Torah (or Law) and the Prophets—and there are other wisdom books outside the traditional canon (the Wisdom of Solomon and Ecclesiasticus, also called Sirach, for example). But the wisdom books are so different from the Law and the Prophets that some people have called them an "alien body" within the canon, and one scholar has said that wisdom "'does not fit into the type of faith'" of the rest of the Bible.[2]

Wisdom books are alien because they make virtually no mention of the historic figures of ancient Israel. You can read through the books of Proverbs, Ecclesiastes, and Job in their entirety and never find any reference to Abraham and Sarah or Jacob and Rachel or Moses or David. Solomon is mentioned, but this exception proves the rule, because Solomon was the legendary patron of wisdom, and so the book of Proverbs (and other materials) is ascribed to him, but that is at best an exaggeration, and more likely fiction (much as the Psalms were ascribed to David). Even so, the stories of Israel's national origins that form the backbone of the Torah never appear in the wisdom books. Wisdom does not engage in tales about what God has said and done, or direct us to the supernatural or the numinous; it directs us to the natural and the normal. It is interested in how ants work, what are proper table manners, and how healthy human relationships function. It is not interested in momentous historical events, but in what happens day in and day out. Wisdom writings frequently are not identifiably Israelite at all. In fact, many of the sayings of the wise in the Hebrew Scriptures are hardly distinguishable from those of other ancient Near Eastern cultures, and one entire section of Proverbs, most scholars agree, was shamelessly plagiarized from an Egyptian source, one Amen-em-opet.

As if the contrast with the narrative portions of Scripture were not enough, the strangeness of wisdom compared to the prophetic books is even greater. Here it is not so much the content of wisdom that appears alien as the methods of inquiry that the sages employed. Unlike the prophets, the sages do not rely on divine revelation, and therefore they

---

2. Walter Eichrodt, quoted in Murphy, *Tree of Life*, 121.

do not preface their sayings with the phrase "thus says the LORD." They do not formally equate what they say with what God says. They do not identify their words as the "word of God." The closest they come to such a theological claim is to posit that reverence for God ("the fear of the Lord," Prov 1:7) is the basis of all knowledge, closely coupled with parental instruction (1:8–9)! For the sages of ancient Israel, observations of the world around them—of everything from locusts to laziness—were observations of the created world, and thus, ultimately, evidence of a divinely instituted order. "Fear" here does not mean fright (although relationships with holiness always involve that—Otto again). I use "reverence" instead to connote respect, awe, and the acknowledgment of authority.

Instead of recipients of supernatural revelation, the sages are investigators of nature. They read the other book of God. Their mode of inquiry is experiential and liberal: experiential in that it involves empirical observations of the world around them, observations that are subject to confirmation or rejection by any objective person; liberal in that they are not bound by conventional ideas but open to virtually all ideas that have to do with the everyday world. So, in a passage from the noncanonical book called Wisdom (aka Wisdom of Solomon), the author suggests that his employment of wisdom has involved the disciplines that we would call cosmology, astronomy, physics, zoology, meteorology, psychology, botany, and pharmacology (Wis 7:17–22). In short, wisdom material is historically untraditional, spiritually unorthodox, and conceptually nonconformist, if not rebellious. Just the kind of material that a "Protestant" (emphasis on *protest*) might enjoy!

One theologian has written a book on wisdom in the Old Testament called *In Man We Trust*, and it has the equally suggestive subtitle, *The Neglected Side of Biblical Faith*.[3] Wisdom has been neglected by the church precisely because it is strange and unorthodox, and because it does not claim to be the absolute word of God. It does not appeal to divine authority in recommending how we should live, but to the authority of experience and common sense. If we ask why we should live a certain way, it does not say, "because God said so," but, "because this is the way that works best for happiness—see for yourself."

Wouldn't it be refreshing if wisdom were not so neglected? Wouldn't it be helpful if people who claim to represent the Judeo-Christian faith would pay as much attention to what we can learn from various human

---

3. Brueggemann, *In Man We Trust*.

disciplines—especially science—as what we learn from divine revelation? Yet we see many people moving in the opposite direction. A group within my denomination, for example, promoted a resolution that says, "All other sources of knowing stand under the judgment of the Scriptures." The wisdom writers would have laughed at this claim, for, ironically, it is not in accordance with the whole Bible. They also would point out that nature is a scripture in and of itself. As one theologian says, "It was perhaps Israel's greatness that she did not keep faith and knowledge apart. The experiences of the world were for Israel always divine experiences as well, and the experiences of God were experiences of the world."[4]

A passage from Proverbs (30:24–28) shows the sage's empirical observation at work. The objects of the wise person's inquiry are such lowly members of the animal world as ants, badgers, and lizards. Here the sages resemble contemporary nature poets, who can contemplate virtually everything in the categories of flora and fauna. From the physical characteristics of the animals they observe, and their behavior, the sage learns something about wisdom. Take the locust, for example, an insect that often devastated crops in the ancient Near East by literally invading the land in waves, as if organized into military battalions. Yet the locusts have no king (Prov 30:27). The sage marvels at such social organization and effectiveness without a political leader at the top, perhaps implying that leaders aren't all that great after all (and this observation was not made in an election year). Here's a good example of a proverb that was surely *not* written by King Solomon.

Above all, the immediate interest of wisdom is not theology or even philosophy, if by the latter we mean abstract thought about concepts like truth, being, and knowledge. The sages were no more like Plato than they were like Moses. They were more like Ben Franklin, Ann Landers, Miss Manners, and Will Rogers. In some ways, they were the ancient world's scientists, fascinated by how nature works, and learning from everyday things how best to live. Their subjects range from those locusts to etiquette to the acquisition of material wealth. They could draw our attention to the sublime wonder of an eagle soaring through the sky, but also elicit our repulsion at a dog returning to its vomit (like fools to their folly [Prov. 30:18; 26:11])! They wanted to know how to be "happy" (Prov 3:13–18), and in this search for happiness they reflect a yearning shared by every human being. Their proverbs have numerous modern counterparts, with

---

4. Gerhard von Rad, as quoted in Bartlett, *Shape of Scriptural Authority*, 94–95.

Ben Franklin being a prominent example—as in, "Early to bed, early to rise, makes a man healthy, wealthy and wise." Or, for a contemporary example, consider a small volume with the title *Life's Little Instruction Book: 511 Suggestions, Observations, and Reminders on How to Live a Happy and Rewarding Life*.[5] It contains such nuggets of wisdom as the following:

> "Return borrowed vehicles with the gas tank full."
> "Don't discuss business in elevators: you never know who might overhear you."
> "Show respect for all living things."

In fact, the same author has a similar book with the pedagogical title *A Father's Book of Wisdom*, a title that also fits the book of Proverbs (3:1, 21; 4:1–5, etc.). The social setting for ancient wisdom was the family, so the sage represents a different communal base than the prophet and the priest.

It was Cervantes who supposedly said that "a proverb is a short sentence based on long experience." Proverbs are pithy observations of the world yielding practical advice on how to live a happy life. The proverb does not so much prohibit or permit certain actions but rather tries to define what happens when people act in certain ways. It describes the consequences of behavior, assuming that people of common sense will avoid negative consequences and seek positive ones. Let a hot spot on your foot go untreated and you will develop a blister and not be a happy camper. But there is a danger in proverbs as well, and it is due in part to their very brevity. If "brevity is the soul of wit" (to cite a Shakespearean proverb), it also risks reductionism. Consider the proverb that says "No harm happens to the righteous, but the wicked are filled with trouble" (Prov 12:21). Our young companion Adrian may have been "filled with trouble" because he was foolhardy, but none of us would have condemned him as wicked. Here a proverb veers into the dangerous realm of moralism. Then there is the problem of a patriarchal culture that could produce the proverb "Better is the wickedness of a man than a woman who does good" (Sir 42:14).

Of course, since proverbs are based on empirical observation, they are thereby subject to refutation. Our experience tells us that harm most certainly happens to the righteous, or at least to people who have done absolutely nothing to deserve it. And two of the wisdom books are at pains to refute such nonsense. So, the speaker in Ecclesiastes says that he

---

5. Brown, comp., *Life's Little Instruction Book*.

has seen the very opposite, the absurdity of wicked people who prosper and righteous people who do not (8:14). Further, the entire book of Job is a passionate exploration of theodicy: the task of justifying "acts of God" when they seem manifestly unjust. Just so, poverty may not be due to laziness (Prov 6:11; 10:4; 28:19) but to an economic system that crushes the poor—here prophets may have an insight that sages need to consider (see Amos 2:6–7; 5:11–12; see also the Excursus, "The Plumbline," below). Similarly, that Ben Franklin proverb that correlates early-morning people with prosperous people ignores the many people who get up early for a job that pays less than minimum wage and are by no means wealthy.

The sages might quickly respond that the appropriateness of proverbs must be determined by the very human faculty that produces them, namely, reason, and that the relevance of a proverb can depend on the context in which it is spoken (or should not be spoken). Abuse results from a proverb's incorrect use, not from the proverb itself. In fact, there are proverbs about the *misuse* of proverbs: "Like a thornbush brandished by the hand of a drunkard is a proverb in the mouth of a fool" (Prov 26:9; cf. v. 7). Proverbs are not intended to fit every occasion. Sometimes one should respond to a fool, sometimes not (Prov 26:4–5). Again, sages do not pretend to promulgate absolute truth, but relative truth—truth that may suit one particular circumstance but not another. The greater part of wisdom is knowing when to use proverbs, and when *not* to use them. When your friend calls to tell you that she has just been fired, it's probably not a good time so say "The wicked are filled with trouble." Proverbial wisdom is contextual; at its best it is "a word in season" (Prov 15:23), for a particular time, not every time. When "fitly spoken," proverbs can be "like apples of gold in a setting of silver" (Prov 25:11).

Martin Luther had a great appreciation for biblical wisdom. Listen to what he said is the purpose of the book of Proverbs, and see if it does not touch on something that is part of everyone's spiritual life: "'to put us at peace and to give us a quiet mind in the everyday affairs and business of this life, so that we may live contentedly in the present without care and yearning about the future.'"[6] Peace, quietness, contentment. If you look at every major religious tradition, not to mention the latest how-to books, you will find some wisdom on how to acquire these attributes. This is what wisdom offers, from the book of Proverbs to the message from Taboose Pass and wilderness pedagogy. Peace, quietness,

---

6. Quoted in Murphy, *Tree of Life*, 60.

contentment—things that are not things but states of mind, "better than silver," "better than gold," and "more precious than jewels" (Prov 3:14–15).

We are fortunate indeed that a book like Proverbs is in the canon of sacred Scripture because its inclusion says to us that every nook and cranny in all the world ultimately is a proper subject of Israel's faith, and therefore of our faith. Every discipline of knowledge, from cosmology to psychology, contributes to our search for happiness in life, and every discipline of knowledge can be used when we must decide how we ought to live. That Proverbs is included in the *canon* (the "rule" of faith)—and that the collection of Israel's Proverbs includes pagan Egyptian sayings—means that we are encouraged by our own religious tradition to learn from others. So, for example, if the Exodus story teaches us something about freedom from political oppression, Swami Amar Tyoti may teach us something about freedom from personal limitations, including the foolish failure to heed advice about hot spots.

Huntfish Falls: Vagabond Stew

Genesis 1:1

I never cease to be amazed at how instinctively we think only inside the box—as Muriel Barbery puts it in her wonderfully unboxed novel, "the inability of living creatures to believe anything that might cause the walls of their little mental assumptions to crumble."[1] Equally amazing is how liberating and enriching it can be when we think outside.

One of our youth backpacking trips took us to Huntfish Falls, in the Wilson Creek Wilderness of North Carolina. On the one hand, I often marveled that I got paid to go backpacking, since leading such trips was part of my work with youth; on the other hand, it wasn't as if I didn't earn my pay on such trips. A number of years after one trip, a college student wrote to me and said, "I know we challenged your patience during our backpacking trips, but at that time we didn't have the patience to wait on the slow old people." For the Huntfish Falls trip, we hiked in to a beautiful mountain stream complete with a waterfall, an enormous swimming hole, and two snakes, who seemed to think that the swimming hole was theirs.

I knew that one of the adults who bravely accompanied me liked to camp and had lots of experience with kids and Scouting. When we met in advance to plan, one of the subjects was, of course, food. What should we bring for dinner? I said that we have always simply asked the kids to bring a freeze-dried backpacking dinner. That way there's no cooking or cleanup. You just heat water to boiling, pour it into each person's foil pouch, let it sit for ten minutes, and, presto, you have beef stroganoff. No

---

1. Barbery, *Elegance*, 18.

fuss, no muss. My only regret, I acknowledged, was that this form of dining seemed to encourage individualism instead of community.

Well, my accomplice had another idea, one that he swore his teenage daughters absolutely loved. He called it "vagabond stew." The idea is quite simple. Each person brings a can of his or her favorite vegetable. We pour all the cans into a giant pot of broth, and, voila, vagabond stew. As he was describing the process, he got more and more animated, as if he was the chef at some five-star restaurant. Why, you can also bring fresh vegetables, like carrots and onions and potatoes. Dice them and throw them in. Or, if you don't have a favorite vegetable, you can bring something else—pepperoni, pasta, or even peanut butter (which, he swore, someone had once contributed).

Well, it was the peanut butter that did it.

"Yuck," I said, at the risk of offending the chef. "Who wants to eat stew with peanut butter in it?"

"Oh, it's wonderful," he vowed.

"But," I said, trying a different tactic, "there's another problem. Backpackers never carry canned food. It's a matter of principle—one of the ten commandments of the backpacker's bible: thou shalt not carry canned food. Too much weight, especially considering that you have to carry the cans out when you leave. Why, some backpackers even remove the labels from tea bags!"

Well, you can probably guess where this story is going. I gave in. After all, it did sound like fun, and it was a way for dinner to be more communal, and our hike in and out was short, so the weight wouldn't make that much difference. And it was the best dinner I've ever eaten while backpacking. There were tomatoes and carrots, peas and corn, pasta, rice, tomatoes, potatoes and pepperoni, all mixed in a broth seasoned with our chef's ground beef recipe, and (thank God) no peanut butter. We were, literally, eating outside the box (or at least the foil pouch).

Wouldn't it be wonderful if we could think outside the box in matters of faith and have the same result—to come up with something so serendipitous; so imaginative; so prone to variation; so inviting of different tastes, textures, and aromas, even at the risk of including something that goes against all of our traditional restrictions—a kind of *spiritual vagabond stew!*

You might say that religion itself is a box, its sides consisting of the Bible and church tradition, worship and ritual, spiritual books and theologians and beyond Western panels, there's Buddhist monks and Sufi mystics. To start thinking outside the box, there's no better place to begin than at the beginning—the opening line of the book of Genesis, indeed, the first word in Hebrew. If you read the NRSV text, here's what you'll find: "In the beginning when God created the heavens and the earth." Oops, wait, there's immediately a footnote (yes, a footnote right there in the Bible). It's footnote *a* attached to the word "created," and here's what it says: "Or, *when God began to create* or, *In the beginning God created*" (italics original). There are two alternatives to the main text. Careful perusal suggests that the main text is a combination of the variants, a kind of compromise. We all grew up with one of the variants: "In the beginning God created the heavens and the earth." I know one scholar who insisted that "that's the way the Bible ought to begin." Nevertheless, the NRSV panel of scholars inserted that word "when"; the NRSV text thereby resembles one variant in the footnote but omits the other word, "began." It's good if you find this confusing, because it means that you're already thinking outside the box.

One of the things that I absolutely love about the Bible is that the very first word is virtually impossible to translate. It's not because we don't know the basic meaning of the root word—it means "begin"; that much is quite clear. It's because we don't know how to translate the word within the syntax of the rest of the sentence, or even if what follows is a sentence, or where it ends. In order to understand this, you're going to need to learn a little Hebrew, a prospect that I'm sure will bring you to the edge of your seat.

Here's the problem. Hebrew was originally written with only consonants and no vowels (modern Hebrew often appears this way). So, the first word would *br'št br'* (the ' being the consonant *aleph* and the *š* the equivalent of our *sh* sound). When you add vowels, the text becomes "pointed." If the text really means "in the beginning God created," then it should be pointed as *bārēšît bārā* (pronounced "bah-ray-sheet bah-rah"; the *br'* consonants are the verb "create"). Or, if it really means "when God began to create," it should be pointed as *bĕrēšît bĕrō* (pronounced "buh-ray-sheet buh-row"). The difference is determined by the vowel markings in the Hebrew: "Bah-ray-sheet bah-rah or buh-ray-sheet buh-row. But we don't have either of those; we have a combination of both: buh-ray-sheet bah-rah. You see the problem, I'm sure.

What difference does it make? It makes a world of difference, quite literally. How we translate the first words determines our theological understanding of how the world began, or at least our understanding of how the biblical author thought the world began—the two, of course, not necessarily being the same. Let's take the traditional translation, ("In the beginning God created the heavens and the earth"). That's the one most of us grew up knowing, along with a traditional understanding that God created the world from nothing, *creatio ex nihilo*, to use the technical Latin term. In the beginning there was absolutely nothing; then, God spoke, and poof! the world came into being. What happens if we take the alternative translation—"When God began to create"? What happens is that the whole doctrine of creation out of nothing proves to be, well, nothing. Instead, it means that in the beginning *something* was already there. That's because the entire sentence reads, "When God began to create the heavens and the earth, the earth was a formless void and darkness covered the face of the deep." It seems as if the earth and the deep are already there. It's as if God is cruising through space and suddenly comes upon this blob of water and says, "Why, look at that! That's a mess! I think I'll make a world of that!" and proceeds to do just that. This is the rendition in the JPS version, which begins, "When God began to create heaven and earth—the earth being unformed and void."[2]

Can you imagine preexistent matter—water at least—lying around for an eternity before God decides to do something with it? To imagine that changes dramatically our understanding of creation and of God herself (just as the pronoun *herself* takes us outside a box). Now God creates by separating what is already there—submerged dry land from water, light from dark, sky from earth. Creation is a matter of rearranging things, not, well, not creating them in the usual sense (that is, from nothing). God the Creator takes something and makes it into something else. That's not what most of us were taught to believe in Sunday school about creation. It's unorthodox—like taking canned vegetables on a backpacking trip.

But to return to the traditional translation takes us from the frying pan into the fire. If we say, "In the beginning God created the heavens and the earth," and then go on to say, "The earth was a formless void and darkness covered the face of the deep," it sounds like God *made* a mess of things, rather than found one. One author translates the phrase "formless void" as "welter and waste."[3] Why would God create a waste? The

---

2. The long explanation in the note to v. 2 suggests that, to ancient peoples, the opposite of created order was not nothing, but chaos, which here God subdues. Nothingness is philosophical; chaos is existential.

3. Alter, *Genesis*, 3. Westermann has a long and intricate discussion of the opening

problem is compounded if we then associate this "void" with chaos. Why would God first make chaos? And what should we make of "the deep"? Put a capital *D* on that and you evoke images of monsters that populate mythic stories already ancient in the biblical author's time. Does such a monster, who unmistakably appears elsewhere in the Bible, appear here? That wouldn't be surprising, since other ancient near eastern creation stories have a monster.[4]

Well, I won't keep you on the edge of your seat any longer. The answer is, permanent ambiguity. We can't resolve the problem, at least not simply on grammatical grounds. What's worse (or better, as we'll see) is that it is only the beginning of such problems in the text. In the very next sentence, we can translate two words as "wind of God" or "spirit of God" or simply "mighty wind." Then the author's cosmology emerges: the earth is surrounded above and below by water (above the sky, below the earth). And then we come to the creation of human beings, whose uniqueness includes the divine order to "subdue" everything and everyone else, an order that we have unfortunately carried out with utter ruthlessness.

In short, this one text alone is full of problems. Some are problems of meaning (what is the text really saying?); others are problems of significance (should we "subdue" the earth?). In order to understand what this text is really saying, and not what you've always *thought* it says, you're going to have to think outside the box. You are going to have to put aside your preconceived notions of virtually everything: the world, yourself, other creatures, and God, to name a few. At some point you may well have to disagree with the text. You may have to say, "I don't believe that God is like that, or that human beings are (or ought to be) like that, or that the universe is like that." To enter into such an *argument* with the text is an exercise of faith. Faith is as much a matter of asking questions as it is in accepting answers (especially answers that someone else has given and that you haven't really thought about). Faith requires that we continually think outside the box, even when the box is Scripture itself.

---

words. For v. 1 he translates "created," not "began to create," but in translating v. 2, he adds a crucial word: "The earth was *still* a desert waste" (*Genesis 1–11*, 76, italics added).

4. Mythological accounts of creation involving a divine battle with a monster are preserved in several biblical texts (Ps 74:12–14; 89:9–10; Isa 27:1; 51:9). The author of Genesis 1 squelched such traditions in vv. 21–23, where God even blesses them. Some texts go further in making the monster a plaything (e.g., Job 40:29; Ps 104:26). An entire issue of *Interpretation: A Journal of Bible and Theology*, is devoted to "Monsters and the Bible" (74.2 April 2020). I alluded to these monsters in "Beach Time" (above).

Why did the biblical authors begin the Bible with a beginning that is ambiguous? We can't know their intention, of course, but I have a hunch that whoever put the vowel markings in the text so that it reads the way it does probably was grinning from ear to ear. "Heh, heh, heh. This will really get them confused," he chuckled to himself. "They'll never get to verse 3." You see, whatever intention was there, the result is that the opening phrase of the Bible requires, in effect, a debate. Does it mean this or mean that? And if it means this, then what? Or if it means that, then what? You could easily spend six months on Genesis 1 alone. And, if you ever finally thought you'd figured it all out, and moved on to Genesis 2, you would be dumbstruck to encounter a different account of creation by a different author with a very different picture of God and plants and animals and humans (not to mention fruit trees and snakes). The argument wouldn't be over; it would be more complicated. And no matter where you go in the Bible, you will often find the same thing—multiple viewpoints side by side, begging you to take sides, or offer another. Just think about the New Testament where there are not only two but four Gospels, each by a different author (or authors), each with a different picture of the man called Jesus.[5] I suggest that we follow the biblical authors' lead. Think outside the box. Think of religious faith not as agreement with a list of propositions (God created the world out of nothing, Jesus was the Son of God, and on and on). Think of faith as the *process* in which you engage the questions that produced such propositions: What does it mean to say that God made the world? How do we account for the astounding impact of the man Jesus on his contemporaries and all of subsequent history?

Bah-ray-sheet bah-rah or buh-ray-sheet bow-ray. The Bible is essentially a literary vagabond stew. It's a wonderful, fascinating, infuriating, inspiring mixture of all sorts of thoughts and opinions, stories and proverbs, prayers and protests. And so is the tradition that follows the Bible, and so is the religion of other cultures. Anyone who thinks that studying religion is boring simply hasn't grasped both its profundity and its puzzlement. The box of religion holds the great mystery that stands behind and beyond all that the sides try to articulate. Here is the most fundamental theological principle behind the opening of Genesis: that mystery, simply because it is a mystery, cannot be contained or controlled by any words or rituals or pictures. Mystery here is not like that in mystery novels, where the mystery is something that is finally solved. No,

---

5. For another dimension of this multiplicity of authors, see "How the Gibeonites Became Israelites," under "Indigenous Peoples' Day" (below).

the mystery of religion is that ineffable reality that stands behind all our attempts to conceptualize it, describe it, and understand it. As the great twelfth-century saint Anselm put it, "God is that than which nothing greater can be conceived."

In an essay prompted by Peter Matthiessen's book *The Snow Leopard*, one theologian has taken the title to suggest something about religious faith.⁶ Matthiessen's title derives from his journey of 250 miles through the Himalayas, accompanied by a biologist. The purpose of their journey was to study the migratory and mating patterns of the Himalayan blue sheep. "But there was also the elusive possibility of seeing the rarest and most beautiful of the great cats, the snow leopard, along the way." This possibility was Matthiessen's most profound fascination, not the blue sheep. As the theologian says, "The snow leopard is a symbol of ultimate reality, that fleeting beauty we see only in occasional snatches. It may never truly be seen by any of us. As [Matthiessen's companion] says, 'Maybe it's better if there are some things that we don't see.'"⁷ Stalking the snow leopard—that is a beautiful metaphor for religious faith. Faith is as much continual searching as finding, as much continual questioning as answering, even as much continual arguing as agreeing.

Bah-ray-sheet bah-rah or Buh-ray-sheet buh-row? From its very first words, the Bible invites you to join in searching and questioning and arguing; invites you to enjoy the rich, multiflavored, multitextured vagabond stew of faith, even with peanut butter.

---

6. Lane, "Stalking," 13.

7. Lane, "Stalking," 13.

Wind River: Beef Stick and Grace

Deuteronomy 8:1–3

One of my backpacking adventures with the Sierra Club took me to the spectacular Wind River Range of Wyoming. At the outset, I was looking at the prospect of carrying upwards of forty pounds on my back, and I worried about making it with my aging, aching, hips. So, when the leaders handed out our snack and lunch rations for the week, I decided to go light. They offered us a huge bag of gorp (nuts, dried fruit, and sunflower seeds), which I reduced to about a third. For lunches, they gave us a bag of bagels, a pound of cheese, and a beef stick for the rest of the week. I weighed the beef stick in my hand and decided not to carry it. After all, it would be healthier not to eat all that fat.

We had only hiked an hour when I got hungry. I pulled out my bag of gorp and I would swear it seemed to have shrunk! Surely, I had brought more than that. I mentally divided it into eight portions and each one looked like about two tablespoons. I ate my day's portion and realized that I was still hungry enough to eat five times that amount. The same thing happened when we stopped for lunch. I was famished, having hiked up a trail that gained a thousand feet in elevation. I pulled out my bagel and mentally marked off eight portions of the cheese. Each one looked like about a two-inch-thick slice, maybe two ounces, not even enough to make a sandwich out of the bagel. The guy next to me had made a sandwich with slices of cheese and beef stick that looked like one of Dagwood Bumstead's. I could smell the beef stick; I could almost taste it. I was going to be hungry all week.

It's amazing what a little hunger will do to you. More exactly, it's amazing what the prospect of continuing, *unrelieved* hunger will do to you. Over the next few days, I found out. At first, I panicked, envisioning myself as collapsing on the trail. Then I tried to take a more philosophical attitude: I would think of the experience as fasting, a noble spiritual tradition. I remembered those words of Jesus about not worrying about what you will eat, and how God feeds even the ravens. That didn't last long, because each day as lunch time approached, I began to hallucinate about beef sticks dangling in front of me on the trail. I became greedy at breakfasts and dinners. In the chow line, I held my cup out for the server a little longer than necessary, hoping I might get an extra spoonful. I elbowed to the head of the line to get second helpings, and even circled back for thirds. Some of those helpings I hoarded for the next day. One night I caught myself inspecting the commissary supplies and thinking for a split second how I could steal some tortillas and no one would know.

Fortunately, reason won out. I realized that I wouldn't starve after all. There would be enough to sustain me, even if I often didn't feel full. I might even lose weight! And at the end of the week, I would go out to a restaurant and feast. And then I began to think about people who don't have enough to eat, and no prospect of a restaurant at the end. What would it be like to be hungry *all* the time with no prospect of *ever* getting enough, much less a feast? What if a slice of cheese and a bagel every day *were* a feast? Compared to chronic hunger, mine was a mere annoyance.

The third day out, bad weather created a major dilemma. It had rained for a day and a half and seemed to be continuing. A number of people had wet sleeping bags and wet clothing, increasing their risk of hypothermia. Our leader, Barbara, decided that if it did not clear off the next morning, we would have to hike out, stay in a motel for one night, and then come back when everything was dried out. And, I thought, when I have had a chance to get that beef stick. When we were alone, I said as much to her, explaining why I hadn't brought it, and how much I wish I had it, even though the last thing I wanted to do was spend a night in a motel.

The next morning the weather cleared. No hike out. No beef stick. Thrilled with the clear skies, we set off to hike over Porcupine Pass, another thousand-foot climb that took several hours, winding back and forth on switchbacks that crisscrossed the steep slope. When we got to the top, it was almost noon. We had magnificent views all around us, so we stopped for lunch and spread out on some boulders. Barbara was off by herself to my left, and I was sort of on the edge of the group, enjoying the view, if not my lunch.

Out of the corner of my eye I saw a movement. It all happened in only a second or two. Silently, almost stealthily, in two steps, Barbara came over to me, bending low, not even standing upright, and in the same flowing gesture held out her open hand containing two slices of beef stick. "Bless you," I whispered. She didn't say a word, didn't linger for a moment, but turned and just as silently as she had come, went back to her perch on the rock. The economy of her movement, I suspect, was to protect the privacy of her gift. No one saw her generosity; no one saw my need.

Grace often happens to us this way—not in a word but in a gesture, one of those little "random acts of kindness." If you were asked to describe grace, how would you do it? Perhaps you would remember a gesture just as simple as the offering of those two slices of beef stick. If this gesture seems a little too crude to qualify as grace, maybe it is because in our affluence we can't recognize grace when it stares us in the face. Two slices of beef stick don't seem like much to people who never go hungry, not to mention in a culture that consumes millions of pounds of beef each day. Here again is why virtually every religious tradition warns against the corrupting effect of wealth—and satiety. The more we have, the less we need to be given anything, and yet the very essence of grace is its givenness.

Grace happens to us not because we have earned it or worked for it or deserve it. More often than not, we *don't* deserve it. One of the problems in being given your food rather than earning it, of course, is that when you eat it you also have to swallow your pride. I didn't deserve Barbara's gift. My anxiety about weight had led to poor judgment and a foolish decision. I didn't deserve to eat well, especially if it meant eating what someone else had carried on her back. What I deserved, I suppose, was to go hungry for the rest of the week, even though I had already learned my lesson on the first day: when backpacking, never skimp on food.

My hunger in the wilderness reminds me of the story of ancient Israel, as interpreted by the Deuteronomist. "Remember the long way that God has led you these forty years in the wilderness . . . God humbled you by letting you hunger, then by feeding you with manna in order to make you understand that humankind does not live by bread alone, but by everything that comes from the mouth of the Lord, humankind lives" (Deut 8:2–3, my translation). Here we must be cautious. The text is not addressed to people who are chronically hungry; it is addressed to people who are chronically full, those who have lived so long in a land of plenty that they can no longer recognize the source of life itself, the one who *gave* them the land in the first place. They have eaten their fill, but instead of blessing God they boast of their accomplishments. "My power and the might of my own hand have gotten me this wealth" (8:17). A people who is chronically full is reminded of the story of when they *would have been* chronically empty were it not for manna from heaven—and for me, those beef stick slices were manna from heaven.

Surely one of the deepest levels of spirituality is the conviction that when all is said and done, we are dependent creatures. In fact, dependence is inherent to the very meaning of the word *creature*. Dependence does not mean that our work and accomplishments are not significant or necessary. But all that we are and do is inextricably interdependent on agents other than ourselves; on the earth, which produces our food; on those who harvest and process it (and, in my case, carried it on her back!). We rely on the cooperation and love of those with whom we live and work, even of those whom we never know. In all of this we are the recipients of grace.

Almost every Sunday we acknowledge our dependence when we repeat this petition of the Lord's Prayer: "Give us this day our daily bread." What could this petition possibly mean if bread for us is not, in some deep sense, a gift? And how can bread be a gift if there is not beyond every "breadwinner" a bread giver?

Most of us, I suppose, at least occasionally "say grace" over a meal. "Say grace" is an interesting phrase. I wonder how often we could "say grace" over some simple gift in our everyday lives, something that we take for granted, rather than for gifted: the thoughtfulness of someone who sends us a greeting card, the memory of someone (like a teacher) who helped us get where we are, one of those naive questions or comments from a three-year-old that makes us look at the world all fresh and new.

In case you're wondering how I made it through the remainder of the week on that trip, I should tell you that when we stopped for lunch the next day, Barbara gave me all the *rest* of her beef stick. She said she didn't really care for it all that much anyway, which I guess was true, because she had hardly eaten any of it in five days. A moment later, someone came by and noticed how much I had left. "How come you still have so much beef stick?" she asked. "Grace," I said. She looked at me quizzically, and when I glanced at Barbara, she gave me a wonderful, conspiratorial smile.

"Do not worry about what you will eat." In my case, at least, Jesus' words proved to be true after all. Maybe the ravens are on to something.

Wind River: Follow the Leader

Barbara (that's Barbara of the beef stick) was slow. When I talked to her prior to signing up for the backpacking trip, going slow seemed like just what I wanted. I have always been terrified of getting on a trip with some twenty-five-year-old hunk who walks at five miles an hour and wants to do fifteen miles every day. Barbara assured me that this was not her style; moreover, she was three years older than me—a senior citizen, no less. This was a geriatric trip!

And she was right. She was slow as molasses. When I walked right behind her, I realized that she took three steps for every one of mine. For people like me with a good dose of type-A impatience, the pace soon became intolerable. Most of the others didn't seem to mind. They herded together, lined up single file right behind her, and plodded along. From a distance, they would have looked like a troop of soldiers marching in lockstep formation. That wasn't for me. I wanted to hike at my own pace, be off by myself.

Now, Barbara would not allow anyone to go in front of her (she was, after all, the leader). So, the only solution was to lag behind (the position is called the sweep). And that's what I did. I would hold back until the troop had moved well ahead of me, and then I would hike at my own pace until I caught up with them. I soon found that there were other advantages to this arrangement. For one, I could stop and look at the beautiful views instead of looking at the backpack of the person in front of me. For another, it was quiet at the rear. Some of my companions kept up a continual stream of conversation and I like to hike in silence. Then as the week wore on, and everyone was further and further away from their last shower, I discovered yet another advantage to being far behind the pack!

My method of hiking by myself worked quite well for the rest of the week, until the next-to-the-last day. That day some of us went off on a day-hike from our base camp, with the goal of climbing to the summit of Square Top Mountain. Barbara led the way. She had done this trip a half dozen times, and knew the route, which often was off trail. After several hours of steep climbing, we came to a snow field just below the summit. (A snow field is what a snowcap is called in climbing jargon.) From miles away, those snowcaps on mountains look like they are about the size of a postage stamp, but close up they can be upwards of several hundred square feet, after which you are talking about glaciers. The snow field that blocked our access to the summit was a relatively small one, but large enough to put a stop to our ascent. We were disappointed, of course, but the hike up and the view from where we stopped were exhilarating anyway, and after lunch and picture-taking, we started down.

This was when my method failed. On the last leg of our ascent, we had climbed over boulders and sometimes rather loose rock at a very steep angle. There was a lot of slipping and sliding, with the danger of starting a rock fall. I saw a better way down. From my usual tail-end position, I branched off from the group and headed off in a different direction. We were above tree line, so it was easy to see the way down. It looked like a fairly gradual descent to the north, then a sharp turn to the south over another gradual traverse, to arrive at the spot where I would wait for Barbara and the others and try to act modest about finding the better route down.

At first, my plan proved true. I made the gradual descent to the north easily—piece of cake. But then I came to the turn toward the south and realized that the rock ledge I thought would be there was not. What was there was a steep stream bed with slippery rocks. With considerable difficulty, I negotiated that but still didn't come to the ledge. Instead, I came to another huge snow field. By now it was too late to go back. It would take too long to catch up with the others, and I didn't want to climb up those slippery rocks. The only way down was over the snow field, and I didn't have a sled, much less skis.

I had heard Barbara and others talk about how dangerous snow fields are. After all, that's why we had turned back. Sometimes people would fall through them where the snow was thin. Even when solid the snow was very difficult to cross without an ice ax and crampons on your boots. Only a fool would try it.

Realizing now my danger I looked around to see if I could spot Barbara, wishing I were *with* Barbara. In fact, she was several hundred yards down below, looking intently at me. When she saw me look at her, she called to me but I couldn't hear over the noise of the stream. Then she made some pantomime gestures suggesting to do something with my hiking stick, but I had no idea what the gestures meant. So, I stepped out on the snow. I took as big a step as I could because the snow had melted along the rock line, exposing a chasm of some fifteen or twenty feet deep along the edge. I jammed my boot heels into the snow with each step, and it worked rather well at first. Then all of a sudden, my left foot gave way and I *was* sledding, but on my butt. For an instant all I could see was a huge boulder dead ahead, and I reminded myself that I *did* have insurance to pay for helicopter evacuation. I flew down the snow field, desperately trying to use my hiking stick to slow my descent, but it was too long and unwieldy. Then, miraculously, by some quirk in the snow that had to be divinely arranged, I turned at the last second and avoided the boulder, coming to rest with my shorts full of snow. What I had found was the fast way down, all right, but certainly not the best way. The best way would have been to follow the leader.

As I walked off the snow field, knees shaking, legs like jelly, there were Barbara and the others. They had watched my little sliding adventure at first with alarm and then with barely concealed humor. Barbara said there was a name for my predicament: I got "cliffed out." That is, I got myself into a spot from which there was no way out but down—or perhaps *over* and down. She then gave me a lesson in snow field navigation. Her previous gestures were trying to show me to telescope my hiking stick to its shortest length, roll over on my stomach, and jam the stick into the snow, thus braking my descent—a pretty wise move. It also would have prevented that load of snow in my britches.

Wisdom says, "Waywardness kills the simple, / and the complacency of fools destroys them; / but those who listen to me will be secure / and will live at ease, without dread of disaster" (Prov 1:32–33).

My story is a kind of parable of the spiritual life. On the one hand, most of us treasure our independence. We don't like people telling us what to believe or what to do. Some of us are, after all, Protestants, a name originating in a rebellion against various teachings of the Church. What is the nature of faith? What does salvation mean, and from what, and for whom? Who decides how the Bible should be interpreted? Protestant churches are rooted in debates about these and other questions that deviated from orthodoxy. That's why Protestants were also called Separatists and Nonconformists. That's why they formed what are called *free churches* (which definitely does *not* mean that they won't pass the offering plate).

We are sons and daughters of the Reformers. We like to go our own way. We like to think for ourselves. That's why "self-help" books on spirituality are so popular (but note that "self-help" here is somewhat self-contradictory!). And all of this, I think, is healthy and even necessary for the development of a mature faith. Often, we do need to be alone, think alone, search alone. To paraphrase Plato, the unexamined spiritual life is not worth living.

On the other hand, there comes a time when we "cliff out." We discover that we cannot really make it on our own. Maybe it's when we first have children and realize that it is extremely difficult to provide them with a spiritual base without some community of faith. Maybe it's when we realize that despite all our solitary searching, there is a hollow place within our souls yearning to be filled. Maybe it's when some crisis—an illness, a death, a major life transition—calls into question all that we thought we had believed. In such situations, we discover that our independence has become what someone has called "me, myself, and I too deep in conversation." We find ourselves looking for guidance from a source *outside* of ourselves. We find that following a leader, a guide who has been there before, is a pretty wise move after all. In a relatively mundane way, the adolescent Adrian learned this lesson with his feet ("Message from Taboose Pass," above).

"Fools despise wisdom and instruction," says the author of Proverbs, "and the complacency of fools destroys them; but those who listen to [Wisdom] will be secure." There comes a point at which people who *only* think for themselves become ignorant rather than wise. Recent reprints of Huston Smith's wonderful book *The World's Religions* have the subtitle *Our Great Wisdom Traditions*. *Religion* seems almost to be a politically incorrect word these days. Some identify it with rigid rules, inflexible dogma, and stifling conformity. Others recoil at clergy sexual abuse, homophobia, and anti-intellectualism (as on climate change and vaccines). Instead of *religion*, *spirituality* is the trendy word. But what if we think of religion as a tradition of wisdom? What if religion is a community's accumulated insight into the meaning of life, a heritage of knowledge and experience that provides a guide for our own lives? One can understand the discipline of philosophy in the same way. As Fideler suggests regarding Stoicism, "Seneca believed that by having access to the philosophical minds of the past, a person will experience a deep sense of happiness . . . enlarged and nourished by a timeless community of the human spirit."[1] Every major religious tradition offers a *way* for people to follow. The Hebrew Bible offers us Torah, a word that means "guidance" or "instruction" as much as "law." Buddhism offers us the Noble Eightfold Path. The scripture of Taoism is called the Tao Te Ching, "The Book of the Way." In some sense, every religion says what the personified Wisdom says in Proverbs, and what Jesus says to his disciples: "Come, follow me."

To some extent, it is unfortunate that our culture seems to value leaders more than followers. How many college or job application forms have you seen that ask for the follower positions you have held? I once heard a politician speak about global trade, saying, "This is not a time to shrink to the future; this is a time to lead to the future." If *shrink* is a pejorative word in global marketing, perhaps it is strangely fitting for spiritual development. Spiritually, there is a sense in which one must shrink in order to grow. There is a degree of humility inherent to the words *follow* and *follower*. To follow is to acknowledge that I do not completely know my way without the guidance of someone else. To follow is to learn from someone else's insight. It is deliberately to participate in a tradition (literally, that which is handed on)—in the case of religion, thousands of years of accumulated experience. The refusal to follow is rooted in the illusion of complete autonomy, and it is the refusal to benefit from a tradition of wisdom. That is why such refusal is foolish and even dangerous. That is how you can "cliff out."

As one author says, "Spiritual life rests . . . entirely on analogies. The Bible provides the analogies that enable the believer to convey meaning to private experience."[2] Note the radical implication: without the Bible (or some other scripture or tradition), one cannot adequately understand the meaning of one's experience. Experience is always interpreted by means of some tradition. The question is, which one (or, perhaps, which ones)?

Faith is a lifelong learning process, from birth to death. It is not an educational experience that we graduate from to get a diploma. Theologian George Lindbeck has described faith as a second language. To become religious, he says, means "becoming skilled in the language, the symbol system of a given religion."[3] Every religious tradition makes use of a vast vocabulary, and to become deeply spiritual within that tradition requires mastering that vocabulary. In our case the vocabulary includes

1. Fideler, *Breakfast with Seneca*, 43, 45.
2. Dupré, "Seeking Christian Interiority," 658.
3. Lindbeck, *Nature of Doctrine*, 34–35. Bellah et al., *Habits*, 152–55, similarly talk about "communities of memory" that employ a "second language."

thousands of words and images. Think just of the book of Exodus, for example. There we need to learn the meaning and significance of Pharaoh, slavery, burning bush, freedom, Passover, pillar of cloud, Red Sea, wilderness, covenant, law, sanctuary, and liturgy. In fact, in its broadest outline, the language of Christian spirituality is rooted in the larger narrative of which Exodus is only a part. As Lindbeck says, a story is not so much a list of things that you have to believe; it is more like "the medium in which one moves, a set of skills that one employs in living one's life." Being religious means "to interiorize a set of skills by practice and training."[4]

Just as it takes a long time and much practice to become fluent in a language, so it takes a long time and much practice to become fluent in a spiritual tradition. To give up on faith without having learned the language well is like learning how to say *Parlez vous Français?* and then thinking, "Well, I don't think French is for me."

To shift the metaphor, learning a language can be compared to learning how to play a game. All games have special words and rules. For example, scoring a "point" in a game could refer to scoring a "touchdown" or a "field goal" or to hitting a "home run." Where is the best place to learn how to play a game? Wherever there are other players, of course! You can't learn how to play soccer by reading a book. You need to join a team. That is to say, you need to immerse yourself in the community that best knows how to play the game (even if they don't always win). On second thought, it would be better to say precisely *because* they don't always win, because that will put you among people who know the game as it really is.

Surely this is true of learning a language. It is difficult if not impossible to speak a language fluently if you do not live for some time among those who are native speakers. And it is so with religion. The best way to learn the language of Christian spirituality is to live within the Christian community where the language is practiced. To be sure, it is where people often fail, but failure is part of the struggle. It won't really help very much to be among people who know only success.

Ultimately a person has to be grounded somewhere, and to be part of a religious community is to acknowledge that that grounding is deeper than our own individual wants and desires, interests and beliefs. It is to shape our values and make our decisions in conversation (and sometimes disagreement) with a tradition that is thousands of years old, an

---

4. Lindbeck, *Nature of Doctrine*, 35.

accumulation of wisdom that often knows far more than we do. To be grounded in this tradition is alternately to be blessed and judged, chosen and challenged, rebuked and redeemed. It is to listen to the stinging words of prophets, the learned words of wisdom teachers, and the puzzling parables of Jesus. In the broadest sense, to be grounded in this "community of language" means to see ourselves as participants in the story of Israel, and the story of the church—Jacob's promise. "The great stories did not happen to the masters of old alone. They happen to us. You and I. This moment. A tale unfolds. For you see, we are the stories."[5]

Robert Bellah sometimes has had students come to him and ask what church to attend, while adding that they don't believe in God. Bellah doesn't make a specific referral, but he says "not to worry about believing in God . . . that if they become part of the life of the church then they will begin to see how the word is used and what it means. Believing in God," he says, "is not something one decides in the privacy of one's room, but something one comes to in a living community, for Christians, the church. Maybe, to be realistic, it depends on the church."[6]

A few years ago, I ran into an old friend from high school whom I had not seen in years. We exchanged the usual stories of what had happened to us, how many kids we had, what work we did, and so forth. After hearing that I am a minister, it took him a moment to recover, but then, I guess *because* I am a minister, he told me of his father's recent death. I asked him how he was doing, and he said a lot better than he had expected. Then he said how grateful he was for how much his church had helped him. I asked if he was referring to a course on grief or to the memorial service. He said that wasn't what he meant. What had helped him most was the accumulation of many Sundays just sitting in worship, lots of book discussions, Bible studies, and a host of other ordinary things that one does in the life of a church. He said it was as if all those years he had been in training for a time like this, and though his grief was still painful, it had a meaning and a significance to him that it could not have had otherwise.

There is a wonderful painting called *Jesus among the Teachers* from the Jesus Mafa community in Cameroon, Africa.[7] The painting shows the child Jesus sitting in a room with the village elders. Jesus is talking and

5. Kushner, *Honey from the Rock*, 15–16.

6. Bellah, "Religious Pluralism," 14.

7. To see the painting, go to https://diglib.library.vanderbilt.edu/act-imagelink.pl?RC=48280.

gesturing with his hands, and the elders are looking at him with stunned amazement and appreciation. The elders are learning from the child, the teachers from one who normally is the disciple, the leaders from one who is normally the follower. In fact, the elders are the first followers of this new way, a way that opens up the realm of God.

The way to avoid cliff-out is to heed the call of Wisdom, thousands of years old. Listening to a tradition of insight that transcends our own way of seeing things just might open up for us a new reality. Becoming a student again (a "disciple") is to be guided by a community of faith whose collective experience is far deeper than that of a single life. It is to follow the leaders through whom we see the reality of God and the truth of life, among whom is the Christ. To be a Christian is to understand what happens to me in the light of the story of ancient Israel and the story of Jesus. It is to "read" my experience through the lens of those narratives (including psalms and proverbs and prophetic oracles). It is because those narratives shape our sense of place and time that we now turn our focus to them, to recall Jacob's promise as well as Jacob's pillow.

PART 2

The Circuit of the Year

Introduction: Jacob's Promise

The woods in winter are lovely, and spiritually deep, but what if it were always winter and never Christmas? In C. S. Lewis's *The Lion, the Witch and the Wardrobe*, that is the dilemma in his mythical land of Narnia under the grip of the White Witch. As one of the characters laments, there "it's always winter, but never Christmas."[1] The deep freeze in Narnia actually has disrupted *two* modes of time, the natural (or cosmic) progression of seasons (no spring), and the historical (no Christmas). Lewis's phrase is a wonderful way to introduce the second part of our look at Scriptures, now shifting our focus to the Bible and the way it informs our spirituality of time and place through the frame of the liturgical year.

One way to begin that shift is to return to the story of Jacob's pillow that introduced Part 1. For, however much we need to regain a sense of natural places and seasonal times as holy, we cannot dismiss the rest of the biblical story, because the shift of focus from Jacob's pillow to God's promise of land is not only pivotal for biblical theology; it is also deeply embedded in Judeo-Christian culture, and especially (North) American culture.

A prominent, current expression of the centrality of the biblical story is the title of former president Barack Obama's recent memoir, *A Promised Land*. The land of promise has been a dominant motif in American religious history from the first European settlements on the continent, one of which came to be called New Canaan. Of course, this history includes the dark irony also evident in the author and title of Obama's book—written as it was by an American whose African heritage includes the "original sin" of slavery, instituted as early as 1619, in which (for the slaves) America was not the promised land but Egypt. So, the

---

1. Lewis, *Lion*, 14. Admittedly, the metaphor assumes a Eurocentric climate, in which Christmas is associated with snowy winters and Easter with warm springs, an association lost on, say, residents of Guatemala and Alaska, respectively.

slaves would compose not only "Jacob's Ladder" but also "Go Down, Moses": "Go down, Moses / Way down in Egypt's land / Tell old Pharaoh / Let my people go."[2] (Further, indigenous *Native* Americans could identify with the disparaging way native Canaanites are portrayed in the Bible [e.g., Deut 20:16; Josh 10:40].) In explaining the title of his book, Obama has said that it expresses his hope that despite all obstacles, we as a nation may yet achieve "a more perfect union," itself a phrase immortalized by the preamble to the Constitution.[3] So, remarkably, "a promised land" has shaped Western history, and especially American history, for thousands of years, all the way back to Jacob's experience at Bethel.

But land was only part of the promise made to Jacob and his family, for the family would become a people, and, when the story turns to the book of Exodus, they become a people *enslaved* by the pharaoh of Egypt, then liberated in the *event* of exodus. Liberated, the people become the covenant community. One purpose of that community was to incorporate their experience of liberation from *their* slavery in Egypt within a polity of law and justice. Their communal identity rooted in the exodus constituted the ethos that governed how they responded to *any one* threatened with oppression (Deut 24:17–21). The communal memory of having been slaves shaped their social ethic.

Later, the promise to the ancestors morphed with the promise of an ideal ruler, prototypically David, whose throne would last forever (2 Sam 7:7–13). The king was the *messiah* (i.e., "anointed"), and the promise of his realm of peace and justice became the dream that motivated both Jews and, later, Christians. The prophets of ancient Israel did not hesitate to condemn the people and monarch when they failed to practice peace and justice, but they also could encourage the hope for fulfillment of the Messianic dream (Isa 9:7; 55:3; Jer 33:15; Ezek 37:24–25; Amos 9:11). The dream lasted long after the Davidic monarchy dissolved.

In the Gospel of Luke, Mary's Magnificat celebrates the annunciation of the coming birth of Jesus by invoking the promise that God "made to our ancestors," as does the expectant father of John the Baptist (1:55, 72). The apostle Paul expands the beneficiaries of the promise beyond the people of Israel when he claims that all people can be "heirs according to the promise" (Gal 3:29).

---

2. Wikipedia, "Go Down, Moses" (https://en.wikipedia.org/wiki/Go_Down_Moses).

3. Obama, interview.

The Christian calendar—and, therefore, the time of our lives—is shaped by the trajectory of the promise because of the way it informs the belief that Jesus of Nazareth is the Messiah who embodies it. We are so used to living in the historical era of AD that we forget how astounding it is that the life of one man could alter our very sense of time. But the liturgical year follows the biography of Jesus and then the movement that his disciples continued. Advent is the season of expectation, awaiting the birth of the Messiah, with Sundays focusing on hope, peace, joy, and love—nowhere more eloquently expressed than in Handel's *Messiah*. Christmas, of course, celebrates his birth over the traditional twelve days, culminating in Epiphany, with the visit of the Magi (a chronology defied by all Christmas pageants), celebrating how Jesus is "a light to the nations" (Isa 42:6). The Magi's arrival in Bethlehem in fact opens the season of Epiphany—seven weeks celebrating the public work of Jesus as God's beloved, a ministry of healing and teaching, a ministry of enlightening. Ash Wednesday introduces the season of Lent. The lectionary reading from Psalm 51 sets the tone, with its acknowledgment of human alienation from God and the need for repentance, atonement, and forgiveness—for "a clean heart" and "right spirit." The penitential mood deepens, culminating in Holy Week: Palm Sunday, Maundy Thursday, Good Friday, and Easter, arguably the most consequential week in history. Then comes the longest season of the year, Pentecost, which tracks the formation and growth of the church, finally taking us back to Advent. On the way back toward Advent, we pause for All Saints' Day, on which we remember those who have died—both famous martyrs and loved ones known only to us.

If the story of Jacob's pillow tells of sacred time and place informed by a creational spirituality—awe in an encounter with the numinous—the story of Jacob's promise leads into historical time. Indeed, this is the great contribution of the Hebrew Bible to Western culture, the notion that time is moving forward, that it has a trajectory, a goal, and, above all, a purpose in accordance with the will of God (however inscrutable!). Thus, some biblical writers can see all of history evolving according to a divine "plan" (Isa 14:26; Acts 2:23; Eph 1:10). Ultimately, the trajectory has not only a beginning (the creation) but an end—not just in the sense of a chronological termination but of an achievement, namely, the realm of God implicit already in the promise to the biblical ancestors. Biblically (in the Christian canon), the grand schema is framed by the books of Genesis and Revelation, and in the latter the risen Christ fulfills the ancient promise: he is "the descendant of David, the bright morning star" (Rev 22:16).[4]

For those who are attuned to it, the liturgical year shapes our spiritual identity. Winter is not complete without Christmas. Halloween is not complete without All Saints' Day; spring is not complete without Easter. Moreover, people really *can* celebrate Christmas in the tropics and Easter in the arctic. Even as we value creation's numinous place and time—our "Bethel experiences"—our daily lives are framed by the story that unfolded from Jacob's promise. These are the seasons of our lives: the hope for peace (Advent), the joy of birth (Christmas), the welcoming of strangers (Epiphany), the reminder of mortality (Ash Wednesday), the yearning for reconciliation (Lent), the excitement of a parade (Palm Sunday), the "night unlike all other nights" (Maundy Thursday), the despair of defeat and death (Good Friday), the ecstasy of triumph (Easter), the encouragement of community (Pentecost), and the grief of loss (All Saint's Day).

Of course, the liturgical calendar is not pure history, unadulterated (as it were) by nature. Dig into the cultural precedents for Christmas and Easter and you'll find the seasons of nature as celebrated by so-called pagans and by Christians of disputed orthodoxy. The early church apparently chose the date for Christmas (a historical datum hardly available from the Gospels) to correlate with the existing Roman celebration of Saturnalia, December 17–24, during which people observed the winter solstice, the longest night of the year, and exulted over the return of longer days that followed. (See "Seedtime and Harvest," above). Indeed, many ancient peoples constructed sanctuaries that were architecturally oriented to channel the sunbeams on the first dawn of spring. A similar kind of solar commemoration was involved in the Norse Yule, hence our Christmas Yule logs. And then there are those evergreen trees and Advent wreaths (the latter originally farming wheels hung up for the winter), not to mention old Saint Nick. Similarly, the name Easter presumably derives from the celebration of the spring equinox involving an obscure goddess named Eostre. And in place of Christmas's decorated trees, Easter has its decorated eggs symbolizing new birth, not to mention the Easter bunny. Even Lent, the most somber of liturgical seasons, derives etymologically

---

4. Arguably, the Hebrew Bible has a similar trajectory. It concludes the Writings (*Ketuvim*) with the book of Chronicles, the last verse of which says "Let him go up," referring to every Jew who wishes to return from exile to Jerusalem to rebuild the temple (similarly, the Passover Seder traditionally proclaims, hopefully, "Next year in Jerusalem").

from words that refer to spring and the lengthening of daylight. Actually, there has been a kind of renaissance of natural celebrations in some Christian communities that by no means consider themselves pagan but recognize how such observances of nature's seasons speak to our spiritual well-being. After all, our very existence on Earth depends on the "circuit of the sun" (Ps 19:4b–6).

But to return to the prior question, What if there were a creation story but no exodus story? What if the Psalms praised the glory of the Creator (19; 104) but not of the Liberator and Savior (105)? For the time of our lives to be complete, we need both pillow and promise. We need the pillow because sometimes "the grace of the world" (to borrow again from Wendell Berry[5]) mediates to us the grace of God, and because our experience of the grace *of* the world ought to lead us to acts of creational conservation *for* the world—the earth and all its inhabitants. But we also need the promise because it calls us into the liberated community whose mission is to ensure freedom and justice for a world still full of Pharaohs who must be brought down from their thrones, as Mary so hoped would happen (see Luke 1:52).

---

5 Berry, *Collected Poems*, 69.

Advent

Keep Awake!

For one first Sunday of Advent, a single line from the Gospel text presents a preacher's dream come true: "Keep awake!" (Mark 13:37). Right there in the lesson, Jesus himself warns listeners not to fall asleep during the sermon. And if they successfully resist nodding off, they will be numbered among the elect when Jesus returns in the clouds of glory. They will also avoid having their name called out loud by the preacher. Random inspections, suggested in the book called *101 Things to Do with a Dull Church*, will ensure that no one is wearing a set of eyeglasses called Wide-Awake glasses.[1] They have photographs of wide-open eyes on each lens. The accompanying tag says, "Sleep in perfect safety while the preacher goes on," and the tag even provides a Scripture reference, Psalm 4:8: "I will both lie down and sleep in peace." This proof text does seem to invite discovery, however, in that lying down in the pew would be a dead giveaway. Perhaps the church bulletin should print a warning citing another text: persons caught wearing the Wide-Awake glasses will be "thrown into the outer darkness, where there will be weeping and gnashing of teeth" (Matt 25:30).

The first Sunday of Advent is called Doom Sunday because the lectionary always calls for readings from the apocalyptic passages of the Gospels foretelling the end of the world. Perhaps we should rephrase a familiar Christmas song to "It's Beginning to Look a Lot Like Doomsday."

---

1. Reith and Wroe, *101 Things*.

Occasionally, astronomers tell us of the possibility that planetary doom may not be just a biblical prophecy. We could be struck by a wayward asteroid, like the one that apparently spelled the demise of the dinosaurs. (One named Bennu may show up in 2182.) Or we could be sucked up by a giant black hole, although presumably there's none close enough at the moment. Astronomy aside, Doom Sunday suggests that the Advent of God's realm has a peculiar temporal configuration, a distinctive sense of time. Entering that realm requires a particular spiritual attitude—watchfulness—in which we wait for the arrival of the Great Mystery into our lives, in this season symbolized by the coming of the Christ child. But the Markan text is not about the birth of Jesus (indeed, Mark has no such story); it is about the *return* of Jesus as Son of Man in the "end time." So, as Advent text, the expectation involves a curious irony, which lies in the very writing down of that vision. Why write down the expectation of an imminent end of the world? Why preserve for future generations the hope of something that is about to happen, as the text says, "in *this* generation" (Mark 13:30)? The very creation of an apocalyptic scripture seems to be a contradiction in terms. It's like those people who put up permanent road markers chiseled in stone saying "Jesus is coming soon" (often on sharp curves).

Of course, when we look at *our* reading of the text the irony is compounded. It's been almost two thousand years (give or take a century) since Mark's text appeared. That's a long time to be watchful for the end time. Why still read this text? And why does church tradition place such a text here, at the beginning of Advent, rather than where it belongs chronologically in the story of Jesus, just before Easter?

One way to respond to these questions is to recognize the distinctive notion of time presented by Mark's text. Just a moment ago I used the phrase "a long time to be watchful for the end time." If Mark were writing that sentence, he would use two different Greek words for time. He would say a long *chronos* to be watchful for the *Kairos*. Greek recognizes two different dimensions of time with these two words. The first word, *chronos*, is the source of our word *chronological*, and it has to do with general, ordinary time, the time that we can measure with clocks and calendars. This is what we mean when we say things like "What time is it?" or "I don't have enough time to go to the grocery store." We could not function without *chronos*. Our everyday lives depend on everyone's "being on time." But if you ask people to talk about the deeply meaningful—indeed, spiritual—times of their lives, they will often be talking about *Kairos*. The word *Kairos* refers not to ordinary chronological time but to a more profound sense of time, to decisive moments or turning points. Amazingly, my word processor automatically capitalizes the word *Kairos*—magically proving my point (Microsoft Word knows!). *Chronos* time is when we arrive somewhere "on time." *Kairos* time is when someone comes "just at the right time." *Chronos* time is signified by the ticktock of a clock; *Kairos* time is more like that *quality* of time signified by our expression "pregnant moment." When a woman is pregnant, we say she is "expecting," and often you will hear the soon-to-be Dad say, "*We* are expecting." Advent is a sense of time that is full of expectation, of something unfolding, of something being created, of a new reality about to happen. In Advent, we are all expecting. We are all waiting for a baby (see "Here I Am," below). When Jesus says, "You do not know when the time will come" (Mark 13:33), he uses the word *Kairos*. Within the ticktock marked by a clock there is an extraordinary reality that cannot be measured by humans but, instead, is the measure by which humans should live.

My favorite illustration of *Kairos* time as an artistic presentation is a scene in the production of *The Nutcracker* ballet, usually performed during Advent. The show begins in ordinary time, with people arriving at a party, celebrating together, and then leaving the party. I have often wished that the production would eliminate this first part, which I find rather tedious, and go directly to the real ballet that follows. Yet to do so would be to eliminate the symbolic division between ordinary time and the dream-time of what follows. The division is marked by that magical moment in which the living room is transformed: the furniture disappears, the Christmas tree ascends into the sky with lights flashing, the music soars, a curtain rises, and a wonderful new world appears before our eyes. We have entered another dimension of reality, with sugarplum fairies, whirling dervishes, and a spinning harlequin. This moment is *Kairos* time.

Physicist Brian Greene has written a popular book called *The Elegant Universe*. It's an introduction to string theory, and I think I understood about one in every fifty pages. In one place, he says that the reality disclosed by modern science is so baffling and so mysterious that it requires us to invent a new set of dimensions of space and time. We are used to several dimensions of space—width, height, depth. But the notion of different dimensions of time is, he says, "truly a bizarre possibility." And then he makes this intriguing remark: "new and previously unknown time dimensions would clearly require an even more monumental restructuring of our intuition."[2] This is what the *Kairos* of God's realm requires: a "monumental restructuring of our intuition."

Keep awake, Jesus says, because such a *Kairos* realm is coming, and if you are not looking for it, you will not see it when it arrives. Now this futuristic prediction of a *Kairos* time near the *end* of Jesus' life bears a striking resemblance to the pronouncement of a *Kairos* time in the present, at the *beginning* of his ministry. In Mark's Gospel, the first words that Jesus utters are these: "The time (*Kairos*) is fulfilled, and the kingdom of God has come near; repent, and believe in the good news" (1:15). Isn't that remarkable! What is projected as a future reality in one text is proclaimed as an immediate reality in the other. In Jesus' present ministry, in the words and deeds of his life, the realm of God has come near. In his teachings, in his storytelling, in his table fellowship, God's realm of forgiveness and peace, reconciliation and compassion, has come near. As so many parables indicate, it is a realm of great joy. It is a realm in which hope comes to those who despair, healing comes to those who hurt, acceptance comes to those who are rejected. It is a realm in which the lost will be found, whether it's a coin or a wayward sheep or a prodigal son. Indeed, one could reduce the gospel message to the three little words, "Lost and found," and although it sounds like the domain of a concierge desk attendant, it is what happens in the realm of God. This realm is present in the "now" of the gospel narratives.

"The time will come; the time is fulfilled." Christian spirituality is "tensed" between these two realities, between the "not yet" and the "now." It is part of our Jewish heritage, epitomized especially in the Passover observance of the "night of vigil" (Exod 12:42).[3] The temporal tension has its counterpart in the spatial one that we looked at previously in the two dimensions of a place like the Jordan River, at once a geopolitical boundary to the land of Canaan and also a spiritual realm, the "fair and happy land" of heaven. The tension between "already" and "not-yet" is one reason why, I think, the biblical authors boldly wrote down those end-time visions of the Son of Man, combining them with the stories of the everyday Jesus. That is why church tradition recommends those visions as Advent lessons to prepare us for reading the *life* of Jesus. Both Scripture and tradition recognize that our personal lives and our public world are a combination of the now and the not-yet. Sometimes

---

2. Greene, *Elegant Universe*, 205.
3. See "Maundy Thursday / Passover" (below).

love, joy, hope, and peace are vitally real. Yet at other times these signs of God's realm seem far off. Sometimes they are a reality for us but not for others, and sometimes for others but not for us. Sometimes we find that we desperately need some good news. That is why Advent hymns are so full of longing: "O come, O come, Emmanuel, and rescue captive Israel, who mourns in lonely exile here."[4] "And you, beneath life's crushing load, whose forms are bending low, who toil along the climbing way, with painful steps and slow."[5] "Rise and shine for One is coming whose love will quench all nature's thirsting to be made whole." These last words come from a hymn titled "Keep Awake, Be Always Ready."[6] (Note how it blends Jacob's pillow ["all nature's thirsting"] with Jacob's promise ["One is coming"].)

To watch for something means to have it and not have it at the same time. To watch is to have the object of our hope by anticipation yet not to have it in its full reality. The time is now; the time is yet to come. Christian spirituality lives in this in-between time. Advent sharpens our awareness of the tension. So does Lent, especially in the Easter Vigil of Holy Saturday. Advent demands that we participate in both the realism and the idealism of Christian faith. The realism is the recognition that brokenness is all around us—that sense of incompleteness evoked so beautifully by those hymns in symbols of mourning, loneliness, exile, heaviness, and pain—the thirst for wholeness. Yet this season also demands that we live by the vision of God's coming realm where mourning is turned to joy, loneliness to community, exile to homecoming, pain to healing. Christian spirituality is a delicate balance between these two realities. To resign ourselves only to the future reality of God's realm is to give up on this world which God loves and where we must live. Yet to dismiss the future and live only in the moment of present incompleteness is to ignore the real *presence* of that realm that has already "come near."

Advent calls us to stay awake lest we miss the time of fulfillment. Advent watching is both ache and expectation, both hurt and hope, both lament and praise. There is a watching in this season that reaches deep into our hearts, beyond all of the things that we want for Christmas. Such watching touches that deep yearning to experience the reality promised to us in these words: "Behold I make all things new" (Rev 21:51). Maybe

---

4. Neale, "O Come, O Come Emmanuel."
5. Sears, "It Came upon the Midnight Clear."
6. Clyde, "Keep Awake."

it's the re-creation of a relationship that now seems broken and dead. Maybe it's our work that has become tedious and pointless. Maybe it's our need to know who we truly are, rather than what we have been. Maybe it's a yearning for healing in body, mind, or spirit. Maybe it's the need to find genuine friendship. Maybe it is our longing to see a better world for others who live in poverty and injustice. Whatever our yearning may be, Advent watching forbids us to give in to that numbing anxiety that says, nothing new can happen to me; nothing new can happen to the world in which I live.

The watching to which we are called is not passivity. It is an active waiting. The metaphor that Mark uses is that of a master who leaves on a journey and charges his servants to keep up with their duties, "each with his work." And he charges the doorkeeper to stand by his post, "to be on the watch," even though the master's return may be delayed (13:32–37). To keep awake means to continue with our everyday lives, to keep hoping our hopes and dreaming our dreams. It means in the midst of brokenness to live by the vision of wholeness; in the midst of darkness, to lean toward the light.

To live by such a time—a time yet to come—is to live in trust and in hope. It is to keep the heart's door open, knowing that only when the door is open will we be prepared for the one who arrives. In one of his writings, D. H. Lawrence puts it this way:

> I am like a small house on the edge of the forest. Out of the unknown darkness of the forest, in the eternal night of the beginning, comes the spirit of creation towards me. But I must keep the light shining in the window, or how will the spirit see my house? If my house is in darkness of sleep or fear, the angel will pass it by. Above all, I must have no fear. I must watch and wait. Like a blind man looking for the sun, I must lift my face to the unknown darkness of space and wait until the sun lights on me. It is a question of creative courage.[7]

---

7. Lawrence, *Phoenix*, 11–12.

"Here I Am"

Luke 1:26–38

Advent is the liturgical season for male envy, the one time of the year in which the lectionary may focus on women, depending on which Gospel text you are following. If you are reading Matthew, the male point of view is maintained, and Mary plays a rather secondary role—never directly addressed, nor does she speak. It is to her fiancé, Joseph, that the angel appears, partly to allay his fears about marrying a woman who is already pregnant. Got to protect that male ego! But in Luke, things are different. Here Joseph takes the back seat and Mary comes to the front, and it is only Luke who tells us about the birth of John the Baptist and his mother, Elizabeth. When the two pregnant women meet, the fetal John the Baptist gets so excited that he performs uterine somersaults. His mother's words to Mary provide a thematic statement of these stories: "Blessed are you among women, and blessed is the fruit of your womb" (1:42).

Advent is the one time of the year when a dimension of spirituality is directly linked to the female body and pregnancy. One poet (and a man) has tried to articulate this in praying for God to make him "Girl-hearted, virgin-souled, woman-docile, maiden-meek."[1]

Now I know that I'm skating on thin ice here! For one thing, an alternative might occur to women: "Why don't *you* have the baby?" For another, some of the qualities that the poet desires have often been used to demean women or to oppress them—weakness, docility, meekness. Historically, in some ways women have been subjected to the same ploy that White masters used on Black slaves, teaching them that docility was their God-given duty in life. Certainly, docility is not a character trait that people (including women) traditionally think of as male. I doubt that

---

1. Everson, *Crooked Lines of God,* 12–13.

many parents have ever said, "Oh, I hope our boy grows up to be weak, docile, and meek." Thanks to the feminist movement, these character traits increasingly aren't seen as typically female either. If you watch any girls' soccer game these days, you would hardly conclude that girls are by nature docile creatures. That notion died long ago when Billie Jean King soundly defeated Bobby Riggs on the tennis court.

It is always dangerous to assign a particular trait exclusively to one gender, including spiritual traits. Yet something rings true in the poet's words. Surely, we can appreciate his words about docility and receptivity as a metaphorical description of a spiritual attitude sometimes manifested in the experience of women. If the metaphor is uniquely feminine, the attitude is not. In fact, I suggest that the story of Mary provides us with a feminine model for a spiritual attitude otherwise attributed (in the Old Testament) exclusively to men. It is not so much that Mary exhibits what is distinctively feminine as that she demonstrates what is distinctly faithful, and in some ways, as we shall see, she outdoes the men.

The attitude I have in mind is expressed by a single word in Greek (and in its Hebrew predecessor), translated as three in English: "Here I am." Since it's always good to know a little Hebrew lest you arrive speechless at the pearly gates, allow me to teach you this one expression: *Hinneni*. It's pronounced "hen-nay-knee." What could be easier, more succinct, or more appropriate when you arrive at those gates than this expression, *hinneni*, "Here I am"?

Grammatically, the root of *hinneni* is the word *hinneh*, which functions as a demonstrative particle or an interjection. The older translation of it was "behold." "Behold, I bring you good tidings of great joy," says the angel. The literal meaning of *hinneh* seems to be something like "look" or "see." So, the NRSV has the angel say, "See, I am bringing you good news." As a demonstrative, *hinneh* functions to point out something. "Look," says God to the heavenly council, "the man and woman have become like one of us" (Gen 3:22). As an interjection, the word functions very much like some of our own expressions. One of my Hebrew professors of Southern birth liked to translate it with "looky here." Young children often use the word "lookit." Or it is like the current use of the word "hey" in midsentence, as in, "I know you didn't start to read this to learn Hebrew, but, hey, I'm giving you the open sesame to heaven."

Now, to continue the lesson, when you add a first-person suffix to *hinneh* you get *hinneni*, "behold me," or "here I am." This is not simply a statement of physical location. It is not the first-person equivalent of one of those signs at the mall that says, "You Are Here." No, "here I am" expresses an attitude of the speaker, especially in reference to someone else. As one dictionary suggests, the expression appears "in response to a call, indicating readiness of the person addressed to listen or obey."[2]

Often, "here I am" appears at critical encounters between God and human beings. When God is about to test Abraham, he says, "Abraham," and Abraham says, "Here I am." When God addresses Moses from the burning bush, he says, "Moses, Moses," and Moses says, "Here I am." When God addresses the boy Samuel in the temple, he says, "Samuel, Samuel." (God sometimes seems to call twice to ensure being heard.) And Samuel says, "Here I am." In each of these stories (Gen 22; Exod 3; 1 Sam 3) the human character says "Here I am" as a way of acknowledging readiness to take on whatever God is about to say. In the case of Moses and Samuel, the address and the response introduce a story of commissioning—Moses to be the human agent of God's liberation, Samuel to be a prophet. So, we could translate the exchange with God saying "Moses," and Moses replying with "Ready."

Early in his Gospel, Luke has used the expression "Here I am" in part because he wants his characters to look "biblical." In other words, Luke is imitating the style of certain portions of the Hebrew Bible, and invoking some of the characters, as a way of showing that his characters represent a continuation of God's involvement with human beings. So, when the angel says, "nothing will be impossible with God" (Luke 1:37) Luke is quoting a line from the story of the birth of Isaac (Gen 18:14). When Luke goes on to have Mary sing what we call the Magnificat (Luke 1:46–55), he is comparing Mary to Hannah, the mother of Samuel, whose piety won her God's favor and a son, and who sang a similar song of triumph (1 Sam 2).

In fact, the entire annunciation story resembles other biblical scenes, like the births of Isaac, Ishmael, and Samson; they all have a common structure with mostly the same key parts. At the same time, the annunciation stories closely resemble commissioning stories, like the story of Moses at the burning bush (Exod 3:1–12). Considering all of these characters, we begin to see how tenuous gender distinctions can be. The commissioning stories are all about men, and their first response to their call is to weasel out by describing themselves as weak and ineffectual. Moses says (I'm paraphrasing), "Who am I compared to the mighty

---

2. Brown et al., *Hebrew Lexicon*, 243.

pharaoh?—what's more, I stutter." Gideon says, "I am in the weakest clan and I am the runt of my family." Isaiah says, "I am a man of impure lips." Jeremiah says, "I am only a boy." And as for the annunciations, when Abraham and Sarah hear of their impending parenthood, they both fall over laughing since they are way past the age of what Sarah demurely calls "pleasure" (see below, "Easter Laughter"). One prophet who also uses Mary's words, "Here I am," is Isaiah, but even he has expressed his ritual inadequacy ("unclean lips"), and it takes a hot coal to his mouth to dispel his diffidence (Isa 6:1–8).

Mary expresses no personal reluctance. Of course, she raises questions, but those questions do not concern a lack of will. At first, she is puzzled by the angel's greeting, a puzzlement deriving from her humility. After all, we easily forget that the first century knew "Hail, Caesar," but no "Hail, Mary." Then she reasonably questions how she will become pregnant when she has yet to have sexual intercourse. Her question has to do with her circumstances, not her personal capability. But she does not try to weasel out of her calling, nor does she demand a sign to prove the veracity of Gabriel's message (cf. Gideon in Judg 6:17). Instead, as the end of the story, she says, "Here I am, the servant of the Lord; let it be with me according to your word" (Luke 1:38).

When Moses said "Here I am," he spoke too soon. It took the secret name of God, three signs, and the promise of a stand-in before he really came around. In Mary, what we have is a woman who, though meek, is far from docile or weak. Instead, she is thoughtful, resolute, ready. And, wisely, she says she's ready *after* she's heard it all (contrast Isaiah: Isa 6:9–13).

Saint Bernard of Clairvaux, according to Luther, said that there are three miracles in our story. There are the incarnation, the virgin birth, and Mary's faith, the third being the greatest. As Luther said, "The Virgin birth is a mere trifle for God; that God should become man is a greater miracle; but most amazing of all is that this maiden should credit the announcement that she . . . had been chosen to be the mother of God."[3] In Mary, a woman, models for us what it means to be receptive of God's presence in our lives, what it means to be "girl-hearted, virgin-souled, woman-docile, maiden-meek," as Brother Antoninus put it. Meister Eckhart put it this way: "What good is it to me if Mary gave birth to the son of God fourteen hundred years ago and I do not also give birth to the son

---

3. Quoted in Bainton, *Martin Luther Christmas Book*, 23.

of God in my time and in my culture? We are all meant to be mothers of God."

"Here I am." "Ready." There are other words, in addition to *receptivity*, that we can use to describe Mary's spiritual attitude: *attention, availability, presentness* (or *watchfulness*; cf. the preceding essay, "Keep Awake!"). What does attentiveness look like? In a letter to an aspiring young author, Flannery O'Connor once suggested that he establish a habit of sitting at his desk for a period of time every day. She said that she did this every morning for two hours. Sometimes, she says, it wasn't productive. Nothing came to her. But, she says, "the fact is that, if you don't sit there every day, the day it would come, well, you won't be sitting there."[4]

Advent asks of us to be attentive to the presence of God in our lives, to be available whenever we are called for some task, to be truly present to and for each other. Advent asks us to be ready because so often we are not. So often we are distracted from the presence of God in our lives. We are victims of a kind of spiritual attention deficit disorder.

One theologian, writing autobiographically, I suspect, confesses to such distraction. He was studiously reading a book when his three-year-old daughter banged at the back door to be let in. When he opened the door, she just stood there.

"Well, come in," he said, quite annoyed.

"No," she replied, whimpering.

"Either come in or stay out," he snarled.

Then suddenly she grew calm, turned her head up, looking into the sky, and whispered, "But Daddy, don't you see the pretty clouds?"[5] All she needed was for him to come outside just for a few minutes and lie down in the grass and look up at the clouds with her, and maybe talk about what shapes they saw. It was a time to be fully attentive, fully available.

Advent is *Kairos* time. As one female author puts it, "We are willing to receive the Spirit. We wait to be impregnated . . . Advent invites us to underscore and understand with a new patience that very feminine state of being, waiting."[6]

---

4. O'Connor, *Habit of Being*, 242.
5. Miller, "Playing the Game," 108–9.
6. Nelson, *To Dance with God*, 61.

Getting Close to Home

Luke 3:1–6

In one of his novels, Wendell Berry describes his fictional town of Port William, Kentucky: "Thousands of leaders of our state and nation, entire administrations, corporate board meetings, university sessions, synods and councils of the church have come and gone without hearing or pronouncing the name of Port William. And how many such invisible, nameless, powerless little places are there in this world . . . invisible to the powers that be?"[1]

The beginning of the Advent Gospel text from Luke is very much like the passage from Berry's novel. Luke wants to place the events he is about to describe on a grand scale, events that, after all, *reshaped* the world of his day (and far more than he could know). Luke is writing a two-volume work, the second of which we call the book of Acts. That book traces the development of the Jesus-movement from Jerusalem to Rome, and ends with a notice about the apostle Paul living in Rome, "proclaiming the kingdom of God and teaching about the Lord Jesus Christ" (28:31). But here, at the beginning of the story of Jesus, Luke reverses the movement. It's as if he gives us a film clip taken from a helicopter that at first lifts up, hovering over the magnificent city of Rome. There's the enormous coliseum, the ancient world's version of a Super Bowl. There's the imperial palace where the latest emperor (Tiberias) lives. There's the senate building and the row of temples for the various gods. We are looking at the metropolitan center of a vast empire.

Now we bank toward the east and fly across the Mediterranean Sea to the land of Palestine and the little province called Judea. There's Herod's magnificent palace in Jerusalem. And there's the even more vast

---

1. Berry, *Jayber Crow*, 139.

compound of the temple, over half a mile in circumference, bigger even than a megachurch in Texas! But here is what is so strange. The helicopter does not land in Jerusalem, at the temple—the center of religious life. It keeps going east, past the hill country and down into the wilderness, the desert area with a little ribbon of water called the Jordan River. And what do we see there in the wilderness? Why, it's a tent with a sign over it saying Teshuvah! ("Revival!" in Hebrew). There is a big crowd gathered around an evangelist named Johnny who's raving and shouting, preaching hellfire and damnation. And now the evangelist is giving an altar call and the crowd is singing "Just as I Am," and there's a whole bunch of people coming down to the front, and one by one the preacher takes them into the river and dunks them under the water and they come out joyfully shouting "Praise God!"

Okay, I admit, that's the way a former Southern Baptist reads the story of John the Baptist (although his title does not refer to a denomination). But my reading is not too far off the mark. Judea and Galilee and Jerusalem loom so large in *our* vocabulary that we easily forget how obscure they were on the grand scale of the Roman Empire. Using contemporary fictional names, the helicopter trip would be something like flying from Washington, DC, to, say, Berry's Port William, or perhaps television's Mayberry. Surely nothing of significance could happen there. Surely, we would never expect to drive down the main street in Mayberry (which is virtually the *only* street), and see one of those commemorative signs saying, "On This Site a Revolution in World History Began." But that is precisely what Luke is saying about the place and time of his story. There are hymns and spirituals about the River Jordan, but I doubt there are any such songs about the River Tiber. In fact, Luke's helicopter goes to a nameless place in the wilderness where a scruffy country evangelist is preaching to a bunch of unknown people. To use Berry's language, the setting of our story is one of those "invisible, nameless, powerless little places" that the world never even sees.

Especially "powerless." That's the other part of the story. Just as Luke's account begins in Rome, so it also begins "in the fifteenth year of the reign of Emperor Tiberius," the most powerful man in the world (at least, as far as Luke could know). Then it moves down the political ladder, as it were, to the regional rulers, including our old friend Herod, and his brother, Philip, whose domain includes Trachonitis, which sounds like a respiratory infection. Then come the high priests in Jerusalem. Why are priests in this list? Because the high priests were the de facto rulers of

Jerusalem. They were part of the political establishment, appointed, in fact, by the Romans, and allowed to run things their way, as long as they didn't let any trouble get stirred up. Luke wants to remind his readers that the spiritual meaning of these stories is inseparable from the political realities of the Roman world. For us it means that these are not just "feel-good" Christmas stories, but stories that challenge the socioeconomic system of our own world.

Will B. Dunn, the preacher in the comic strip *Kudzu*, lives in the godforsaken little town of Bypass, and that's what Luke does to Jerusalem in this story—turns it into Bypass. He does the same thing with the rulers, from the emperor on down. Or, to pick up on Luke's theology, that's what the "word of God" does—it bypasses Rome and emperor, Judea and Herod, Jerusalem and high priest. Only at the end of Luke's helicopter ride does he tell us that the route is the trajectory of the word of God. The word of God does not come to the centers or the people of power; it comes to that raving evangelist, John, and the crowds come to John—ordinary people, powerless people.

John is not an emperor or a ruler or a high priest. John is a prophet. That is what it means to say that the word of God comes to him. The political context in which this word comes is by no means new. In fact, mixing the political with the religious is what the prophets were all about (they would have trouble with our neat distinction). A prophet was a combination of a Henry Kissinger, Billy Graham, and Jesse Jackson, all rolled into one. Think of Micah, whose book begins like this: "The word of the LORD that came to Micah of Moresheth in the days of Kings Jotham, Ahaz, and Hezekiah of Judah" (1:1) Or think of Hosea: "The word of the LORD that came to Hosea son of Beeri, in the days of Kings Uzziah, Jotham, Ahaz, and Hezekiah of Judah, and in the days of King Jeroboam son of Israel" (1:1) Or consider Jeremiah's autobiographical version: "The word of the LORD came to me saying, / . . . / I appoint you over nations and over kingdoms, / to pluck up and to pull down, / to destroy and to overthrow, / to build and to plant" (1:4, 10).

Wait a minute! Did he say "overthrow"? "To destroy and overthrow"? Yes, he did. If you read through the books of Kings, and read the prophets, you will find that they are frequently embroiled in politics, especially vis-a-vis the king. The prophets were troublemakers who were frequently involved in what the late civil rights activist and congressman John Lewis (1940–2020) called "good trouble" (see below in the Excursus on prophecy, "Naboth's Vineyard"). That trouble could extend to threats against national security: in the word that came to the prophet Amos, God threatened to "rise against the house of Jeroboam with the sword" (7:9).

Be that as it may, prophets had a long track record of just happening to be around when a government was overthrown. So, prophets were dangerous people to those in power (except, of course, for the "false prophets" who supported the royalty: see, e.g., Jer 23:23–32; 28). Here the plot of Luke's story thickens considerably. John the Baptist is a prophet reciting the words of another prophet (see Isa 40:3–5) about the coming (that is, advent) of the Lord. He is calling on people to "prepare the way" for this advent.[2] John is saying, along with his predecessor Isaiah, that such preparation will involve leveling mountains and raising up valleys, making crooked things straight and rough places smooth. No, he is not talking about another Department of Transportation highway. He is talking metaphorically about his hierarchical society. And if you are at the top of the political and economic and social hierarchy, leveling is not something you find attractive. You'd like to keep the mountains and valleys just the way they are, thank you. John seems to be announcing a new order of things. And there he is, out in the wilderness, with what looks like a mob all fired up and ready to go.

Here is a deeper dimension of Luke's geographical and political language. He starts his story with Rome because his story is really about an alternative empire, as it were. The story that is about to unfold is a profoundly political story because it involves the creation of a new government. That government, of course, will soon be identified by John's most precocious revival participant as the "realm of God," that participant, of course, being Jesus. It is for that realm that people are called to prepare. That is what advent means—the coming of a new order. Because the Lord does not come to be a subject; the Lord comes to rule. That is why Luke speaks of the "reign" of Tiberius, uses the word "governor" and (three times) the word "ruler." The story is about the conflict between two sovereignties—the reign of Tiberius and the reign of God.

Immediately after the passage that we have read, Luke tells us that "the people were filled with expectation," wondering if John himself is, in fact, the Messiah (3:15). Here our familiarity with the word robs it of its radical nature. When the people of John's day thought of the messiah, they did not have in mind "little Lord Jesus asleep on the hay." They had

2. In the Isaiah text, the subject is not people but the heavenly council as God's agents, as in 40:1–2.

in mind a political leader (a *real* Lord) who would revive the ancient Davidic monarchy. In fact, Luke has already used this language in the angelic annunciation of the birth of Jesus: "the Lord God will give to him the throne of his ancestor David. He will reign over the house of Jacob forever, and of his kingdom there will be no end" (1:32). For her part, Mary seems to get the message when she says that God "has brought down the powerful from their thrones, and lifted up the lowly" (1:52). Such language did not play well in Jerusalem.

Even as a newborn, John's role in the new order was clear. As his father, Zechariah, says (his muteness miraculously overcome), God has "raised up a mighty savior for us," because God "has remembered his holy covenant, the oath that he swore to our ancestor Abraham" (1:72–73). Here Luke employs the deep meaning of divine memory that is far more than mere recall. It's not as if God says, "Let's see. Who was that guy way back when I started everything? What was his name? He was married to a woman named Sarah. They had a kid named Isaac. What *was* his name? It began with an *A*—Aaron, Abimelech, Ahijah? No, that's not it. Oh, now I remember—it was Abraham."

But that isn't what it means to say "God remembered." God's remembering is not simply the recalling of facts; rather, it is the reclaiming of a promise, Jacob's promise, which, of course, goes back to Abraham. Jacob's pillow focused on Jacob's experience of the numinous at Bethel; Jacob's promise focuses on the way God's presence is experienced in the history of the people Israel, projected into future generations. When God remembers the promise, the world is rerouted, as it were, to the trajectory of the way God wants it to be. When God remembers, the world returns to a proper relationship to God, in a word, to righteousness. As Zechariah says, the purpose of God's remembering the promise to Abraham is that people might serve God in righteousness. Righteousness means being attuned to the way of God in the world, which Zedekiah says is "the way of peace" (1:79).

When Luke has Zechariah referring to God as remembering Abraham, Luke no doubt has in mind the way the word is similarly used in other biblical stories. In the primeval flood story (Gen 7–9), after the entire earth is submerged, God "remembered Noah and all the wild animals and all the domestic animals that were with him in the ark. And God made a wind blow over the earth . . . and the waters gradually receded from the earth" (8:1). At the opening of the Exodus story, the enslaved Israelites "groaned under their slavery, and cried out." God "remembered his covenant" with their ancestors, and Pharaoh soon found out what that meant (Exod 2:23–25). When the Israelites were hauled off into exile in Babylon, the word came to the prophet Jeremiah, saying, "Is Ephraim my dear son? . . . I still remember him" (31:20; cf. Isa 49:14–15; 42:4). Accordingly, the Persian king Cyrus issued an emancipation proclamation, not only freeing the exiles but authorizing the construction of a new temple (2 Chr 36:22–33). Each of these texts refers to God's remembering, and in each case memory is the catalyst for momentous change: creation saved from chaos, slaves saved from bondage, exiles saved from captivity. In the latter two cases, God's memory challenges political power: Pharaoh and Babylon.

Much of Christian piety suggests that salvation is a spiritual transformation that happens within a personal soul (and, for many, saves them from the fire of hell, a notion not completely inconsistent with John's preaching [Luke 3:9]). But however important that may be, Luke's opening stories about John and Jesus suggest something more. Salvation also involves the political, economic, and religious institutions of empire and temple. Salvation is not only redeemed souls but a redeemed society, not only spiritual development but the development of a just social order. The reversal involves an economic redistribution of resources, with the rich becoming empty and the hungry full (1:53).

That Jesus did not, in many ways, fulfill those expectations is a large part of the burden of the Gospels. To understand who Jesus is in the Gospels is to understand how he redefined what it meant to be the Messiah and redefined the nature of the realm over which the Messiah rules. I use the present tense because it points to a reality that would have astounded not only Tiberius and Herod and High Priest Caiaphas but even Luke himself—to think that two thousand years later, there are millions of little bands of people still gathering together in the name of the one announced by John, and that when they think of their connection with one another, all over the world, they constitute an "empire" far more vast than the most grandiose dreams of Caesar. If Luke were alive today, he would be pleased to know that when people speak of Rome they often mean the church, and never mean the empire. Our very designation of time displays this imperial revolution, for we live in the year AD (*Anno Dominus*), not AT, *Anno Tiberius*.

If we could find the spot in the Jordan River where John had his revival (as no doubt some tourist venue claims to have done), we could put a commemorative sign there saying, "On This Site a Revolution in World

History Began." How did it begin? Theologically, it began when the word of God came to John in the wilderness. Humanly speaking, it began in the hearts and souls of a few members of the revival meeting who not only could tolerate John's preaching but were convinced by it, convinced to change the way they lived and how they related to one another. The revolution began when a few people committed themselves to be citizens of the new order first, and citizens of the old order only secondarily. Perhaps that is the most stunning part of Luke's picture, that the revolution that changed the world began with a handful of worshipers who were nobodies in the middle of nowhere.

Another way to imagine Luke's helicopter ride from Rome to the Jordan River is to translate the various personal names and place-names in a way that literally brings them close to home. This is the function of Scripture, after all, that the movement of the word of God recorded there continues here, in our own place and time. Imagine that the word of God is using Google Earth, and it starts with the whole earth in view but, with incredible speed, zooms in not on the River Jordan but where you are. You can fill in the blanks for yourself: In the administration of President _____, in the governorship of _____, under mayor _____, the word of God came to members of _____ in the town of _____, next to Biscuitville (my own location!). This is where the revolution begins. (You could also add whatever "high priestly" figures you deem appropriate.) The revolution begins in the hearts of people in one of those "nameless places"—not in the White House or the state house or city hall. In fact, sometimes those so-called high places are obstacles to the new order. But sometimes, if we are honest, so are we. So, as one Advent hymn says, "Let us each our hearts prepare for Christ to come and enter there."

What does such preparation involve personally? Each of us has to answer that question for ourselves. Only we—and those closest to us—know the "rough places" in our hearts that need to be made smooth. Only we know the "high places" of pride that need to be humbled (Ebenezer Scrooge). Only we know the low places of discouragement that need to be raised up (George Bailey in *It's a Wonderful Life*). Or those crooked spots in our souls that need to be straightened (the Grinch). A character in a recent novel is an example. After many years of estrangement and separation, she and her husband have gotten back together. She says, "Something felt ironed out, smoothed down and pressed flat."[3]

---

3. Hinton, *Friendship Cake*, 23.

But the political language of Advent—the coming of God's government—insists that preparation is not only introspective. Advent is not just personal, but social and political (that is, a matter of polity, of communal identity and ethos).[4] In a sense, Advent is subversive. It demands that our allegiance is first to God's realm and not to Caesar's realm. As Luke's language of leveling suggests, Advent looks toward the formation of an alternative community in which the values of wealth and power are overturned by the values of sharing and cooperation. Low places—places of hunger, homelessness, and loneliness—need to be filled. High places—places of discrimination, hatred, and abuse—need to be brought low. That is the dream of Advent, and of Jacob's promise.

"On This Site a Revolution in World History Began." The sign could go anywhere, whether it's Port William or Mount Pilot or Bypass. It's no more unlikely to begin there, in a little group of worshipers, than it was on the banks of the Jordan River. It is no more unlikely to begin close to home than it was with those people whom John baptized, coming out of the water filled with a new sense of life and hope and joy because they now were living in the new order of God, that strange realm that both is and is yet to be.

---

4. For Luke's answers, largely socioeconomic, see the next section, "Getting Ready for Christmas" (below).

Getting Ready for Christmas

Luke 3:1–17

Every year the lectionary texts for Advent present a strange contrast to the popular notions of getting ready for Christmas. The popular notions offer us cheerful songs like, "It's beginning to look a lot like Christmas, everywhere you go." Advent texts offer us "signs" of apocalyptic distress: "people will faint from fear and foreboding of what is coming upon the world" (Luke 21:26; see "Keep Awake," above, on Doom Sunday). Who can stand the day of the Lord's coming? asks Malachi. "For he is like a refiner's fire and like fullers' soap" (3:1–2). Fuller's soap was a caustic bleaching agent. So, getting ready for advent here is like being burned with fire and then dipped in Clorox. And the story of John the Baptist offers only more of the same. John lambastes his audience as a bunch of snakes, likens them to trees about to be cut down and burned, and warns that if they are *not* ready when the Messiah comes, then the Messiah will burn them "with unquenchable fire." Somehow this does *not* look a lot like Christmas!

Why does the church insist that Advent is as much a time of judgment as of joy? The insistence is rooted in the acknowledgment that there is something in most of us that *resists* the coming of the Messiah. Flannery O'Connor filled her stories with numerous characters who experienced grotesque mishaps because they were resistant: "This notion that grace is healing omits the fact that before it heals, it cuts with the sword Christ said he came to bring."[1] Something in us instinctively holds back from the meaning that his advent might have for our lives. One source of our resistance is the fear of change. We are afraid that if we are truly prepared for the coming of the Messiah, then something in us will have to give way.

---

1. O'Connor, *Habit of Being*, 411.

GETTING READY FOR CHRISTMAS 129

Something will have to be different from the way we are now. To "prepare the way" is, in some sense, to repair ourselves, and repair sometimes can be threatening and painful. A resident at a halfway house for former drug offenders said that to recognize his addiction he had to repair himself, had to accept the truth about himself that his fellows would not let him avoid, and, he said, such truth "hurts." At the same time, another resident praised *God* for repairing her. When I asked the minister who was their counselor about the difference, he said that they would both agree with each other.

Just so, the metaphors of refining metal and bleaching cloth imply that spiritual transformation cannot take place without spiritual discomfort. One cannot become gold and still retain all the dross. One cannot (like the garment in Clorox ads) "look like new" and still have all those old stains. And getting *rid* of the dross and the stains may involve some uncomfortable changes. It is because Advent involves such change that getting ready for Christ is not necessarily the same thing as getting ready for Christmas. It may even at times be the *opposite* of getting ready for Christmas.

John the Baptist is so named, of course, because of his activities, not his denominational affiliation. Following tradition, Luke identifies John with the figure in the book of Isaiah who issues the command, "prepare the way of the Lord" (3:4; cf. Isa 40:3). The central words and gesture of this preparation appear in John's preaching and baptizing. He proclaims "a baptism of repentance for the forgiveness of sins." Such repentance is how people get ready for the Messiah. What does this mean?

The words *repentance, forgiveness,* and *sin* are so laden with moralistic baggage that we need to continually redefine them. Sin is that "something" that closes us off to spiritual transformation; sin is our resistance to change. Repentance is the process of changing, and forgiveness is the act of releasing or letting go of sin. Baptism is the ritual that (for adults) initiates the process of repentance. It is not necessary for such repentance, and, interestingly enough, Jesus never performed baptisms, as far as we know.

Now let's look more closely at that phrase "repentance for the forgiveness of sins" (Luke 3:3). Literally we could translate it "changing into releasing" of sins. Repentance *means* change, transformation, conversion. To repent is to change, to turn around. It is to change into releasing whatever separates us from the truth about ourselves and how we ought to live. The word *forgiveness* means "release" in a quite specific way: it refers to the gesture in which we open up our hands. When we open up our hands, we let go anything that resists the changes that we need to make and, at the same time, our open hands make us ready to receive the truth that Christ brings. To celebrate Advent, to prepare the way of the Messiah, to get ready for Christmas, means to change into releasing. It is as simple as the gesture of opening one's hand, and yet often as difficult as it is simple, because to be open is to expose ourselves to the *pain* of the truth.

Let's look even more closely at that word "release," and the gesture of opening the hands. Perhaps we have something to learn here from our Buddhist friends. Buddhism teaches that the root problem of existence, that which prevents us from attaining true enlightenment is our preoccupation with grasping. We are always grasping for things: money, power, status, appearance, achievement, security. We become attached to these things, hold on to them, and all of this grasping makes it impossible for us to release our grasp and be open to that illumination that will set us free. This image of grasping provides a helpful analogy for the Christian image of forgiveness and releasing. The hand that grasps cannot release; the heart that holds on cannot let go; the soul that is closed cannot be open to receive.

In our culture, at least, getting ready for Christmas often seems like an extended exercise in grasping. Consider a *For Better or Worse* cartoon that appeared at the time of Halloween but also refers to Christmas. The older daughter, Elizabeth, has just finished helping her little sister, April, put on her first Halloween costume and equipped her with a jack-o'-lantern collection bucket. Elizabeth is excited that April is now old enough to know the meaning of holidays like Halloween and Christmas. When Elizabeth presents the costumed April to their dad, April holds up her bucket and says "Gimme." The cultural image of Advent preparation is grasping, buying, acquiring, consuming; the spiritual image is releasing, letting go, giving up. What then shall we do? I am not suggesting that we no longer give each other presents, for such giving can reflect that love which is at the heart of this season. But I would suggest that we hear how Luke answers this question as well. "What then, shall we do?"

Luke is the only Gospel author whose characters *ask* this question of John. Only Luke gives us some examples of what "changing into releasing" looks like, at least here in the story of John. "What then shall we do?" ask the crowds. It's really quite simple, says John. If you have two coats, give one to someone who has none. If you have food, give to those who are hungry. Note that John does not answer with a list of religious exercises. He does not say, prepare for the Messiah by praying, fasting, studying Torah, worshiping, observing dietary regulations, or lighting your menorah. Such exercises can be meaningful ways of spiritual preparation, but instead John demands only an act of generosity at the most basic levels—clothing and food. Repentance is not simply changing one's mind; it is also something enacted in one's lifestyle. It is not simply something that you feel in your heart; it is something that you do with your hands. You let go. You release. You relinquish something that is yours yet is needed more by someone else. Repentance is a lesson in being dispossessed.

Then come the tax collectors and soldiers, and they too ask, "What should we do?" Tax collectors often cheated people by inflating their taxes; soldiers often used their authority to extort money by intimidation. So, repentance for both of these groups meant releasing greed and power, releasing their grip on innocent victims, and performing their jobs with honesty and compassion. They do not need to change *jobs;* they only need to change the way they *do* their jobs (much as *we* might want tax collectors to desist!). So, in the stories of Jesus, it is repentant tax collectors (like Zacchaeus) who continue to be tax collectors and yet are also model citizens of the realm of God (see below "Palm Sunday").

Getting ready for the Messiah means giving instead of getting. Here's a novel way to get ready for Christmas. Go into your closet or your dresser drawer and find a coat or a sweater (if you have two) and give one to the local clothing closet. Maybe it's the sweater that someone gave *you* last Christmas! Go into your cupboard and find a can of beans and donate it to the local food bank. And if a single coat or a can of beans seem insubstantial tokens, please note that John didn't limit giving to *only* one item!

But don't stop with your closet. Go into your workplace, and if you use your power to manipulate or control people, release it. But don't stop with your work. Go into your heart, and let go of whatever resists being open to the inbreaking of God's realm, resists what you know must change in order for spiritual transformation to take place. Maybe it's an old grudge that you have nurtured for years; maybe it's a negative attitude that sees every cup as half empty.

And what may happen if we do change into releasing? A contemporary poet puts it well when she writes, "As closed hands open to each other / Closed lives open to strange tenderness."[2] "Strange tenderness." Perhaps that is what we are really waiting for in Advent.

John came preaching a baptism of repentance for the forgiveness of sins, a changing into releasing. Prepare the way. Get ready for Christmas, but also get ready for the Christ. Open your closets, open your cupboards, open your work, open your homes, open your hearts and hands to that "strange tenderness" that the Messiah brings.

---

2. Sarton, "AIDS," 147.

Christmas

The Stable Animals' Reunion[1]

Many, many years ago—indeed, some two thousand years ago—on the first birthday of Jesus, there was a most unusual gathering in Bethlehem in the land of Judah. Jesus himself was not there for his birthday celebration. In fact, we know very little of what happened to him until he became a grown man and began his ministry of teaching, healing, and storytelling. But on this night—Christmas Eve, it would later be called—there was a reunion of the animals that had been there one year ago on the night of Jesus' birth. How they arranged the meeting and how they were able to travel there, no one can know. But then there is much about that night that is beyond human understanding. In the words of the Christmas chant *O Magnum Mysterium*, "O great mystery and wondrous sacrament, that animals might see the birth of the Lord as he lay in the manger."

Those who gathered on that birthday night were a camel who had carried one of the wise men, the donkey who had carried Mary, a sheep who had come with the shepherds, and two turtle doves who just happened to have a nest in the stable.

After greeting each other and talking about their journeys and what had happened to them over the past year, the animals began to reminisce about the night of Jesus' birth. The camel, who had traveled farther than anyone to get there, was the first to speak.

---

1. An imagined background for the traditional hymn "Jesus, Our Brother, Strong and Good," albeit with the addition of a camel and the exclusion of the cow.

"It's wonderful to be together again, but all of us are not here. I wish the cow had come. After all, it was her manger . . ."

The donkey interrupted: "I heard that the cow's owner sold her because she kicked over a milk pail."

"That's a pity," said the camel. "Some humans can be so thoughtless, and, I must say, I'm glad none of them are here tonight. I don't know about the rest of you, but that night I felt that, if it hadn't been for us, the humans just might have botched the whole thing."

"You can say that again," said the donkey. "I couldn't believe how dumb humans can be. I carried poor Mary all day long from Nazareth. Joseph just had to get to Bethlehem before the tax deadline, as if he couldn't file an extension under the circumstances."

The camel nodded and said, "You don't need to tell me how stupid humans can be—at least the men. You all remember why the wise men were the last to get to the manger. It was because they had trouble following that star, and they refused to stop and ask for directions until they got lost. And they call them 'wise' men," he snorted.

"Well," said the donkey, "we finally made it to Bethlehem, and way past my dinnertime, I might add. We were all as hungry as could be. Mary was so big with child I thought she was going to give birth right on my back. I admit we were getting a little desperate to find a place, but guess where Joseph stopped. It said Royal Bethlehem Inn over the front door. They called it that because King Herod had slept there once. Reason enough not to stop, if you ask me. And from the looks of the place, I'd call it the No-Tell Hotel, if you know what I mean. Why, it was little more than a saloon with a few rooms up above. And there was all this loud music and shouting going on in the dining room. What a zoo."

"I'd rather you not use that word pejoratively," said the camel.

"Oh, right," the donkey replied, looking rather embarrassed. Then he said, "Anyone could see that the 'no vacancy' sign was all lit up, but that didn't stop Joseph. He went into the inn and came right back out, said there was no room. Well duh! Before he could say another word or even grab the reins, I moved off and headed in the direction of the barn. Joseph was yelling and screaming behind me. 'You stupid donkey!' he shouted. But I knew where I was going. I can smell oats a mile away. And I knew we would be warm in there and far away from all the noisy partying in the hotel.

"I stopped right next to a big pile of hay and the cow's manger, figuring that's where the oats would be. By this time, I could hear Mary groaning. Joseph came running up behind me and put his arms up to help Mary down. It's amazing how little men seem to understand about childbirth. Any fool could see that she was having a contraction. Well, he finally got her down and at least had the sense to make a kind of bed for her out of the hay pile.

"The next few hours or so were hard to bear. Poor Mary went through the birth pains, and Joseph helped as best he could. Did a pretty good job, if you ask me. Then the baby was born, making the most beautiful sound I've ever heard, a strange little cry that sounded like . . . let's see, it was like . . ."

"Like the cry of a little lamb?" suggested the sheep.

"Yes, that's it!" the donkey replied. "That's exactly what it sounded like—the cry of a little lamb. Well, Joseph looked around frantically for something that would serve as a cradle. Of course, that was the other reason I'd stopped by the manger. It looked like it would be a good spot to put that baby, even if it is a place where we animals feed. So, while Mary was giving birth, I did my part by eating all the oats in the manger. Then I licked it clean as a whistle."

"Yes," said the sheep, "it was nice and clean, but the wood was still hard and cold. We needed something soft and warm, and that's when we sheep saved the day, if I may say so. We knew right away how we could keep that baby warm. The problem was how to get the idea across to those dense humans, and in such a way that they thought it was their idea. Simply saying 'baa' wouldn't work.

"So, we sheep huddled together and came up with a plan. Then we broke into small groups (we were the first to think of this way of accomplishing a task), and each group went to a shepherd. The shepherds were standing there oohing and aahing over the baby, not even realizing that he was cold as the River Jordan.

"The shepherds carried their shears in a kind of bag, and they had all put their bags on the ground. One sheep from each group went to a shepherd's bag and picked up the shears in his teeth, while the rest of the group lay down as if they were about to be sheared. I guess the shepherds were still too dazzled by the baby because they looked at us with their brows all furrowed as if they were trying to figure it out. Then one of them actually said, 'Sheep are so dumb. That one thinks it's a goat and can eat anything, even those shears.' And they all laughed as if this was the funniest thing they had ever heard."

"Then one of us had a brilliant idea. She put the shears in her mouth, walked over to the manger and opened her mouth and dropped the shears into it. All the other sheep then did the same thing. Then all of a sudden one of the shepherds finally got it. 'Hey,' he said, 'I've got a great idea. Why don't we shear some wool from the sheep and put it in the manger to keep the baby warm?'"

"I told you," said the camel. "Not only are men slow to ask for directions; they are pretty slow understanding them as well."

"Well," said the sheep, "they finally got the manger fixed up proper for the baby, and Joseph moved the manger next to Mary and put the baby in it. Jesus was still fussing, though."

"No wonder he was fussing," said one of the doves. "There were all those enormous birds singing so loud the little fellow could never get to sleep."

"Birds?" asked the camel.

"Yes, those enormous birds with those huge wings. I didn't know we had such big members in the bird family."

"Do you mean those creatures that had hands and faces that looked like humans?" asked the camel.

"Yes, those were the ones," said the dove.

"Those weren't birds," said the camel, with a hint of disdain. "Those were angels."

"Well, I'll be," said one dove. "I thought they were enormous parrots since they were singing like humans. I always wondered how they could do that. But they sang so loud, it was a blessing that their song was short. Then everything got quiet and Mary started singing the baby a lullaby."

"Oh boy, do I remember that," said the other dove. "I know Mary was the 'handmaid of the Lord' and a saint if there ever was one, but, with all due respect, that woman could not carry a tune. So, I said to Jonah, my husband, I said 'Come on, Jonah, we're going to sing that baby to sleep' (Jonah has a rich baritone voice). So, we flew down to the manger and perched on each side, right next to the baby's ears. Jonah took the left, and I took the right."

"No dear," said Jonah, "it was the other way around."

"Jonah, I know I took the right ear," Jonette insisted

"No Jonette," Jonah replied, but then the camel interrupted, clearly annoyed. "Whatever!" he said. "Get on with the story."

"Well Jonah and I cooed ever so softly in the baby's ears, and in no time, he was fast asleep," said Jonette, looking quite pleased with herself.

"That was when you started us all laughing," said the sheep to the donkey. "I always wondered what got you to laughing so."

"Well, I couldn't help it," said the donkey. "I stood there looking at this scene and the absurdity of it all suddenly struck me. I laughed as hard as I've ever laughed."

"Heehaw! Heehaw!" brayed the donkey, and all the other animals laughed along with him, as they had done that night, tickled again by the donkey's funny voice.

"How could you not laugh?" said the donkey. "Here was the Messiah lying in a feeding trough that belonged to one of us. You would have thought that God would have arranged things so that he could be born in a nice bed in the palace, but no, he's born in a stable. And who gets to witness his birth—the royalty, the rich and powerful? No. It's a bunch of shepherds, scruffy and dirty, and smelling like . . ."

"Watch it!" warned the sheep.

"Oh, sorry," said the donkey. "Well, let's just say they weren't the type you would expect to be invited. But the angels chose them to be the ones who heard of Jesus' birth, and to go to the stable and see him with their own eyes."

"Maybe," opined the camel, "that is because it takes humility to know that you need to be loved, need it more than anything money can buy."

"Yes, I suppose you're right," said the donkey. "And here was another funny thing: the other humans who got to see the baby were not only foreigners; they were astrologers. Pagans! Yet they were there at Jesus' birth."

"Maybe," said the camel, "that is because they had not forgotten to look up at the stars shimmering in the clear, desert sky; they had not lost their sense of wonder at the world around us."

"Yes, that must be it," agreed the donkey, clearly impressed with the camel's wisdom. "And," he continued, "here was the funniest thing of all, that *we* were there. Animals. I mean, God obviously has to have a sense of humor. So, I laughed—heehaw, heehaw, heehaw!" All the other animals laughed once more, making the most joyous sound.

When the laughing finally stopped, a silence grew over the animals, as if each was thinking over the role that he or she had played in the drama.

Finally, the camel spoke again: "You know what humans say about a silence like this, the silence that suddenly comes over a group?"

"No, what?" asked the sheep.

"They say that it means an angel is passing over," the camel answered.

"Well," said a dove, "now that I know what they are, I sure would like to see one again."

"I'm afraid that's all in the past," said the donkey. "And as pleasant as it is to remember what happened that night, I'm afraid the show is over, as it were. We played our part quite well, but there's no role left for us to play. We will always have this wonderful memory of that night, but no one will remember us, I can assure you. If the humans ever tell the story of his birth, I bet they'll leave us out. The shepherds and the wise men will get all the attention."

"Doomed to obscurity," commented the camel sadly.

Silence grew over them again, and as it deepened, the stable seemed to grow darker and darker. Then in a flash the stable filled with an incredibly bright light that seemed to come from all over the room but from nowhere in particular, and the animals huddled together, trembling in fear.

"What's happening?" whispered the sheep.

"Listen!" said Jonette the dove. "Hear that sound? Believe me, that's the sound of wings."

"Angels!" they all gasped.

Then the light seemed to draw itself together into a ring, and the ring was divided into four columns, and each column became an angel. The angels stood in front of the cowering animals, each holding a flaming sword.

"Do not fear," said one of the angels. "For we have not come to harm; we have come to bless, and to honor. Donkey, come and stand before me."

The donkey looked at his friends with wide, amazed eyes, then stood before the angel with head bowed. The angel slowly lowered the flaming sword onto the head of the donkey, and even though the sword seemed to be made of fire, yet it did not burn. Then the angel said, "Because you carried the Christ child and his mother, and found for them a stable and a manger, I commission you to carry the Christ once again. When he enters Jerusalem, the Holy City, with the crowds shouting 'Hosanna,' he will ride upon your back. As you laughed at his birth, so you will laugh even louder on Easter morn, for laughter is the surest sign of the holy in your midst."

When the angel lifted his sword, there appeared over the donkey's head what looked for all the world like a golden halo.

Then a second angel spoke: "Jonette and Jonah Dove, come forward and bow your heads." The two doves lifted their wings and fluttered over to the angel. Then the angel lowered her sword on the heads of the doves, first Jonette and then Jonah, and said, "Because you comforted the Christ child in his manger bed, you will have a child, and she will be the one whose shape the Holy Spirit takes when she descends upon Jesus at his baptism. Because you brought peace to this child, your kind shall always be a symbol of peace for all the world."

The angel lifted her sword and there above the heads of Jonette and Jonah were golden halos, just like the donkey's.

Then the third angel summoned the sheep, who went and knelt before him. The angel lowered his sword upon the head of the sheep, and said, "Because you gave your wool for the Christ child's bed, he will be called the Lamb of God, for the greatest power on earth is the gentleness of love." The sheep beamed from ear to ear, so that the corners of her mouth almost touched the halo that had appeared above her head.

Finally, the fourth angel called the camel, who knelt before her, and the angel placed her sword upon his head, saying, "You who bore the wise men to the Christ child's side have shown yourself to be as wise as they (if not a bit wiser!), for you have helped your friends to see the true meaning of Christ's birth. It is the meek and lowly who know him best, and those who still can wonder at a starry sky are the ones who will enter the realm of his great mystery. Because of your wisdom, you will be in one of his most vivid proverbs: 'it is easier for a camel to go through the eye of a needle than for someone who is rich to enter the realm of God.'"

Such was the stable animals' reunion that Christmas Eve so long ago. The touch of the angels' swords must have filled them with some mysterious force, for each of them lived to be far, far older than the allotted times of their species—long enough to see the fulfillment of the angel's promises, some thirty years away.

"O great mystery and wondrous sacrament, that animals might see the birth of the Lord as he lay in the manger." And now at last their story is known, and each of them—camel, sheep, doves, and donkey—remind us of the truth that Christmas brings: that wonder is the beginning of wisdom, and humility is its end; that love is our soul's greatest need, no matter how many things we have, or how many things we want; that peace is as beautiful as the turtledove's song; and that laughter is the sound of a sacred joy that seeks to fill every human—and animal—heart.

Epiphany

A Kingdom of Kudzu and Crud

Matt 2:1–12; Luke 13:12–21

Epiphany—which means "manifestation" or "revelation"—is about the first encounter between Christ, the Messianic king, and the Gentiles, or non-Jews. The lectionary for Epiphany Sunday calls for a reading of the nativity story from the Gospel of Matthew because that story tells about the three foreign astrologers who came to see the newborn king. Despite what numerous Christmas carols, church pageants, and popular legends suggest, these guys were not kings. The Greek word is *magoi*, so instead of "kings" some English renditions use the more literal "magi." Etymologically, the word stands behind our words *magic* and *magician*. In the ancient world magi engaged in various seemingly unorthodox spiritual practices, sort of the New Age contingent of the times, sometimes frowned on by more traditional folk. The way some contemporary Christians have condemned the Harry Potter stories for their promotion of "wizardry" provides a rough parallel. But in Matthew there is no hint of condemnation; rather, the magi "represent the best of pagan lore and religious perceptivity which has come to seek Jesus through revelation in nature."[1]

---

1. Brown, *Birth of the Messiah*, 168.

So, the story features both of the books of God, the scripture of creation and the scripture of the Torah (broadly construed), for the magi are led to the newborn Messiah by the star in the heavens, but they are also guided by the Jewish scholars who know that the location—Bethlehem—is "written" in the book of Micah (5:2). Indeed, one could say that the scripture of creation takes precedence, for it is the magi to whom the birth is first revealed by the star, and even after the magi learn of Bethlehem from the scholars, the star leads them to the place.

Because Christianity rapidly became a religion that embraced all peoples, this story of royal birth and pagan veneration indicates at the outset what this ruler's kingdom will be like—it will be a realm for outsiders as well as insiders. The inclusion of the "other" was only enhanced when later legends filled out the portrait of the magi by identifying one as Black.

The stories of Jesus as a teacher and healer confirm the indications already present in the infancy narratives. Here Jesus appears as a teacher of wisdom who employs proverbs, aphorisms, and parables to describe the realm within people's hearts, here and now. He does not talk so much about supernatural things as natural things of the everyday world. Often, he does not even mention God at all, except to say that these otherwise secular stories are what God's realm is like. "The two subjects, ordinary life and the transcendent, are so intertwined that there is no way of separating them out and, in fact, what we learn is not primarily something about God but a new way to live ordinary life."[2]

But if Jesus used the conventional speech forms of wisdom, what he said was far from conventional. In fact, his sayings and stories were often puzzling and frequently shocking. There is a kind of unreality in the parables that should make listeners scratch their heads and say, "Wait! What is he talking about?" If we do not react that way, perhaps it is because we do not see their strangeness. They have become too familiar to us, and, as proverbial wisdom says, "familiarity breeds contempt." Truly to grasp a parable may leave us with more questions than answers, and yet, like those astrologers, perhaps "overwhelmed with joy" at this realm manifested to us (Matt 2:10).

Consider the parable of the mustard seed (Luke 13:18–19). "What is the kingdom of God like?" asks Jesus, "and to what should I compare

---

2. TeSelle, *Speaking in Parables*, 45. Much of what follows derives from critical research on the parables, especially Scott, *Hear Then the Parable*, chapters 15 and 19; and Crossan, *Historical Jesus*, chapter 12.

it? It is like a grain of mustard seed that someone took and sowed in the garden; it grew and became a tree." At first sight, the parable presents us with a vivid image, but it is in no way shocking. The parable seems to be a brief story about the growth from a tiny thing to a big thing, from a seed to a tree, suggesting something unsurprisingly obvious: "Tall oaks from little acorns grow."

But, as obvious as the image of growth may be, when offered as a simile for the realm of God it would have struck Jesus' audience as strange indeed. To begin with, the general expectation of Jesus' day was that God's realm would arrive in power and majesty on the spot. It was not something that would appear virtually unseen and develop slowly. It would appear with cosmic upheavals and, above all, with political and military clout, driving out the hated Romans and restoring Israel to her former national glory. Those who longed for this realm expected big things first.

If one were to choose an appropriate botanical image for the realm of God it would be what Ezekiel calls the "noble cedar" (17:22–24). Native to Lebanon only, the cedar was a variety that grew to a height of one hundred feet with a trunk of similar proportions. Though not nearly as tall, the "noble cedar" was to ancient Palestinians what our giant Sequoias might be to us—a fitting symbol of national power.

But Jesus does not compare the realm of God with a cedar; he compares it to a mustard plant. Botanically, it was no more appropriate to speak of a mustard tree than it is to speak of an azalea tree. Mark is closer to the truth when he calls it a "shrub" (4:32). Luke probably used the word "tree" to suggest the future dimensions of the Messianic realm, but, even so, it is clear that the mustard plant was far from noble. In fact, it is ignoble. It is more like a weed than a vegetable plant, and, like many weeds, it is invasive. It tends to run wild and take over. Planting it in one's garden would be something like planting kudzu in ours.

But the mustard plant was unfit for normal gardening in another way: it was forbidden by religious law. Since it was a plant cultivated for its seeds rather than its fruit, it was ritually unlike vegetable plants. So, planting it in a vegetable garden was taboo, impure, profane. To do so was considered unnatural, or what the law called "unclean," and the garden and the gardener became ritually contaminated. According to the Israelite view, it was a violation of the natural order to mix things that did not belong together. So, Leviticus forbids mixing two different kinds of seed in a garden, as well as using a cloth blended from two different kinds of fiber (no wool and cotton blend slacks; they mix animal with vegetable; Lev 19:19). The same notion of what was natural and unnatural, of course, produced laws regulating not only gardening but sexuality and eating (no Oysters Rockefeller). Anything or any activity that appeared to be unnatural was unholy, and therefore the last thing that one would think of in comparison to the realm of God.

Cedars or Sequoias, yes; mustard or kudzu, no. And that is why Jesus's parable of the realm was so shocking. The realm is not simply like an acorn growing into an oak; it is more like kudzu growing into a tree—not on trees but as trees. Can you imagine a forest of kudzu? Can you imagine your next-door neighbor *planting* kudzu? That is what the realm of God is like! The comic strip called *Kudzu* is close to the truth in the parable because there is something essentially comic about Jesus' description of the kingdom as an invasive annual weed (see below, "Easter Laughter").

Now if this parable about the kingdom as kudzu isn't enough to surprise you, consider the following one. "And again he said, 'To what should I compare the kingdom of God? It is like yeast that a woman took and hid in three measures of flour, till it was all leavened.'"[3]

Again, at first sight, this parable presents an unsurprising image. When we think of leaven, we think of those neat little foil yeast packets that we buy at the grocery store. And we think of the wonderful aroma of rising dough. The parable is like the superficial impression of the preceding one—it is a story about growth and expansion. But in the ancient world, they didn't have Fleishmann's yeast packets. Leaven was a piece of dough saved until it fermented. Leaven was rot, or, to choose a word alliteratively akin to kudzu, it was crud.

As necessary as it was for baking regular bread, leaven was profane and unholy. In the ancient world, it was a symbol for moral corruption, putrefaction, and degeneration. It was the opposite of the holy, namely, unleavened bread. It was unleavened bread that was eaten at Passover, when leavened bread was forbidden to be found in any household (much like mustard seeds were forbidden from any garden [Exod 12:19]). The apostle Paul repeats the negative connotation when he talks about the "old leaven of malice and evil" and the "unleavened bread of sincerity and truth" (1 Cor 5:7). Leaven is corrupt, profane, unholy, impure. Yet it is what the realm of God is like.

---

3. Following the optional translation, NRSV note (instead of "mixed in with"). See below.

And the parable goes further. The kingdom is like a *woman* using leaven. It is not surprising for a woman to be using leaven, but in first-century Judaism, it is surprising for a woman to be part of an analogy for the realm of God. Women were considered inferior to men, as even Paul suggests when he says that men were the image and glory of God whereas women were the glory of men (1 Cor 11:7)! Yet Jesus says that a woman's everyday action is like the kingdom. And notice the final straw—the woman's action is described as suspiciously furtive. She *hides* the leaven in the dough. The world of Jesus' day expected a kingdom that looked like this: holy, male, and open (that is, manifest—Epiphany!). Jesus said it was cruddy, female, and hidden.

You see, Jesus himself—in his teachings and in his life and death—changed the very meaning of the word *epiphany*. No longer does it mean a manifestation of royal power in majesty and glory. At least, that is not the beginning of epiphany. It may end there, and certainly does in Christian faith, in which the risen Lord is worthy "to receive power and wealth and wisdom and might and honor and glory and blessing," to quote the book of Revelation (5:12). But the kingdom does not begin that way. It begins with kudzu and crud. And that makes it all the more subversive.[4]

One of the ironies of the epiphany story in Matthew is that pagan astrologers announce the birth of the Messiah. Like the psalmist, they have seen God's glory in the sky (Ps 19), even as others cannot see it because they have their eyes on the ground. Those whom some Jews would not even touch, much less eat with, are the ones who genuinely worship the newborn king of Israel. Far from worshiping the Messiah, Herod and the religious authorities are rightly frightened by the news of his birth. Herod proceeds with the slaughter of the innocents, and the religious authorities later will plot to kill Jesus. And no wonder, because his kingdom of kudzu is more insidious and uncontrollable and therefore more dangerous to political power than any noble cedar. And his repudiation of the laws of taboo, his willingness to associate with Gentiles, to touch lepers, and to welcome social outcasts threatened the power of the religious establishment and a social order rooted in spiritual chauvinism that excluded people from the realm of God.

---

4. The mountaintop transfiguration story provides a momentary illustration of epiphany as glorious, but Jesus declines the offer to create a shrine at the place, and immediately upon descending he warns the disciples of how he must suffer and die (Matt 17:1–13; cf. "Tent or Temple?" above).

A kingdom of kudzu and crud. The function of these parables is to "subvert [our] dependency on the rules of the sacred, the predictability of what is good."[5] Epiphany is about the inclusiveness of the realm of God, about the acceptance of people whom the moral majority thinks of as weeds and rot. Perhaps that is why when the astrologers came to the place where the star of Bethlehem stood suspended over the newborn Christ, "they were overwhelmed with joy"—because, pagan though they were, the door to the kingdom was opened to them, and they had seen the light.

---

5. Scott, *Hear Then the Parable*, 328.

Baptism of Christ: The Uncongealed Word

Matt 3:13–17; Mark 1:4–11; Luke 3:21–22

At an ecclesiastical meeting I once gave a little impromptu speech about biblical interpretation and made the mistake near the beginning of asking the question: "What is the Bible?" Before I could answer the question, someone shouted "the Word of God!" Now, I'm not the kind of person who thinks fast on his feet (I'm more the kind who thinks slow on his butt). So, of course, I didn't come up with the response that I carefully honed in my mind all the way back from the meeting. Here's what I *would* have said if I had my wits about me: "No sir, the Bible is not the Word of God, and anyone in the Reformed tradition (which includes the United Church of Christ) should know that." Jesus the Christ is the Word of God, not the Bible. In Reformed tradition, the Bible at times *becomes* the Word of God when it functions to instill faith and obedience. But to say that the Bible *is* the Word of God is to give it a status that it does not rightly have. In fact, it easily produces a heresy that I call "Quadritarianism"—God in four persons, Father, Son, Holy Spirit, and Holy Book.[1]

Obfuscation about what the word *is* can mean became infamous when president Bill Clinton defended his statements about the Monica Lewinski affair by saying, "It depends on what the meaning of the word *is* is." But putting Clintonian political spin aside, it is nevertheless true that the meaning of the word *is* can be highly debatable, and especially in theological discourse. If you don't believe me, check out the ecclesiastical debates on what the word "is" means when we say of the eucharistic bread, "This is my body."

---

1. As Stroup notes, Karl Barth represents the classic formulation, in which "Scripture is not itself God's Word," but, as a witness and by God's grace, "may *become* God's Word" (*Promise*, 46; italics added).

The same ambiguity appears when we take the sentence "The Bible is the Word of God." Or consider an even simpler sentence: "God said," or "God says" or "God spoke," which, after all, *leads* to words of God. The two words "God spoke" produce the simplest of grammatical sentences—subject and verb. But those two words are profoundly difficult to understand. In terms of content, "God spoke" is probably one of the most complicated sentences that one can utter. What does it mean? Unless you believe in a literal sense (God spoke audible words that humans could hear), what sense it makes is by no means immediately clear.

What sense do you make, for example, of those billboards that (for a mercifully brief period) were signed by God? At first, they seemed warmly invitational: LET'S MEET AT MY HOUSE BEFORE THE GAME. —GOD. But a mile down the road, the message became threatening: DON'T MAKE ME HAVE TO COME DOWN THERE. Then a mile later the threat became utterly concrete: KEEP USING MY NAME IN VAIN AND I'LL MAKE RUSH HOUR LONGER (that will *really* produce a "Goddamned traffic jam"!). I had never believed that these messages had any validity until one day when I was driving to a meeting and happened to be going through a stretch of I-85 known as "the highway of the shadow of death." All of a sudden, I realized that I had been thinking about something other than my route, and became alarmed that I had missed the exit. And then looming above me was another of those messages from God: DO YOU HAVE ANY IDEA WHERE YOU'RE GOING?

Somehow, I don't think God is in the outdoor advertising business. If she were, I wish she would say more things that I can agree with, starting with BILLBOARDS ARE VISUAL POLLUTION. To me, there's something presumptuous, even arrogant, in those billboards. As if some human can actually speak for God. But what then do we do with other texts, like the Bible, that say over and over again "God said"? Are those words not also presumptuous, if not arrogant? What makes the billboards less valid than the Bible?

The voice of God is central to the lectionary texts for the first Sunday after Epiphany, celebrating the baptism of Christ. None of the texts say explicitly "God said," but a voice comes out of heaven and speaks, and there is little doubt to whom that voice belongs.[2] What is the relationship between the Word of God (usually spelled with a capital *W*), the words of God (as in the Bible), and human words (what the author writes)? "A

---

2. The Gospel of John, as usual, is the odd one out on this, saying that the voice comes from "the one who sent me" (1:33).

voice came from heaven"—the words of the author; "'you are my Son, the Beloved'"—the words of God. What is the Word of God here? It is something like this: Jesus is the definitive model of an authentic human being, someone who is in a completely trusting and obedient relationship with God, the way we were all created to be. But that is an abstraction. The Word of God here appears in the words of God that name Jesus as "Son," and the words of God are, of course, the words of the author just as much as the descriptive words "a voice came from heaven." It is impossible to separate the words of the author and the words of God.

Over and over again you hear people citing the words of God in the Bible with the assumption that they are the Word of God, and not human words. I'm afraid I have some bad news for such people: there is no unmediated Word of God. That is, every word spoken by God and written in the Bible is a human word. The Ten Commandments (literally "ten words") are one of the most important examples of words that God says in the Bible. But, as one scholar puts it, when all is said and done, "at some point in the formation of the tradition, someone placed these words in [God's] mouth."[3] The implications of that claim are enormous, determining what we mean by truth and revelation and morality—ultimately, what we mean by "God." The authorial agency behind the words of God leads to a critical judgment: the Word of God is not limited to or confined by the words of the biblical texts, although the words may point to the Word. The Word of God is, in fact, beyond words, even if we must use words to talk about it.

The first time I read the Tao Te Ching, the "Bible" of Taoism, I was struck by the similarity between the Tao and the Word. *Tao* means something like "way of being," and the opening lines of the Tao Te Ching say: "The tao that can be told / is not the eternal Tao. / The name that can be named / is not the eternal Name."[4] Note that the pair tao/Tao corresponds with word/Word. Certainly it is true that the word that can be told is not the eternal Word. Indeed, in a phrase attributed to the Jewish philosopher Martin Buber, he mirrors the Taoist when he says that biblical stories are trying "to name the Unnamable." For Buber, our words about God are "legitimate stammering" (a phrase inspired by the figure of a stuttering Moses, Exod 4:10).[5] If everyone (and especially every Christian) would

---

3. Patrick, *Rhetoric*, 71.

4. Laozi, *Tao Te Ching*, 1. See n 1, above.

5. McConnell, "Introduction," 17, who also cites Buber's phrase. Theologian David Kelsey develops the metaphor of stammering in *Human Anguish*, especially in chapter 11.

understand that and live accordingly, there would be a lot less divisiveness, bigotry, hatred—and, yes, violence. The word that can be told is not the eternal Word. The name that can be named is not the eternal Name. To get back to our biblical text, that means that the particular expression of the Word in the words "you are my Son, the Beloved" is not completely revealing of who Jesus is, or who God is. No words can be. The problem comes when people forget that Jesus is the Word of God and insist that these *words* are the Word.

The word that can be told is not the eternal Word. The man who insisted that the Bible *is* the Word of God did not understand that. In the context of the main issue at our meeting (welcoming gays and lesbians into the church), he insisted that the Word of God is completely and eternally expressed by one verse in Leviticus—after all, the words of God (18:1). The verse concerns sexual relations, in particular, *homosexual* sexual relations (18:22): "it is an abomination." But what do we do when a word of God contradicts another word of God?

Consider another story in which the heavens open and a voice speaks, in this case, to the apostle Peter (Acts 10). Peter is confronted by a spiritual dilemma—welcoming a Gentile (Cornelius) into the church, something that according to his Jewish heritage he considered unacceptable, indeed, "unlawful" (10:28). (Lest we throw stones, we must recognize the same prejudice in North American racism, in which "It was taboo for blacks and whites to sit, stand, or eat in the same space at the same time or even to use the same utensils."[6])

In praying about it, all of a sudden Peter realizes that he is really hungry, and while he is waiting for lunch to be served, he falls into a "trance." He sees the heavens opened, and a sheet descending, miraculously containing his lunch! Bon appétit! But there's a problem: lunch includes all sorts of foods that are explicitly forbidden for Jews to eat (including reptiles!). And Peter has *never* eaten anything that according to the Levitical rules, is "profane or unclean."[7] But the voice from heaven replies, "What God has made clean, you must not call profane" (10:15). Peter wisely gets the message: Gentiles should be welcomed into the church. The same interpretive movement is evident when Jesus says that it is not what people ingest as food that defiles (makes them "unclean")

---

6. Wilkerson, *Caste*, 292.

7. For "four-footed creatures," cf. Lev 11:27; for reptiles, Lev 11:42. Also taboo are shrimp, clams, oysters, and crabs (Lev 11:9–12). I have discussed the biblical texts involving homosexuality in Mann, *Book of the Torah* (2nd ed.), 223–28.

but what they emit, namely, "evil intentions" (Mark 7:17–23). And the greater significance of sources of contamination is evident in Jesus' touching an untouchable leper, who was required to warn off others with the cry, "Unclean!" (Matt 8:1–4; Lev 13:45).

And here is the message about the Word of God. It is not eternally expressed in the words of the Bible *without* being subject to reinterpretation. In the story about Peter, the words of God spoken from heaven *contradict* the words of God spoken to Moses. The new words annul the old words. The revised legal ruling overrules the former law. The new ethic rejects the old. Belonging in an inclusive community overrides believing in an exclusive dogma. Genuine tradition is an ongoing reinterpretation, the "living faith of the dead," in contrast to traditional*ism*, which is "the dead faith of the living," to paraphrase the ecclesiastical scholar Jaroslav Pelikan.[8] The man who insisted that Lev 18:22 is the Word of God was in error because he did not know what the meaning of the word *is* is.

"Someone placed these words in God's mouth" is another way of expressing the Taoist saying, "the tao that can be told is not the eternal Tao." But it is still possible (indeed, desirable) for us to say that sometimes the words of God *are* the *Word* of God when they function to challenge us both personally and corporately to live in a relationship of integrity with God and with each other. When these words become part of our very identity, as they certainly do in Christian spirituality, they become God's Word for us. The transformation from word to Word is a gift of the Spirit. To say that an author placed words in God's mouth is to say that the biblical authors' work is "fictive." Wherever the Bible says "God said," it is a human author who is saying it. These are works of fiction. In a sense, it is no less presumptuous than those billboards. Whether or not it is arrogant depends on the extent to which we are willing to acknowledge that the words of God are not the Word of God (and that neither has to do with billboards).

To say that the biblical words of God are fictitious is not to say that they are false. After all, Jesus's parables are all fiction, but for many they reveal the Word of God. The story of the prodigal son or the good Samaritan are fiction; we do not ask if they are reporting things that actually happened, nor do we ask who the characters really were. But we recognize that the stories *really* describe the human condition. Indeed, it is realization of that descriptive power that *makes* the stories bearers of

---

8. Among numerous references, see Wikipedia, "Pelikan, Jaroslav."

the Word. To use the word *fiction* is to recognize that the biblical Word is fluid. Simply by being in the context of a story, the Word is fluid, and not fixed. Or, prompted by an interesting passage from Gail Godwin's novel *The Finishing School*, we could say that the Word is uncongealed. One character, Ursula, is talking to the narrator, Justin: "There are two kinds of people," she says. One kind has "congealed into their final selves" and will never change. The other kind "keep moving, changing." "They are fluid." That's what keeps them alive. Then she warns, "You must be constantly on your guard, Justin, against congealing."[9] If it is true that a congealed human being is not truly an alive human being, then it's all the more true that a congealed Word of God is not the *living* Word of God. To say that the Bible *is* the Word of God, and by "is" to mean that the Word of God is *fixed* in the words eternally, is to congeal the Word of God. It is to make it into verbal Jell-O, Jell-O that has been chilled and turned from its fluid state into the (relatively) solid state, the kind of Jell-O that you can pop out of a mold at a picnic.

Although sometimes it comes dangerously close (Deut 4:2; 12:32; Rev 22:18), the Bible does not attempt to congeal the Word of God, primarily because the dominant way of talking about God is through story or narrative. God is a character in a story, not a concept captured in a definition or a creed. And by nature stories present truth in fluid, uncongealed form. Stories always allow for ambiguity, for moving and changing, for surprise, as Godwin's character says. For the biblical critic Robert Alter, "fiction was the principal means which the biblical authors had at their disposal for realizing history." Narrative fiction is the artistic form that "left little margin for neat and confident views about God," and it suited their perception of the "profound and ineradicable untidiness in the nature of things."[10]

Compared to the Hebrew Bible's theology, the Gospels push the story form to the extreme. The sentence "God said," in various forms, must occur thousands of times in the Hebrew Bible, but it only occurs twice in the Synoptic Gospels[11] (and there indirectly)—once at Jesus' baptism, and once at his transfiguration, the story that brings Epiphany to an end

---

9. Godwin, *Finishing School*, 4 (italics original).

10. Alter, *Art of Biblical Narrative*, 32, 154.

11. That is, Matthew, Mark, and Luke. The Gospel of John is in many ways unique in its presentation of Jesus. For example, in one anecdote, "a voice came to him from heaven," and refers to Jesus's "glorification," but even here the people who hear it think it's thunder, or an angel speaking (12:28).

(e.g., Mark 9:2–10), thereby framing the life of Jesus. In the transfiguration story, God says to several disciples, "Listen to *him*." In the Gospels we learn who God is by listening and watching what this *man* says and does, how he relates to other people, whom he touches, with whom he eats. (And in the transfiguration story, Peter has yet another revelation, that the Messiah is not a militant political hero but a suffering servant). Jesus *never* says, "God says." He *lives* who God is. What he says and does *represents* who God is. In this role of mediator, Jesus continues a tradition established by Moses, of whom Karl Barth wrote, "to look to God meant to Israel to look to this man, to hear God to hear the word of this man, to obey God to follow his direction, to trust God to trust his insight."[12] (Indeed Jesus can say, in contrast to what God said, that what he says is better!—e.g., Matt 5:21 and Exod 20:13; cf. above on Acts 10). *Theology* becomes his *biography*, or, as the Gospel of John says, the Word becomes flesh (John 1:14).

Short story author and novelist Flannery O'Connor once said, "The fiction writer presents . . . grace through nature, but when he finishes there always has to be left over that sense of Mystery which cannot be accounted for by any human formula."[13] She writes "Mystery" with a capital *M*, because, I think, it is equivalent to the Tao that cannot be told, and "Word" with a capital *W*. Mystery is the uncongealed Word of God.

You must constantly be on your guard against congealing. That is true whether we are talking about our own souls or our words about God. We must constantly resist allowing either to turn into Jell-O.

---

12. Barth, *Church Dogmatics* 4/1, 430. Remarkably, as Friedman notes (*Commentary*, 240), starting with Moses "all revelation to Israel is mediated by a prophet. God never speaks directly to the people again in any book of the *Tanak* [i.e., the Hebrew Bible]."

13. O'Connor, *Mystery and Manners*, 153.

Lent

Ash Wednesday

The Sting of Death

Philippians 2:1–11

One a bright summer morning I was walking through the woods at a local park at my usual fast clip when yellow jackets stung me several times on the ankle. Within seconds, my palms and scalp and the soles of my feet began to itch as if I had instant poison ivy. For reasons I can only grant to providence, some voice inside me said, "Run like hell to the car," and I did. In retrospect, running may not have been the best idea in terms of blood circulating the venom, but it got me there quickly. By the time I got home my tongue was beginning to swell, and there was little question about what was happening: I was having an allergic reaction to the sting, incipient anaphylaxis. I had never had such a reaction before; in fact, only a month or so previously I had been stung while out backpacking, miles from the nearest road. Had the allergic reaction happened then, I would have died.

When I got home, I popped a couple of Benadryl tablets and my wife, Connie, drove me to the emergency room. Never had traffic seemed so slow or red lights so long. When I got there, Connie went off to fill out forms and I was promptly installed in a bed, hooked up to an IV, and pumped full of *more* Benadryl. Within seconds a doctor joined the nurse and asked if I was having trouble breathing. I admitted to some difficulty, and he said to let them know if it got worse. The problem is that your bronchia and tongue can continue to swell to the extent that it closes off breathing and you're a goner. I wondered if that could happen so fast that I would not be *able* to let them know.

By then Connie was back and I think I actually whimpered a bit, because I was thinking that I was too young to die, that I had all these things I wanted to do, and that it wasn't fair. Most of all, though, I was in shock—to realize that within minutes you could go from fitness walking to death, so I recall the major thing going through my mind was, "This can't be happening!" But it was.

Fortunately, they did not have to give me epinephrine, which can have its own side effects; the Benadryl was enough, and within an hour or so I was on my way home, bolstered by a strong dose of steroids. The next day I got an epinephrine pen to carry with me everywhere at all times, along with chewable Benadryl tablets. I also came away with a new sense of reality to what Saint Paul calls "the sting of death" (1 Cor 15:55).

For about two weeks after my scrape with death, the whole world looked wonderful, sort of the way it does for George Bailey at the end of *It's a Wonderful Life* (even that loose banister knob). Nothing that used to seem so problematic or annoying or frustrating seemed that way anymore. The people I loved seemed dearer than ever, and I even felt love for people I didn't know at all. Stoplights?—no problem; I had all the time in the world. Slow traffic?—relax and go with the flow. Worries about the church seemed to float away. Internal pressure to finish a writing project gave way to more gardening. When people would greet me with the casual question, "How are you?" I would think, "Terrific, seeing as how I'm not dead." It was great just to be alive. Then, about two weeks out, I found myself sitting at a stoplight, getting irritable at how long it was taking to change. Only two weeks out and I needed to be stung again.

Saint Paul says that in baptism we have been buried with Christ into death so that we might walk "in newness of life" (Rom 6:4). Christian spirituality wants to provide us with a sting such as mine every once in a while, and particularly during the season of Lent. That's the purpose of the Ash Wednesday ritual of rubbing ashes on our foreheads, reminding us that "we are dust, and to dust we shall return," *so that* we might walk in newness of life. Ash Wednesday is a ritual yellow jacket sting that wants to remind us that life is wonderful. I even heard of a minister who, to get the point across vividly, had an empty coffin at an Ash Wednesday service, and he invited people to come forward and try it out. That may sound more like Halloween, but I suspect that those who took him up on the offer didn't forget the service any time soon.

Paul connects the experience of burial with baptism, which is why some Baptists argue that baptism *should* be all the way under and not just a wet thumb. When I was baptized as a child, the Southern Baptist minister held a handkerchief over my face and leaned me back under the water of the baptismal pool. I always thought he held me under just long enough to make me wonder if he was going to let me up (a trick of the trade, no doubt). But baptism is a ritual expression of a spiritual reality that doesn't need water, whether in a pool or on a wet thumb. (Quakers do quite well without it.) The ritual symbolizes a spiritual movement that is central to Christian faith—the reenactment of Jesus' death *so that* one may also reenact Jesus' "newness of life," which is what Easter is all about. Nature has its own reenactment every year that offers a parallel to the story of Jesus, as much Easter hymnody recognizes: "Now the green blade rises from the buried grain," and "Spring has dawned on earth today."[1]

It seems that sometimes it takes something shocking—lying in a coffin, almost dying of an insect sting—to help us see how wonderful life is. As one author says, "Not being isolated, not being in pain, and not yet being dead are privileges which we relish most after we endure [isolation and pain] and a glimpse of death."[2] A college student found a smart way to apply the principle. She wrote a letter to her parents in which she informed them that her dorm had burned down, but she was out of the hospital, and she had moved in with her boyfriend, who had promptly got her pregnant. Then she added a postscript: "There was no fire, my health is perfectly fine, and I am not pregnant. In fact, I do not even have a boyfriend. However, I did get a D in French . . . and I just wanted to make sure that you keep it all in perspective."[3] No doubt, her parents were so grateful by the time they finished reading the postscript that the D in French didn't really matter in the grand scheme of things. They died a little death in reading the body of the letter so that when they read the PS they could walk in newness of life.

Paul's model for the Christian life is, of course, the life and death and resurrection of Christ. The spirituality that Paul describes in Romans

---

1. Crum, "Now the Green Blade Rises" (hymn 238) and John of Damascus, "Come You Faithful" (hymn 230).

2. Lustbader, *Counting on Kindness*, 26.

3. Quoted in Klein, *Healing Power of Humor*, 13–14.

is a reenactment of the movement of the Christ in the Philippians hymn (2:1–18). The one who was equal to God did not hold on to that status; instead, he "emptied himself, taking the form of a slave." "He humbled himself," even to the point of death on a cross, the most ignoble way to die in first century Palestine. "Therefore," Paul says, God has exalted him as "lord," above even the powers that put him to death.

Now, Paul says, this movement of letting go, of self-emptying and humility, is the model for the way we should live (see above, "Getting Ready for Christmas"). "In humility regard others as better than yourselves. Let each of you look not to your own interests, but to the interest of others." It takes a little death for us to regard others as better than ourselves. That is a very difficult thing to do, whether the others are husband or wife or partner or parents or friends or—especially—strangers. Our big, fat egos get in the way. We want to hold on to the feeling that we are better than others. We are afraid to let it go, because to let it go makes us feel insecure and vulnerable. To "give up" is often judged negatively, but giving up of oneself is essential for spiritual growth. As one spiritual author says, "In learning to give up ourselves we learn both to live and to die—to die not only our final death, but those many deaths of daily living by which we become more alive."[4]

What keeps us from giving ourselves up is what Paul calls sin. Sin is a refusal to leave the "old self" behind and live as the new self that has died and risen in Christ. Without the theological language, it is a process sometimes accomplished on a therapist's couch. Sin is whatever prevents us (usually pride) from letting go of the feeling that we are better than everyone else. Sin is that false sense of security that prohibits our taking the risk of vulnerability that will lead to newness of life.

There is yet another dimension of our reluctance to die the little deaths that lead to newness of life. To do so means not only to see others as better than ourselves but also to give up the notion that we are in control of our lives. I remember that morning when I was speed-walking in the woods, feeling self-assured of my physical condition for someone pushing sixty. Our culture gives us all these images of how we can control how long we live by controlling our behavior. Take control of your life, say the ads. Eat right, exercise often, and practice some spiritual discipline, for example. And if we do become ill, we have all those powerful drugs that can control the illness. Some people well into their eighties would

---

4. Stendl-Rast, "Learning to Die," 36.

have died years ago were there not medications for high blood pressure and a host of other ailments. We are used to being in control. Then along comes a little yellow jacket and everything is turned upside down—or a lethal virus, like COVID-19, that kills millions of people, healthy or not.

To experience the newness of life in its deepest sense, we have to give up the illusion that we are the masters of our existence. In fact, the word *master* is the equivalent of what Christ is declared to be after his self-emptying. God pronounces him to be *kurios*. The Greek word refers to someone who has the power to decide, and it means "lord" or "master." But Christ is the "master" only after he has let go his power and become powerless.

The doctrine of the atonement is by far one of the most complex and baffling of all Christian concepts. What does it mean to say that "Jesus died for our sins"? On the surface, it seems rather simple, but the more you inquire about it, the more complicated it becomes. How does it "work"? Is it a sacrifice or a vicarious punishment or the payment of a debt? Is it something that happens without our participation, or something in which we must be deliberately involved? There are no easy answers to these questions, but I think we have before us one model among many other possibilities. The self-emptying of Christ, his dying to self, is, for us, the human model of openness to life as the gift of God. When we participate spiritually in that death, when we are, in some sense, "buried with Christ," then we too are set on the path that leads to "newness of life." Reenacting the death leads to reenacting the life. This is the way that leads from Ash Wednesday's sting to Easter's claim: he is risen!

To be "saved" here does not mean to have something done to you against or at least without your will.[5] It is not some sort of magic trick that God plays in which God, like a wizard, turns you into something you are not. On the other hand, it also does not mean something that you accomplish by yourself. Salvation here is not simply a new insight into who I am and how I am to live. Instead, salvation here means my identifying with the story of Jesus—in particular with the story of his death—to the extent that I *participate* in what happens to Jesus. My identification with the story is what it means to obey him, and in that identification I am crucified with him and raised with him. I too become the *child* of God, which is to say that I have a "new and right spirit within me." That is the goal

---

5. Arguably, other biblical authors entertain the possibility of a more radical, unilateral "operation," a heart replacement (Jer 31:33; Ezek 36:26–27, in tension with 18:31). Cf. Deut 30:6 with 10:16.

of Ash Wednesday, recited every year from Ps 51:10. The psalm employs a subtle spiritual synergy. Asking God to "create" a new heart uses the Hebrew word *bara'*, a verb exclusively used with God as subject. We may think of human beings as "creative" in many skills, but in Hebrew thought only God can *bara'*. But, in a sense, God cannot create a new heart for us unless there is a sign of receptivity. To use a medical metaphor, we have to sign a consent form. The psalmist's plea is a consent, a "change of heart" that opens up the possibility of receiving a new heart. As one author puts it, "Dying is something I must do. It can't happen unless I give myself willingly to change. I die to what I was and come alive to what I will be."[6]

This way of understanding salvation takes with utmost seriousness the power of a story. As one New Testament theologian says, a story has the "power to lead hearers into an experience of identification with the story's protagonist."[7] This power is outside the hearer, and in this sense the story does something to the hearer—it leads us. This is how the Spirit creates a new spirit in us. But in listening to the story and participating in it the hearer also exercises her imagination and so, you might say, cooperates with that power. To pursue the opening metaphor, the story provides the sting.

In a newspaper article a woman talked about her experience with breast cancer. First, she was terrified. The oncologist called the tumor "a very small ductal carcinoma in situ," but all that meant to her was death. Then she got angry. "Why was this happening to me?" she asked. "I exercised, ate right, went for checkups." Like most of us, she was in control of her health. Then her reaction was "spiritual." She asked, "What was I being punished for? What sin had I committed to deserve this?" Apparently, she got out of that sick theology rather quickly. And after surgery and radiation, she apparently recovered. But the experience has dramatically altered her life. "From the day that I got this diagnosis I have been a changed person," she writes. "I try to find the joy in life and take advantage of each day. Little things don't irritate me anymore. My motto is, 'It's only (fill in the blank); it's not life.' Fill in the blank with anything from dust on the coffee table to a worn-out heat pump."[8]

The yellow jacket stings on my ankle led to a dying and an awakening to newness of life. Rightly understood, ashes on the forehead can

---

6. Stendl-Rast, *Gratefulness*, 11.
7. Hays, *Faith of Jesus Christ*, 252.
8. Motsinger, "Disease Taught Lessons," A1.

accomplish the same transformation. Emily Dickinson puts it well: "A death-blow is a life-blow to some / Who, till they died, did not alive become."[9]

9. Dickinson, "A death-blow is a life-blow to some," 204.

Eat Less, Chew More

Philippians 2:2–3

Lent begins on Ash Wednesday, when Christians mark their foreheads with ashes and hear the words, "You are dust, and to dust you shall return." One year I wasn't there to administer the ashes; instead, I was home recovering from surgery. It's traditional to give something up for Lent, and I had given up my prostate. When I first heard the diagnosis of prostate cancer, I said to the surgeon, "But I thought I would live to my nineties like my parents." "You still might," he said. But I didn't want "might," I wanted "will."

In the long process I found myself on the receiving end of my congregation's caring in an unusual way, a caring expressed with food and drink, books and puzzles, emails, and, of course, greeting cards. Some of the cards were funny, some serious, but all were welcome as a ray of sunshine on a dark day. On the serious side, one person wrote about my diagnosis, saying, "the explosion of such news is so insulting to our sense of security and well-being." That is certainly true, and largely the subject of what follows. On the lighter side, one card expressed the sender's apology for not being able to find a box of beer-flavored chocolate. Another posed a riddle: what did the doctor say to the patient after surgery? "That's enough out of you." I couldn't have agreed more. And one person wrote simply "Damn the Big C."

Among all these cards, one seemed to come straight from a Zen master (although the proverb proved to be Swedish): "Eat less, chew more." There were other such recommendations, including "talk less, say more." Fortunately, the sender did not underline that one, thereby preventing a defensive reaction on my part. But since fasting is a traditional Lenten discipline that requires eating less, we'll focus on that for a moment. Could it be that such a proverb is not only applicable to someone going through an illness but to everyone, simply going through life, and particularly in the season of Lent? The hospital may give you little choice: they *make* you eat less, and for a while all you get to chew is ice chips. But what about our normal life? Sometimes, I think, the proverb calls for something we need to do voluntarily; sometimes circumstances force us into it.

It doesn't take much reflection to realize how countercultural our proverb is. Have you ever seen an advertisement for a restaurant where you pay according to how *little* you can eat? No, it's always *all* you can eat. Do fast food restaurants compete in offering the smallest burger? Of course not. McDonald's offers a Quarter Pounder. That's nothing, says Burger King, we offer the whopper, and if that isn't enough, we'll give you a *double* whopper. Poo, says Wendy's, we carry a Triple with cheese. You're all wimps, says Hardee's. We serve a Monster Thickburger (amounting to one thousand four hundred calories, and that's without the Biggie Fries). For a while, McDonald's started a marketing campaign on offering Super Sizes. Instantly our language grew to include the new verb, *supersize*, as in supersize me a milkshake. Then a film called *Super Size Me* poked fun at the dietetic disaster of fast food, and the name disappeared.[1]

But the reality of super sizes dominates our culture. As Americans, we are accustomed (some would say addicted) to bigness. Our choice of cars has grown from sedans to station wagons to minivans and SUV's. The original Hummer epitomizes supersizing. It looks like a family assault vehicle. The same is true of houses. By 2004, the average house size had grown from 1,600 square feet to over 2,300 square feet. In one town in California, where dot-com money abounds, the typical new home is larger than the town's 8,500 square foot city hall. But such houses simply mirror the rise of big-box stores like a Wal-Mart Supercenter. And, of course, these examples of supersize cars, houses, and stores require a supersize share of energy to heat and cool, producing supersize greenhouse gases.

Expand your horizon beyond individual consumers to our nation and it's not hard to see how, compared with much of the world, we eat more than our share of just about everything. I suspect that we coined the terms "shovel it in" and "wolf it down" to describe gorging on food, one metaphor being mechanical, the other animal. But shoveling it in is what the church names as one of the seven deadly sins—gluttony. Lenten

---

1. Spurlock, dir., *Super Size Me.*

spirituality says "eat less, chew more." But fasting can apply to other forms of consumption in addition to food, such as watching TV, driving cars, or shopping. In the lectionary, Lent begins with the story of Jesus' temptation in the wilderness, where he refuses to give in to the desires for food, for supernatural protection, and for political power. You are hungry, says the devil, turn these stones into bread. You are invulnerable; jump off the roof. You can be powerful, just worship me. But Jesus says no. (See Matt 3:1–11.)

One of the primary texts for Lent is Philippians 2. The apostle Paul is encouraging the Philippians to practice a Christian spirituality based on the model of Jesus (see also above, "The Sting of Death"). Paul's purpose is not so much to teach them doctrine as to instill in them a certain mental attitude, "being of the same mind." This does not mean agreeing on everything; it means having the same spiritual orientation. That orientation is defined by this verse: "Do nothing from selfish ambition or conceit, but in humility regard others as better than yourselves" (2:3)

In a sense, Christian spirituality is refined within the relationships of a community; the goal is to become smaller, not bigger. The goal is to empty yourself, not be full of yourself. When we say that someone is "really full of himself," we mean that he's too big for his britches, has a swelled head. Such fullness often takes the form of pride, the opposite of humility.

Jesus shows another way. Elsewhere it is called the "way of the cross." Although Jesus could have exploited his closeness to God, instead he "emptied himself." He humbled himself by living as an ordinary human being, not as some supernatural, divine being. He could have strutted around the way kings do; instead, he lowered himself to the status of a slave. He could have held on to the royalty of the title Son of God; instead, he assumed the posture of the servant of the Lord. Jesus became "his royal lowness." Ultimately, his call for everyone to exercise such lowness led the high and mighty, whose power was threatened by that call, to put him to death. But this is the one whom God exalted, whose title is Lord, while all the Caesars and high priests of the world are brought low.

The spiritual attitude of emptying oneself is expressed in different ways throughout the New Testament. Jesus' disciples must take up their cross and follow him. They must lose their life if they want to save their life. They must be crucified with him in order to live with him. They have to become like the grain of wheat that falls into the ground and dies if they want to sprout and bloom. Having the same mind in emptying ourselves is what Buddhists talk about in terms of "mindfulness" and "emptiness." Here's how the Tao Te Ching puts it: "if you want to become full, let yourself be empty. If you want to be reborn, let yourself die. If you want to be given everything, give everything up."[2]

As Marcus Borg says, taking up your cross means "dying to an old way of being and being raised into a new way of being."[3] Such dying is hard work. It means letting go of your pride, letting go of your desire for invulnerability, letting go of fear, and stepping into that strange "new creation" that is what Paul calls life in Christ. To return to our proverb, dying means taking one nibble at a time rather than a big bite; it means chewing slowly and truly enjoying what you are eating rather than wolfing it down and wanting more.

In his book *Peace is Every Step*, Thich Nhat Hanh remembers what it was like to be a child eating a cookie. He says "I always went to the front yard and took my time eating it, sometimes half an hour or forty-five minutes for one cookie. I would take a small bite and look up at the sky . . . , and take another bite . . . I was entirely in the present moment, with my cookie . . . and everything." (Clearly, as a child he would have passed the famous "marshmallow test" involving delayed gratification!) He then offers a "Tangerine Meditation" on eating slowly, followed by his appreciation for "The Eucharist," suggesting that Jesus "knew that if his disciples would eat one piece of bread in mindfulness, they would have real life."[4]

About a week after I was home from the hospital, I decided that I was ready to go for an extended walk. What an adventure *that* proved to be! I was still feeling unsteady, so I took my set of trekking poles and headed out. My usual route took me from my house over to a parcourse several blocks away. The farther I walked, the slower my pace became. By the time I reached the parcourse, I doubted whether I could make my usual one loop around, and almost headed back, but some stubborn pride pushed me on. Then it occurred to me what I must look like to someone else: in two words, *very old*. I was literally creeping along, barely getting one foot completely ahead of the other, leaning on my poles. Here was an old man with gray hair, stumbling along at a snail's pace, while everyone else zipped by.

2. Laozi, *Tao Te Ching*, 22.
3. Borg, *Heart of Christianity*, 93.
4. Nhat Hanh, *Peace Is Every Step*, 20.

But this was the place where I always prided myself in walking 3.7 miles per hour. (I know because I used a GPS system and a pedometer to measure my accomplishment.) I used to take a smug satisfaction when I *passed* people who *appeared* to be *jogging*—even people younger than me. Now circumstances were forcing me to observe the apostle's command: "Do nothing from conceit, but in humility regard others as better than yourselves." I was in the slow lane, and that proverbial snail could easily have passed *me*. But such thoughts did not occupy me for long. Instead, I found myself *laughing* at myself, which is often the beginning of spiritual growth. Besides, I suddenly realized that I was having the best time I'd had in weeks. I was enjoying being outdoors, enjoying the sunshine and blue sky, enjoying the chill in the air, enjoying the trees waiting for spring. In short, I was enjoying immensely every slow step. I was enjoying simply being alive. With my feet, as it were, I was eating less and chewing more.

As I concluded my walk, the meaning of Thich Nhat Hanh's book took on a new dimension because I could appreciate it literally as well as figuratively—*Peace Is Every Step*. Walk less, step more. Eat less, chew more. "If you want to become full, let yourself be empty. If you want to be reborn, let yourself die. If you want to be given everything, give everything up." And here's the rest of that Swedish proverb: "fear less, hope more; whine less, breathe more; hate less, love more, and all good things will be yours." If you need something to remind you to practice your Lenten discipline, you can even buy a spoon that has those key words engraved on it: "eat less, chew more."

Holy Week

Palm Sunday

Two Parades, Two Kings, Two Crowds

Holy Week is incomprehensible without politics. (As I have pointed out before, by *politics* I do not mean partisan competition but the polity of a society; see below.) Most of us, I would guess, don't think of this week in that way, if we think of it at all. It is a religious week, stretching from Palm Sunday to Easter, not a political week. For many Christians, this is the holiest time of the year, and the reason for that has nothing to do with politics. It is because this week includes Good Friday, the day on which Jesus was crucified. That horrible day is called "Good" because it was the day on which Jesus died for their sins. As Paul puts it, "God put [him] forward as a sacrifice of atonement by his blood" (Rom 3:25). Accordingly, one can think of the events of this week as part of the "plan" of God for the redemption of humankind (Acts 2:23; Eph 1:10, 3:9).[1]

But if we read the Gospels without that interpretive lens, we see a different picture. We see an unfolding of events determined by political power. The death of Jesus is a result of fears about his religious *and* political intentions, as perceived by political authorities. He is executed by the Romans as a threat to political order. It is the religious establishment in

---

1. For a different interpretation, one more in line with what follows here, see "Passion of God" (below). Borg and Crossan, "Jesus' Final Week," 28, also allude to such a "plan."

collusion with the Roman authorities who sacrifice Jesus on the altar of the empire.

I am not suggesting that Holy Week is only political; but I am suggesting that it is *not* only religious, if by *religious* we mean reduced to the state of individual souls and having nothing to do with the soul of a society. Jesus was an innocent victim of capital punishment carried out in the most ghastly way that the Romans could devise—as Raymond Brown says, "one of the most terrible deaths known to antiquity."[2]

Starting with the story describing Jesus' triumphal entry (as it is called) into Jerusalem, we can understand the story of Holy Week as a tale of two parades, two kings, and two crowds. Perhaps the primary question that Holy Week poses for us is not "have you been saved?" but "to what crowd to you belong?"

But first, the parades. New Testament scholars Marcus Borg and John Dominic Crossan have traced the developments of Holy Week with particular attention to the Gospel of Mark and the political dimensions.[3] They suggest that the week began with two processions entering Jerusalem. I don't think they mean that these processions literally happened simultaneously, but the timing is not significant. What *is* significant is the time of year and who was riding on the lead float, as it were.

The time of year is the annual Passover celebration. Indeed, some of the accounts of the Last Supper say that Jesus was celebrating a Passover meal with his disciples.[4] Passover, of course, is the annual festival that celebrates the release of Israelite slaves from the power of Pharaoh's Egypt (see below, "Maundy Thursday / Passover"). As one line in the ceremony says, "We were Pharaoh's slaves in Egypt, and God brought us out with a mighty hand." The current ceremony ends with the words "Next year, in Jerusalem." That could mean to the celebrant "Next year I'll celebrate in Jerusalem," but it could also mean, "Next year Jerusalem will be free." So, Passover was very much like our celebration of Independence Day. But of course in Jesus' day, Israel was *not* independent; Israel was a colony of the Roman Empire. So, imagine how the Roman authorities in Jerusalem must have felt as Passover arrived. It was not uncommon for Jewish rebels to take advantage of the patriotic fervor and incite an insurrection, which is precisely what would happen in 66 CE. The situation put everyone on

---

2. Brown, *Death of the Messiah*, 855.

3. Borg and Crossan, "Jesus' Final Week."

4. In the narrative chronology of the Synoptic Gospels, the entry occurs before the Last Supper. John 12:12 ties the entry to Passover.

edge. Extra security forces were needed in case riots broke out, and potential rebels had to be swiftly and severely punished. The last thing the Roman authorities needed was some kind of Jewish Independence Day parade.

What *was* needed was a show of force, so the Romans had their own parade. The governor of the colony, named Pilate, who lived in the coastal town of Caesarea, rode up to Jerusalem at the head of an imperial troop of soldiers and cavalry. The parade served "as a deterrent against and preparation for any possible trouble." The procession entered Jerusalem from the west. As Borg and Crossan say, this parade "symbolized and actualized Roman imperial power."[5]

Then we have another parade, the one celebrated on Palm Sunday: Jesus' triumphal entry into Jerusalem, coming from the east. This parade is remarkably different. There is only one man. He is not riding in a chariot surrounded by armed soldiers. He is riding on a donkey. (Think of it as a bicycle, not a Humvee.) Matthew's Gospel explicitly makes the connection that the others imply when he says that this scene is a fulfillment of prophecy from the book of Zechariah (Matt 21:4–5; see Zech 9:9): "Look, your king comes to you; / triumphant and victorious is he, / humble and riding on a donkey, / on a colt, the foal of a donkey." And consider the rest of the passage: "He will cut off the chariot from Ephraim / and the warhorse from Jerusalem; / and the battle bow shall be cut off, / and he shall command peace to the nations; / his dominion shall be from sea to sea, / and from the River to the ends of the earth" (v. 10). In fact, Borg and Crossan suggest that Jesus' parade was deliberately confrontational of the political and religious authorities, although intention is difficult to prove.[6] In any case, one thing is clear: he is an altogether different kind of king. He does not exercise his rule through violence, but through nonviolence. He brings peace, not war, and it is universal peace, a "dominion" (read "empire") that stretches from sea to shining sea. The shout of the crowd that watches this strange king pass by only reinforces his image of royalty. "Hosanna!" they shout, meaning "Save us!" And then "Blessed is the king who comes in the name of God!" In Mark's Gospel, they say "Blessed is the kingdom [read: "empire"] of our father David that is coming." Palm Sunday's Hosanna echoes the promise of Jacob's dream, the fervent expectation that it is about to be fulfilled. Numerous times, Mark

---

5. Borg and Crossan, "Jesus' Final Week," 29.
6. Borg and Crossan, "Jesus' Final Week," 28.

tells us how the political and religious authorities are afraid of the crowd of Jesus' supporters (11:18, 31; 12:12; 14:2).

It is important that we not spiritualize the cry "Hosanna!" by ignoring its political meaning. "Save us!" does not have anything to do with sin, but it has very much to do with evil. The crowd is not begging for forgiveness; it is pleading for justice. *We* may enter Holy Week thinking about personal salvation, but they are yearning for political liberation. They are living under one of the most powerful and oppressive regimes of the ancient world, an oppression imposed primarily by the imperial tax system.[7] There were agricultural taxes, sales taxes, taxes on land and personal property, tariffs on imported and exported goods, a per capita ("poll") tax and a household tax. The tax system itself was only part of a larger economy that brutally exploited those who were least able to pay, namely, the peasantry. One analysis suggests that tolls and taxes were a minimum of about half and as high as two-thirds of a peasant's resources.

Moreover, wealthy landowners and moneylenders also took advantage of the poor. The prosperous were able to buy up land and reduce the former owners to sharecroppers or even slaves. The wealthy were able to invest their resources in loans and demand high rates of interest or huge fines for nonrepayment. So the average peasant who came into financial difficulty could find himself forced to sell his land for a pittance, forced to live on that land as a sharecropper. According to some studies, the exploitive tax system combined with exorbitant interest rates on loans finally drove the peasantry below poverty, which was widespread and normal, and into absolute destitution.[8] As one scholar puts it, "'Judaean society rotted from within because of the social imbalance caused by excessive wealth" at the top.[9] (Does this sound familiar?) When the crowd shouted, "Save us!" they were calling for relief from systemic political evil, not the burden of personal sin.

It isn't difficult to imagine how the Roman authorities would have reacted to this alternative parade, especially in the context of Passover. Humble or not, here was a man who drew large crowds of people. They hailed him as if *he* were their emperor, or at least *would* be their emperor when he came into power, which they seemed to think would happen soon. And what did Jesus do next? He proceeded to the temple and drove out the money changers. These merchants exchanged Jewish coins for

---

7. Crossan, *Historical Jesus*, 218–24.

8. Crossan, *Historical Jesus*, 221.

9. Crossan, *Historical Jesus*, 221, quoting Martin Goodman.

Roman coins. The people were there to purchase offerings for sacrifices that the priests would offer for them. The money changers had a monopoly on the exchange, and the priests, of course, had a monopoly on sacrifices. It was a set-up for the exploitation of the poor. Moreover, the temple authorities were in cahoots with the political authorities because they both benefited financially from Roman power.

"Blessed is the king who comes in the name of God." There are two parades, two kings, and two crowds. This crowd represents the supporters of Jesus. They have been impressed with his wisdom and his parables; they have been moved by his healings; some of them who are known as "sinners," social outcasts, have been grateful that he has welcomed and accepted them at table. This crowd yearns for the kingdom that he talks about, or, to use parallel political terms, the government, the empire, the administration—one that will turn upside down the socioeconomic system that oppresses them. They are ready, they are waiting, and they are a threat.

And here is an irony: Jesus did not prove to be the savior they were yearning for. He did not liberate them from imperial Rome. He did not save them in this way. His way of saving people was different, but it was not just saving souls, either, and the best example of that salvation is the story of Zacchaeus (Luke 19:1-10), so here we digress.

"Zacchaeus was a wee little man and a wee little man was he." People who grew up learning songs about the Bible in Sunday school know he was a "height challenged" man who climbed up a tree to see Jesus. As is often the case, the story was taught and learned on a child's level, a process that often results in moralizing. The "point" of the story became something like how we value spiritual curiosity and ingenuity. But in reality, this "wee little man" was an evil little weasel because he was an agent of the economic system of imperial Rome—a tax collector.

The personal Zacchaeus is appealing and winsome. But the public Zacchaeus is another matter. Tax collectors were not so much direct agents of the government as private entrepreneurs. Tax collecting was a business farmed out to the highest bidder. The collector paid the government for a license, then tried to profit from the collection. "Chief" tax collectors like Zacchaeus would hire subordinates to do the actual collecting. He is a businessman who has gained his wealth by his participation in the economic system. Some of his wealth, by his own confession, came through dishonest means—through fraud. But much of his wealth also came through perfectly legal means, simply by taking advantage of the system. *He* didn't write the tax code; *he* didn't regulate debt foreclosures or interest rates. People in Rome did that.

Tax collectors were widely reviled by the populace. Rabbinic sources often use the phrase "tax collectors and robbers" as if the two were synonymous. Similarly, the New Testament speaks of tax collectors and sinners, classifying them along with prostitutes and moral outlaws. And aside from the economic burden, there was the political resentment in that the taxes went to the occupying military power. If you already resent your taxes going to Washington, imagine how you would feel if they went to, say, Beijing, and you'll sense the resentment that accompanied paying taxes to Rome.

The economic and political background of the Zacchaeus story radically alters what salvation means. Zacchaeus, the chief tax collector, reviled and ostracized as a sinner, is the one with whom Jesus chooses to dine—indeed, Jesus invites himself to lunch at Zacchaeus's house. There is a feeling of urgency here, expressed two times with the word "hurry," and Jesus' conviction that he "must" visit with Zacchaeus (Luke 19:4-6; cf. 2:49). In this simple but most profound of human gestures—sharing a meal—Jesus accepts the personal Zacchaeus for who he is apart from the public Zacchaeus, and Zacchaeus experiences a new and strange and wonderful richness—the richness of the realm of God, an economy based on grace, not greed. The most dishonorable of men is honored to be the host of the Messiah, and—this is most important—the one so honored becomes honorable, becomes what he is, in fact, named—Zacchaeus, "righteous one."

In short, what happens here is what should happen whenever the grace of the gospel is encountered—justice. In this case, justice means the redistribution of material resources, prompted by the experience of the wealth of God's love. As Douglas Meeks puts it, "in general the biblical faith teaches that there is enough if the righteousness of God is present and acknowledged as the source of life."[10] Justice is the ethical response to God's bountiful love. For Zacchaeus, the acts of justice are as extravagant as the act of grace, of the Christ having dinner with the crook. Alluding to Jewish law, first he vows to give half of his possessions to the poor, presumably referring to that wealth gained by legal use of the system. Then he vows to pay reparations, that is, punitive damages, "four times" what he took by fraud. If we want to see the full import of the

---

10. Meeks, *God the Economist*, 174.

Zacchaeus story, we must attend to both the public and the personal face of this chief tax collector. When we hold both faces in view, the story is not only about personal spiritual transformation but also about political transformation that must take place for "salvation" to come. When Jesus says, "Today salvation has come to this house" (19:9), it means that Zacchaeus is saved from sin, it is true—but it also means that because of the economic expression of Zacchaeus's repentance, salvation has come to some of those oppressed by an unjust system. The immediacy of "today" exemplifies what Jesus means elsewhere when he says that the realm of God has "come near" (10:9; cf. above, "Keep Awake!").

"Save us!" the crowd shouted, but Jesus did not institute a political revolution, much less a military coup. The salvation he effected *could* relieve them of their oppression, but only if the model of Zacchaeus were duplicated by a kind of tax collector movement that eventually would lead to systemic change. In that case, the nonviolent power of grace would transform an individual, but, if picked up and augmented by a community, and then by a society, it would transform the world. Of course, even if he *had* intended the revolution that the Roman and religious authorities feared, Jesus could not have implemented it, because, to return to the subject of crowds, there are *two* of them, and the other one soon is shouting something quite different from "hosanna." They are shouting, "Crucify him!"

The scene shifts from the parade route to the plaza outside what in effect was the courthouse where Jesus is on trial before Pilate. The legal procedures include both the religious authorities and then the Roman authorities. But in the end Pilate finds no fault in Jesus. He will not condemn him to death and says that he will release him. But then the other crowd comes into play, one manipulated by the religious authorities. According to Brown, this crowd is "misled by the chief priests" and quickly falls prey to the influence of "mass persuasion."[11] Borg and Crossan suggest that this crowd does not include common people but only "supporters of the authorities."[12] In any event, this crowd becomes an angry mob who is as hostile to Jesus as the other crowd was sympathetic. Apparently, there is a custom during Passover for the authorities to release one prisoner, and the crowd insists that Pilate release a man named Barabbas, known as a bandit. And when Pilate asks what he should do with Jesus,

---

11. Brown, *Death of the Messiah*, 808. Cf. Borg and Crossan, "Jesus' Final Week," 31, who point out that the courtyard was not accessible to ordinary people.

12. Borg and Crossan, "Jesus' Final Week," 31.

the crowd shouts, "Crucify him! Crucify him!" And that is what Pilate does, "wishing," as Mark puts it, "to satisfy the crowd" (15:15).

Christian history is riddled with slander of the Jewish people as a whole as "Christ killers."[13] But the story of Jesus' trial and execution suggests something far different. Both crowds in the story are Jewish crowds. Only one is against Jesus. And that crowd consists of the party loyalists of the priestly establishment, which, itself, is in league with the financial and political power of the empire. In John's account, Pilate points to Jesus and says to the "chief priests," "Here is your king!" And the chief priests say, "We have no king but the emperor" (19:14-15). As Brown puts it, "In all the Gospels the mass opposition to [Jesus] is what ultimately forces Pilate to accede to the crucifixion."[14]

Two parades, two kings, two crowds: the story of Holy Week begins and ends with a political drama, mirroring how the story of Jesus began. In Matthew, "in the time of King Herod," the magi come to Bethlehem seeking the newborn "who has been born king of the Jews" (Matt 2:1-2). In Luke, Mary's Magnificat praises God, who "has brought down the powerful from their thrones" (1:52), and John the Baptist's father blesses God, who "has raised up a mighty savior," the descendant of King David, so that the people "would be saved from our enemies" (1:69-71). Yes, the poem promises "forgiveness for their sins" (1:77), but the "oath" that God swore to Abraham (1:73) is also Jacob's promise, and in its most expansive vision it signifies "the way of peace" (1:79), and there can be no peace without justice.

The story of the two parades that ushers in Holy Week raises questions about political allegiance, *not* in the sense of a partisan political party, but of the extent to which a society's polity—that is, its government, its body politic—does or does not provide the justice and peace that the biblical heritage demands—or, to quote the words of one political vision, "liberty and justice for all." Here again is a reason why we need both books of God, for Easter is more than some natural process that leads from dying to rising, like spring bulbs; Easter is also a profoundly political event that celebrates the victory of a political prisoner who was tortured and executed by the power of the state. Had Jesus died a natural death at a ripe old age, his resurrection might signify something like nature's movement from winter to spring. But Easter is the victory of God's

---

13. Borg and Crossan, "Jesus' Final Week," 28.
14. Brown, *Death of the Messiah*, 809.

power over the imperial power of the world, the realm of God over the realm of Caesar. This is why one triumphant Easter hymn rejoices that "Spring has dawned on earth today," but also invokes the Exodus story: "loosed from Pharaoh's bitter yoke, Jacob's sons and daughters."[15]

Palm Sunday poses a challenge: to choose to be part of one crowd, and not another, to commemorate one parade and not the other, pledging allegiance to one ruler, and not the other. One ruler is "Caesar," the other is the one whose title was written on a sign and nailed on the cross on which he was executed: "The King of the Jews." At his birth the Roman imperial king resorted to murder to stop him (Matt 2:16–18). But he is the Messiah, whose dominion of justice and peace reigns from sea to sea, because, when the week is over, God will fulfill the prophecy of Zechariah: God will make the Messiah "triumphant and victorious," and, in our own time, a crowd of millions and millions will gather for an Easter parade, and some will congregate to join in singing Handel's magnificent chorus—hallelujah to the King of Kings.

---

15. John of Damascus, "Come, You Faithful."

Passover / Maundy Thursday

The Man with the Tattooed Arm[1]
Exodus 12

"Time is one of the world's deepest mysteries. No one can say exactly what it is. Yet, the ability to measure time makes our way of life possible. Most human activities involve groups of people acting together in the same place at the same time. People could not do this if they did not all measure time in the same way."[2] This is the opening paragraph in an encyclopedia article on time. It suggests the almost paradoxical nature of that "fourth dimension" of reality, as it has come to be known since Einstein. On the one hand, time is a philosophical and scientific subject that eludes precise definition and leads the investigator into models of reality that defy ordinary experience. "Einstein," for example, "demonstrated that time is, in fact, elastic and can be stretched and shrunk by motion."[3] On the other hand, virtually all human activities (at least in so-called civilized societies) would be thrown into confusion if we did not treat time as an utterly practical dimension that we can neatly measure and record. Time is that easily quantifiable part of our experience that we can follow with incredible precision on an inexpensive digital watch.

Here again are the questions that I raised at the outset of this book: How do we measure the time of our lives? How do we "tell time"? The utterly ordinary categories that we use in fact have little or no basis in physical or astronomical reality. The same encyclopedia article points

---

1. This essay (here with some changes) originally appeared as Mann, "Passover," 240–50.
2. *World Book Encyclopedia*, 1988 ed., s.v. "Time."
3. Davies, *God and the New Physics*, 120.

out that our twelve months (etymologically related to *moon*) "have no relation to the moon's actual cycle." Similarly, our division of months into weeks, days into twenty-four hours, hours into sixty minutes, and minutes into sixty seconds are impositions of measurement that do not necessarily fit with the physical universe. And if these measurements are arbitrary, how much more are such notions as the weekend. In short, the most fundamental categories of time that govern our lives are a synthetic framework—a fiction, you might say—that gives shape to an otherwise protean mystery.

How we measure the time of our lives is more than a scientific question that can be answered with "hours" or "minutes," or with sophisticated corollaries of quantum theory; it is also a metaphorical question that demands to know the very meaning of our lives. The way we answer this question reveals the extent to which that meaning is spiritual or merely secular.

Christianity enjoys a kind of monopoly on time in that the entire world follows a calendar that is *anno Domini* "in the year of the Lord," namely, the Christ. Yet Christianity shares with all religions the observance of sacred times during each year, times that are correlated with sacred stories. Telling time means telling stories. The liturgical seasons of the Christian calendar are symbolic reminders of the gospel, the sacred story of the Christian faith. Sacred stories of any culture are sacred not simply because they are about gods, but because they create and shape our "sense of self and world." Such stories "orient the life of people through time, their lifetime, their individual and corporate experience . . . to the great powers that establish the reality of their world."[4] In a way far more profound than terms like *hour* and *day* and *year*, such sacred stories provide the framework within which we determine who we are and how we are to live. They give a shape to time, and thus to our lives. As one theologian suggests, "Our sense of personal identity depends upon the continuity of experience through time . . . Even when it is largely implicit, not vividly self-conscious, our sense of ourselves is at every moment to some extent integrated into a single story."[5] Just so, in one of those fascinating parallels between science and religion, a professor of theoretical physics puts it this way: "Our very notion of personal identity—the self—the soul—is closely bound up with memory and enduring

---

4. Crites, "Narrative Quality," 295.
5. Crites, "Narrative Quality," 302.

experience. It is not sufficient to proclaim 'I exist,' at this instant. To be an individual implies a continuity of existence together with some linking feature, such as memory."[6]

The preceding remarks about time, sacred times, and sacred stories, bring us to a consideration of the Passover narrative in chapter 12 of Exodus.[7] Eventually, our attention will include references to the contemporary Passover ritual, as well as comparisons with the Lord's Supper.

"This day shall be a day of remembrance for you . . . throughout your generations" (Exod 12:14). Passover is Israel's "linking feature" of "memory." The Passover narrative is arguably the most important section of the entire book because it is primarily here that the experience of exodus is communicated not simply as a moment in historical time (in the past) but as a perennially recurring moment in the present life of those for whom the story is sacred. The word *communicate* here means far more than to convey information. Communication here includes the religious connotations associated with the closely related word *communion*. The Passover narrative elicits a communion between past and present, and joins past and present together in anticipation of the future.

The Passover narrative communicates between past and present because the literary unit contains not only narrative but also liturgical "ordinance."[8] The unit is composed of the skillful editorial weaving of story and liturgy (or, to use the terms of comparative religion, *myth* and *ritual*). Of course, story and ordinance cannot be completely separated, largely because of the use of dialogue as the literary means to represent ordinance. If we had only the story (Exod 12:29–39), we would have only history. Unleavened bread would be a scarcely remembered detail, something that the ancient Israelites once had to eat because there was no time for using yeast in the midst of a hurried escape (v. 39). With the ritual, we have not merely history but drama. Unleavened bread is what the contemporary Passover service calls "the bread of affliction,"[9] a sacramental food that communicates the experience of affliction as well as redemption for those who reenact the story (cf. the "bitter herbs" of the ritual [v. 8] with the bitterness of the Egyptian oppression [Exod 1:14]). Similarly, in the contemporary ritual the eating of parsley dipped

---

6. Davies, *God and the New Physics*, 119–20 (italics original).
7. All verse references are to chapter 12 unless otherwise specified.
8. Exod 12:14, 17, 24, 43.
9. Goldberg, *Passover Haggadah*, 8.

in salt water symbolizes "both the idea of spring and redemption and the memory of enslavement, the salty water of tears."[10] Thus, the Passover meal is a somatic ritual in which one *tastes* both bondage and salvation (cf. above, "Spiritual Phenomena").

The dramatic "presentness" of the Passover narrative appears most concretely in the "dress code" of the ordinance: "'Buckle your belts, put on your sandals, grab your walking stick, and eat fast" (Exod 12:11, my translation). The rule applies not only to the historical people in the story—the people who actually left Egypt—but also to all future generations. Even a contemporary celebrant is supposed to eat the Passover meal in traveling clothes, ready for a trip. And where is the contemporary celebrant—living, say, in New York or London or Moscow—going? Why wear these traveling clothes? Because the celebrants are about to embark on a journey to freedom, a journey taken by millions of predecessors for several thousand years, and yet a journey that is as personal and recent as the liberation of an individual soul from its own secret bondage. The best way to embark on this journey is to dress for the part, to appear, as it were, in costume at the Passover table.

"Buckle your belts, put on your sandals, and grab your walking stick." It's the equivalent of "fasten your seatbelts." This verse from the ancient Passover narrative contains a metaphor for all of worship, both Jewish and Christian, especially when we consider the context of a sacred meal, and the connections between the Lord's Supper and Passover in the New Testament. The church or synagogue is a kind of repertory theater. We are the actors, and the story of the Bible is our script. Each time we come together for worship we are reenacting one of the world's great dramas—indeed, many would say the greatest drama ever written, with the longest-running production in history. Reasonably intelligent people will read the same books, listen to the same symphonies, and watch the same ballets over and over again. After all, one definition of a classic is a book that is worth reading numerous times. We would think anyone boorish who declined an invitation to hear a live performance of Beethoven's Ninth Symphony by saying, "Oh, I've heard that one before." We recognize that such classics are worth experiencing numerous times partly because each experience holds the possibility of a new revelation—something we had not seen or heard or understood before.

---

10. Trepp, *Judaism*, 310.

The same possibility resides in the repetition of the biblical drama: the possibility that a hope will be rekindled, that justice will prevail, that wounds will be healed, that broken relationships will be mended, sins forgiven, new life experienced—in short, a new experience of exodus. But there is something quite unusual about the production of the biblical drama. It is a drama that we do not simply observe as passive spectators. Rather, as the Passover narrative demands, it is an "observance" in the sense of reenactment (Exod 12:26; the word literally means "work" or "service," as in the Greek origin of "liturgy," which means the "work of the people"). We are the actors; we are onstage. The biblical authors demand that we be more than an audience; they demand that we assume the parts of their characters.

The "casting" of contemporary celebrants as characters in the Passover drama is the primary means by which the celebrants identify with the characters and thus "communicate" with the experience of exodus ("going out"). In the contemporary Passover ritual (or Haggadah ["narration"]), the celebrants say, "We were slaves of Pharaoh in Egypt and the Eternal our God brought us out from there."[11] Such a statement, of course, is a complete fiction. It is not historically true. It is no more true for Passover celebrants to say that they "remember" the exodus than it is for North Americans to say that we were the Pilgrims who left the old world for the new—but it is no less true either. For some, fiction (say, the parables of Jesus) communicates a spiritual truth that is far deeper than facts. Such fiction becomes a story about us, a story by which we transcend the categories of space and time and participate in the reality that it narrates. When the Passover celebrants say, "We were there," they are also saying, "The exodus is here"—the experience of freedom is not simply a historical memory; it is a living reality, here, in the reenactment of this play. The reenactment transcends the present, but it is also infused with a transcendent presence, the presence of the God of exodus.[12]

The spiritual identification between contemporary celebrant and biblical character appears in the Passover Haggadah commentary when it says, "In every generation one must look upon himself as if he personally had come out of Egypt."[13] This process of identity formation is the primary reason for reenacting the play over and over again. Hal Holbrook

---

11. Goldberg, *Passover Haggadah*, 9 (italics added). Cf. Deut. 6:20–25.
12. For a discussion of these terms of transcendence, see Pilgrim, "Ritual," 572–75.
13. Goldberg, *Passover Haggadah*, 23.

played the elderly Mark Twain so many times that for years producers invited him to play only older men. It took him four hours to put on his makeup. But when he took to the stage, he was *Mark Twain Tonight!* "That's the point of acting the whole part," he once said, "You are whom you portray."

One of my favorite children's stories is called "Upstairs and Downstairs."[14] It is about an owl who at first appears more silly than wise. He lives in a two-story house with a twenty-step staircase. One day he decides to try to be upstairs and downstairs at the same time by running as fast as he can. But no matter how fast he runs, he cannot be in two places at the same time. After exhausting himself, "he sat on the tenth step, because it was the place that was right in the middle."

The conclusion of the story is richly ambiguous. Has Owl succeeded or failed? In the end he is not upstairs or downstairs, so he appears to have failed. Yet, when he sits down on the tenth step, right in the middle, in between upstairs and downstairs, has he, in fact, found a way to be in both places at one time? The latter possibility is not as irrational as it may seem. Physicists tell us, in fact, that if Owl could have run fast enough, he could have outrun time and accomplished his goal. Of course, he would have had to travel faster than the speed of light, but in principle "it can scarcely be said to be a self-contradictory property to be in two places at the same time any more than . . . to be at two times in the same place."[15]

Passover is about being in two places at the same time and at two times in the same place. In the book of Exodus, the Passover narrative comes in between oppression and liberation, and the Passover meal is to be eaten "at twilight," literally "between the two evenings" (Exod 12:6). In fact, the inclusion of the liturgical ordinances functions to retard the progression of the story of the last plague, thereby heightening the feeling of suspense. As a result, the time before the actual departure from Egypt seems to be stretched, as it were. Or, to use a spatial metaphor, the Israelite characters stand poised on the threshold of freedom, frozen in a tableau in their travel costumes. It is a liminal (threshold) time and space. The characters are in Egypt and yet by anticipation out of Egypt. They are in the midst of oppression and yet already have a taste of freedom. The contemporary Passover Haggadah puts it best, using both spatial and

---

14. Lobel, *Owl at Home*.
15. Gerhart and Russell, *Metaphoric Process*, 180.

temporal categories: "Now we are here; next year may we be in the Land of Israel. Now we are slaves; next year may we be free."[16]

One verse from the Passover narrative (v. 42) perhaps best signifies the mood of the story and the ritual: "That was for the Lord a night of vigil, to bring them out of the land of Egypt. That same night is a vigil to be kept for the Lord by all the Israelites throughout their generations." An alternative translation would be "a night of watching." The mood is one of both anxiety and excitement, fear and hope. In this sacred time, God watches over Israel, and Israel watches (waits) for God.

The anxiety of the Passover night, of course, derives in part from the terrifying event that is about to unfold: the death of all the firstborn in Egypt. Only a streak of lamb's blood on the doorpost stands between the Israelites and the Destroyer who moves in the darkness (v. 23). The presence of the Destroyer gives a kind of primitive, numinous quality to the narrative, and thus to the corresponding ritual. It is a dreadful night. While the narrative does not flinch from attributing this horror to the God of Israel (v. 12), contemporary readers may well be reluctant to interpret the story in a literalistic way. But in the overall context of the book of Exodus, the death of the firstborn appears to be the tragic consequence of Pharaoh's stubbornness. It would certainly not be the last time that innocent civilians would suffer as a result of official government policies. As Moshe Greenberg has noted, Pharaoh refuses to surrender his "claim to ultimate, self-sufficient power." Instead, he arrogantly "resists, careless of the cost, unto death."[17] Even so, the narrative in no way dwells on the death of the Egyptians, much less exults over their fate, and contemporary seder texts include a lament for those who died.[18]

In the context of the larger exodus narrative, the anxiety of the ritual also derives from the unresolved tension of the plot. Will Pharaoh let Israel go, or not? For it is not until after Pharaoh has made his last move, not until his forces are drowned in the sea and Israel is really out of Egypt, that redemption from slavery will be complete—"at the morning watch"

---

16. Goldberg, *Passover Haggadah*, 8.

17. Greenberg, *Understanding Exodus*, 181. Greenberg may also have Hitler in mind (see below).

18. One Haggadah, for example, says: "Our triumph is diminished by the slaughter of the foe," and cites the ancient rabbinic tradition: "When the Egyptian armies were drowning in the sea, the Heavenly Hosts broke out in songs of jubilation. God silenced them and said, 'My creatures are perishing, and you sing praises!'" (Bronstein, ed., *Passover Haggadah*, 48–49).

(Exod 14:24). Thus, the words of Psalm 130 would be an appropriate supplement to the Passover ritual: "I wait for the LORD, my soul waits, / and in his word I hope; / my soul waits for the Lord / more than those who watch for the morning, / more than those who watch for the morning" (vv. 5–6).

One of the most intriguing aspects of Jewish and Christian spirituality is the way both traditions created two of their most significant rituals out of "a night of watching" and not "the morning watch." Both the annual Passover meal and the perennial (for some, daily) Lord's Supper lift up, as it were, the night before redemption. Of course, Christians moved their sabbath to the first day of the week, in recognition of the day of Christ's resurrection. Moreover, both Passover and the Lord's Supper incorporate the "day after" (liberation from Egypt, resurrection from death). They are thus "festivals" of freedom (cf. Exod 12:14). But the setting of both rituals is the "night of watching."

"Why is this night different from all other nights?" asks the Passover Haggadah.[19]

"On the night of betrayal and desertion, and on the eve of death," says one version of the eucharistic words of institution.[20]

Considering another possibility for Christian ritual perhaps will underscore the ambivalence of both the Lord's Supper and Passover. What if the church had adopted for its primary symbol not the cross but a rainbow over an empty tomb? What if the primary text and corresponding ritual were the Easter morning breakfast that the risen Jesus had with his disciples (John 21:1–14)?

In short, the sacred time of both Passover and the Lord's Supper incorporates being "in two places at the same time [and] . . . at two times in the same place." This time is a "night of watching" that looks forward to "the morning watch." Theologically, both the commonality and differences between the two rituals and corresponding religious traditions are reflected in a poignant aphorism: "The Jews say, 'The world is so evil; why has the Messiah not come?' The Christians say, 'The Messiah has come; why is the world still so evil?'" Perhaps the greatest contribution of the Passover tradition to both Judaism and Christianity is its stubborn insistence on incorporating the continuing reality of both redemption and evil into the order of the ritual.

---

19. Goldberg, *Passover Haggadah*, 8.
20. United Church of Christ, *Book of Worship*, 47.

Many years ago, I was invited to attend a seder at the home of some Jewish acquaintances. I had participated in seders along with fellow Christians in an attempt to reclaim our Jewish heritage, but I had never been part of a seder in its native context. At the time, I was teaching courses in the Old Testament and in biblical Hebrew, so I approached the evening as one who has learned a language and a culture and finally gets to test his knowledge in the field. I arrived with high expectations of a moving spiritual experience, but at first these hopes were dashed. At this seder, at least, the religious elements were intertwined with ordinary dinner-table conversation, often with much laughter. I also quickly discovered that the host, who was leading the ceremonies, often did not know Hebrew as well as I did and showed some surprising ignorance of the text of Exodus, so I found myself mentally giving him an examination as if he were one of my students. But near the end of the evening, I found that it was I, in fact, who was being examined. It happened when something caught my eye that I had not seen all evening: the man had a tattoo on his forearm. It was not a tattooed picture, but a number, of about five or six digits. It was the kind of tattoo that was stamped on the arms of concentration camp prisoners in Nazi Germany. This man had been in Auschwitz, or some such camp. Suddenly the entire evening changed, and along with it the seder and its meaning.

This is the question that haunted me then and haunts me still: how could this Jew who had been in Auschwitz celebrate the Passover? In the shadow of the Holocaust, in which six million Jews were murdered, how could he read these lines from the seder: "[God] brought us out from slavery to freedom, from anguish to joy, from sorrow to festivity, from darkness to great light"?[21] My host, of course, had survived, but for millions of others—perhaps his own relatives—there had been no exodus, only slavery, anguish, sorrow, and the final darkness. From this perspective, the ambivalence of the ritual deepens into paradox: Passover celebrates liberation even in the face of suffering and evil that are unrelieved by liberation. In fact, more recent versions of the Passover Haggadah include explicit references to this paradox, as in this one: "in the brutal days of Holocaust, we drank the cup of poison, foretold by the prophet Zephaniah: 'That day is a day of wrath, a day of trouble and distress, a day of waste and desolation, a day of darkness and gloom, a day of clouds and

---

21. Goldberg, *Passover Haggadah*, 24.

thick darkness."[22] Here is a midrashic move that only Jews should make, but from which we may well learn.

How can a Jew celebrate the seder in the face of Auschwitz? We may pose the question more generally: what is the relationship between ritual forms and suffering? When contemporary Jews celebrate the seder, they are obeying a command that is thousands of years old. In a sense, the celebration of the seder is a "command performance." Granted, the celebrants may not consciously think of it that way. If you asked them, "Why are you doing this?" they might not say, "Because God told us to." But that is what is happening. Even for Jews who consider themselves largely secular, participating in this ritual in effect identifies them with the characters in the ancient biblical drama who follow divine orders. "The LORD said to Moses . . . this day shall be a day of remembrance for you. You shall celebrate it as a festival to the LORD; throughout your generations you shall observe it as a perpetual ordinance" (Exod 12:1,14). We could just as well translate "you must celebrate it," "you must observe it," and note that the command is described as "a perpetual ordinance." An "ordinance" is a type of law; celebrating Passover is a "law-abiding" activity, an act of obedience to what "the LORD said."

What is the result of such obedience after Auschwitz? According to Emil Fackenheim, a Jewish theologian, it is to maintain one's Jewish identity and therefore to triumph over Hitler. "Jewish opposition to Auschwitz cannot be grasped in terms of humanly created ideals," he says, "but only as an imposed commandment . . . , an imperative as truly given—as was the Voice of Sinai" (referring, of course, to the giving of the Ten Commandments).[23] In an incredibly daring move, Fackenheim compares the commanding voice of Sinai with "the commanding voice of Auschwitz." And what does it command? Just this: "Jews are forbidden to hand Hitler posthumous victories. They are commanded to survive as Jews, lest the Jewish people perish. They are commanded to remember the victims of Auschwitz lest their memory perish. They are forbidden to despair of man and his world, and to escape into either cynicism or otherworldliness."[24]

Observing the ordinance of Passover reactivates memory, at once both painful and redemptive. In the ritual, the memory of suffering

---

22. United Jewish Appeal, *United Jewish Appeal Israel Independence Day Haggadah*, 6–7.

23. Fackenheim, *God's Presence in History*, 83.

24. Fackenheim, *God's Presence in History*, 84.

refuses to deny or escape from its reality; but the memory—and hope—of liberation refuses to despair or succumb to suffering. Similarly, the Lord's Supper lifts up the brokenness of Jesus, and therefore our brokenness, yet it is called "the joyful feast of the people of God." In this ritual we share with our Jewish brothers and sisters the paradox of anguish and joy. To recall the metaphors of the children's story, we are in two places at the same time—downstairs and upstairs. The same combination is evident in the old African American spiritual: "Sometimes I'm up, sometimes I'm down; nobody knows the trouble I've seen—glory, hallelujah."[25] Rituals of great spiritual depth keep us honest, but also hopeful.

The recognition of both suffering and redemption is the primary spiritual substance of what it means to be in two places at the same time. The fusion is achieved not only by the content of the Passover story but also by the form of "ordinance." Just as the Passover narrative (or Haggadah) is conformed to an ordinance (or seder [order]), so the story of the Last Supper is conformed to an "Order of Word and Sacrament." Here in ritual form is explicit reference to a quality shared implicitly by virtually all artistic forms—from stories to paintings to dance—especially when these forms attempt to tell us something about suffering. As one author puts it, "Form is the negation, the mastery of disorder, violence, suffering, even when it presents disorder, violence, suffering . . . The work of art sets its own limits and ends according to its own law: The 'form' . . . makes the intolerable tolerable and understandable, it subordinates . . . the evil to 'poetic justice.'"[26]

If the order of worship masters suffering even as it presents it, perhaps we can better understand why worship is demanded and not simply recommended. The Passover ritual is ordinance as well as order, making participation a form of obedience as well as the voluntary acceptance of an invitation. American individualism along with its ecclesiastical companions like my own Congregationalism resist such notions. We do not like to think of worship as doing something that we are told to do. One communion invitation even says, "Come not because you must, but because you may."[27] Yet there are also traditions in which participation in the Lord's Supper is complying to an "ordinance" and therefore an obligation of church membership. It used to be that people in the Evangelical and

---

25. See Cone, *Spirituals and the Blues*, 63–64.
26. Marcuse, *Essay on Liberation*, 43.
27. United Church of Christ, *Book of Worship*, 80.

Reformed churches were required to attend Holy Communion at least once a year in order to maintain their standing. When they did so, they filled out a communion card and put it in the offering plate, and their attendance was dutifully recorded (and no doubt reported to the pastor!). In theory, at least, failure to comply with the ordinance could mean excommunication, a contemporary analogue to the original Passover ordinance excluding from the community those who refused to participate in the eating of unleavened bread (Exod 12:15, 19). As authoritarian as the contemporary Christian "ordinance" may seem, the idea was not so much to keep people in line as to ensure that they would reaffirm their identity as Christians, that they would remember the gospel story, that they, too, might be helped to experience "exodus" despite the reality of suffering. Extending the sense of liturgy ("the work of the people") to ordinance ("the obedience of the people") recognizes that rituals can be the way to redemption, and law the means to grace.

Just as the liminality of the Passover story speaks to us in a personal way, it also has political implications. The exodus story as a whole provides an important antidote to any Christian spirituality that would see worship as divorced from the reality of oppression and the need for redemption in our own time (cf. Fackenheim's warning about "otherworldliness" in the above quotation). The ritual drama demands an ironic identification with the oppressed as well as the liberated, the victims as well as the victor—indeed, the participants are both at the same time. Thus the "ordinance" of the ritual effects the same spiritual and political empathy as do the "ordinances" of the law (Exod 24:3). Those who have been oppressed aliens must not themselves become the agents of oppression (22:21; cf. 3:7–10). As Deuteronomy makes especially clear, those who genuinely "remember" the story of the exodus will reenact it not only in dramatic ritual but also in acts of justice on behalf of the poor (Deut 15:15; 24:17–18, 21–22). Justice is the ethical form of liturgical memory.

Throughout our generations, Passover is the time of our lives, continually calling us to face the darkness of our night even as it lifts our eyes to the light of the "morning watch."

Good Friday

The Passion of God

In 1989, ninety-six fans were crushed to death in a soccer stadium in Sheffield, England. At one of the hospitals to which these victims were taken, an attending surgeon spoke to the parents who had come to find out the fate of their children. The surgeon read the names of those killed, expressed his sympathy to the parents, and then said that as a Christian he believed that God understood the parents' grief and was with them in the time of need. One father bitterly responded: "What does God know about losing a son?"[1]

Holy Week can also be called Passion Week, beginning with Passion Sunday, the alternate name for Palm Sunday, but the word *passion* focuses on the death of Jesus on Good Friday. *Passion* at one point was a hot word in our culture, thanks to the movie by Mel Gibson, *The Passion of the Christ*. I haven't seen the film and probably won't. For one thing, I have grown incapable of watching graphic violence. But more to the point, I think that the movie perpetrates a dangerous understanding of Christian faith. That understanding appears in one traditional notion of the atonement, evidenced already in the New Testament. John Calvin puts it in sharp form: "[Jesus] bore the weight of divine severity, since he was 'stricken and afflicted' by God's hand and experienced all the signs of a wrathful and avenging God."[2] Jesus is the ultimate sacrificial victim who bears the sins of the world, thereby obtaining forgiveness for all.

There is no doubt that the passion story, including Easter, is central to Christian faith. As Marcus Borg says, "death and resurrection . . . [are]

---

1. "Good Question," 6–7.
2. Quoted in Brock and Parker, *Proverbs of Ashes*, 29. Calvin is probably quoting Isa 53:4. Cf. Rom 3:25.

the psychological-spiritual process at the center of the Christian life."[3] But the centrality of this metaphor does not require that we buy into a theory of Jesus' death as a sacrifice, that such a death is part of the plan or will of God. Have you ever really thought about that? Do we really want to believe in a God who would deliberately condemn his own son to be tortured and murdered, for *any* cause? Can you imagine any human parent doing that?

Consider the story of Jesus praying in the garden of Gethsemane. As Donald Capps says, "It is a story in which a son pleads with his father to be spared the death that almost certainly awaits him, and who believes that his father has the power to intervene in his behalf but chooses not to."[4] Do we want to say that God would subject *anyone* to such cruelty, but especially God's own child? As Rebecca Ann Parker suggests, "To say that Jesus' executioners did what was historically necessary for salvation is to say that state terrorism is a good thing, that torture and murder are the will of God."[5] Such a view amounts to "cosmic child abuse." Consider the irony: here is our society, post-911, still wounded by and fearful of terrorism, yet many people are enthralled by a story in which terrorism is an act of God—not in the sense that insurers use that term, but literally: an act of murder willed and sanctioned by God.[6]

Parker has coauthored a book that shows how the Christian validation of sacrifice and violence in the atonement can be dangerous especially for women and children. Consider the woman who was beaten repeatedly by her husband and went to her priest for counseling. The priest said that she should rejoice in her sufferings because they brought her closer to Jesus. "He said, 'If you love Jesus, accept the beatings and bear them gladly, as Jesus bore the cross.'"[7] Preachers for slave owners

---

3. Borg, *Heart of Christianity*, 107. In regard to what follows, Father Richard Rohr suggests that the substitutionary atonement doctrine "has kept us from a deep and truly transformative understanding of both Jesus and Christ. Salvation became a *one-time transactional* affair between Jesus and his Father, instead of an ongoing *transformational lesson* for the human soul and for all of history" (*Universal Christ*, 141; italics original).

4. Capps, *Child's Song*, 116.

5. Brock and Parker, *Proverbs of Ashes*, 49.

6. New Testament theologian Walter Wink puts it adamantly: "God did not kill Jesus or have him killed or even allow him to be killed, and every view to the contrary depicts God as committing an unconscionable sin" (*Human Being*, 109).

7. Brock and Parker, *Proverbs of Ashes*, frontispiece (the full account appears later in the book).

in the American South employed the same theology to keep their slaves "docile" (cf. 1 Pet 2:18–25).

"If you are willing," Jesus prays, "remove this cup from me; yet, not my will but yours be done." Yet Jesus receives no answer. Do we want to think, then, that God *is* willing that he die such a death, but refuses to help? I, for one, do not think so. I think that Jesus's torture and death do not show the will of God but the will of human beings who are so caught up in evil that they cannot or will not see that the will of God is totally opposed to everything that such violence signifies. Jesus challenged the system—both religious and political—and, like so many before and so many after, the system responded with terror and death.

There is another alternative in imagining a response to Jesus' prayer (and imagination expressed in metaphor is all we have). It is to imagine God as the parent who in fact would do *anything* to rescue his son, but *cannot*. It is to imagine God as powerless to stop what is happening to God's son. It is to imagine a God who suffers the deepest, most devastating grief that *human* parents can suffer, the death of a child—no, worse, the torture and murder of a child.[8]

A traditional Holy Week hymn says "God's own sacrifice complete." A revised version says "God's own child is sacrificed."[9] The two are radically different: one talks about how humans have killed Jesus *as if* he were a sacrificial animal; the other says that the sacrifice was God's own doing. I'll go with the former.

In two of the Gospels, Jesus dies crying to God, "Why have you forsaken me?" The other side of the metaphor would have to imagine the agony of God as the parent who can do nothing but watch. It is as if Jesus is in one of those interrogation rooms with a one-way mirror, and God is on the other side looking in and can see what is happening but cannot do anything, cannot even be heard, and Jesus cannot even see that God is there.

We should not adopt a theology in which God causes the suffering of Jesus or controls it or sends it for some good purpose, any more than we should hold that God causes, controls, or sends the suffering of others.

---

8. In Kelsey's terms, the inability of God to intervene is a dimension of God's "sovereign self-regulating," in which God does not violate "the ontological integrity of the creatures and their creaturely powers" (*Human Anguish*, 364, 367). Presumably, that would include Jesus's executioners. Indeed, Kelsey boldly characterizes this self-restraint as "the uselessness of the triune God" (367).

9. Montgomery, "Journey to Gethsemane."

Rather, as David Kelsey argues, "As exemplified in Jesus' crucifixion . . . God actively resists horrendous suffering by entering into it fully . . . , by freely being closer to us *as we are experiencing such suffering* than we can be to ourselves in the experience of suffering."[10] And the way that God does that with Jesus is by being the grieving parent. As one theologian says regarding the dying of his own son, God's role is not that of providing "supernatural escape" from suffering, "but the faithful companion in the Valley."[11] Kelsey goes on to say that we can and should trust that it is "a companionship ordered to some good," but whatever good may come of it, it is not as escape, nor is it part of a divine plan for which suffering was the strategy.[12] In Christian tradition, Easter is the good that God creates *out of* Jesus' suffering, God's No! to the imperial power that put him to death.

This brings us back to our opening scene in the hospital room after the soccer game disaster, and the parent's anguished question: "What does God know about losing a son?" Christian faith says, Everything and more, because the death of God's son is not only an accident, tragic as that is, but torture and murder. In Christian faith, God is a parent who grieves and mourns the death of a murdered child. As one author has written, this is "A Grief Like No Other."[13] Christian faith says that God has experienced that grief. That is God's passion. God is a *pathetic* God, not an *a*pathetic God.

The metaphor of God as a parent who can do nothing to save her child is not exclusively Christian. Rabbi Jeremy Kalmanofsky has written an essay about "Parents at Prayer." He begins with a situation in which a parent falls on his knees before a physician and begs him to say that his two-year-old son will be all right, that he will not die of cancer. "What could it be like," the rabbi asks, "to see before him the tortured father of a

---

10. Kelsey, *Human Anguish*, 358–59 (italics original).

11. Richard Lischer, quoted by Kelsey, *Human Anguish*, 404. The "Valley" is "the darkest valley" (NRSV) or "valley of the shadow of death" (NRSV footnote), Ps 23:4.

12. So also Kelsey: "God freely places Godself in those experiences of deep suffering to bring some good out of them" (*Human Anguish*, 364). To pursue the parental grief metaphor, an analogy could be the ways grieving parents create organizations to counteract whatever evil caused the death of a child (e.g., Mothers against Drunk Driving [MADD] to curb drunk driving or Sandy Hook Promise to curb gun violence).

13. The title of an article by Eric Schlosser in the *Atlantic* in September 1997.

tortured child? What could he say? Nothing except exactly what he said: 'I cannot do that.'"¹⁴

Kalmanofsky then talks about how his own parenthood has changed his understanding of God. God can no longer be for him the "Big Daddy" who protects us from danger. Now, he says, he sees the "spiritual power" of God's parenthood not from the perspective of a powerless child, but in his "experience as a powerless father, who prays holding babies." "If I could only keep them from bullies and nightmares, unreturned love, leukemia, bulimia, depression, bipolar disorder, cocaine, car accidents, flunking math, AIDS, rapists, Osama bin Laden. *But I cannot do that. And I would not even if I could.*" Why not, we must ask? And he says, because it would rob them of their full humanity—the need to grow, to gain wisdom, courage, and kindness, "to become fully realized human beings." "They can attain this," he insists, "only if our power to protect them is limited, even as our love is infinite." So, Kalmanovsky concludes, we and God "are parents together, loving beyond any promise of comfort."¹⁵

"We and God are parents together." Perhaps that is the clue to at least one meaning of Christ's death that avoids the pitfalls of divine child abuse. Alongside the passion of Christ, which teaches us about dying and rising, there is the passion of God. God is the parent who suffers a grief like no other. And, if there is any comfort in any of this, perhaps it is that the God who suffers is closer to us than any Big Daddy God whose power is unlimited. In one of the novels of Cormac McCarthy, one of his characters says, "those who have suffered great pain of injury or loss are joined to one another with bonds of a special authority . . . The closest bonds we will ever know are bonds of grief. The deepest community one of sorrow."¹⁶ We are used to hearing about Jesus as "the man of sorrows, acquainted with grief" (see Isa 53:3), but is this not also true for God, the grieving parent? And does this not mean that we might be joined to God precisely in the experience of deepest sorrow? And does this not mean that a crucial role of the church is to be a community of sorrow—as well as joy? As the apostle Paul says, "If one member suffers, all suffer together with it; if one member is honored, all rejoice together with it" (1 Cor 12:26).

---

14. Kalmanofsky, "Parents at Prayer," 56.
15. Kalmanofsky, "Parents at Prayer," 57 (italics original).
16. McCarthy, *All the Pretty Horses*, 238.

One of the most profound books written on the death of a child is that of Nicholas Wolterstorff called *Lament for a Son*. On one page he gives this advice to would-be comforters. Don't try to minimize the loss. Don't say foolish things about silver linings or "getting over it." I think he would agree with a character in a novel by Kent Haruf, a father who says to his daughter, whose own daughter was killed in a car accident, "You don't get over it, do you. When a child goes. You never do."[17] Correspondingly, Wolterstorff says, "I need to hear from you that you are with me in my desperation. To comfort me, you have to come close. Come sit beside me on my mourning bench."[18] That is what the passion of God means. God has come close to us and is with us in our desperation, whatever it might be. God sits beside us on the mourning bench.

In a letter to a theological magazine, a writer says that his son was killed accidentally just before his fifteenth birthday. "In an instant," he says, "my reliance on the sovereign control of God was undone." After the funeral, he purchased a crucifix, an unusual move for a Protestant. He hung it on the wall over the kitchen table, and, he says, "every evening, when I had to stare at [the] empty chair in front of me, I could lift my eyes to the crucifix and remember God had suffered a grief such as mine . . . I find it easier to love the God who suffers than I did the one who controls. Twelve years later I still look to that crucifix and find solace and hope."[19]

"What does God know about losing a son?" Everything, and more. Easter cannot take that grief away completely. God does not "get over it" any more than a human parent gets over it. How could God get over it, when violence takes the lives of thousands of his children every day? Nor does Christian spirituality get over it. After all, traditionally the cross is our primary symbol, not a rainbow over the empty tomb, and the Last Supper is our primary meal, not a sunrise breakfast (see "Passover / Maundy Thursday," above). Easter comes, it is true, and thank God, but Easter cannot remove the pain of that day strangely named Good Friday. Nothing can *remove* such pain, but such pain can be *relieved* when it is shared. "The closest bonds we will ever know are bonds of grief. The deepest community one of sorrow." No matter what our grief, even "a grief like none other," God, in her passion, comes to sit by us on the mourning bench. That for us is the best place for God to be.

---

17. Haruf, *Benediction*, 110.
18. Wolterstorff, *Lament for a Son*, 34.
19. Hosick, "After a Child Dies," 45.

Easter Laughter

One year not long before Easter I happened to see somewhere a list of church bulletin bloopers. Here are a few examples:

Offering: Please place your donation in the envelope along with the deceased person you want remembered.

Attend this luncheon program and you will hear an excellent speaker and heave a healthy lunch.

This evening at 7 P.M. There will be a hymn sing in the park across from the Church. Bring a blanket and come prepared to sin.

The visiting monster today is Rev. Jack Bains.

The study series Women in the Word starts next week. There are several different studies to choose from. Ladies, make sure you sign up for a stud before next week.

Brother Lamar has gone on to be the Lord.

Mrs. Jones has not had any clothes for a year and a half and has been visited regularly by the clergy.

The sermon this morning: "Jesus Walks on the Water." The sermon tonight: "Searching for Jesus."

Hymn: "Wise Up, O Men of God"

That Easter I read some of these at the outset of the service. Later I discovered that I was in line with an ancient tradition, with a Latin name, no less—the *risus paschalis*, the "Easter joke." Some traditions celebrate it on Easter Monday, leading me to wonder if they are not quite comfortable with laughing on what for some is the holiest Sunday of the year. My congregation had no such reservations. In fact, in ensuing years I was inundated with so much comedic material that I had enough for a hundred Easters. I could have switched professions and become a standup comic.

Is comedy a part of faith, laughter a dimension of spirituality? You may be surprised to learn that there are a number of scholarly books about laughter. One is part of a series of books on Phenomenology and Existential Philosophy, which already suggests that scholars have a weird sense of humor. Another book even has the title *Taking Laughter Seriously*. The author says something that may surprise you even more, namely, that because Christianity highly values solemnity it unfortunately tends to stifle laughter.[1] I noticed this once when visitors to our church communion service complained that young children "came running and laughing up to the communion table." God forbid that they should enjoy it, even though we had declared it to be a "joyful feast." On the other hand, at another eucharistic celebration, after enjoying the feast, a four-year-old announced proudly and loudly to her mother, "Mommy, I ate it all up!" Wisely, her mother did not shush her, or express any disapproval of this interruption, but said, "Good for you!" And everyone laughed.

Now it is true that in the Old Testament, God is not often given to mirth, except in a kind of derisive snort (e.g., Ps 2:4), and Jesus is never portrayed in the Gospels as laughing. I have seen a painting of a laughing Jesus, an encouraging sign in iconography, although the guy looks more like a pale Charlton Heston than a swarthy Yasser Arafat. But there is one story in the Old Testament in which laughter is thematic—the annunciation and birth of Isaac, the son of Abraham and Sarah. In fact, the very name "Isaac" means "he laughs," (*yitsaḥ* in Hebrew, pronounced "Yitsak") but that is to get ahead of the story. You won't find this story in the lectionary for Easter, but it should be, for it foreshadows the *risus paschalis*.

The story appears in several parts (Gen 17:15–23; 18:1–15; 21:1–7). In what is probably the oldest version (Gen 18:1–15), Abraham is sitting outside his tent on a hot afternoon when three men show up. The narrator tells us that these men are in fact divine messengers, including God (early Christian interpreters had a field day with this, arguing that the visitors are none other than the Trinity, which, of course, presumes a preexisting Christ).[2]

---

1. Morreall, *Taking Laughter Seriously*, 125–26.
2. The author of Hebrews (13:2) resisted that move, referring to the visitors as angels.

Exhibiting typical Near Eastern hospitality, Abraham promptly invites the visitors to dinner, which means that he orders his wife, Sarah, to get busy in the kitchen. After they have eaten, one of them says that they will return, and when they do, Sarah will have a son. Sarah has been eavesdropping at the tent door, and she bursts into laughter. The narrator tells us why: the couple is "advanced in age" (Gen 18:11); Sarah is postmenopausal. No wonder she laughs! But the Lord (being omniscient) is not happy and asks why Sarah laughed, adding, "Is anything too wonderful for God?" (18:14, reflecting the Septuagint). She lies and says, "I did not laugh," but God correctly says, "Oh yes, you did laugh" (18:15).

Apparently the annunciation is news to Sarah, although—in the canonical sequence—it is not to Abraham, for he has already heard it in the preceding story (17:15-23). His response there is even more incredulous than Sarah's here: "he fell on his face and laughed" (v. 17).

Those unfamiliar with biblical language might think from this that Abraham has difficulty standing up, but the reference—usually—is to an act of reverence. In the presence of God, you fall on your face. You've probably seen the gesture in TV pictures of Muslims at prayer, kneeling with their heads to the floor and their arms stretched out in front of them. It is a gesture of humility and obedience, both appropriate spiritual attitudes for mere humans in the face of God Almighty (for Muslims, Allah). And, in fact, the annunciation was preceded with precisely this gesture at the outset (17:3).

But the second occurrence of this phrase is hardly accompanied by reverence. If anything, it is irreverence. Abraham cracks up. He falls down laughing at God Almighty. It says something about the patience of God that Abraham isn't zapped on the spot. When Saint Paul praises Abraham's faith, saying that he did not "weaken" or feel any "distrust," despite being a centenarian, Paul conveniently leaves this little incident out of his argument (Rom 4:19-20). Instead, Paul bases his description of Abraham on another text in which Abraham is the model of the trusting soul (Gen 15:6). I really wish Paul had at least added a few qualifying phrases, something like "Of course, Abraham had his faults. He didn't always believe. Sometimes he doubted, just like you and I. Once he even laughed in God's face." But Paul doesn't do that, and taken alone his description of the faith of Abraham presents an unfortunate ideal that few can attain (cf. Heb 11:8-19). (Paul also omits that little incident in which Abraham palms off Sarah as his sister in order to save his own skin [Gen 12:10-20].)

No, according to our story, Abraham was most definitely not always "fully convinced that God was able to do what he had promised" (Rom 4:21). The man certainly had reason enough to laugh at what God offers. As Abraham says to himself, "Can a child be born to a man who is a hundred years old? Can Sarah, who is ninety years old, bear a child?" (Gen 17:17). He can't believe it. It's too good to be true. So, the promise of a son is unexpected and surprising. The story is about infertility and a child, homelessness and a homeland. And at this point in the story, this old man and woman are childless and homeless.

So, who wouldn't laugh at the absurdity of the situation? Who wouldn't laugh at the sheer incongruity between what is promised and what is real? As feminist biblical scholars point out, it is a symptom of a male-dominated culture that Sarah learns of the promise only by eavesdropping, and only when she laughs does God speak directly to her. In fact, the only words ever addressed directly to her in the entire narrative are when God chastises her for snickering.

Of course, when Abraham laughs, he doesn't say to God what he has said to himself. Instead, he immediately composes himself and offers a more practical solution to the problem. Why not use Ishmael? Ishmael is Abraham's son by his housemaid Hagar. Lest you think of this as an illicit love affair, it was apparently customary in ancient Near Eastern culture for childless women to use their housemaids as surrogate mothers. Jacob (Abraham and Sarah's grandson) ended up with two wives, two housemaids and thirteen children! However morally questionable this practice might be for us, it was not a moral problem for the author of Genesis. (These stories profoundly complicate what one might mean by "biblical family values"!)

In the annunciation story, the appeal for Ishmael is a rational rebound from the laughter. Or maybe we should say that it is rationalistic. In the laughter, Abraham entertains the possibility of the impossible: can an old couple really have a child? The laughter, of course, is incredulous because the possibility itself seems incredible, so the possibility is posed in the form of a hypothetical question. But then Abraham does a 180-degree turn. You might say his thinking shifts from right brain to left brain. Reason takes over from imagination. The security of a plan replaces the insecurity of a promise. "Let's use Ishmael. He's here already" (Gen 17:18). Ishmael is known. The child of the promise is unknown, and therefore risky.

We tend to think of Abraham's laughter as the opposite of faith because it reflects his doubt that God can do what God has promised. But could it be that the moment of his laughter was more like faith than the alternative plan he proposed? In a comment attributed to him, theologian Reinhold Niebuhr says, "Humor is the prelude to faith, and laughter the beginning of prayer."[3] Perhaps his suggestion will help us understand the role of laughter in our story, and in our own stories as well.

When Abraham laughs at God's promise of a child by Sarah he is laughing at the incongruity of it all. God's promise doesn't make sense. It doesn't fit with what Abraham knows. It's inconsistent with his physical condition. It's absurd considering *Sarah's* physical condition, because absurdity is "senseless, illogical" and "laughably foolish" (Webster's dictionary).

Just because there are very few references to laughing in the Bible, does that mean that there is no sense of humor in the Bible? Perhaps the problem lies with our inability to see it. For example, we might find Jesus' parables funny if the language were as powerful for us as it must have been for his listeners. Jesus says that the realm of God is like all sorts of crazy things. In one parable that realm is like bread mold that a woman hides in some dough. You probably don't find that funny, but to the original audience the very incongruity of the realm of God (holiness) and bread mold (called leaven, which is unholy), not to mention a woman, and hiding it, would have been scandalously humorous. It's screwball comedy, like a camel going through the eye of a needle (Matt 19:24; see above, "A Kingdom of Kudzu and Crud").

In fact, in his study of laughter, John Morreall concludes that incongruity is one of the basic dimensions of humor. "Humor," he says, "is based on novelty and incongruity, on having one's expectations violated."[4] That's what is happening to Abraham; his laughter is a result of the radical incongruity of the situation. In the face of infertility, it is the very incredibility of the promise of a child that makes it funny, ridiculous, and ludicrous. This is why, at the birth of the child, Abraham names him "He laughs." And Sarah says, "God has brought laughter for me; everyone who hears will laugh with me" (Gen 21:6). "Laughter" is the son of the promise.

---

3. https://www.quotemaster.org/q908fdaa8241c169c8ddfa618043b9446/.

4. Morreall, *Taking Laughter Seriously*, 128.

In fact, when you think about it, isn't the Bible full of such incongruities from one end to the other? There's Moses, a man who stutters called to be God's spokesperson. There's David, the runt of his family, called to be king. There's Amos, a rustic fruit farmer called to be a prophet. And isn't the gospel itself full of incongruities? There are those "realm-of-God" parables with kudzu trees and holy rot, useless jewels and stolen treasure. There's the Messiah in the manger, visited by lowlife shepherds and pagan magicians. There's the Son of God partying with sinners, the King on the cross, God's foolishness wiser than human wisdom (1 Cor 1:25). There's losing your life to find it—and finally, the incredible, unbelievable, incongruous story of Easter. Jesus was not what the Messiah was expected to be. Isn't the Bible, therefore, one huge example of incongruity, and so one huge joke? And shouldn't our first response to it be laughter? Isn't that why "humor is the prelude to faith, and laughter the beginning of prayer"?

Laughter is our response to the appearance of the unexpected, the incongruous. Earlier I said that Abraham "cracks up," and that is a rather interesting expression. There are several meanings to "crack up": to have a collision, to have a physical or mental breakdown, and to laugh boisterously. To pursue the expression, maybe we could say that laughter is the prelude to faith precisely because it "cracks us up." And perhaps all three senses of the expression come into play here. To crack up is not only to laugh but also to collide with something totally unexpected and to see our previous categories of reality break down. Faith then sometimes begins with a collision, a breakdown, and a laugh. Indeed, one theologian has suggested that the spiritual process of "conversion" involves a "collision of narratives" in which a person's identity "may be altered and reality perceived in a radically new way."[5] Surely that was the case with the "expecting" parents, Abraham and Sarah.

Another author puts it this way: "laughter is the sign of one's approach to the absolute . . . Our behavior is maladapted when we act like programmed robots rather than living creatures in a perpetual state of creative improvisation."[6] Traditional piety tells us that the first time Abraham falls on his face (Gen 17:3), we see how to approach the absolute, God Almighty. But maybe the second time he falls on his face (17:17), we see another, equally compelling approach. For a moment

---

5. Stroup, *Promise of Narrative Theology*, 171.
6. Tournier, *Wind Spirit*, 29.

(before he reverts to the Ishmael solution), Abraham cracks up, which means that laughter opens him up to the possibility of the unexpected, to novelty. "Can a child be born to a man who is a hundred years old? Can a woman who is ninety years old bear a child?" (17:17) The promise of a child is an invitation to join in God's "creative improvisation."

Perhaps one of the reasons that we fail to see the humor in a Bible full of it is because we no longer expect to find anything different from what we already know. Perhaps the reason that worship sometimes leaves us unsatisfied is because we have not really opened ourselves to the "new creation" that is there. Maybe one of the reasons that people give up on religious faith and the church is that they know too much and expect too little. When the little girl at our communion service announced, "Mommy, I ate it all up!" it was, in effect, a "creative improvisation" of the liturgy, and we cracked up at her childish expression of accomplishment in "cleaning her plate," reminding us that the Eucharist is, indeed, a joyful thanksgiving for grace, shared at table in fellowship with others who are hungry to be blessed. And when her mother said, "Good for you!" we realized that the child's joy was good for us, as well.

I heard a story once about a group of Blacks who, in the early '60s, went to a segregated restaurant somewhere in the Deep South and sat down at the counter. They sat there for a long time until, finally, instead of a waiter, the manager appeared, glared at them, and growled, "We don't serve Negroes here."

"No problem," one of them said, "we don't eat them either; we just want hamburgers." They went away empty-handed, but I suspect they also went away laughing with a sense of victory. In this case, humor empowered them to make a joke of an outrage—and thereby to keep going in the fight for justice. Here laughter took the form often used to put down the mighty—satire (remember the folktale "The Emperor Who Had No Clothes"?).

In his book about surviving the Nazi concentration camps, Victor Frankl describes an even more radical situation. The prisoners would make fun of each other's emaciated bodies in the showers. They even devised "a kind of cabaret" in which they sang songs and told jokes about camp conditions. "Humor," he writes, "more than anything else in the human make-up, can afford an aloofness and an ability to rise above any situation, even if only for a few seconds."[7] A Jewish tale reflects the same

---

7. Frankl, *Man's Search for Meaning*, 61, 63.

way in dealing with suffering. An old man was on his deathbed, comforted by his wife. He reminisces on all sorts of hardships that they weathered together—a terrible pogrom, beatings, being robbed, living in the ghetto. With each remembrance, his wife nods and says, yes, she remembers all that, and affirms that she was with him all the time. Then there is a pause, and the man looks at her with a twinkle in his eye, and says, "You see, Golda, I think you were bad luck."[8]

Laughter can also play a role in similar (albeit radically different) occasions of grief. In our memorial services there is almost always laughter, usually in the stories that people tell about the person who has died. I vividly remember one service for a prominent church member who was a gifted therapist and brought healing to many people. Among other things, she was renowned in the youth group for her talks on sexuality and the time that she used a banana to demonstrate the use of a condom. I and others told such funny stories about her, and, as one person was leaving the service, she said to me, "I never knew it was possible to laugh and cry at the same time." Laughter is the flip side of sorrow, the side that insists, despite all evidence to the contrary, that life is greater than death, that peace is greater than violence, love stronger than hate.

What would happen if we looked at faith itself differently? Instead of seeing it as "been there, done that," what if we saw it as "a perpetual state of creative improvisation"? What if our reading of the Bible became a process of continual reinterpretation in which we are open to surprise and transformation? What if religious fellowship was an ongoing conversation in which we listen to and offer differing points of view (including with some prostrate Muslims)? What if being a Christian meant being engaged in an exploration of new ways of thinking about God and human beings and the earth. "Creative improvisation" in fact is what life demands of us anyway. That is what relationships are all about—and parenting and learning and working. That is what is involved in growing older gracefully, in dying peacefully. The difference for us is that our improvisation is rooted in the tradition symbolized by the one who says, "I am making all things new" (Rev 21:5).

Can a child be born to a man who is a hundred years old? Can a woman who is ninety years old bear a child? Hah!

※

---

8. Biro, *Two Jews*, 102.

All Saints' Day

Watching over One Who Grieves

On All Saints' Sunday my church provides candles for those who are remembering someone who has died. There is a table set up at the front of the sanctuary, and people place one or more candles in the candleholders on the table and light them, sometimes saying out loud the name of the loved one, or simply in silence. By the time the ritual is over, the table is illuminated by scores of flames, each representing someone whose life burned bright and is no more with us. For a number of years now, I have lit one in memory of my wife, Connie, who died at the relatively young age of sixty-seven and quite unexpectedly, and I am still grieving, albeit not as acutely as at first.

    Among a vast field of contenders, one of the most eloquent writers on the subject of grief is the late Nobel laureate Elie Wiesel. And one line from his writings has stuck with me more than any other: "To watch over one who grieves is a more urgent duty than to think of God."[1]

    No one knew better about grief than Wiesel. He was a Holocaust survivor whose family was murdered by the Nazis, and who himself experienced the horrors of Auschwitz. He wrote of his harrowing experience in his book titled *Night*. So, Wiesel's assertion is not one of those simplistic dismissals of the profundity of grief in which one is encouraged to make lemonade out of lemons. On the other hand, we should also

---

1. https://www.quotemaster.org/q253a0e36ca0df7c9fc5c054242b2fadf.

not underestimate the gravity of the second half of his assertion, the part about thinking of God.

Wiesel was a Jewish writer who struggled with the immense theological problem of how to believe in God after Auschwitz (see "Maundy Thursday / Passover," above). That struggle is as old as the biblical book of Job, and as current as today's inexplicable tragedy. Thinking about God is, usually, the most important activity that a pious Jew is called to do, and, I would argue, it is no different for Christians. The word *theology* means "word about God," alike in etymological structure to other words like *geology* or *psychology* or *entomology*. Just as the chief duty of a geologist is to think about the earth, and the psychologist to think about the mind, and the entomologist to think about bugs, so the chief duty of the theologian is to think about God. But it would be a mistake to assume that only professional theologians *are* theologians, or that theology requires an advanced academic degree and a teaching position in a divinity school, because everyone who, in the slightest degree, believes in God, is called to think about God as their highest duty. Indeed, foremost in that thinking is the difficult task—the lifelong task—of defining for oneself what it *means* to believe in God, which is no small feat.

Both the Hebrew Bible and the New Testament attest to this duty to think of God in the so-called great commandment: "Listen, O Israel. Love Yahweh your God with all your soul, with all your heart, indeed with your full capacity" (Deut 6:4–5, my translation). When asked what is the greatest commandment, Jesus wisely quoted this one, called the Shema in Judaism. In Matthew's version, he adds the phrase "with all your mind," which is simply a logical extension of the Hebrew anthropology, in which heart and soul and mind are an expression of the full human self. Wiesel's words are each highly significant: thinking of God is a duty. It is a responsibility, a requirement. Thinking of God is part of the obedience demanded by that great commandment. The love of God here is not so much emotion as it is *devotion*—it is loyalty, and involves pledging one's allegiance to God as the ultimate concern in one's life. And because it engages the whole self—body, mind, and soul—it is urgent. It demands immediate attention. Compare the response demanded by the military command "Attention!" That is the urgency with which one must think about God.

But that brings us back to the first part of Wiesel's assertion: "to watch over one who grieves is a *more urgent* duty." Perhaps now we can understand how remarkable Wiesel's claim is. How could there be anything more urgent that the total devotion of oneself to God? And yet, there is. It is "watching over" another fellow human being who is in grief.

I have read dozens of books on grief, and, in my own inadequate way, talked with people who are grieving, but to experience grief is far different than to know about it from books or even from the testimony of others. So it was with Connie's death. Over the course of months, people often said to me, "I can't imagine what you are going through," and my response was usually "No, you can't, nor could I have before it happened." So, wisely, no one said to me, "I know just how you feel," because we cannot know that about another person, no matter how similar our loss may be.

But there are, of course, similarities. One of my favorite books on the subject is called *All Our Losses, All Our Griefs*,[2] and the major theme of the book is how *all* losses cause grief, and how the dynamics of grief exhibit commonalities across the board. One of the most interesting dynamics is the way otherwise desirable events sometimes involve loss and grief. A job promotion, for example, may be what one has longed for, but suddenly you are moved upstairs to a different office and different colleagues and new responsibilities, and the loss of the familiar leads to grief. But the loss of a spouse is a lot deeper than a loss of an office or of colleagues, and yet, even so, not as deep as the loss of a child. Whatever the loss, at some point—early on—comparisons break down and become meaningless.

But critical to every experience of grief are those who watch over the grieving. Anniversaries are some of the hardest times, and in the summer after Connie died my daughter, Mary Liz, and I observed an anniversary—our annual beach trip with friends, the eldest of whom I have known for almost fifty years. There was no way that we could go through that week without somehow recognizing our mutual grief, so several days into the week we assembled down at the water's edge in our beach chairs, late in the day, after margaritas, when the tide was out. And our friends read some texts from the Bible and from Mary Oliver. And then we built a very rudimentary sandcastle, little more than a mound, unadorned with turrets and such finery, underneath which we buried some of Connie's ashes. Then our friends gracefully left us alone and went up for dinner.

---

2. Anderson and Mitchell, *All Our Losses, All Our Griefs*.

Mary Liz and I decided that we wanted to wait until the tide came in and our sandcastle began to disintegrate, yielding to the water that would take it into the sea. It took a long time, but finally the water came, and when it encircled the sandcastle, we were ready to leave the beach and go back to the cottage for a late dinner, assuming that our friends had already finished. But it wasn't a dinner alone after all, for they had waited for us, and watched us, down on the beach—watched *over* us. And no one ate until we were all there, and we gave thanks for food, and for friendship, and we lifted our glasses in a toast to the Spirit among us, and to Connie. Companionship, from the Latin, meaning "with bread."

One of those friends *is* a professional theologian, which means that he thinks about God for a living, is even paid to do so! I don't know what he was thinking as we sat on the beach, but at one point, he reached over and held my hand, and I can still feel the warmth of his.

"A Meeting in the Air"

1 Thessalonians 4:17

"There's going to be a meeting in the air, / in the sweet, sweet by and by; / I'm going to meet you, meet you over there, / in that home beyond the sky. // The singing you will hear never heard a mortal ear, / 'twil be glorious I do declare; / and God's own son will be the leading one at that meeting in the air." Those words are the refrain from an old gospel song recorded years ago by the Carter family. No doubt the composer of the song had in mind one of the lectionary texts for All Saints' Day: "then we who are alive, who are left, will be caught up in the clouds together with them to meet the Lord in the air." It's the "rapture."

As is often the case, fundamentalists have so monopolized this corner of biblical imagery that little of it seems left for us. In mainline churches, talk about the rapture is rarely heard. *The Encyclopedia of the Reformed Faith* does not even have an entry for it. In fact, I confess that I sometimes use "rapture language" jokingly, as in, "on the day that my lapel mike works perfectly we can expect to see Jesus coming on the clouds of glory." My jocularity is shared by one church's long-range planning committee, who decided to call themselves "until the rapture."

For most of us, I suspect, the rapture is not high on our list of preoccupations. We are more concerned with making it through the day. Faith has to do more with everyday life than with an afterlife. And this attitude, I would say, is justified both biblically and theologically. As the Jewish philosopher Martin Buber puts it, the primary focus of our Judeo-Christian heritage is "to hallow this life,"[1] to perceive the sacred in the everyday and live accordingly. Yet the everyday life is certainly not all there is to Christian faith, for this faith is rooted in the claim of the gospel

---

1. The title of one of Buber's books.

story, "Jesus is risen," and the promise that the resurrection of Jesus reveals to us what our own end will be, indeed, what the end of the world will be. As the United Church of Christ statement of faith says, it is the promise of "eternal life in [God's] realm, which has no end."[2] All Saints' Day invites us to think about eternal life by reminding us that we are part of the *communion of saints*, a community that includes both the living and the dead. Invariably, the lectionary includes for that day a reading from the apocalyptic vision of the book Revelation, such as this verse: "I looked, and there was a great multitude that no one could count from every nation standing before the throne and before the Lamb, robed in white, singing 'blessing and glory . . . honor and power . . . be to our God forever and ever! Amen!'" (7:9, 12).

How shall we understand the "meeting in the air," or the gathering around the throne? How important is the end-time communion of saints for the present-time community of the church? How central is the hope for a life after death in Christian spirituality?

"We will be with the Lord forever," says the apostle Paul to the Christians in Thessalonica. Paul's letter to them is the oldest document in the New Testament, dated to around 50 CE, predating all of Paul's other letters and all of the Gospels. Here is the earliest Christian spirituality, scarcely more than fifteen years after the death of Jesus. Paul is addressing a particular problem having to do with those who have died (or, literally, "fallen asleep"). Christians who are alive are worried that those who have already died will not be included in the rapture. Paul assures them that not only those who are alive but also the dead will be part of that "meeting in the air."

Paul is speaking to a Greco-Roman audience. In their culture, there were two options regarding death. On the one hand, there was the belief that death was the end of all life, that nothing waited beyond the grave. As a Roman writer, Lucretius, put it, "death is nothing to us" (*On the Nature of Things*). Since the person has no existence after death, says Lucretius, no one should be afraid of it, because if you are nothing, there is nothing to fear. On the other hand, there was the belief in the immortality of the soul, championed by Plato and others. According to this view, death did not really happen to the *soul*, only to the body.

Paul opposed both of these views. Yes, he says, there is life after death, but no, it is not the immortality of the soul. Rather, it is life in a

---

2. United Church of Christ, *Book of Worship*, 513.

resurrected body. Paul's anthropology is Jewish rather than Greco-Roman. The human person is not a soul embedded (much less imprisoned) in a body. The human person is a spiritual entity that is inherently and indivisibly soul and body. What we now call the psychosomatic integrity of the self is thoroughly Israelite in origin. And because this is the nature of human life before death, it will be the nature of human life after death. As Paul puts it, what is a "physical body" will become a "spiritual body" (1 Cor 15:44). The transformation from the physical to the spiritual does not remove the somatic.

It was Descartes who said, "I think, therefore I am"—a statement that came to epitomize the Enlightenment. Unfortunately, this anthropology in which the mind was everything and the body merely the container has proved disastrous in many ways, a problem now recognized by many disciplines of thought (especially ecology). In contrast, Israelite anthropology recognizes the psychosomatic unity of the self, recognizes that our personal identity is very much wrapped up (as it were) in our bodies.

Once when I was teaching a religion class of female college students, I asked them to imagine what it would be like to wake up the next morning in the body of their roommate. One of the young women, apparently unsatisfied with her own body, quipped, "I wish I *could*!" But the truth is that we can't really imagine that because who we are is inextricably tied up with our bodies, warts and all, and biblical anthropology affirms the goodness of ourselves as bodies. The belief in a resurrection of the body is an affirmation of the goodness of God's creation, the goodness of all material things, of matter itself. Belief in the resurrection is not a denial of the value of this life: on the contrary, it is the ultimate acknowledgment that life as created by God is infinitely precious, so precious that God wills for it to continue after death.

"There's going to be a meeting in the air." The Judeo-Christian affirmation of the bodily nature of *human* nature leads immediately to an affirmation of the *social* nature of human nature. We are essentially social beings. As the creation story says, "It is not good that the man should to be alone" (Gen 2:18). To be completely human, Adam the earthling needs a "partner fit for him." As the Jewish philosopher Martin Buber put it in his classic book *I and Thou*, "all real living is meeting." That is, to be human is to be in relationship with others. As Buber says, "I become through my relation to the Thou; as I become I, I say Thou."[3]

---

3. Buber, *I and Thou*, 11.

"All real living is meeting." Please do not confuse this sentence with "all real living is meetings"! If heaven is simply "another meeting to go to," it might qualify better for hell. But that obviously is not what Buber (or Paul) has in mind by "meeting." Rather, meeting here signifies the interrelationships within a community that define both individual and group identity. Indeed, "meeting" also signifies *spiritual* identity because in Jewish and Christian tradition the meeting is not only with each other but also with God. That is why the earliest sanctuary in ancient Israel was called the "tent of meeting." It's why Quakers refer to their services as "meetings."

For Paul, then, life after death means not only the resurrection of each person as a "spiritual body," but also as part of a social body. This is why for Paul those who have died remain "asleep in Christ" until the return of Christ. In other words, for Paul the communal connection is so critical that he believes everyone will get to heaven together, not one by one. Of course, Paul at first expected the return of Christ soon, certainly within his own lifetime. He could not have dreamed that two thousand years would leave us in precisely the same position of his Thessalonian audience. Perhaps if Paul were here with us today, he would want to change that view.

Paul was a complex creature of first-century Judeo-Christian, Greco-Roman culture. His thinking about life after death—and resurrection—was a development of one stream of Jewish tradition, namely, apocalyptic. For at least fifteen hundred years before him, Jewish spirituality had no concept of life after death, except for a vague, shadowy underworld. Ancient Israelites found life to be meaningful and good without any belief in life after death. Furthermore, there are even biblical passages that are at best skeptical. Ecclesiastes thinks that we are no different from the animals and suffer the same fate: "as one dies, so dies the other; all are from dust, and all return to dust again" (3:19). "The living know that they will die," he says, "but the dead know nothing . . . , and even the memory of them is lost" (9:4). (He and Lucretius would have gotten along quite well.)

In the second-century BCE, religious persecution changed all that. Apocalyptic thought arose in the midst of political oppression of the Jews by non-Jewish rulers. The torture and murder of Jews simply for confessing their faith led some of them to believe that there would be justice in the end, beyond this life, since there was no justice in this life (Dan 7; 1 Macc 1:20–64; 2 Macc 6–7). Life after death became an answer to the cry of the persecuted whose murderers went unpunished.[4] Today that cry would be deafened by the echo of the six million Jews who were slaughtered by Hitler, but also by the cry of millions of others, whether Jewish or Christian or not, who have suffered a similar fate—from the peasants of Cambodia to the campesinos of Guatemala to the African slaves and indigenous peoples of America. In Judeo-Christian spirituality, life after death is a matter not only of personal survival and social identity: it is also a matter of the faithfulness of God and ultimate justice. That is why martyrs figure prominently in the celebration of all saints, both ancient and modern—the latter including (unofficially) bishop Oscar Romero, Dietrich Bonhoeffer, and Martin Luther King Jr.

"There's going to be a meeting in the air." Is it possible for contemporary people to believe this? I do not pretend that it is easy. And I certainly do not argue that one *must* believe it in order to live a Christian life of integrity. It is surely possible to follow Jesus—to love God and neighbor—in this life without thinking too much about an afterlife. God knows there are enough causes that deserve attention right here on earth. But on All Saints' Day, I suggest that we consider what it might mean for us to extend Buber's comment that "all real living is meeting" to the possibility of a meeting beyond death.

Surely one of the major barriers to our own belief is the biblical language itself. It may have made sense to Paul, but we find it hard to believe that God will blow a trumpet, Jesus will descend, and we'll all gather together in the clouds. Our meteorological understanding of the world defies such pictures. Also, we can't resist all sorts of questions: Where is heaven? How could it be a *place* in any meaningful sense of the word? Will there be room for everybody there? How could you find anyone? What if you didn't *want* someone to find *you*? What is a "spiritual body"?

As natural as such questions are, they ignore a crucial aspect of the biblical language, namely, that it is metaphorical. As is often the case, literalism is the enemy. When questioned about the resurrection, Jesus rejected a literalistic question posed to him by a faction of Jews who did not believe in it (the Sadducees; Luke 20:27–36). They are trying to trick Jesus so that he will make some outrageous gaffe and lose his popularity. So, they pose a ridiculous hypothetical situation based on the tradition in which the brother of a dead man married his widow so that she could bear children in the dead man's name (Deut 25:5–6). What if (they asked)

---

4. Segal, *Life after Death*, 262–72.

there were *seven* brothers who all died, each having married the wife of the first to die? To whom would she be married in heaven? In this case, the poor woman would probably have thought *life* was hell, and the last thing she would want would be to continue her misery as a reproduction machine in *heaven*. Jesus responds by saying that the Sadducees are like the children's-book character Amelia Bedelia. She takes everything literally and gets into lots of trouble as a result. Jesus says that the Sadducees have a literalistic view of heaven—that is, of the resurrection—according to which people have ordinary bodies and function just as they do on earth. But heaven is a completely different reality where people are "like angels and are children of God," not simply resuscitated corpses (see Matt 22:23–33; Mark 12:18–27; Luke 20:27–40).

Biblical descriptions of life after death are trying to describe a reality that no one has experienced directly. Whatever it is, it is certainly a reality that is beyond our ordinary categories. A United Church of Christ *Book of Worship* liturgy for All Saints' Day talks about the company of "all believers in every time and beyond time." The "communion of saints" refers to a coexistence of both the living and the dead within a single ontological reality that transcends our categories of space (earth/heaven) and time (alive/dead). Theologian Sallie McFague describes this communion as a kind of cosmic ecology: "we do not have to leave God when we die, nor do we join God in heaven . . . [Rather,] we are with God whether we live or die, for whether our bodies are alive or return to the other form of embodiment from which they came, they are within the body of God."[5] Similarly, a memorial-service liturgy recognizes the inconceivable nature of that reality by referring to it with a biblical quotation: "ear has not heard, nor eye seen, nor human imagination envisioned, what [God] has prepared for [us]."[6]

Strangely enough, contemporary science may help us in recognizing the possibility of such a reality. Consider just a few examples. We used to think that atoms were the smallest unit of matter, but now we know that there are subatomic particles with strange names like gluons, quarks, and leptons, but we can't see them. Astronomers tell us that there are black holes in the universe, pinpoints of unbelievably intense gravity that suck in everything around them, so intense that even light cannot escape, so we can't see the black holes either, but they are there (currently, not too

---

5. McFague, *Body of God*, 176.
6. United Church of Christ, *Book of Worship*, 68, 373, based on 1 Cor 2:9.

close!). And consider what we think about the origin of the universe, the big bang, and how the universe is continually expanding from that explosion. What is beyond that expanding edge? What was there before? Even within the universe, there may be "10 billion trillion habitable planets."[7] There is even a theory that there are parallel universes connected by something called "tubes" (could one of those be "heaven"?).

The reality of the world as science describes it is at least as incredible as Paul's meeting in the clouds. As one book suggests, much of scientific knowledge does not result from direct observation of reality but from instruments that *suggest* that reality. As a result, the authors say, "The world that we know is a world of our imaginations, a world that is 'made up' of our largely second-order mediated experiences."[8] Theologian Hans Küng echoes this thought when he quotes a scientist who says, "'The range of the real world must transcend quantitatively and qualitatively by inconceivable dimensions the horizon of knowledge available to us.'"[9] And Küng himself says "God's consummation is beyond all human experience, imagination and thought. The glory of eternal life is completely new, unsuspected and incomprehensible, unthinkable and unutterable."[10]

"What ear has not heard, nor eye seen." Because the reality that we call heaven can only be described metaphorically, I suggest that we use a piece of contemporary fiction to do so. At the height of its popularity, I picked up a copy of *Harry Potter and the Sorcerer's Stone*. I wanted to see what all the hullabaloo was about—that is, both the enormous popularity of the book and its sequels among young (and some old) readers, but also why some Christian groups want it banned. The reason for the latter is that the hero, a boy of ten, is a wizard, and most of the plot takes place in a boarding school for wizards called Hogwarts. For the most part, these are good wizards, not bad wizards.[11] After reading the book, it seems to me that the religious critics are much like Harry's disgruntled uncle, described as someone who disapproves of imagination.

Early in the book, Harry has been summoned to the school of wizardry, ordered to report to "platform nine and three-quarters" at the train station for an eleven o'clock train. When he arrives at the station,

7. Frank, "Truth May Yet Be Out There," A19.
8. Gerhard and Russell, *Metaphoric Process*, 23.
9. Küng, *Eternal Life?*, 224, quoting Hoimar von Ditfurth.
10. Küng, *Eternal Life?*, 220.
11. No doubt such critics invoke the biblical condemnation of wizards, as in Lev 19:31; 20:6, 27.

his unimaginative uncle, who sneers at the whole idea of wizardry, sarcastically observes that there is a platform nine and a platform ten, but no platform nine and three-quarters, and leaves the boy standing there baffled and forlorn. The ticket office says there is no eleven o'clock train either. Then Harry sees several other kids about his age with their parents, carrying luggage just like his, and he guesses (correctly, it turns out) that they too are headed for Hogwarts. Then the strangest thing happens. As he watches one of the boys, the boy heads off to platform nine, and just as he is about to run into the wall that separates it from platform ten, he disappears into thin air. Now Harry approaches one of the parents and confesses that he doesn't know how to get to the right platform. She encourages him not to be afraid but to just run straight towards the wall, and that is what he does, but instead of a bruising crash he instantly finds himself on the other side. Looking back, he sees a sign saying Platform Nine and Three Quarters, and there waiting to take him to Hogwarts is "a scarlet steam engine." He has entered another dimension of place and time.[12]

But that fictional scene may not be as fanciful as it seems—may, in fact, have its parallel in the science of quantum mechanics. As one University of Chicago scientist suggests, that field of research is "extremely counter-intuitive," posing a realm of reality that "we don't see in our world today." In fact, the "properties of matter" in quantum mechanics "could allow you to walk through a wall."[13] Quantum mechanics evokes a reality that eye has not seen, just as the liturgical language does. Maybe getting into Hogwarts is not all that different from getting into heaven. As a correspondent wrote to me in an email, "there's no good choice other than to keep moving with faith and awe towards the wall."[14]

12. Rowling, *Harry Potter*, 93–94.
13. Public Broadcasting Service (PBS), "Race to Develop Quantum Technology." Remarkably, walking through a wall is a phenomenon described of the risen Jesus in the Gospel of John (20:19, 26).
14. Genie Carter, email to the author, July 25, 2021.

Holidays

New Year's Day

A Time for Janus

In the year of our Lord, 2006, New Year's Day fell on a Sunday. I didn't take a poll, but I'm sure that no one came to church that morning wondering what I would say about the presentation of baby Jesus in the temple. That was the story in the Gospel reading from the lectionary, it being the first Sunday after Christmas (Luke 2:22–40). Mary and Joseph bring the eight-day-old Jesus to the temple for a kind of postpartum ritual in which the mother presents the child to God and states his name. But, for those who stumble out of bed on New Year's Day, the liturgical calendar is not usually on their mind; rather, it is the seasonal calendar, and the only "post-partum" significance might be post-Christmas exhaustion or New Year's Eve hangover. If the liturgical calendar claims December 25, the secular calendar claims January 1, whether a Sunday or not. Actually, the first Sunday of Advent is the beginning of the liturgical year, about as close as Christians come to a New Year's Day. But most of us, I'm sure, are more in an end-of-the-year frame of mind when Advent rolls around. New Year's is more popularly known as the day on which one makes resolutions, often having to do with dieting following all the binging of "the holidays."

Our Jewish heritage celebrates the New Year, only it follows the Hebrew calendar and comes usually sometime in September. It's called

Rosh Hashana, which means "head of the year." Followers of other faiths have New Year's celebrations too (Muslims and Hindus, for example). And the Chinese New Year celebration makes our New York City Times Square display seem tame. The Christian calendar eventually won out, designating all of historical time to be either before Christ (BC) or in the year of the Lord (Latin: *Anno Domini* = AD). To be more inclusive of non-Christians, we have changed these designations to BCE and CE: Before the Common Era and (in the) Common Era.

It's not that the Christian liturgical calendar doesn't recognize New Year's Day, and I suppose some of the more liturgically observant churches celebrate it. After all, (North) American churches have incorporated Thanksgiving, essentially a national commemoration, although there are no lectionary readings for July Fourth (US Independence Day). In the year 2006, however, the readings for the baby Jesus trumped that other baby that sometimes appears in New Year's iconography. Otherwise, for New Year's, every year there are the same readings (Eccl 3:1–13; Ps 8; Rev 21:1–6; Matt 25:31–46), which are the same readings for New Year's Eve ("Watch Night") perhaps for those who don't make it up the next morning. Fittingly, the reading from the book of Revelation, the major biblical entry in the apocalyptic genre, includes the vision of a new heaven and earth and the divine promise, "See, I am making all things new." Similarly, the Gospel reading describes the last judgment scene, concluding with the alternative verdicts of eternal life or eternal punishment (perhaps enough to make for a more sober celebration). The Psalm praises God for creating humans "a little lower than God" (more accurately, than "divine beings"), certainly a positive anthropology with which to begin a new year.

My own preference would be for the reading from Ecclesiastes, that great impious, rather curmudgeonly, skeptic of the Bible, sort of our religious Cynic, if that isn't an oxymoron. The reading is the passage introduced by the words "For everything there is a season, and a time for every matter under heaven" (3:1), probably best known to many people not because of their frequent Bible reading but because of the folk song called "Turn! Turn! Turn!" written by Pete Seeger and performed by numerous folk musicians. That song, I would argue, appealed to people in the 1960s primarily because of the closing phrase, "a time for peace," to which Seeger added, "I swear it's not too late." Although the song faithfully follows the biblical text in acknowledging that there is a time for love and for hate, for war and for peace (among other pairs), it clearly encourages us to "turn" toward peace.

The Ecclesiastes text is a kind of compendium of human experience, posed in pairs of "seasons" and "times," some of which are opposites, sort of a biblical yin/yang: love and hate, war and peace. Some pairs can be more like the swings of a natural pendulum: planting and harvesting, or discarding stones (say from a field) and gathering them (say to build a wall). Birth and death, of course, are opposites, but they do not involve human volition in the same way as love and hate; rather, they are the ineluctable natural rhythm of human life, in some ways correlated to the emotions of laughing and weeping, or dancing and mourning. New Year's Eve and New Year's Day combined tend to encourage our reflections on the experiences of the preceding year and expectations for the year ahead. The memories may well include times both happy and sad, gains and losses (including in the stock market!), successes and failures, just as the expectations may well include hopes as well as fears, wishes as well as worries. The time of our life "turns" on what has been and what will be.

January is the namesake of the Roman god Janus, a theological etymology shared by March (Mars), May (Maia), and June (Juno). Janus presents a fitting image for the beginning of the year, because Janus is a god with two faces. One face is looking back, the other looking forward. The two faces, in turn, represent what we might call the existential character of Janus—he is the god of gates and doorways. A doorway, after all, can lead in either of two directions, out or in, backwards or forwards, both in the dimension of time as well as space. A door can close off but also open up. A door can shut out but also welcome in. The Latin word for doorway or threshold is *limen*, giving us the adjective "liminal." Doorways symbolize the liminal nature of our experience. Jewish homes recognize this by placing a mezuzah on the doorpost (which is what the word *mezuzah* means) containing a passage from the Torah (the Shema) and the commandment to write the words on the mezuzah (Deut 6:4–9).

Many years ago, theologian Stephen Crites wrote an influential article titled "The Narrative Quality of Experience," in which he pointed out how our lives are really stories. Our identity is best understood in terms of a narrative—what has happened to us in the past, what is going on now, and what will (or might) happen in the future. So, we are a combination of memory and expectation, both experienced in each fleeting moment of the present. When you get to know someone really well, they will eventually tell you stories about their past, present, and future. They will tell you their memories—some joyful, some painful, some happy, some sad; they will tell you of what is going on now in their lives; and they will tell you their expectations—some optimistic, some fearful, some hopeful, some anxious. Personal identity, Crites says, is a combination of "the chronicle of memory and the scenario of anticipation."[1]

Each of us, then, is like Janus, with one face looking back and one face looking forward. Every moment of our lives, of course, is a liminal moment, because every moment leads ineluctably from past to future. And there are some liminal experiences that stand out, major steps that we take in one direction or another—leaving home, as for college or some other endeavor; starting a new job; getting married; having a baby; grieving a loss—all special "times" or "seasons." More than any other day of the year, New Year's Day represents the liminal quality of our experience. New Year's Eve is the night we look back over the past year. Television programs often review significant events of the past year and remind us of prominent people who have died. But it is also a night to look forward to the year ahead. On this one night, at least, maybe it is good for us to flirt with Janus, if not to worship him.

Each of us is a chronicle of memory and a scenario of anticipation. Remembering and anticipating make us who we are; without them, we lose our identity. One of the most tragic illustrations of what happens when memory is gone appears in people with Alzheimer's disease. That disease robs people of their past. They can no longer remember the face of a loved one; in a sense, they can no longer remember their own face. Though less dramatic, the loss of anticipation can also produce a loss of identity. Such loss is the source of the proverbial recognition that at some age you realize that your face will not appear on the cover of *Time* magazine as the person of the year, that you probably won't discover the cure for cancer, nor will you become a best-selling author. In each case, the reality of who you are is changed by the limitations of what you might be, or what might happen.

If the loss of memory and anticipation can be problematic, so can their persistence. We have a word for a dysfunctional memory—*nostalgia*—a word derived from the Greek words for "pain" and "return home." Strangely, the theme song of New Year's Eve smacks of nostalgia rather than anticipation: "should auld acquaintance be forgot and never brought to mind?" the song asks. No, we'll sing "for auld lang syne," literally, for

---

1. Crites, "Narrative Quality," 303.

"long time since": in other words, for the good old days. On the threshold of the new year, the song seems only able to look backwards, a one-faced Janus.

I don't know of a one-word equivalent for *nostalgia* that names the anticipation for something yet to be which is, in fact, unrealistic. We talk about someone living in a "dream world," or we say, often sarcastically, "in your dreams." This is not to say that dreams, in the deepest sense, can't envision a future worth working for; one need think only of Martin Luther King Jr.'s most famous speech, arguably a version of Jacob's promise. But, like memories, dreams can also trap us in an unhealthy spiritual state. People who live in anticipation of something that is simply not going to happen live in a state of delusion or denial. One can even argue that hope itself prevents us from truly enjoying living in the present moment, that wishing for tomorrow robs us of simply being fully in the here and now. Just as it's possible to become mired in your chronicle, it's also possible to become stuck in your scenario.

The trick, of course, is to live in such a way that neither memory nor anticipation imprisons us in nostalgia or delusion. To negotiate the doorway in any moment requires a difficult discernment of what is healthful and what is not. Sometimes we need to shut the door on the past and move on (as Ecclesiastes says, "a time to throw away"); sometimes we need to open it and revisit ("a time to keep"). From the prophetic perspective, Second Isaiah (a prophet during Judah's exile in Babylon) exhorted the exiles not to remember the "things of old" (i. e. the good old days), because God was doing "a new thing" (43:18–19); on the other hand, he could say, "Remember the former things of old" (46:9). Memory recalls the faithfulness of God, which is the grounds for hope. Memory without hope is nostalgia; hope without memory is merely wishful thinking.

For many months during 2020–2021—the time of COVID-19—we learned in a grim way the truth of Ecclesiastes' words: there was "a time to refrain from embracing," and only gradually have we experienced anew how wonderful is "a time to embrace." And the same is true for the future. Sometimes we need to find the courage to open the door whose threshold we've always wanted to cross. But sometimes we need to acknowledge that a door is closed and cannot be opened, that we need to see another door that is open, leading to something new. Sometimes we can only know how to go forward by looking backward—which often is what we mean by learning from our mistakes. But sometimes we have to anticipate the future so that the past does not drop us into despair. We really do have to be like Janus, having two faces that oscillate, as it were, on the threshold, now looking back, now looking forward. That is the only way to know who we are, and who we may become.

Martin Luther King Jr. Day

The View from the Mountaintop

On the night before he was assassinated, Martin Luther King Jr. addressed an audience of largely Black garbage workers in Memphis, Tennessee. His speech, as often was the case, rose to a crescendo at the end in the style of Black preaching. He spoke of threats to his life, and then he said that he had gone to the "mountaintop" and seen the promised land.

Aside from Valentine's Day, about the only saint's day that most of us lower-church Protestants observe is Saint Patrick's, and that celebration probably owes its popularity to consumption of green beer. It's unfortunate that there are no lectionary readings for the King holiday. Our national calendar of holidays offers numerous presidents and historical occasions, but only Martin Luther King Jr. Day offers us a role model who stands out from all the others. King was a prophet. Ask almost anyone what a prophet is and they will quite likely tell you that a prophet is someone who can predict the future. If that is the criterion, then King was a prophet on the night before his death, for in this speech he seemed possessed with clairvoyance, the tragic accuracy of which would prove true within twenty-four hours.

But anyone who has read the Hebrew Bible carefully will tell you that clairvoyance in that sense is not the primary characteristic of a prophet. *Clairvoyance* means "seeing clearly," but what the biblical prophets saw most clearly was the present. They saw things that almost everybody else either could not or would not see. Much of what they saw can be summarized by one word—injustice. And when prophets looked to the future, their intent was not so much to predict what would happen as to envision what might happen if people lived according to the will of God. There is a special word in Hebrew, *ḥazah*, that refers to prophetic vision, this unusual way of seeing how things are and how they might be. Perhaps King was feeling the inspiration implied in that word when in the Memphis speech he drew out the word "seen." Similarly, King's more famous speech, "I Have a Dream," was the epitome of a prophetic vision.

It is impossible fully to appreciate and understand who Martin Luther King Jr. really was unless we see him as a prophet. Of course, we can and should look at him from other perspectives. The political scientist can analyze King's tactics and strategies, and discuss his debt to Mahatma Ghandi. The sociologist can examine his roots in the Black community, and the ethnic groups and social classes of his followers or his opponents. The psychologist can analyze King's behavior, showing us that King—like anyone else—was a man with flaws. But, for all that, King must be understood as a religious figure if he is to be understood at all, and if the larger movement that he led is to be understood as well.

I suspect that if most of us had been in the room when King was speaking, and heard him say that he'd gone to a mountaintop, we would have turned to each other and asked, "What mountaintop? There aren't any mountains around Memphis. I thought he spent the day meeting with his staff and the garbage collectors' union. When did he have time to go to the mountains?" Such questions would have been something like the comment that an FBI agent, on the scene of King's famous "I Have a Dream" speech in Washington, reportedly made to one of his colleagues over a walkie-talkie: "Find out what's behind this dream."

But King did not take his text from nature's scripture, as in John Muir's "divine manuscript"; he took it from biblical Scripture. He said that he'd been to *the* mountaintop, and the definite article is like that in Jacob's dream (The Place). King's predominantly Black audience in Memphis knew in an instant what King meant. They knew the mountaintop to which he referred, so they responded with "yessir" and "amen." King's audience knew what the mountaintop was because they knew their Bibles. They knew that scene at the end of the book of Deuteronomy where Moses, the great leader of Israel, who had led his people out of bondage, stood on Mount Nebo and looked over into the promised land, a land that he would not enter. No doubt they remembered how the scene closes as well, how Moses dies and the people mourn for him for thirty days. Perhaps they could even recite the closing words of the text (and of the Torah): "Never since has there arisen a prophet in Israel like Moses, whom the LORD knew face to face. He was unequaled for all the signs and the wonders that the LORD sent him to perform in the land of Egypt, against Pharaoh and all his servants and his entire land, and for all the mighty deeds and all the terrifying displays of power that Moses performed in the sight of all Israel" (Deut 34:10–12). King had been to the mountaintop and he had seen the future, or, to put it more accurately, he had been shown the future. God had revealed to him the promised land, which meant, of course, the freedom of his people from the iron grip of segregation and prejudice. God showed King the coming realization of his dream. So, King's mountaintop speech evokes the promise that we have been tracing from another dream—Jacob's at Bethel—all the way down to almost half a century after King's death, when a former Black president would write a book titled *A Promised Land*.

There are two contexts in which we should consider King's mountaintop vision. One is liturgical. In Year C of the lectionary, the Epistle readings for the Sundays before and after the holiday are from 1 Corinthians 12, where Paul spells out his well-known image of the church as the body of Christ. The social and political implications of the body metaphor suggest interesting comparisons with King's vision. Paul says that everyone must live and work in a way that serves the "common good" (12:12). That suggests a remarkably different culture from our own, in which people tend to live and work in such a way that serves what is good for them. Then society constitutes a collection of individuals looking out for "number one."

The other context is the growing realization that political liberalism has grown anemic and uninspiring because it is self-consciously secular. Liberals tend not to want to appeal to religious tradition, lest they tear down the wall separating church and state. At worst, liberals have adopted a purely materialistic worldview in which only what is objective and empirical is real, and anything that is "spiritual" or "religious" is dismissed as irrational. The result is that the religious Right can lay sole claim to the spiritual meaning of people's lives and claim to represent their religious values (see below in the Excursus on Prophecy, "A Poor Man's Coat").

Rabbi Michael Lerner has offered a trenchant critique of secular liberalism in his book *The Left Hand of God*, with the subtitle *Taking Back Our Country from the Religious Right*. As Lerner suggests, "Americans hunger for a framework of meaning and purpose to their lives that transcends their own individual success and connects them to a community based on transcendent and enduring values."[1] This is a spiritual hunger

---

1. Lerner, *Left Hand of God*, 44.

that those on the Left have ignored or, worse, ridiculed. People are looking for meaning and purpose that transcends their own self-interest and particularly the drive for financial success. They are looking for community rooted in transcendent values. They want a framework that pulls together all of the elements of this hunger, something that impels them, lifts them up, and gives them a reason to live in a certain way. In other words, they are hungering for exactly what King saw—a vision, a dream, a community of peace and justice rooted in the will of God, precisely what Paul describes: a community in which all work together for the common good.

Like Moses, King had been to the mountaintop, and the view from the mountain was very different from the view down below. Down below, within one day, King would be dead. But from above, the view was clear and the goal was in sight. This view from the mountaintop was not merely a momentary fantasy any more than King's prophetic clairvoyance was a crystal ball. No, the view from the mountain was a pervasive vision, a religious conviction, which undergirded King's entire career, and the work of most of his followers. It was a vision of none other than the realm of God. This vision was the driving force of King's life and the civil rights movement. If we do not see that vision, and march to its drums, then we will understand neither who King was nor the compelling motivation of that mission.

King's vision provided the spiritual framework of meaning that liberalism has largely lost. That framework was narrative in form, and it included above all the story of creation, in which God created every human being in God's image, male and female—people of every race and color and ethnicity. This is arguably the foundational story that at once validates all human beings as children of God (across all religious differences) and charges them with careful stewardship of the earth and all its creatures. The framework narrative included the story of the exodus, in which God liberated slaves from oppression, called them into a covenant community, and gave them a land where liberty and justice could rule. And it included the story of Jesus, one sent from God whom the world tortured and murdered, a story with which Blacks could all too well identify. In his book on *Religion in the Old South*, historian Donald Mathews shows how Black slaves received the Christian message "as the primitive Christians had—as a message . . . about God's act in history which proclaimed 'liberty to the captives.'" In their emotional worship services, Blacks did not wallow in guilt, like their White evangelical counterparts.

No, "Blacks were lifted up, enabled to celebrate themselves as persons because of their direct and awful [i.e., awe-full] contact with divinity which healed their battered self-esteem with the promise of deliverance, the earnest of which was the vision itself."[2] That is, the vision itself was already a form of deliverance, couched in the emotional ecstasy of worship. This was King's vision, and the vision that drove the civil rights movement.

Lerner also refers to King and how the biblical vision provided the framework that enabled him to "ensoul politics."[3] In other words, King's vision produced a soulful politics that was the spiritual "soul food" that fed the hunger for meaning and purpose beyond individual self-interest. As Lerner describes it, this vision lives in the hope for "a world of caring, for a genuine connection and mutual recognition, for kindness and generosity, for connection to the common good, to the sacred, and to a transcendent purpose for our lives."[4] That is also a wonderful description of what Paul means by Christian community (and from a rabbi, no less!)—a community of caring, of mutual recognition, of kindness and generosity, of concern for the common good, a connection to the sacred, and to a transcendent purpose for our lives.

Perhaps the primary reason to become part of a religious community like a church, synagogue, or mosque is to be nurtured by its caring and guided by its values—above all, to be inspired by that same story of creation and exodus, justice and peace, that is the heart of King's vision: to be heirs of the promise of both Jacob's and King's dream. In the failure to learn that story, and to teach it to each generation, the vision will be lost. And, as Proverbs warns, "When there is no prophetic vision (ḥazôn), people lose their grounding" (Prov 29:18, my translation). In a sense, to identify with that story is to stand on that same mountaintop as Moses and King and to look into the promised land, living (and dying) in the hope that one day we as a community and as a society will get there. Put on your hiking boots; it's time to climb.

---

2. Mathews, *Religion in the Old South*, 213–15.
3. Lerner, *Left Hand of God*, 158.
4. Lerner, *Left Hand of God*, 15.

Excursus: Prophecy

A Poor Man's Coat

If you take your neighbor's overcoat in pawn, you shall restore it before the sun goes down; for it may be your neighbor's only clothing to use as cover; in what else shall that person sleep? And if your neighbor cries out to me, I will listen, for I am compassionate. (Exod 22:26)[1]

Thus says the Lord to the houses of worship: Seek me and live; but do not seek one of your religious sanctuaries, or enter one of your famous churches, for they shall come to nothing.

I hate, I despise your religious festivals, and I take no delight in your worship services. Even though you offer me your monetary offerings, I will not accept them. Take away from me the noise of your songs; I will not listen to the melody of your organs. But let justice roll down like waters, and righteousness like an ever-flowing stream. (Amos 5:4–5, 21–24)

As I suggested above, Martin Luther King Jr. is best understood, at least from a religious perspective, as a prophet, and the holiday that commemorates his life and work provides a fitting context for an excursus on the prophetic movement of the Hebrew Bible. King was assassinated in April 1968, when he led demonstrations to launch what was known as the Poor People's Campaign. The title of that campaign could serve as a description of a major concern of the biblical prophets. In our exploration of prophecy, we are looking for the religious motivation for liberal moral values, motivation that ought to help shape public policy.

---

1. The texts in italics are somewhat paraphrased to suggest a contemporary audience.

My interest in the prophets comes from my conviction that our prophetic heritage is at the heart of our faith, and that without an understanding and affirmation of that heritage, religious communities remain half-baked. Another influence has been reading Jim Wallis's book *God's Politics*. Wallis is an evangelical who founded the magazine called *Sojourners* and the network that goes by the same name. He brings enormous integrity to the word *evangelical*. Wallis is also the founder of Call to Renewal, "a national federation of churches and faith-based organizations working together to overcome poverty by changing the direction of public policy."[2]

The subtitle of Wallis's book points to his major critique of religion and politics in America: *Why the Right Gets it Wrong and the Left Doesn't Get It*. The Right gets it wrong because fundamentalists have succeeded in redefining what "moral values" means. Their values are really an example of mora*lism*: reducing moral values to a narrow set of issues, primarily having to do with sexuality, while ignoring those *social justice* issues that so dominate prophetic theology. The Left doesn't get it because some liberals are paranoid about religion in public life. They suffer from what I would call "theocraphobia"—the fear that basing public policy on anything religious will lead inevitably to a kind of Orwellian (or Falwellian) theocracy. The Left willingly identifies with secular humanism, thereby yielding to the Right any appeal to what after all should inform the decisions of all voters of religious faith, namely, their religion! And when the Left *does* make the rare foray into religious language, the result sometimes is laughable, as when presidential hopeful Howard Dean proclaimed that his favorite New Testament book is Job.

Some people think that we should stop using models for God like "king," or "lord," not only because they are masculine, but because they are political (after all, we could also use "queen" or "lady"). But I think this would be a mistake. The political titles remind us that faith and politics are *not* separate, even though church and state may be separate (by "politics" I mean polity; see "Getting Close to Home," above). The political model resists any notions of spirituality that are exclusively individualistic. The political model rejects notions of salvation that focus on personal sin and do not include the evil lurking in social and economic institutions—especially our own. As Wallis says, the political model questions those of us who say that we "aren't 'religious,' just spiritual."

---

2. From the dust jacket of his book.

"The problem for all of us well-meaning 'spiritual folks,'" he says, "is that we've lost the social, unifying, and liberating aspects of biblical faith."[3] The biblical covenant model is all of those—social, unifying, and liberating—and that is the prophetic model.

Anyone who reads the book of Amos will immediately see why Wallis's critique is right on target. Imagine the scene: Amos shows up one day at a popular religious gathering. It could have been at one of the national shrines, like Bethel, the "house of God" founded in the story of Jacob's pillow that we read in the Introduction to Part 1. The service is well underway when Amos storms into the room, stomps down the center aisle, pushes the priest aside, and starts shouting (paraphrasing): "Thus says the Lord: don't expect to find me here at Bethel. And don't think that I enjoy all your praise songs, or need your offerings. In fact, I hate all of that. I despise your worship services. Here's what I want from you: Let justice roll down like waters, and righteousness like an ever-flowing stream" (5:4–5, 21–24).

From Amos's words we learn a number of key factors in biblical prophecy. Amos uses a "messenger formula," "thus says the LORD," to show that he is speaking for God. As Amos says elsewhere, "Surely the Lord GOD does nothing, / without revealing his secret / to his servants the prophets" (3:7). It is a bold claim, and it is a claim affirmed by the community of Israel who preserved Amos's words. The second factor is the prophetic criticism of religious piety that is politically bankrupt. By "politically" I mean having to do with social policies and practices, primarily economic. For now, we note the two key words that together summarize prophetic theology: justice and righteousness.

Justice and righteousness often appear together in prophetic speech. *Righteousness* refers to "right relationship"—being in the right relationship to God and to each other. Righteousness is an attitude of the heart. *Justice* is the active form of righteousness; it is putting righteousness into practice in the community. Justice is the public policy expression of the individual spiritual condition of righteousness.

As one scholar has said of our passage from Amos: "'We are dealing here with the first radical critique of religion, which denounces it as spiritual alienation.'"[4] People come to church to be close to God. Amos says that you cannot be close to God if you and your society are unjust

---

3. Wallis, *God's Politics*, 37.
4. Georges Casalis, quoted in Wolff, *Joel and Amos*, 267.

EXCURSUS: PROPHECY 229

to your neighbor; in such a circumstance worship is a hypocritical sham. There's an irony in Amos's critique of religion in that the synagogue and church have preserved it in the very book that is the *foundation* for their religion. The critique is in the Bible that many Christians carry around with them and bring to church, and it's like carrying a time bomb. To read the prophets is to put oneself at risk.

If you ask, Well, what is justice? the answer is best given in a story, like the one Jesus told when asked what it means to love one's neighbor (see Luke 10:25–37). We know the story only from an archaeological discovery.[5]

FIGURE 2

An excavator uncovered a note written by a farm worker to a city official. In the ancient world, paper was quite rare, and notes were written

5. Albright, "Letter," 568; and Yavne-Yam Ostracon.

on potsherds, little pieces of broken pottery. Here's what this one says, paraphrasing somewhat: "Let His Honor the mayor hear the word of his servant." The writer uses the polite way of referring to himself as the servant of the one to whom he is speaking. It goes on: "your servant was reaping in the field, and had finished; and I gathered in about a bushel before my rest. When I had finished reaping, there came Hashabiah the son of Shobai, and he took your servant's overcoat. And all of my fellows will witness on my behalf . . . that truly I am free of guilt. Restore my overcoat. Do not leave me helpless."

We can't be sure of what happened, but apparently the foreman accused the worker of some wrong—maybe he hadn't reaped his quota, or perhaps the foreman thought the worker stole some of the crop for himself. But the worker declares his innocence, and appeals to the mayor for help.

Taking an overcoat may not sound like much, but to the ancient peasant it was an essential piece of clothing. The overcoat doubled as bed and blanket. Think of how homeless people today wrap themselves in an overcoat to fight off the night chill, and think of someone confiscating that overcoat, and you'll have a sense of what is happening here. This is why biblical law forbids confiscating an overcoat and keeping it overnight. As the law says (with God speaking), "for it may be your neighbor's only clothing to use as cover; in what else shall that person sleep? And if your neighbor cries out to me, I will listen, for I am compassionate" (Exod 22:26).

The potsherd is my favorite illustration of what justice is because it reports the experience of a real, live person, an experience that the law says *should not* happen—and, to top it off, both experience and law are part of Amos's critique. Elsewhere he condemns those who keep a peasant's overcoat overnight, and the wrong is compounded in that the garments are used in the context of immoral sexual behavior, and in a sanctuary, no less (2:8)!

The Hebrew canon is divided into the Law, the Prophets, and the Writings. Only the first two existed in canonical form in the time of Jesus. When Jesus issues what we call the Golden Rule, of treating others the way we want to be treated, he says that in this one rule *all* of the Law and the Prophets are contained (Matt 22:40). So it is with our potsherd: here is all the Law and the Prophets, and here is the concern of justice and righteousness.

But justice is not simply a legal matter. Abraham Heschel puts it well: "Justice exists in relation to a *person*, and is something done by a *person*. An act of injustice is condemned not because the law is broken, but because a *person* has been *hurt*."[6] Here is the central concern of biblical prophecy, to address the ways people hurt each other, not only in terms of individual relationships, but also within social and economic systems. Prophecy is primarily concerned with healing human hurt. As the law on the garment suggests, prophecy is the voice of social conscience that hears the cry of the oppressed, and the voice of God who answers that cry with compassion, the same reaction that impelled the Israelites' exodus from Egypt (Exod 2:23–25).

In the book of Exodus, the law about the overcoat is part of the two trajectories that result from Israel's liberation from Egypt. One trajectory leads to worship. Worship is the liturgical form of memory, best seen in the liturgy for Passover, when the celebrants say, "We remember that we were Pharaoh's slaves in Egypt" (see Deut 6:20–21; and "Passover / Maundy Thursday," above). The other trajectory leads to the establishment of a covenant community in which justice rules. So, many of the laws conclude with the same memory: "Remember that you were a slave in Egypt" (see Deut 5:15; 15:15; 16:12; 24:18, 22). If worship is the liturgical form of memory, justice is its ethical form. The purpose of both the liturgy and the law is to *extend the experience of liberation to all people in every generation.* Injustice happens when liturgical memory does not carry over into ethical memory. When Israelites will not hear the cries of the oppressed, God does not want to hear their songs of praise. "What God wants is not for the faithful to follow the rules for correct worship, but for the faithful to live in the right way."[7] Or, to give the priests their due, perhaps it would be better to say not *only* to follow the rules of correct worship.

I said that the story recorded on the ancient peasant's potsherd leads us to the heart of justice, but the peasant's words are not really a story in the complete sense. A story involves a situation that produces tension, and then resolves that tension. In the potsherd message there is no resolution. We do not know if the mayor helped the peasant or not. The mayor is in a position of power, but we do not know if he abused

---

6. Heschel, *Prophets,* 216 (italics added).
7. Olson, *Depths of Life,* 88. Cf. Jas 1:16–27.

that power or used it in the cause of justice. If the mayor acted on behalf of the peasant, then he resolved the story. But we can go further: if the mayor helped the peasant to get his overcoat back, then the exodus from Egypt happened all over again. And that is the purpose of both liturgy and law: to make the exodus—the liberation from bondage—happen all over again, again and again.

Outside the main door to the Southern Poverty Law Center in Birmingham, Alabama, there is a stone fountain. The top is a large, flat surface, and out of its center water bubbles up and flows out over the entire surface. Around the edge of the top are inscribed the words of Amos that I quoted above: "Let justice roll down like waters, and righteousness like an ever-flowing stream." The fountain is an artistic expression of the prophetic word. Rather than an "eternal flame," it is an "eternal stream." Amos's image is that of a deep stream or river, continually surging and moving on, instead of an arroyo, a gully that is dry most of the time and only occasionally wet. Heschel points out how different this image is from our Western icon of the blindfolded lady holding scales that are evenly balanced. That image is static and composed, symbolizing a *concept* of equity. But Amos's perpetual stream portrays justice as "God's *power* in the world, a torrent, an impetuous drive, full of grandeur and majesty."[8] Over against the "noise" of "solemn assemblies," justice is the sound of a surging waterfall that cannot be stopped.

Ultimately, the prophetic heritage poses a question to each of us, and to the society in which we live: will you contribute to the sound of that waterfall? Will you act in such a way that the exodus is a perpetual stream, happening again and again, helping those who are hurt, replacing injustice with justice? If so, then, as Moses says, "it will be righteousness to you before the Lord your God" (Deut 24.13, RSV). But if not? Well then, as Amos says, "the end has come . . . prepare to *meet* your God!" (4:12).

---

8. Heschel, *Prophets*, 213 (italics added).

The Plumb Line

FIGURE 3

To return to Jim Wallis's book for a moment, he argues that one of the failings of the Left is its refusal to use religious language in talking about politics, that is, economic, social, and foreign policies. I suggest that the prophets provide that language, and that those who take liberal positions on issues ought to know that language and be willing to use it. It is a question of nothing less than the motivation for liberal moral values, and the insistence that the Religious right has no monopoly on our biblical heritage. Liberals who do not know that heritage may need a little remedial education.

> *This is what [the Lord God] showed me: the Lord was standing beside a wall built with a plumb line, with a plumb line in his hand. And the* LORD *said to me, "Amos, what do you see?" And I said, "A plumb line." Then the Lord said, "See, I am setting a plumb line / in the midst of my people Israel; / I will never again pass them by."* (Amos 7:7–8)

For those of you who don't work as a carpenter or a mason or dabble in home construction, and don't know what a plumb line is, it's a simple device that uses gravity to tell us if a wall or doorframe or chimney is straight up and down—that is, if it is "plumb."[9] If the wall doesn't follow

---

9. The picture above is of a plumb line resembling one given to me by a parishioner who, as a mason, knew its use in constrction, but also who, as a Quaker and

the string, then the wall is crooked, or "out of line." A plumb line is a way to measure the uprightness of the wall. And if the wall is crooked, the only thing to do may be to tear it down, because if you start with a crooked wall, everything else will be crooked too, and end up like the leaning tower of Pisa.

Now let's use some imagination. What if there were a plumb line that measured the uprightness of a society? What if we could hold up such a line to our government, our health care system, or our tax laws, for example? Indeed, what if we could hold up such a line to our churches, and to ourselves? What would we see?

The prophet Amos is reporting a vision. God is the source of the vision, so Amos says "thus the Lord God *showed* me." The word for "show" here is the ordinary word that means "to see," but it is in a conjugation that means something like "to *make* to see" or "to *cause* to see." God causes Amos to see God standing on a wall, holding a plumb line.

Amos does not describe the nature of his vision in any detail. He does not indicate that he was in some kind of trance or having an out-of-body experience or anything "supernatural." Perhaps Amos was just walking around town and noticed a laborer holding a plumb line, but Amos was "made to see" something that most of us would not. He does not stop to analyze the process of seeing, but visionary seeing is the most basic aspect of biblical prophecy. The prophet can see things in a way that most other people cannot—and sometimes *will* not. The prophet is a poet, not simply because he often writes poetry, but because he is someone whose insight allows him to "see into" the way things really are. Prophet and poet know how to see in this way because they have learned how to *look,* an art that most of us have lost. Prophetic vision is a state of "heightened consciousness."[10]

By itself the vision of the plumb line does not tell us very much about what it means. But what God says in the vision suggests that the wall is crooked, and the wall represents the people of Israel. Then God concludes with these ominous words: "I will never again pass them by." In two visions preceding this one—visions of a locust plague and drought—Amos has pleaded for God's forgiveness for Israel, and God has granted it. But now Amos makes no such plea, and God says, in effect, "this time I am coming and I am really ticked off."

---

antiwar activist, knew how Amos employed the metaphor to detect the moral status of a society.

10. Wolff, *Joel and Amos*, 299.

The plumb line has uncovered the crookedness of Israel. What does Amos see that is crooked? He might have witnessed this little scene involving another prophet—Elisha—described in the book of Kings (2 Kgs 4:1): a woman "cried to Elisha, 'Your servant my husband is dead; and you know that your servant feared the LORD, but a creditor has come to take my two children as slaves.'" In the previous section above, we heard the cry of a farm worker who had his coat taken illegally. Now we hear the cry of a woman whose children are about to be taken as compensation for an unpaid debt of her deceased husband. The word "cry" here does not refer to weeping but to a cry of distress, a plea for help. But the woman's situation is different from the farm worker's in that what is about to happen to her is perfectly legal. Maybe there had been a drought and her husband's crop had failed, and he had to borrow grain just to survive, and then he died, and the woman had no means to repay the debt, and the law said that the creditor could take her children as payment. To be sure, they were not literally "slaves," but "indentured servants," their service limited to a mere seven years, but imagine how the woman's grief over her husband would now be deepened, and imagine what *she* would think of the law on bankruptcy. The wealthy and powerful benefited from the law at the expense of the poor.

Such a scene *is* apparently what Amos saw, because he includes it in a list of indictments against Israel.

> *Hear this, you that trample on the needy, and bring to ruin the poor of the land, / saying, . . . "When will the sabbath be over, / so that we may offer wheat for sale? We will make the cup measure small and the pound measure heavy, and practice deceit with false balances, buying the poor for silver and the needy for a pair of sandals, and selling the sweepings of the wheat."* (Amos 8:4–6)

Abraham Heschel imagines what a student of philosophy might think upon encountering the prophets. He might "feel as if he were going from the realm of the sublime to an area of trivialities. Instead of dealing with the timeless issues of being and becoming . . . he is thrown into orations about widows and orphans, about the corruption of judges and affairs of the market place. Instead of showing us a way through the elegant mansions of the mind, the prophets take us to the slums."[11]

Amos takes us to the village market, and holds up his plumb line and he sees vendors who cheat their customers by using "loaded dice,"

---

11. Heschel, *Prophets*, 3.

as it were—a measuring cup that holds less than it should, scales that are rigged, a weight that is too heavy. He sees merchants who sell floor sweepings as if they were top quality. He sees how immoral business corrupts religious traditions: they spend the Sabbath day scheming on how to ply their illicit trade the next day. And he sees that widow who is losing her children, only here it is for a mere pair of sandals. She bought a pair of sandals for her kids on credit and can't afford to pay her bill, but the law says that the creditor can take her kids away.

But Amos also takes us from the marketplace and the slums to the "other side of the tracks," where the middle class and upper classes live.

> *Alas for those who lie on beds of ivory, and sprawl on their couches, and eat lambs from the flock, and calves from the stall; who sing idle songs to the sound of the harp, and like David improvise on instruments of music; who drink wine from bowls, and apply the most expensive lotions to their skin, but are not grieved over the ruin of their country! Therefore, they shall now be the first to go into exile, and the revelry of the loungers shall pass away.* (Amos 6:4–7)

> *Hear this word, you wealthy ladies who live in Green Acres, who oppress the poor, who crush the needy, who say to their husbands, "Bring me a martini, will you, darling?"*[12] *The Lord God has sworn by his holiness: The time is surely coming upon you, when they shall take you away with hooks; through breaches in the wall you shall leave, each one straight ahead, says the Lord.* (Amos 4:1–2)

> *I will make the sun go down at noon, and darken the earth in broad daylight. 10 I will turn your feasts into mourning, and all your songs into lamentation; I will bring the black clothing of grief on everyone, I will make it like the mourning for an only child, and the end of it like a bitter day.* (Amos 8:9)

Amos was not exactly the life of the party, and in Amos's time, those who were well-off had lots of reasons to party. It was a time of great prosperity for some. Business was booming; international trade was flourishing. The well-off increased their wealth by taking the land of those who defaulted on loans, just as they could take their children. Houses were bigger and ornately furnished, with bedroom suites made out of

---

12. The usual translation is, "Hear this word, you cows of Bashan / . . . / who say to their husbands, 'Bring something to drink!'" Amos sharpens his deprecatory "cows" with the reference to Bashan, a lush agricultural region, and here no doubt referring to rich pastures.

expensive carved ivory. People feasted on leg of lamb and veal scaloppini, and washed it down with so much wine that they needed bowls instead of glasses. The wealthy ladies who lived in exclusive neighborhoods led a life of drunken leisure, oblivious to that destitute widow and her children. Indeed, those children might be the servants who would have to wait on the ladies hand and foot. None of the partygoers seemed to be aware of how their lifestyle was built on an economic and legal system that exploited the poor. As one commentator describes the time, "The rich became richer while the poor became poorer,"[13] or to use Amos's more vivid language, the rich trampled on the poor and crushed them (2:7; 5:11).

All of the corrupt merchants, ruthless creditors, heartless landowners, extravagant partygoers, and hypocritical worshipers, are the ones that God will no longer pass by. The prophet's warning is very clear—they will go into exile. The image of the wealthy ladies is most graphic—they will be led through the destroyed walls of the city like cows with hooks in their noses. God has stood on the wall with a plumb line and found it crooked, and now the wall will come down. The prophet's warning of exile was quite real, because that was the relatively new policy of the Assyrians (the superpower of the day). If a country's rulers would not submit to them, the Assyrians would either kill or exile the rulers and exile the upper classes of the entire populace. Within fifty years of Amos's warning, it came true.

Let's focus again on the image of the plumb line. If we held up the plumb line of justice (for that is what it is) to our own society, what would we see if we looked through the prophet's eyes? First, we need to acknowledge that the prophet's plumb line is not the one that we usually look at. We have other plumb lines that are intended to measure other strengths and weaknesses. We see them every day in the newspaper and on the evening news. They include the "leading economic indicators"; the Dow Jones; the NASDAQ; indices for small-, medium-, and large-cap stocks; the yields on treasury notes; and the gross national product. And there are other plumb lines—the State of the Union address, and the State of the State address.

What if every night on the evening news, and every morning in the newspaper, you would see *prophetic* plumb lines?—the leading poverty indicators, the leading health crisis indicators, the leading

---

13. Wolff, *Joel and Amos*, 90.

inadequate-housing indicators, the leading hunger indicators. What if we held up that plumb line to bankruptcy legislation or to proposals to privatize Social Security or to tax breaks for the wealthy or to the refusal to extend Medicaid? Perhaps we should heed another president's words, those of Theodore Roosevelt: "'The test of our progress is not whether we add to the abundance of those who have much; it is whether we provide enough for those who have too little.'"[14]

Years ago, Bob Riley, the Republican governor of Alabama, was moved to hold up the prophetic plumb line to his state, and then to govern accordingly. He was persuaded by an essay written by Susan Hamill, a law professor who was taking a sabbatical at evangelical Beeson Divinity School. The title of Hamill's essay was "The Least of These: Fair Taxes and the Moral Duty of Christians."[15] Hamill's plumb line showed that Alabama had a sales tax on basic foods of up to 11 percent, but property taxes were the lowest in the nation. People who made little were hit with a relatively large income tax. But taxes on major businesses, like the timber industry, were extremely small. Big Timber owned 70 percent of the land and payed 2 percent of the taxes. As Hamill says, "I was talking about lowering taxes for a lot of families and raising taxes for others so that the result would be just. I said a family of four struggling at below the poverty-wage level is very different from a family of four whose breadwinner earns $200,000 a year."[16]

When asked about federal tax regulations, Hamill noted the same discrepancy, the tax burden shifting from the wealthiest individuals and corporations to the middle class. She was appalled by the lack of moral discussion on tax laws. "People in Washington," she says, "are asking only whether the cuts will stimulate the economy . . . That is not a moral analysis by itself . . . If a community is run by the market, then Mammon has triumphed over God."[17] Hamill's criticism echoes that of Jim Wallis, who suggests that "budgets are moral documents."[18]

Governor Riley's modest tax reform failed by 2 to 1. He stated that "his own Bible-based beliefs about Christians' duty to care for the poor inspired him to take his stance," but most of his fellow Christians didn't see it that way. They thought charity could take care of the problem.

---

14. Roosevelt as quoted in Century Marks, *Christian Century*, 6.
15. Hamill, as quoted in "Unjustly Taxed," 28
16. Hamill, as quoted in "Unjustly Taxed," 28.
17. Hamill, as quoted in "Unjustly Taxed," 28.
18. Wallis, *God's Politics*, 241.

Hamill's view is thoroughly prophetic: charity is not justice. Handouts cannot solve problems created by a corrupt economic *system*. Hamill puts it colorfully: "An A+ record in charity can't turn an F in injustice into a C average."[19] That's an economic plumb line.

"This is what the Lord God showed me: the Lord was standing on a wall with a plumb line in his hand." In an interview playwright Edward Albee was asked what the purpose was behind much of his work. Albee said, "Art holds up a mirror to the audience and says, 'this is you. If you don't like what you see, change.'"[20] That's what Amos's plumb line does for us and for our society. Amos's analysis of his own society is so relentlessly negative that it is easy to overlook the faint note of hope that undergirds it—the hope that Israel will do just what Albee suggests, change.

"Seek good and not evil, / that you may live; / and so the LORD, the God of hosts, will be with you, / just as you have said. / Hate evil and love good, / and establish justice in the [courts]; / it may be that the LORD, the God of hosts, / will be gracious to the remnant of Joseph" (Amos 5:14–15).

Naboth's Vineyard 1 Kings 21:1–24

So far in our exploration of biblical prophecy we have focused on a poor farm laborer whose coat was illegally confiscated, and then on a poor widow whose children were taken in accordance with bankruptcy law. Now we focus on a man who is murdered because he will not give up his property. This man is not poor, but he is the victim of injustice nonetheless. It is a story of how royal authority is used to make someone powerless. The story illustrates Lord Acton's famous warning: power corrupts, and absolute power corrupts absolutely.

In exploring biblical prophecy, we are looking for the motivation behind moral values. Why should we be good? A difference in values appears immediately in our story in King Ahab's apparently simple request. He wants the vineyard next to his royal palace, owned by Nabath. His offer seems reasonable enough and not the least coercive. He will either give Naboth a better vineyard or pay him whatever price he wants. But Naboth does not want another vineyard or money. He wants *his* vineyard.

---

19. Hamill, as quoted in "Unjustly Taxed," 28.
20. Interview with Edward Albee.

It is his "ancestral inheritance," literally "the inheritance of my fathers" (1 Kgs 21:3)

Naboth and Ahab are operating on two different economic assumptions about real estate, that is, land. Naboth comes out of the ancient tribal culture in which a person's land is a sacred trust. There is a deeply personal attachment to the land. No land is really privately owned, for all the land belongs to God, and humans "are but aliens and tenants" (Lev 25:23). However, as a gift from God, a particular family's land was inalienable—that is, it belonged to a family forever, "their possession for all time" (25:34). That is why there is legislation called the Jubilee Year, according to which all land that has been sold can be redeemed by the family to whom it originally belonged. Even if the family cannot afford the property, it becomes theirs again: "in the jubilee it shall be released" (25:28). But, you say, the present owner will lose, and you are correct: the right of private ownership is rooted in land as family inheritance, not in land as financial investment. This is biblical "family values."[21]

Ahab comes with a different set of values. To him, the vineyard is simply a piece of real estate that can be bought and sold or traded. Land is a commodity, and its worth lies in its *commercial* value. Presumably, here that commercial value lies in the productivity of the land—it will grow great fruit! Ahab is operating on marketplace values.

With his offer turned down, Ahab goes home, gets in bed, and pouts. Enter Jezebel. The queen more than makes up for the king's lack of assertiveness. "Some king *you* are," she says, adding "*I* will give you Naboth's vineyard," showing who really wears the crown in the family. So, she arranges to have Naboth framed and executed. The charge is cursing God and king. Cursing God was such an unspeakable offense that the author writes the opposite—"bless God"—as a euphemism. To Jezebel, cursing God and king are pretty much the same thing.

Now, Jezebel was not an Israelite; she was a Phoenician, and her marriage to Ahab was one of those political arrangements that royal families used to expand and secure power. Jezebel worshiped the god Baal. Baal was a thunderstorm god just like Yahweh, the God Israel, and

---

21. There is no evidence that the Year of Jubilee was ever enacted. In his so-called inaugural address at Capernaum (Luke 4:16–19), in proclaiming "good news for the poor," Jesus apparently called for its enactment ("the year of the Lord's favor"), with allusions also to Isa 61:1–4. The word "release" is the same used in the Lord's Prayer (Luke 11:4), suggesting that "debts" may be the better alternative to "transgressions" (cf. Matt 6:12), a reading that could unsettle a capitalist economy.

so a rival deity. Scholars have dismissed Phoenician mythology as "nature worship," a move that has had disastrous consequences for Christianity's attitude toward nature. But that problem aside, it is true, as far as we know, that the Phoenicians' mythology focused on the cycles of nature rather that a god acting in historical events.

So what? you may say. Better to worship a tree than destroy a rainforest, and I would agree. But there *is* a problem with a religious tradition that is *only* oriented toward nature. Here we return again to the complementary balance of Jacob's pillow and Jacob's promise. The problem arises if there is no religious or moral significance in the way human beings act with one another. What really matters is that spring comes again, and so you tell the story of Baal's triumph over death, and you live in that story (and it has its own beauty and creational significance). But while ancient Israel certainly did not exclude a celebration of spring, that was not the heart of their story. As I have already suggested, the heart of their story was that *exodus* comes again, that is, that liberation from oppression happens again, and the way it happens is for the community of Israel to be a community of justice.

Given Ahab's submissiveness in this story, it should not surprise us that he also submits to Jezebel's religion. He became a convert to Baal. As a previous passage says, "he went and served Baal, and worshiped him. He erected an altar for Baal in the house of Baal, which he built in Samaria" (1 Kgs 16:31–32).

For people of a liberal persuasion one of the highest values is pluralism, or better, the affirmation of pluralism as a good in itself. We like to think that all religions are pretty much the same and equally valid, and of course there is some truth to this. All religions have some version of "Love your neighbor as yourself," for example. But all religions are *not* the same, and our biblical story gives us a fine illustration of this.

Jezebel came from a culture in which the power of the monarchy apparently was absolute. Might makes right. But such a view of monarchy was inconsistent with Israelite culture and tradition. There the monarchy was embedded in a covenant community, a community of justice structured in law. The king was supposed to be the defender of justice who redeemed the powerless "from oppression and violence," because "precious is their blood in his sight" (Ps 72:1–2, 14). The actions of Jezebel and Ahab violate that law, and the Ten Commandments in particular. Note the key words: Jezebel and Ahab *coveted* Naboth's vineyard, and Jezebel arranged for two scoundrels to *bear false witness* against him by accusing Naboth of cursing God, thereby they were *taking God's name in vain*, with the result that they had Naboth *murdered*. In this one-sentence summary, four of the Ten Commandments are broken.

But the law itself was rooted in something even more fundamental—a particular story—the exodus story. The Ten Commandments all follow upon the preamble: "I am the LORD your God, who brought you out of the land of Egypt, out of the house of bondage" (Exod 20:2). It is the kernel of a story that determines how the community should live. The basis of law—and therefore the basis of all moral values—lies in this story. As one scholar says, the law is simply the "socioeconomic *content*" of the story of liberation.[22] The flip side of this story, as it were, is Israel's affirmation of identity: "We were Pharaoh's slaves in Egypt."

It ought to be a platitude, but probably is not, that the exodus story is the bedrock of our motivation in developing our position on public policy. Of course there are many other parts of the story, especially the life and teachings of Jesus. But to be a Jew or a Christian means to claim ancient Israel's story as our own, to find *our* spiritual identity in the same affirmation: "We were Pharaoh's slaves in Egypt" (see Deut 6:21; and above, "Passover / Maundy Thursday").

But that isn't true, you might say. Of course not, if by *true* you mean that we were literally there, but then the story would only be true for the small number of people who experienced the historical event. Then every Jew or Christian since then would be a liar to claim that he or she was Pharaoh's slave. But we're not dealing here with story as fact; we're talking about story as ethos, the story that provides the crucial identity for a community. In his book, *A Community of Character*, Stanley Hauerwas says, "Our first moral question must be of what history am I a part and how can I best understand it?"[23]

Note how fundamental this story is: Before we develop our laws and ordinances, before we formulate our moral values, before we decide what is right and wrong, we have to decide what story provides our communal identity. In the exodus story, the primary motivation for morality is in the movement from bondage to liberation. The story imposes an identity on us that our culture fervently resists—the identity of the powerless and the oppressed. In the story, we are not on Pharaoh's side, we are on the side of the oppressed. The story forces us to identity with the powerless, not

---

22. Gottwald, *Tribes of Yahweh*, 59 (italics added).
23. Hauerwas, *Community of Character*, 100.

the powerful, and to see the world through the eyes of the powerless—the eyes of that farm worker deprived of his coat, of that widow deprived of her children; through the eyes of Naboth, deprived of his land and even life itself. And notice how radical *politically* this story is in that it forces those who *are* in power and claim the story as their own to *govern* on behalf of the powerless and not the powerful.

With the story of Naboth's vineyard in mind, listen now to the words of another prophet, Micah: "Alas for those who devise wickedness / and evil deeds on their beds! / When the morning dawns, they perform it, / because it is in their power. / They covet fields, and seize them; / houses, and take them away; / they oppress householder and house, / people and their inheritance. // Therefore thus says the LORD: Now, I am devising against this family / a calamity from which you cannot remove your necks; / and you shall not walk haughtily, for it will be an calamitous time. // On that day they shall take up a taunt song against you, / and wail with bitter lamentation, / and say, 'We are utterly ruined; / the LORD alters the inheritance of my people; / how he removes it from me! / Among our captors he parcels out our fields.'" (Mic 2:1–4).

"They covet fields and seize them," precisely what Ahab and Jezebel have done. The punishment fits the indictment: those who have taken the inheritance of others (cf. 1 Kgs 21:3) will have their inheritance taken from them, their fields parceled out by their captors.

In an essay called "The Common Good," Jonathan Rowe describes what happened to public lands called "the Commons" in eighteenth-century England. The commons were public lands open to all for farming, hunting, and pasture. But with the rise of the industrial revolution, the British Parliament decided that the Commons were worth more in the hands of private owners, so they "evicted commoners, abolished their traditional rights, and declared the Commons private property. Land became a commodity and so did the commoners themselves, many of whom had to sell their labor to mill owners."[24]

Rowe points out that the same process is all too much with us in what the George W. Bush administration did to increase logging in national forests, open wetlands to development, and drill for oil in the Alaskan National Wildlife Refuge. That "refuge" is about to become the Naboth's vineyard of our country's profligate waste of energy, another

---

24. Rowe, "Common Good," 54.

commons turned into a commodity. Other Naboth's vineyards include family farms displaced by agribusiness, mountaintops valued for their ore rather than their beauty, and Amazon rainforests, turned into pasture for cattle for fast food hamburgers, just to mention a few.

In his book called *Pathologies of Power: Health, Human Rights, and the New War on the Poor*, Paul Farmer describes what happened to poor people in Haiti who for generations had lived and farmed in a beautiful valley. But the government, aided by the United States, decided to flood the valley to build a dam for hydroelectric power. The farmers were evicted and forced to live on land with poor soil. Worse, *they* did not benefit from the installation of electricity. They are called "water refugees," and they refer to their former habitat with a phrase that sounds just like Naboth's—their "'ancestor's gardens.'"[25]

Things don't go so well for Ahab and Jezebel. God sends the prophet Elijah to meet Ahab who has "gone to take possession" of his vineyard. The prophet's message for Ahab is gruesome: "In the place where dogs licked up the blood of Naboth, dogs will also lick up your blood" (1 Kgs 21:19) The sentence is appropriate for the king who did *not* see the blood of the powerless as "precious" (Ps 72:14). Jezebel's fate is even worse: dogs will eat her entire body (21:18–24). If you wince at the gruesome fate that awaits Ahab and Jezebel, you wince at the wrong place. The narrator winces at the murder of Naboth and celebrates the death of the "royal family." In a sense, this is a typical story of the triumph of good over evil, and in such stories the bad guys often come to a violent end.[26]

After hearing the preceding sermon, someone suggested to me that we need to start a movement of religiously informed political action called "Plumb Line Politics." That's a wonderful phrase, and a wonderful idea, worthy of a Jesse Jackson. In an earlier incident involving King Ahab and Elijah, the king accuses the prophet of being the "troubler of Israel." Elijah turns the accusation around: "'I have not troubled Israel; but you have'" (1 Kgs 18:17). The prophet's role is to be immersed in the trouble caused by those in power. The late congressman John Lewis immortalized the expression "good trouble," referring to the fight for racial justice and other causes. Getting into "good trouble" is the work of Plumb Line Politics. But the phrase won't work if people do not know that it

---

25. Farmer, *Pathologies*, 32.

26. The circumstances of their deaths do not completely fit the prediction; see 1 Kgs 22:37–38; 2 Kgs 9:30–37.

EXCURSUS: PROPHECY 245

refers to a passage from the prophet Amos, and that the significance of that passage itself is rooted in Israel's story of liberation, and that that story is our story. I suspect that if a politician were to call for Plumb Line Politics to a liberal, Christian audience, most of them wouldn't have the least idea what she was talking about (just as they wouldn't know what mountain King climbed). A conservative Evangelical audience probably would. Maybe a little Bible study is in order.

Feeling Rachel's Pain

In the following passages, we hear numerous voices: the prophet Jeremiah, God, and the people of Israel. In the final passage the prophet speaks about Rachel. Rachel was the wife of Jacob, from whom came the twelve tribes of Israel (Jacob had children by three other women! [Gen 29:31—30:23; 35:16-20]).

> *Jeremiah 8:18—9:1; 31:15*
> *Jeremiah: My joy is gone, grief is upon me, my heart is sick.*
> *19 Hark, the cry of my poor people from far and wide in the land:*
> *The people: Is the Lord not in Zion? Is her King not in her?*
> *God: Why have they provoked me to anger with their images, with their foreign idols?*
> *The people: The harvest is past, the summer is ended, and we are not saved.*
> *Jeremiah: For the hurt of my poor people I am hurt, I mourn, and dismay has taken hold of me. Is there no balm in Gilead? Is there no physician there? Why then has the health of my poor people not been restored? O that my head were a spring of water, and my eyes a fountain of tears, so that I might weep day and night for the slain of my poor people!*
>
> *Jeremiah: Thus says the Lord: A voice is heard in Ramah, lamentation and bitter weeping. Rachel is weeping for her children; she refuses to be comforted for her children, because they are no more.*

Michael Moore's controversial film *Fahrenheit 911* was a scathing attack on President Bush's war in Iraq. Among the various scenes in the film, the one that was the most poignant and moving to me featured a woman who had lost her son in the war. She was standing outside the fence that surrounds the White House, where she had been denied an audience with the president, and she was weeping. She was literally doubled over with her grief, bent at the waist, clutching her stomach as if in physical agony, and she could not be consoled. She was a contemporary Rachel, and she was feeling what a prophet feels, deep down in his heart. As the inheritors of the prophetic heritage, our most fundamental calling is to empathize with that woman, to feel what she feels. Bill Clinton liked to say, "I feel your pain." Comedians came to make fun of those words, perhaps in part because they became a cliché. But Clinton's instinct was right, and, knowingly or not, his words expressed how a politician ought to approach public policies from a prophetic perspective. The core of prophetic consciousness is not thoughts about God or critique of social policies or threats of punishment—the core of prophetic consciousness is feeling pain.

We have looked at a farm worker deprived of his overcoat, a widow deprived of her children, and an vineyard owner deprived of his land, and even his life. Prophetic consciousness forces us to look at these incidents, rather than to look away or to pretend that we don't know about them. More, the prophets insist that we try to imagine what it would *feel* like to be one of the victims. What would it feel like to be a homeless person who has to sleep outside on a cold night without any covering? What would it feel like to be a woman who has just lost her husband and is in debt and now has her children taken away? What would it feel like to be a man who is falsely accused of a crime and lynched by a mob? (Black American history is full of this.) Before anything else, the prophet says—*feel* this!

To feel what someone else feels is to empathize. The word *empathy* comes from the Greek word *pathos*, which means "a feeling of suffering." *Pathos* has come over intact into our vocabulary, meaning "a quality, as of an experience or a work of art, that arouses feelings of pity, sympathy, tenderness, or sorrow."[27] *Sympathy* usually means feeling *for* someone; *empathy* means feeling *with* someone. Their opposite is *apathy*—the inability or refusal to feel *anything*.

Empathy can never be complete. It is wrong and even insensitive to say to someone, "I know just how you feel," even if the same things have happened to you. Perhaps, again, this was the false note in Clinton's expressions of empathy. But it's impossible, I think, to watch the woman in Moore's film and *not* feel *something* of her grief—impossible, that is, unless you are apathetic. In her book on suffering, Dorothee Soelle says, "apathy flourishes in the consciousness of the satiated," that is, in

---

27. *American Heritage College Dictionary*, 4th ed. (2002), s.v. "pathos."

the consciousness of those who have more than they need.[28] American culture exhibits such consciousness in the phenomenon known as conspicuous consumption: buying luxury items as a display of one's wealth, whether it is cars or jewelry or houses, a high-end watch instead of a perfectly functional (albeit lowly) Timex (see "Eat Less Chew More," above). We saw conspicuous consumption in those wealthy revelers measured by Amos's plumb line.

Prophets, then, are "pathetic" figures, not in the secondary sense of arousing scornful pity, but in the primary sense of arousing compassion, a word that literally means "suffering with." And prophets are pathetic because they speak for a pathetic God. The prophet's pathos empathizes with God's pathos.[29] The biblical authors audaciously claim to speak God's words: "thus says the Lord." But behind those words is an even more audacious claim—to feel what God feels. So closely do the prophets identify with God's feelings that at times we are not sure if they are speaking for themselves or for God.

On the other hand, the prophet also feels what his people feel, or, more accurately, what they are *about* to feel, because, in the present, they are apathetic—they do not feel the farm worker's shivering or the widow's grief or the vineyard owner's outrage and despair. Because they cannot or will not feel the pain of others, what they are *about* to feel is their own pain. The time for grieving is at hand, and it is Rachel who will be grieving.

> "Thus says [the God] of Hosts: Consider, and call for the professional mourners to come; send for the skilled grievers to come; let them quickly raise a dirge over us, so that our eyes may run down with tears, and our eyelids flow with water. For a sound of wailing is heard in Zion: 'How we are utterly ruined!'" (Jer 9:17–19)

But no one will listen. *"To whom shall I speak and give warning, that they may hear?"* Jeremiah asks. *"See, their ears are closed, / they cannot listen"* (6:10). They hear what their leaders *want* them to hear—the king and nobles and elders, priests and scribes and—yes, other so-called prophets. All of them are like Mr. Goodvibes. All of them are saying that happy days are here; everything is just fine. No need to worry, much less to grieve. No need to be alarmed. Jeremiah can see the enemy coming, with destruction in its wake, but Israel's leaders see only what they *want*

---

28. Soelle, *Suffering*, 40.
29. Heschel provides a classic statement of this in *Prophets*, especially 23–26.

to see. "*From prophet to priest,*" says Jeremiah, "*everyone deals falsely. // They have treated the wound of my people carelessly, / saying, 'Peace, peace,' when there is no peace*" (6:13–14).

"Everyone deals falsely," says Jeremiah of Israel's leaders. Sometimes it seems that way with our own when they weaken air-quality standards and call the policy "Clear Skies"; when they cater to the timber industry and call it "Healthy Forests"; when they censor environmental reports on climate change by deleting scientific information; and, of course, when they launch a preemptive war when there is nothing to preempt. It is a ludicrous irony that Donald Trump could suggest swallowing Clorox as an antidote for COVID-19, while continually berating various TV networks and journalists as proponents of "fake news."

Public officials do not want to admit failure or talk about suffering or consider the possibility of defeat or acknowledge the reality of violence and death. And we all too willingly play along with this denial. We would rather be entertained by stories about a runaway bride than informed about a runaway national debt, much less the horrors of war. The call to feel pain goes against our natural tendencies. In a *Kudzu* cartoon Preacher Will B. Dunn reads about predictions of horrible catastrophes from the book of Revelation, when someone in the congregation raises a hand and asks if the TV program *American Idol* will still be on. No one considers the irony that the show *American Idol* might *be* an idol, a "foreign god" who lures us away from the real world and the real God. Such an idol anesthetizes us from pain, just as the show *Survivor* ignores the plight of millions for whom that word is not make-believe.

"*My joy is gone, grief is upon me, / my heart is sick,*" says the prophet (Jer 8:18), and then God's words: "*Why have they provoked me to anger with their images, with their foreign idols?*"(8:19) And then the prophet again: "*For the hurt of my poor people I am hurt, / I mourn, and dismay has taken hold of me /. . ./ O that my head were a spring of water, / and my eyes a fountain of tears, / so that I might weep day and night / for the slain of my poor people!*" (9:1).

Amos said, "Let justice roll down like waters." Jeremiah says, Let your eyes overflow with tears. The prophets use various literary forms to express their feelings: legal indictment and trial, satire, diatribes, liturgies, proverbs. But the one that best expresses their pathos is the lament or dirge, the formal expression of grief. Amos used the same form: "*Hear this word that I take up over you in lamentation, O Israel: Fallen, no more to rise, / is maiden Israel*" (5:1–2). For the prophets' audience, hearing such words would be like looking in the morning newspaper and finding your own obituary. No wonder the prophets were such popular figures!

So closely is Jeremiah associated with the dirge that he gave his name to a noun—*jeremiad*, "a literary work or speech expressing a bitter lament or a righteous prophecy of doom."[30] But notice what the prominence of lament says about the nature of prophetic discourse: while it speaks of God's anger over injustice and idolatry, anger is not the dominant feeling. Grief is the dominant feeling, and for the prophet it is not only his own grief, but also God's. When he says *"For the hurt of my poor people I am hurt, / I mourn, and dismay has taken hold of me,"* he is speaking for God. The prophet has moved into the mystery of God's interior life. He feels what God feels. Walter Brueggemann puts it eloquently: "[God] is no longer an enemy who must punish or destroy but the helpless parent who must stand alongside death, like Mary at Calvary, like David over Absalom, 'My child, my child,' but he is helpless and can only grieve."[31] The "God of the Old Testament" is often caricatured as a "God of wrath," ignoring that she is also and more so a God of grief.

The prophet feels what God feels, and he calls us to feel it too. That is the role of the church, first to feel what the prophet feels, and then to say to our society, you must feel this too. Pathos is the platform for Plumb Line Politics.

Our role is neither pleasant nor popular. It is controversial and counter cultural. The prophet believes in the power of negative thinking, that unless a society faces the realities of injustice and falsehood and violence, that society faces its end. The Negro Spiritual affirms that there is a balm in Gilead; the prophet wonders if it is so. In calling us to grieve, the prophets foreshadow the words of Jesus when he says, "Blessed are those who mourn"—blessed because the only way to healing is not the denial of pain but the feeling of pain, which is the work of grief. Brueggemann again puts it well: "The riddle and insight of biblical faith is the awareness that only anguish leads to life, only grieving leads to joy, and only embraced endings permit new beginnings."[32]

---

30. *American Heritage College Dictionary* s.v. "jeremiad."

31. Brueggemann, *Prophetic Imagination*, 58. For this grief metaphor applied to Good Friday, see "Good Friday: The Passion of God" (above).

32. Brueggemann, *Prophetic Imagination*, 60.

"There Is Hope for Your Future":
Jeremiah 31:7–9, 15–20, 26

Jeremiah has been dreaming. That's what the last verse in these readings tells us, that the vision of Israel's future described in the preceding verses is a dream. "Thereupon I awoke and looked, and my sleep was pleasant to me" (31:26). It is the same dream that appears in the Psalms: "When the LORD brought back those who returned to Zion, we were like those who dream" (Ps 126:1). Together the texts give us a vision of restoration anticipated and restoration fulfilled.

Probably the most common misunderstanding of prophecy is the assumption that it involves nothing more than prediction—predicting what will happen, something like consulting a crystal ball. Prophets do that, of course—they predict things—but only when they have finished their main purpose of examining the moral integrity of a society. It is often said that prophets do not simply foretell, they also "forth-tell," that is, they put forth a critique and issue a warning.

Sometimes prophets used physical signs as well as words to forth-tell. Isaiah walked naked through the city for three years to dramatize how exiles would be stripped and led away (Isa 20:1–6). God commanded Ezekiel to lie on his side for 390 days (the duration of exile; Ezek 4–5). Jeremiah wore a yoke around his neck to symbolize Israel's submission to the Babylonians (27:2). Six years later, with Jerusalem under siege, and one year before the Babylonians destroyed it, Jeremiah performed another sign. He bought a field in his hometown. The account of his purchase carefully spells out the legal details involved, the "terms and conditions" of the purchase, the signing of the deed, and the presence of witnesses. Then Jeremiah says, "thus says the LORD of hosts, the God of Israel: Houses and fields and vineyards shall again be bought in this land" (32:15).

Jeremiah's purchase was more than a shrewd instance of real estate speculation (buy low, sell high). It was literally an investment in the future. He bought a piece of land in what was soon to become occupied territory because he trusted in God's promise that beyond Jerusalem's destruction there would be a restoration; beyond exile, there would be a return. In other words, Jeremiah acted in hope even in the midst of despair.

When we say that someone is living in a "dream world," we mean that she is out of touch with reality. A dream world in this sense is unreal, and anyone who lives in it is naïve at best, and self-delusional at worst. They need to "get real." We noted that prophets have a special kind of insight—they can look into things and see what the rest of us cannot. Maybe the same preposition—"into"—applies to their vision of the future. They see *into* the future because they live in hope, and they insist that this future—this vision, this dream—is real (or will be).

But there is a difference between living *into* a dream and living *in* a dream. Living *in* a dream implies that you are pretending that everything is really all right when in fact everything has gone to hell; living *into* a dream is inclining *toward* a reality that is yet to be, a reality that is promised but not yet fulfilled. When Martin Luther King Jr. gave his famous "I have a dream" speech, he was not suggesting that everything was OK; he was calling America to live into a reality that was yet to be. There is an important detail in the story of Jeremiah's purchase. God tells him to put the legal documents in an earthen jar and bury it "in order that they may last for a long time." And it would be a long time indeed, some fifty years, during which Jerusalem would be destroyed and many Israelites taken into exile in Babylon.

Exile was the extreme form of divine punishment. All through this series we have heard the prophets' warnings, but not asked about the nature of the judgment they pronounced. In the biblical world, natural disasters and war were often considered to be divine punishments. In Israel's covenant tradition, such disasters were part of the sanctions intended to ensure obedience. The result of obedience was divine blessing; the result of disobedience was the divine curse (e.g., Deut 28). That's why I have suggested that the prophets could never say "God bless Israel" without also entertaining the possibility that God would curse Israel (see "Indigenous Peoples' Day," below).

And curse is what God did! Amos talks about various disasters that God inflicted on Israel: famine, drought, crop diseases, locusts, military defeat, and plague (compared with the plagues against the pharaoh in Exodus, no less [4:6–11]). Yet Israel did not repent of the social injustice that Amos criticized. So, the prophet warned: "the end has come" (8:2). And it did. In 721 BCE the Northern Kingdom of Israel fell to the Assyrians, and all the "notables" who had ignored Amos's warnings were carried off to exile. They became the "ten lost tribes of Israel."

We cannot operate within this worldview. We cannot make causal connections between natural disasters and a people's moral stature. It would be obscene to tell people that they have suffered from a hurricane because of their sins (although some "evangelists" are willing to do so). We cannot keep a straight face and tell a farmer that his crops have failed because our nation's neglect of the poor is unjust. We certainly cannot tell the innocent victims of war that God is punishing them.

Divine curse will have to mean something different for us, namely, the consequences that follow from the decisions we make. Decisions and actions have consequences, either good or bad, and often those consequences are punishment (or reward) enough. A punitive God does not cause drought, but foolish energy policies and global warming do (see "Seedtime and Harvest," above). God does not cause wars, but reckless political policies do, and the suffering that results is a consequence of those policies. We cannot adopt a prophetic worldview in which God is the agent of these disasters, but we can adopt a prophetic politics that stands in judgment of the policies that *lead* to such disasters.

In addition, here the sages of wisdom may supplement the prophetic critique. Sometimes we are cursed by our own actions. Those who refuse or fail to learn the lessons of experience are foolish. They bring "calamity" upon themselves; it is "the fruit of their way" (Prov 1:20–33). In fact, with climate change in mind, the rebuke of Wisdom (a personified figure here) is all the more suggestive. Fools have refused Wisdom's counsel, scoffed at her knowledge, turned a deaf ear to her warnings. In rejecting her they have also disdained reverence for God (v. 29). Had they responded otherwise, they would be "secure," and "live at ease, without dread of disaster" (v. 33). But now, she says, "I also will laugh at your calamity; / I will mock when panic strikes you, / when panic strikes you like a storm, / and your calamity comes like a whirlwind" (vv. 26–27). The language for calamity here—severe weather—is figurative; for victims of climate change, it is literal. Rather than the wrath of God, it is more fitting to see natural disasters as the revenge of Gaia.

Ancient Israel's understanding of divine blessing and curse also tells us that divine election does not mean impunity. To be God's "chosen people" does not make that people immune to the consequences of injustice. Amos puts it succinctly in a passage I have already quoted: "You only have I known / of all the families of the earth; / therefore I will punish you / for all your iniquities" (3:2). God is not a permissive parent, and Israel is no spoiled child. Interpreted through the eyes of Lady Wisdom, this means that sometimes our foolish actions have punitive consequences.

Moreover, even forgiveness does not mean impunity. To be forgiven of one's sin does not mean that the consequences of that sin magically disappear. In Israel's covenant with God, the ultimate curse would be destruction—a warning that is used over and over. Forgiveness means that God will not exercise this ultimate curse; God "will not come to destroy," as Hosea puts it (11:9 RSV), but only after he has acknowledged that the "sword rages in their cities" (11:6).

Horrifying as the curses are, they reflect the real world in which Israel lived. The warlords of the Assyrians and Babylonians punished their rebellious subjects in just the way that Israel conceived of God punishing them. Blessings and curses, rewards and punishments, were simply a given if one used a covenant model for the relationship between God and Israel. Such a model has serious shortcomings, especially when applied to the suffering of an individual person, like Job. Above all, the model raised the question of how such a God could also be merciful.

The Babylonian captivity was the most cataclysmic event in ancient Israel's history. The words of the prophets had come true. The end had come. And yet, it had not. In 538 BCE—fifty years after Jeremiah purchased his field—the Persian king Cyrus, successor to the Babylonian rulers, issued an "edict of restoration" that granted the Israelite exiles the right to return to their homeland and rebuild their temple. Second Isaiah called Cyrus the Lord's Anointed—Messiah (Isa 45:1).

None of the prophets except Second Isaiah could have foreseen the rise of Cyrus, but they still envisioned a future for Israel on the other side of exile. A modern proverb puts it well: the role of the prophet is to afflict the comfortable and comfort the afflicted. Despite all their indictments and predictions of catastrophic punishment, the prophets also proclaim God's merciful forgiveness and restoration. Through Hosea, God warns, "I will destroy you, O Israel" (13:9), but also "I will heal their disloyalty; / I will love them freely" (14:4). Joel foresees "the day of the LORD" (Judgment Day; 2:1), when God will punish Israel, but also affirms that God is "gracious and merciful, slow to anger, and abounding in steadfast love" (2:13). Amos, as we have seen, warns "prepare to meet your God" (4:12; quoted on many a roadside sign in my part of the Bible Belt), that there will be "wailing" in all the city plazas (5:16), that God "will destroy [Israel] from the face of the earth," and yet, in the *same* sentence, "except that I will not utterly destroy the house of Jacob" (9:8). Indeed, the book ends with a glowing vision of restoration of the Davidic realm and "the fortunes of my people Israel" (9:11–15). Ezekiel can invoke the horrific curses of the covenant tradition, including famine so horrendous that people resort to cannibalism (5:9–12),[33] but the book ends with beatific descriptions of restoration, including a new temple in Jerusalem (chs. 40–45) from which will flow a river that nurtures a garden of trees, providing year-round fruit and "leaves for healing" (47:12; cf. Rev 22:1, "the river of the water of life"). Isaiah can say, "your city lies desolate" (1:7), but give us that wonderful Advent reading about Jerusalem and about swords beaten into plowshares (2:2–4), and virtually all of Second Isaiah (Isa 40–55) is about the "good tidings" of God's re-creation of exiled Israel, when "all the trees of the field shall clap their hands" (40:9; 55:12).

To use Jeremiah's words (which, of course, are also God's words), "there is hope for your future" (31:17). What was the foundation for that hope? If the God of the covenant's last word was a curse, what could be the source of blessing? The answer is so simple that it seems almost embarrassing to say it—the source of hope is love. "Is Ephraim my precious child? Is he the child I delight in? As often as I speak against him, I still remember him. Therefore I am deeply moved for him; I will surely have mercy on him, says the LORD" (Jer 31:20). "For I have become a father to Israel, / and Ephraim is my firstborn" (31:9). Forgiveness means the continuation of God's love.

The model of God has shifted. Here God is not the covenant Lord exacting a legal curse, but the gentle, loving parent pronouncing a familial blessing. The blessing is not without judgment—God still "speaks against him"—but God also "remembers him." What does that mean, that God remembers him? It isn't as if God has forgotten who Israel is; it isn't that kind of memory. It is more like the literal meaning of the word *recollect*—God re-collects who Israel was to begin with. It is as if God pulls out all the baby pictures in the family scrapbook and recalls what this child was like. Further, the scrapbook includes pictures from *before* Israel's birth, pictures of the expectant parent, with all the hopes and dreams that expectant parents have. And when God remembers that, God is deeply moved.

The overt language for God here is masculine ("father"), but there is also an underlying feminine counterpart when God says "I will surely have mercy on him." Phyllis Trible has observed that the root of the word

---

33. See Deut 28:53. Cannibalism within besieged cities is attested in ancient Near Eastern documents and in 2 Kgs 6:24–32. The same desperation happened during the Nazi siege of Stalingrad (1942–1943), and within the Donner Party in California in 1846.

EXCURSUS: PROPHECY   255

for "mercy" derives from the word that means "womb."[34] To "have mercy" is, as it were, to have a womb. There is something intrinsically maternal about mercy, even though, of course, fathers can be merciful too. But, to pursue the maternal metaphor here, God remembers what it was like to be pregnant with her child. There are the pictures of her in those billowing maternity dresses. Similar maternal images of God in childbirth appear in Second Isaiah: "I will cry out like a woman in labor, / I will gasp and pant" (42:14). God is the mother who has birthed Israel and "carried [her] from the womb" (46:3). The "creator of Israel" (43:15) is also the *procreator* of Israel. And when God remembers all of this, the hopes and dreams, God also remembers the promises she made to this child, the promise to nurture and love him no matter what (it is a version of the promise to Jacob/Israel). And in these memories, God is "deeply moved." It's one of those biblical metaphors that sound funny to us. It literally means "my guts are wrenched." Perhaps our metaphor of "heartache" comes closest, because it connotes psychological as well as physical pain: God's heart aches for her child. That ache is part of the pathos of God that we looked at in the terms of feeling Rachel's pain, "weeping for her children"—indeed, Jeremiah's dream of hope is immediately juxtaposed with that despondent image, with the hopefulness signaled by God's new word: "Keep your voice from weeping" (31:15–16). Womb-feeling and heartache—that is what it is for God to remember her child. That is what it is to feel love, especially when your child has gone astray. And that heartache is the source of Israel's hope.

"Thereupon I awoke and looked, and my sleep was pleasant to me." Jeremiah has been dreaming. It is a pleasant dream, not the nightmare that he saw so often before. The nightmare will come to an end, but is *not* the end. "There is hope for your future." What you must do now, says Jeremiah, is to live *into* that dream.

I think we can distinguish between two types of hope—*hoping for* and *hoping forward*. Hoping for has an object, something that we want. Hoping forward does not have an object. Hoping forward is the hope that one must have when hoping for seems, well, hopeless. Hoping forward is an attitude of openness to the possibility of grace, to be surprised by grace. Hoping forward does not have an object because we don't know what the future will bring. For Jeremiah's people, the basis for hoping forward is rooted in the heartache of God. Living into the dream means

---

34. Trible, *Rhetoric*, 31–71.

living toward something that is yet to be and cannot be defined. As the apostle Paul says, "hope that is seen is not hope" (Rom 8:24). The dream is not something we can control. We cannot know in what concrete ways the dream will be fulfilled. It is sobering to know that Jeremiah never got to enjoy the field he bought, as far as we know, because the last we hear of him, he has been taken against his will to Egypt (Jer 43:1–7). But we should not confuse the field with the hope. The field is a *sign* of hope, hope for the people, not just hope for the prophet. Jeremiah did not return to his field, but Israel returned to the land.

To live in hope is not to wish for some particular outcome; it is to trust yourself to the womb-feeling heart-aching love of God, "because," as another prophet says, "you are precious in God's sight, and honored, and he loves you" (Isa 43:4).

Earth Day

United Nations Environmental Sabbath / Earth Rest Day

The Fungus among Us

There seems to be a custom by which we name certain foods with foreign words or unfamiliar words because if we called a spade a spade we might not eat the food to begin with. *Escargot* comes to mind, the French word for snails—a wonderful appetizer almost indistinguishable from its garlic sauce. Then there's truffles, a very expensive delicacy, partly because they are very difficult to cultivate and must be found in the wild. Truffles are fungi. That doesn't sound too appetizing, does it? "Would you like some fungus in your omelet?" the waiter asks, having removed the snail plate. Descriptions of the smell of truffles do not sound too pleasant to me, ranging from dirty socks to ripe seafood.

Truffles are like mushrooms: they are the fruit of a fungus. The smell may be produced by Betaproteobacteria, probably not listed in the ingredients. We normally think of fungus as destructive when it's on our vegetables or on rosebushes or in clothes as mildew. Truffles are sort of like an apple on an apple tree, but here the "tree" is a vast network of tiny threads of fungus that grow underground. And these fungi are critical to the life of a forest, and ultimately to us.

If there is one fundamental principle of ecology celebrated on Earth Day, it is this: all of life is interconnected and interdependent. Theologian Larry Rasmussen puts it succinctly: "That nature is a community is *the* scientific discovery of the twentieth century," and, he continues, that earth "is *also* a community" ought to be a central starting point for theology and ethics—hence the title of his book *Earth Community, Earth Ethics*.[1]

---

1. Rasmussen, *Earth Community*, 15 (italics original).

Ian Barbour, writing on the interface of science and religion, adds, "The chemical elements in your hand and in your brain were forged in the furnaces of stars."[2] John Muir had his folksy way of putting this: "When we try to pick out anything by itself, we find it hitched to everything else in the universe."[3]

My botanical observations about fungi are taken from a fascinating book by Jon Luoma called *The Hidden Forest*—hidden because much of the book has to do with the soil under the forest. When we think of a forest, most of us just have in mind the trees above ground, and perhaps various other flora and fauna that live there. But increasingly scientists are learning that that is at best only half of the story. Under the ground is where much of the action is, and the action is largely the work of micorrhizal fungi.

Dig into healthy forest soil, especially in an old growth forest, and you will find fungi everywhere, and they are crucial to the health of the ecosystem. The fungi live deep in the soil, so they cannot photosynthesize; they cannot use sunlight to produce food. Instead, they survive by joining themselves to tree roots. They wrap themselves together with the very cells of fine roots, sometimes growing between the roots' cells, and sometimes even penetrating into the cells. Once in place, they survive by taking food from these fine rootlets. High overhead the leaves of the tree produce sugars and other nutrients, and down below in the earth the fungi invite themselves to dinner.

You might call the fungi parasites, but here's the really fascinating thing about them. They have a relationship with the trees, a kind of mutual feeding and protection society. The fungi and the tiny roots join together so closely that they work virtually as one, supporting each other. In effect, the fungus web extends the root system of the tree. The strands connect trees with as much as one thousand times more soil area than the roots themselves. The fungi feed on the sugar from the roots. The trees feed on water and nutrients that the fungi draw from the soil.

And here is the most amazing thing: the fungi form a kind of protective armor against disease-causing bacteria around the roots. In some cases, the fungi even inoculate the soil with antibiotics that kill the

---

2. Barbour, *Religion in an Age of Science*, 147. Buddhists affirm a similar worldview: "Everything is too interconnected for anything to have independent, self-sufficient existence" (Wright, *Why Buddhism Is True*, 233).

3. Muir, *Nature Writings*, 245. Cf. Simard, *Finding the Mother Tree*, 283: "everything in the universe *is* connected" (italics original).

bacteria. It's as if the tree says to the fungi, "Help yourself to dinner," and the fungi say to the tree, "Here's some vaccine to keep you from getting the flu." As Luoma says, "there is an exquisite symbiosis among living tree [and] living fungus" that ultimately includes all other flora and fauna.[4] The forest is actually a community of interdependent organisms. Indeed, scientists have discovered that trees also communicate with one another, sounding alarms about imminent dangers, such as insect invasions. "Brainless, stationary trunks are protecting each other."[5] And we humans are tied to the fungi as well, inasmuch as the fungi make for healthy trees, and trees produce oxygen, which makes our life possible. As Luoma points out, "Virtually all of the oxygen in the air we breathe was made by green plants, photosynthesizing over hundreds of millions of years."[6] Moreover, when the trees absorb carbon dioxide, they are retrieving carbon from the atmosphere and storing it in their woody bodies, as well as in the fungal fibers, and thus ameliorating in a major way our pollution of the atmosphere with its resultant global warming. The more the fungus the healthier the trees, the healthier the trees, the healthier are we. So, the relationship between fungi and trees includes us, as well. We breathe in the oxygen that the trees breathe out, aided by their underground companions.

It is always helpful to remember that the essential (that is, natural) meaning of the word *spirit*, at least in the Hebrew of the Old Testament, is "wind" or "breath." We humans are animated—literally "inspired"—by the breath of God (Gen 2:7), but so are all other breathing creatures (Ps 104:27–30; Eccl 3:19). Whatever differences there are between humans and other creatures, we have a spiritual bond with them. Moreover, all flora and fauna also share the same physical origin, made "out of the earth" or soil (Gen 2:7, 9, 19). As Muir says, "One fancies a heart like our own must be beating in the plants and animals."[7] The fungus and the tree are not two separate things. They are part of an enormous web that includes mammals and insects and bacteria and ultimately us. Wait, you say, bacteria? It's more than enough to be related to fungi, but surely we

---

4. Luoma, *Hidden Forest*, 111. Cf. also Simard, *Finding the Mother Tree*, 59–60, who uses the word "mutualism."

5. Simard, *Finding the Mother Tree*, 229.

6. Luoma, *Hidden Forest*, 74.

7. Muir, *Nature Writings*, 245.

are not related to bacteria! Therein lies another chapter of our biography and—to cite a poem by Mary Oliver—"The Family" to which we belong.[8]

The fungal family has a long history. Sometime around one and one half billion years ago, the world greeted one of our first ancestors. I don't think it's scientifically proper to say that this ancestor was male or female, but someone has given him the name Prospero (we could just as easily call her Prospera, I suppose). The name is fitting in that this little critter prospered indeed. When I say little, I mean infinitesimal. Prospero stood tall at about three one-thousandth of a millimeter. You'd need a powerful microscope to see him. Of course, Prospero didn't literally stand up on anything resembling feet. In fact, it would be difficult to say which end was up or down. Scientists aren't even sure what kind of critter this was. Some think it wasn't a critter at all but a plant, some think it was a critter (that is, an animal), and some think it was neither of the above. And here's the most shocking fact of all: Prospero was the offspring of a bacterium. For shame! You know what bacteria are, I'm sure. They're those "bad germs" that we are afraid of catching, and we run around with bottles of disinfectant to kill as many of them as we can. (We forget that there are also "good" germs, but we'll come back to that in a minute.)

Actually, Prospero is the personal name for the ancient organism. The usual scientific name is *eukaryote* (pronounced "you-carry-oat"). That first syllable *eu* means "good" or "well." Prospero was a good little karyote because he learned how to do something that was totally new to the world: he "invented respiration, the power to deal with oxygen."[9] Of course, he didn't use lungs to breathe as we do, but he learned how to absorb oxygen from the air, something like the way a sponge soaks up water. You may think, so what? Well, Prospero's invention was a really big deal, because without it you and I wouldn't be here, nor would any other animals that live on the land.

You see, Prospero had an ancestor too, another little critter called a *prokaryote* (meaning "first karyote"). The poor little thing has no personal name, as far as I know. The prokaryotes had already been around a while—two billion years or so. They produced oxygen, and in two billion years even teeny tinies can produce a lot of oxygen. But too much oxygen is not a good thing. That's why we have all kinds of food packaging that says the food contains "antioxidants." Too many oxidants can break

---

8. Oliver, *New and Selected Poems*, 215.
9. Swimme and Berry, *Universe Story*, 98.

down the cells in your body, and that's what would have happened to all the prokaryotes if our little fellow Prospero had not come along. By learning how to use the oxygen for energy, Prospero cleared the air, as it were, and—here's the really big deal—that meant that life could evolve into much more complex organisms, including us. Thanks to Prospero, another one and a half billion years or so later, our species emerged on the scene—*Homo sapiens*.

Now it isn't as if eukaryotes and prokaryotes aren't around anymore. They are around in the gazillions, the prokaryotes proudly bearing the old family name bacteria. Some of them we could do without—the ones that cause food poisoning, like Salmonella, for example, or, to recall our lesson in forest soil ecology, the bacteria that attack tree roots (in which case, the descendants of Prospero are in a civil war with their ancestors). But some are good for us. In fact, given Prospero's achievement, scientists can say that bacteria are "The greatest chemical inventors in the history of Earth," and they are "no more 'germs' than the plants that feed, clothe, and house us are 'weeds.'"[10] Moreover, if bacteria weren't around to help living animals process food and to decompose dead things, living things (like us) would have a hard time surviving. Indeed, as I write, bacteria are helping us survive the COVID-19 virus, because one vaccine begins with a long bath in a solution energized by trillions of modified E. coli! And let's not forget that bacteria are the active agents that create foods like cheese and yogurt. Those popular yogurts touted as probiotics contain such bacteria as lactobacillus acidophilus. And eukaryotes are around also, especially in the form of those fungi that we have met already, like those mushrooms in our omelet, and the yeast that infuses our bread. And, yes, eukaryotes as fungi can cause problems, like athlete's foot, ringworm, or worse, meningitis. But both prokaryotes and eukaryotes are to be thanked for wine.

It may surprise you to know that we are eukaryotes too, because eukaryotes have cells with nuclei, which is true of all plants and the creatures in the kingdom that biologists call Animalia. If you consider this bad news, I'm sorry to be the one to tell you that if you trace your family tree way, way, way back, back to one and a half billion years ago, you will find Great-to-the-umpteenth-degree Grandpa Prospero (or Grandma Prospera). You come from a family that includes fungi and, further back, bacteria. Our evolutionary connection certainly will come as bad news

---

10. Margulis and Sagan, *What Is Life?*, 58–59.

to those people who don't believe in evolution, at least of humans. At one time those unbelievers numbered more than half of Americans. A lot of unbelievers are running around trying to force public school science teachers to teach creationism or "intelligent design" along with evolution, but evolution is science, and the other two are religion. These people apparently are ashamed to think that they "came from apes," as they say. Imagine what they would think about coming from bacteria!

Many people don't believe in evolution because, they say, it's "only a theory." But this objection misunderstands what a theory is in science. Gravity is a theory too, but I don't see any of those people jumping off buildings to prove that it's wrong. Others don't believe in evolution because they think that it rules out any involvement of God. Some scientists, of course, agree with them, saying that the fact of evolution proves that there is no God. But here scientists are meddling with religion! Still, it is true that evolution happens (is still happening) because of chance mutations and the process of natural selection. Even Einstein wasn't comfortable with such uncertainty. "God doesn't play dice with the universe," he said. But fellow physicist Neils Bohr replied, "Who is Einstein to tell God what to do?"[11]

But what if we think of God as working in and through a process of creativity whose outcome is uncertain? Maybe God likes things to be open-ended rather than controlled and planned. The Myers-Briggs personality inventory has a set of categories which show that a person is more likely to want to control things (a J type) or more likely to appreciate spontaneity (a P type). I suspect that God is a strong P, much as I hate to be on the opposite side of God.

Artistic creativity provides a wonderful analogy here. In the book called *Creative Spirituality: The Way of the Artist*, a potter named Willi Singleton describes how he makes pots. He uses a wood-fired kiln, refusing the convenience of gas or electricity. Firing with a wood kiln is a "chaotic situation," he says; "'the wood kiln basically does things to the pots that I don't do to them . . . I didn't make the firing. I participated in the firing . . . Nature makes the fire.'"[12] For Singleton, using an electric kiln only enhances "the potter's control over the process . . . rather than letting larger forces play a role." It is a "domineering" approach to the clay. The wood kiln, instead, allows for unanticipated results, and, the author of

---

11. https://en.wikiquote.org/wiki/Bohr%E2%80%93Einstein_debates.
12. Wuthnow, *Creative Spirituality*, 114 (italics original).

the book concludes, "the unanticipated ways in which a wood-fired kiln produces its effects are [Singleton's] metaphor of the sacred."[13]

The process of the potter's "creative spirituality" is remarkably similar to the way some theologians want to think of God. Gordon Kaufman, for example, thinks of God as that process of "serendipitous creativity" that we can see at work in the process of evolution. To paraphrase the potter, we could say that God didn't make the world but participated in its making. To call God Creator is to use a symbol for that process of serendipitous creativity. And what a wonderful coincidence that one biblical story of creation pictures God as a potter. In fact, the process here involves trial and error. God realizes that the man (literally "earthling") is lonely, so God forms "out of the ground (earth)" all the fauna. But they won't do, so God performs a little surgery on the man and, voila, the perfect "partner," woman. Moreover, the process of creation in the opening Genesis account is cooperative as well. For example, God gives the command for the earth to "grass grass" (Gen 1:11, my translation). Here the first word is a verb, the second a noun based on the verb stem. So, the earth participates in the creation of all plant life.

Kaufman puts it this way: "To be devoted to God the creator is to be devoted to that ultimate reality—that ultimate mystery—which expresses itself in and through all that exists, including the evolutionary and historical development of the ecosystem that has given birth to us and to many other creatures."[14]

Instead of being ashamed of our microbial ancestors, perhaps we should stand in awe and humility before our humble origins and wonder at the creative process that produced us. To acknowledge Prospero is to affirm that we are part of a vast community that includes all creatures, all plants, all rocks, all rivers. Indeed, our community stretches back beyond the formation of Earth, back to the big bang that started the whole process. In his book *Religion in an Age of Science,* Ian Barbour says that science shows "the interdependence of all things. We are part of an ongoing community of being; we are kin to all creatures, past and present."[15] Kaufman says, hopefully, that the latest expression of the evolutionary process is the "dream of a new humanity living on a new ecologically ordered earth." The forest, with its interdependent ecosystem literally

---

13. Wuthnow, *Creative Spirituality,* 129.
14. Kaufman, *In Face of Mystery,* 330.
15. Barbour, *Religion in an Age of Science,* 147.

rooted in fungi, has much to teach us, as does the evolution of those fungi in the first place. The fungus is among us not only in the ground beneath the trees, but in our family tree as well. Earth is "a linked biological and physical system with a beating, photosynthesizing, rainmaking heart of wild woods."[16] You and the tree in your backyard came from a common ancestor a billion and a half years ago.

The word *eukaryote* is sometimes spelled with a *c* instead of a *k*, and in that spelling it appears in my dictionary right above the word *Eucharist*. Both words have the same prefix, *eu*, meaning "good" or "well." At the Eucharist we give thanks for the good work of God in the world, especially in the life of Jesus the Christ. But it is appropriate also to give thanks to that good process of serendipitous creativity, including our lowly ancestor, the eukaryote. And don't forget, it is because of the eukaryotes that we have the bread and the wine!

---

16. Reid and Lovejoy, "We Can Still Save Earth's Forests."

Independence Day / Thanksgiving Day

The Heart of a Pilgrim, the Mind of a Prophet

Deuteronomy 26

I suspect that I am not alone in wishing that "America the Beautiful" were our national anthem. For one thing, it doesn't have any "bombs bursting in air," nor does it require a famous singer with a 100-megawatt voice to do it justice (and wouldn't it be more patriotic if we *all* sang the national anthem anyway?). Another aspect of "The Star-Spangled Banner" makes it unattractive: the composer, Francis Scott Key, was a slave owner, and the third verse (though it is rarely sung) rebukes slaves who might have gone over to the British forces. "America the Beautiful" is more like a hymn, with its stately rhythm and frequent references to God, although the theological language might breach constitutional restraints. But for me the most important reason for choosing "America the Beautiful" would be for the words "God mend thine every flaw" and "may God thy gold refine." The clear implication of these words involves a capacity for self-criticism that is missing from "The Star-Spangled Banner." The hymn *assumes* that the nation is flawed and impure, in need of mending and refining. The hymn allows for no slogan like "My Country—Love It or Leave It." Instead, it calls for a different attitude—love it and *relieve* it. The country is deserving of our love, but its flaws require our participation in its relief.

Behind the phrase "God mend thine every flaw" there lies a long theological heritage that stretches back to ancient Israel and the Hebrew Bible. This heritage has shaped our national identity from the outset and ought to inform our understanding of patriotism. I suggest that we can formulate what it means to be a true patriot in these terms: to be true patriots is to have the heart of a pilgrim and the mind of a prophet.

Ancient Israel held a kind of annual July Fourth and Thanksgiving Day celebration all rolled into one. The liturgy for the occasion appears in Deut 26, itself a revision and expansion of the ancient firstfruits ceremony.[1] In its literary context, this chapter comes after the "articles of the covenantal polity" in chapters 12–25,[2] something like Israel's constitution, and the ceremony in chapter 26 serves to reinforce the people's communal identity and allegiance. In this liturgy, the celebrants affirm "This is who we are."

The setting of the entire book is Moses's farewell sermon to the people of Israel before they enter the land of promise. The point of view is that of someone looking over the Jordan River to the west, yearning for a homeland. The setting of the ritual for Moses and his audience is that time in Israel's immediate future when that yearning will be fulfilled; but for the author and his audience, the ritual evokes that future as past. The purpose of the ritual is to force every Israelite throughout history, at least once every year, to identify with the Israelites who waited on the other side and then crossed over. The ritual forces everyone to identify as an immigrant—indeed a refugee—given that the memory of being slaves in Egypt is still fresh (5:15; 10:19; 15:15; 24:18, 22).

The setting of the book and the ritual of chapter 26 are both reflected in American history, as I noted in the introduction to Part 2. Pilgrims who saw their destination as the promised land would name a town in Connecticut New Canaan, and Moses's homily has its counterpart (including quotations from Deuteronomy) in the illustrious sermon of John Winthrop, "A Modell of Christian Charitie," delivered onboard the ship *Arbella* in 1630 as it approached the shore of New England (see "Indigenous Peoples' Day," below).

In the biblical ritual, the Israelites take some of their first agricultural products—say spinach and scallions—and present them at the sanctuary as a gesture of gratitude, and there are also words prescribed for the ritual. Everyone is supposed to say to the priest, "Today I declare to the LORD your God that I have come into the land that the LORD swore to

---

1. Deut 26 appears in the lectionary for Thanksgiving Day, Year C; Deut 8:7–18 is suggested for Year A.

2. This construal of ancient Israel's covenant law was coined by S. Dean McBride Jr. in his notes to Meeks, gen. ed., *HarperCollins Study Bible* (p. 287), and most definitively in his article "Polity of the Covenant People."

our ancestors to give us" (Deut 26:3). Isn't that remarkable? The author's audience was probably living at a time some five hundred years after the time of Moses. But every person, no matter how far removed historically from the first immigrants, is required to assume the identity of the immigrants in the story. "Today I declare that . . . I have come into the land." To create an analogy in US history, rather than going to the central sanctuary, celebrants would go to Ellis Island once a year to identify with immigrants as they stepped off the boat there.

But there is more. The worshiper is now required to recite a kind of historical narrative that begins with, "A wandering Aramean was my ancestor" and ends with that wanderer settled in "a land flowing with milk and honey" (Deut 26:5–9). The "wandering Aramean" refers first to Abraham and then to Sarah and then to their descendants, the founding family of Israel, but the recital takes in all of Israel's history up to and including the original settlers in Canaan. In between, of course, is the core of Israel's historical identity, the story of the exodus. It is a story of the liberation of oppressed slaves and their formation as a community chosen by God, their liberator. The celebrant in the ritual is called to identify with the immigrant in the narrative. In fact, the recital immediately shifts to first person plural: "the Egyptians treated *us* harshly" (v. 6) The purpose of this identification is for the worshiper to experience the brutality of oppression but also the joy of someone who tastes liberty for the first time. This identification is central to the Jewish celebration of Passover, in which the celebrants say, "We were Pharaoh's slaves in Egypt" (see "Passover / Maundy Thursday," above).

But there is more. This is a land flowing with milk and honey, which means a bountiful land, with enormous natural resources. It is "a land with flowing streams, with springs and underground waters welling up in valleys and hills, a land of wheat and barley, of vines and fig trees and pomegranates, a land of olive trees and honey, a land where you may eat bread without scarcity, where you will lack nothing, a land whose stones are iron and from whose hills you may mine copper" (Deut 8:7–9). The only thing that's missing, as former Israeli prime minister Golda Meir once complained, is oil. These resources are part of God's blessing on this people. The ritual therefore *commands* the people to *enjoy* their blessings, and *rejoice* before the God who gives them.

"A wandering Aramean was my ancestor." "I have come into the land." "So now I bring the first of the fruit of the ground that you, O LORD, have given me" (26:10) The heart of an immigrant bursts with joy and gratitude for the political freedom that makes life possible, for a land that provides a secure home, and for all of the material things that make life pleasant. The immigrant *loves* his country, and loves the God who is the source of "Life, Liberty, and the pursuit of Happiness," to borrow from our Declaration of Independence.

Many years ago, long before the collapse of the Iron Curtain that separated East from West Germany, a newspaper article appeared on July Fourth about an immigrant who had fled from East Germany and found his way to America. In the accompanying picture, the man was sitting at a desk, and on the desk was a framed copy of the United States Constitution and on the wall behind was an American flag. The man had been in this country for *thirty years*. Yet his words reflect that sense of fresh gratitude that the biblical ritual wants to instill: "You can't appreciate freedom unless you've lived in a country where it doesn't exist."

But there is still more in our biblical model—there is the demand for justice. No sooner have the Israelite immigrants rejoiced over their freedom and material blessings than they are also required to say "I have neither transgressed nor forgotten any of your commandments" (26:13). Just as the immigrants are not to forget their personal identification with Israel's history, so they are not to forget the moral responsibility that goes along with that identity. Immigrants are members of the *covenant* community. They are not isolated individuals who enjoy life without a care for the needs of others. The function of liturgical memory is to instill a social morality. The text makes clear who those others are—they are especially "the resident aliens, the orphans, and the widows" (26:13), a biblical phrase that refers to the most vulnerable in their society. These are people who do not have all the advantages of an independent, self-sufficient citizen, and who have no one to protect and defend them. Indeed, "resident aliens" *are* immigrants, similar to someone residing in the United States with a green card. These are people who are particularly prone to poverty and often exploited by the powerful. The Israelite immigrant is urged to enjoy the "bounty" of the land but also to ensure that these vulnerable people also "may eat their fill" (26:12). The pilgrim is to have the mind of a prophet.

The demand for justice is at the heart of biblical prophecy, just as it is at the heart of biblical law (see the Excursus on Prophecy, above). So says the Torah: "Justice, and only justice, you shall pursue, so that you may live and occupy the land that the LORD your God is giving you" (Deut 16:20). So says the prophet Isaiah: "Learn to do good; / seek justice,

/ rescue the oppressed, / defend the orphan, / plead for the widow (1:17). The sages agree: "To do righteousness and justice / is more acceptable to the LORD than sacrifice" (Prov 21:3). And the psalmist confirms that the responsibility of the king (that is, of the government) is to provide the "poor with justice" (72:2).

But it was primarily the prophets of ancient Israel who called the king and the people to account. The prophets were the conscience of the nation. They were both social critics and poetic visionaries. In other words, they were people of unusual insight who could see the flaws of the nation but also could nurture the dream on which the nation was founded. They reminded Israel of their covenant responsibility and warned of the consequences of disobedience—namely, loss of both land and liberty. At the extreme, Jeremiah would even call for none other than the acceptance of defeat, of surrender to the enemy, and insist that this was the will of God. God in his sovereignty has created the world and confirms any ruler that fits God's purpose. God can even refer to the enemy king, Nebuchadnezzar, as "my servant," and order Israel to "serve the king of Babylon and live" (27:17). Defeat is the way to life. The prophets "spoke truth to power," and because of that some of them (including Jeremiah) wound up in jail, setting a precedent for numerous contemporary protestors. From the prophetic perspective, there can be no unqualified allegiance to king or country, because the primary allegiance is to God. I've always admired the Jehovah's Witness kid who many years ago refused to put his hand over his heart while reciting the Pledge of Allegiance, because he confessed to "love *God* with all his heart," as Deuteronomy says. The trial went to the Supreme Court, and he won.

The prophets were the ones who believed that God would mend Israel's every flaw, and refine Israel's tainted gold. As Malachi says, "God will refine them like gold and silver" (3:3). To be a true patriot is to have the heart of a pilgrim and the mind of a prophet. It is to be able and willing to see not only the gold but also the dross, not only the beauty but also the blemish. To be a true patriot is to live within a spiritual and ethical tension. It is to love one's country but also to relieve one's country. It is to get a lump in your throat when you sing, "God shed his grace on thee" but also to get a fire in your belly when you sing, "God mend thine every flaw."

Sister Miriam Therese Winter has written a contemporary version of "America the Beautiful," extending its prophetic dimensions.[3] First, of course, there is inclusive language regarding gender: we are "a sisterhood and brotherhood." There is also a recognition not only of Pilgrims but also of Native Americans: "indigenous and immigrant." Our national flaws appear more concretely: "the bloodshed through the years," demanding that we have "the wisdom born of tears" and "the courage to repent." Where are our flaws more evident than in the genocide committed against Native Americans and the slavery inflicted on African Americans? For the ancestors of African Americans, America was not the promised land. It was the "house of slavery" (Exod 20:2) or Babylon, the land of exile (Ps 137:1–3). Finally, in Winter's version, there is a universal horizon, including "two continents," recognizing that America is both North and South America. And there is "that dream of peace, nonviolence, all people living free."

It wouldn't be difficult to list other flaws in our country that need mending: environmental pollution that obscures our "purple mountain majesties," questionable war that belies "that dream of peace," North American greed that ignores "a hemisphere where people here all live in harmony" (Winter's version). But our biblical model suggests a particular focus. The biblical ritual centers in enjoying and sharing food. The equitable distribution of food is, after all, the most basic example of justice. In fact, the "sacred portion" of food is that shared with the needy (Deut 26:13). As I write these words (in December, 2020), the evening news is showing endless streams of cars lined up at food banks across the country, because the COVID-19 catastrophe has left millions of people out of work and out of food. Yet for months Congress has been incapable of providing the relief that justice requires, incapable of mending the flaw of hunger.

A true patriotic speech will call on us to both rejoice and repent, but we don't often hear the latter. We are much fonder of expressing the heart of a pilgrim than the mind of a prophet. Many churches are prone to waving the flag in one hand and the Bible in the other, not recognizing that sometimes the two are in conflict. Then on June 1, 2020, there was Donald Trump's use of the Bible as a prop for a photo op after marching down Pennsylvania Avenue, which was cleared of peaceful protesters by

---

3. Winter and Bates, "How Beautiful, Our Spacious Skies."

mounted police and tear gas.[4] No speech in our history better combines the heart of a pilgrim and the mind of a prophet than Martin Luther King Jr.'s "I Have a Dream." His words are a model of how biblical language can serve as a powerful motivation for true patriotism. King knew how to hold the flag in one hand and the Bible in the other because he recognized that sometimes the Bible stands in judgment of the flag.

Let us have the heart of an immigrant, rejoicing in liberty and the bounty of our land, but let us also have the mind and conscience of a prophet, relieving the downtrodden and the hungry. Israel's thanksgiving celebration retells their story of immigration, recognizing that it is a story shared by countless others. Indeed, it is literally a story shared by virtually all human beings, as Mohsin Hamid argues in an article in *National Geographic*, "We are All Migrants." The claim goes to the heart of the focus of this book—place and time: "None of us is a native of the place we call home," he says, "And none of us is a native to this moment in time." All of us ultimately come from a different place, and every moment of time "slips away" and "is irrevocably lost."[5] A subsequent article in the same issue ("Who Were the First Europeans?") follows the recent use of DNA research in archeology in showing that "Europeans living today, in whatever country [which would include the Americas], are a varying mix of ancient bloodlines hailing from Africa, the Middle East, and the Russian steppe ... In an era of debate over migration and borders, the science shows that Europe is a continent of immigrants and always has been ... There are no indigenous people."[6] Even Native Americans are not native!

Folk singer John McCutcheon has said that "stories are the connective tissue between human beings," and he has composed a song titled "Immigrant," in which he evokes phrases from the Statue of Liberty— give me your tired, your poor, your huddled masses yearning to be free. In his song, the immigrant sings, "I am *your* story."[7] The song mirrors the conclusion of Hamid's essay: "It is the central challenge and opportunity every migrant offers us: to see in him, in her, the reality of ourselves."[8]

---

4. Crowley and Dias, "Trump's Visits to Church and Shrine."

5. Hamid, "We Are All Migrants," 17.

6. Curry, "Who Were the First Europeans?" 100, 104. Hamid, "We Are All Migrants," 17, argues that even contemporary Africans in the Rift Valley are not strictly indigenous.

7. McCutcheon, "Immigrant" (italics added).

8. Hamid, "We Are All Migrants," 20.

A wandering Aramean was my ancestor. Can we see the error in presuming that we did not all, in some metaphorical sense, come through Ellis Island? Almost every political speech in the US ends with "May God bless America"; maybe we should get into the habit of adding, "and mend our every flaw."

Laboring on Labor Day
Exodus 16

Moses was not the kind of leader whom you would want to follow into the wilderness. The wilderness in this story is not like those often pictured on Sierra Club posters with lush forests, azure lakes, and thundering waterfalls. It is a desert, where water and food are hard to find, or nonexistent. The Israelites have just come out of Egypt—the place of their former slavery—and they are on their way to the promised land. In the immediately preceding story, they had nearly died of thirst. Moses didn't think to bring any bottled water. Now they have no food. Moses seems to have forgotten the chuck wagon also.

The people's need is real—they do have to eat and drink. But the expression of their need to Moses is hysterical and irrational (herewith paraphrased): "If only we had died by the hand of Yahweh in the land of Egypt, when we had pot roast and French bread, salads with spinach and cucumber and Ranch dressing. But you have brought us out into this wilderness to starve us to death." What an incredible accusation! The immediate need for food is expressed as a suicidal wish. The State of New Hampshire's license plate says Live Free or Die. The Israelites are saying the opposite, we'd rather die than be free if we also have to be hungry. And they romanticize the past—the long years of forced labor when they cried out to God now becomes a place where they ate like kings rather than slaves. Even worse, they have distorted the very purpose of God's act of deliverance. In their anxiety about the future, they have turned the God of grace and love into a sadistic God whose design for them is death rather than life. In fact, their assessment of their situation is framed by images of death: we would rather have died; God is out to kill us.

What has happened to the people who only six weeks before, stood on the shore of the Red Sea and sang a song of praise to God for rescuing them from the Egyptians? Why does this people, whom God has chosen as "a treasured possession out of all peoples" (19:5), now want to return to Egypt and belong to a tyrant? Why has the future that God has promised them in the land of Canaan lost its compelling power? The immediate lack of food is a problem, but is it that big a problem? As the story unfolds and food is provided, it becomes clear that food is not the primary issue.

Now, there is a natural explanation for what the manna probably was. There is an insect in the Sinai Peninsula that produces a kind of sweet, white substance. If the idea of eating something like that repels you, consider that honey is just such a substance. The substance called manna is rich in carbohydrates and sugar, and is still eaten by bedouin today, sometimes baked as cakes. But even if this natural explanation provides a historical explanation for the food, historical truth is not what the story is about (it rarely is in the Bible). This is why the author emphasizes the miraculous circumstances in which the manna appears. The manna shows up, on schedule, every morning, six days a week. But on the sixth day there is twice as much, and on the seventh day, none at all. The seventh day is the Sabbath, and the insects know enough to rest, even if some people don't.

The Sabbath is a kind of weekly Labor Day, and one of ancient Israel's greatest gifts to the world. It is a day to stop work completely. Orthodox Jews, for example, will put their Shabbat meal in a crockpot on Friday before sundown so they won't have to work on the Sabbath. So, there is twice as much manna on the day before the Sabbath—enough to last until the Sabbath is over. While any leftovers will spoil during the week, manna on the sixth day will not spoil overnight, so there will be food on the Sabbath day. And there is yet another miraculous aspect: no matter how much or how little the people gather, each person gets just what she needs.

This story is a narrative presentation of God's economy. There are enough resources to meet everyone's needs. The supply is regular and reliable. People do not have to compete. No one can have too much; no one has to get by with too little. Everyone has equal access to food if they are willing to do the work of gathering. In other words, there is equality of distribution. There is no necessity for accumulating more than one needs, no reason for hoarding resources. In fact, what is hoarded rots and stinks (except on Shabbat)! Similarly, work has the finite goal of gathering what one needs. Once those needs are met, there is no reason to work an extra day. It is time to rest, time to tell stories about the escape from Egypt, put a patch on your tent, build sandcastles with the kids, take a nap.

But it immediately becomes clear that the real problem is not the lack of *physical* food; it is the lack of spiritual *fortitude*. The real problem lies in Israel's anxiety over the future, and that anxiety stems from a lack of trust in God. The people's distrust appears in their attempts to achieve for themselves what God has already given them as gifts. They insist on laboring for what God has already labored. Moses tells them that God will give them the manna every day. It is literally their "daily bread," to recall that phrase from the Lord's Prayer. It is given for this day only (except, again, on the day before Shabbat). It requires a good deal of trust to rely on that bread, and on the God who gives it. What if it does not arrive tomorrow? It is no wonder that some of the people ignore Moses's instructions and hoard the manna overnight. What if it isn't enough? So, some of them go out on the Sabbath looking for more manna even though they have been given a double portion the day before.

In short, the story addresses a situation in which the need is real, but so is the likelihood that the need will be met. They should know that God will provide their daily bread, but they want to make their own provisions just in case. They become what we call "survivalists," stocking up on food in preparation for the day when they won't be able to find any. The author suggests that this situation is a test of the people's trust in God: "In that way I will test them, whether they will follow my instruction or not" (16:4). Some of them get an F.

What happens when they fail the test? Does God withdraw the food as a way of punishing them? No, the daily bread continues. What they lose is not God's care for them but the integrity of their relationship to God. The result is a most unflattering picture of people desperately working for something that is already offered to them as a gift, people laboring for more than they need. They work tirelessly to care for themselves, because they do not acknowledge how much God cares for them. As a result, their work in gathering food becomes obsessive. They must have more than a day's worth—more, more, more. They even work overtime on the Sabbath in order to produce what they desire, but already have!

If there is a story in the Bible that we should read over and over again in thinking about how God's economy works in contrast to our economy, this is it. Our economy says consume as much as you can ("shop 'til you drop"). Our economy says eat more than you need (see above, "Eat Less, Chew More"). Our economy says that it is not grace that governs distribution of resources, but greed. Or at least earning enough money is what makes it possible for people to have enough to eat. The only way for each to gather as much as they need (to use the words of our story) is for each to earn as much as they can.

The characters in the story cannot stop working. They are too anxious that they will not have enough simply from what God has given them and what they have already gleaned. So, they continue to work. To say that they cannot stop is to say that they cannot *shabat*, to use the Hebrew verb, and therefore they have no *Shabbat*, to use the noun—they have no Sabbath. That's what the root word for "Sabbath" means—"stop." Stop working. Stop laboring. Stop doing. Rest, relax, just be. Previously, we looked at the Sabbath tradition in regard to enjoying beach time, and observed that even God needs beach time to be "refreshed" (literally "re-souled"). The text that uses that word precedes it with the verb *shabat*, saying that God "stopped and was refreshed" (Exod 31:17, my translation). The reason that God could be refreshed was because God stopped (i.e., stopped working). But the characters in the Exodus story are not capable of cessation; they are workaholics.

Labor Day is a time for idleness, but our multitasking, goals-driven, type-A culture is haunted by the old proverb, "idle hands are the devil's workshop." Indeed, stigmatizing idleness is part of American religious tradition. It was our Puritan ancestors who invented what is called the "Protestant work ethic," which, as Albanese suggests, engendered a sense of "not having enough to rest content."[1] A recent book about "time management" makes a similar point. For medieval farmers, time was not abstract; it was concrete in nature's rhythm. But at some point "'time became a *thing* that you *used*,' a resource that you could feel bad about mishandling."[2] Puritans could easily support their views on industry by citing Scripture: "a little folding of the hands to rest, and poverty will come upon you like a robber" (Prov 6:10–11). The creation story says just the opposite: idle hands are the only way to rest. In fact, folded hands are the only hands that can be lifted up in prayer, because they are not collecting manna or holding a plow or scattering seeds or picking vegetables, or for that matter typing on a keyboard. Recently, someone in China began what soon became known as "the lying flat movement," in

---

1. Albanese, *America*, 109.
2. Williams, "Life's a Leaky Boat," C4.

which people who felt increasingly overworked simply stayed home and took to bed. "Rest is resistance," one of them writes.[3]

In Wendell Berry's novel *Remembering*, a character named Matt tells a story from when he was a boy. He had been working for his uncle in a cornfield, increasingly exhausted by the heat of the day, when his uncle said to stop and take a break, and they flung off their clothes and jumped in the cool water of a flowing stream. In fact, the rest of the day, they would stop whenever they got too tired and repeat the same refreshment. "I thought of all the times I'd worked in that field, hurrying to get through, to get to a better place, and it had been there all the time," he says, "redemption . . . a little flowing stream."[4]

---

3. Rosenblum, "Work Is a False Idol," A23.
4. Berry, *Remembering*, 58–59.

Indigenous Peoples' Day / Columbus Day

How the Gibeonites Became Israelites

Josh 2:1–24; 6:1–27; chap. 9

One Sunday morning I had scarcely walked through the church door when a frantic Sunday school teacher came running up to me in the hallway looking utterly frazzled.

"What am I going to do?" she said, "The lesson this morning is about Joshua's conquering Jericho and I read the story in the Bible and it has this horrific ending where they kill everyone in the city, including women and children! And God told them to do it! What am I going to do?" she repeated. "I don't believe all this."

"Then tell them what you believe," I said. "Tell them the truth, as you see it. Tell them that we do not believe in a God like that. Tell them that here the Bible is wrong."

When we had both calmed down a bit, we agreed that she could just tell the usual version of the story and leave out all the violence—after all, her pupils were elementary age.

Most people know the book of Joshua primarily because of the story of Jericho (Josh 2:1–24; 6:1–27), a victory achieved when the Israelites parade around the city for seven days with a trumpet band loud enough to knock down the walls. Even people who don't know the story itself have heard the spiritual, "Joshua Fit the Battle of Jericho." The word "fit," of course, is a dialectical version of the word *fought*, and Joshua is full of fighting. That's the major problem with the book for most of us, and the story of Jericho provides a good example. It's a colorful story that makes for great pictures in children's Bibles, but the primary color is blood red. After the walls of the city miraculously collapse, as God has planned, the

Israelites fall upon the hapless citizens and slaughter every one of them (well, almost; Rahab and family are spared, but we'll come back to that). As one verse puts it: "They devoted to destruction by the edge of the sword all in the city, both men and women, young and old, oxen, sheep, and donkeys" (6:21). That's the verse that so disturbed the teacher, who, to her credit, had actually read the full text and not just the version in the curriculum. Children's Bibles don't show that, thank God. We sanitize the story for kids, not wanting them to see the wanton violence, the brutality, the horror of genocide.

But maybe that is a mistake—surely not for the youngest children, but maybe for older ones, and certainly for youth. People ought to be exposed to such biblical stories at *some* stage in their learning before adulthood, lest a children's version is all they know (and may have ever read!). And they should read the stories not in the sanitized version, but in the original, with all its raw violence. Why? Because such stories raise fundamental questions about the nature of God and about what it means to be a human being, and wrestling with those questions should be part of our spiritual education. In the Jericho story, the violence is not initiated by humans alone, as the teacher correctly observed. God *orders* the violence, orders the slaughter. "To devote to destruction" is a sacred act of dedicating the victims (and sometimes even confiscated property) to God. This is *holy* war. The book of Joshua is probably not high on the list for family devotions, largely because of *this* horrible meaning of "devote." Skip over to Judges and you will find even more violence, including the charming story of Jael, a woman who kills an enemy general by giving him a sleeping potion and then driving a tent peg through his skull (Judg 4:17–24).

There's another perspective to take in studying this story, namely, a perspective in light of our own history in the Americas, a history that includes the near annihilation of Native Americans.[1] Only fairly recently has our secular calendar listed Indigenous Peoples' Day, alongside (or in place of) Columbus Day. Native Americans are the "Canaanites" in American history; just as according to Israel's national myth the Canaanites fell into Israelite hands, so the native peoples of the Americas succumbed to conquistadors in South America and conquests by US soldiers in North America. Our national myths tend to emphasize times of friendly relations between the European immigrants and the indigenous

---

1. See Mann, *1491*.

peoples, with Thanksgiving being one such occasion. But for indigenous peoples, the arrival of the colonists more often led to hostility, violence, disposition, and exile. Death came not only from warfare but also from diseases like smallpox (sometimes deliberately inflicted on them) to which indigenous peoples had no resistance. Within two hundred years of European colonization, their numbers were reduced from an estimated one hundred million to ten million. We celebrate Columbus as the one who "discovered" America, even though indigenous peoples had been here for thousands of years.[2] He may be joyfully celebrated as a hero to the descendants of the colonists, but to Native Americans his successors brought the Trail of Tears and Wounded Knee. Consider just the words of General William Tecumseh Sherman: "We must act with vindictive earnestness against the Sioux, even to their extermination, men, women, and children."[3] His words evoke the very horrors of the full Jericho story, in particular that verse left out of children's Bibles: "They devoted to destruction by the edge of the sword all in the city, both men and women, young and old" (6:21).

Here's something even stranger than reading the book of Joshua: sometimes the reason to bring your kids (and yourself) to Sunday school is to teach them (and yourself) what is wrong about the Bible. Parents often say, "I want my child to know the biblical stories." Well, at some point, when they are old enough, certainly by adolescence, they need to begin to wrestle with the question, Which stories are normative for me, and which must I reject? Which stories model for us how to be people of spiritual depth and moral integrity, and which stories show us how religion itself can turn us into inhuman monsters? If such a critical approach *does* sound strange to you, rest assured that the same approach is in the Bible itself. Many (probably most) biblical texts were not composed by a single individual, but by numerous writers and editors over a long period of time. The Bible values differences of opinion (see above, "Vagabond Stew").

I once attended a Columbia University seminar on the Hebrew Bible. The scholars in the seminar were disproportionately Jewish. At

---

2. Recent archaeological research has discovered footprints in the Southwest dating back over twenty-three thousand years.

3. On this quotation and more such travesties in American history and their analogies in the book of Joshua, see Mann, *Book of the Former Prophets*, 23–24. As noted there, similar atrocities were also committed by Native Americans, but not on such a scale.

the first seminar I was stunned at the aggressive manner in which these scholars attacked each other. And I do mean "attacked." One would have a thought that their lives were at stake over the meaning of some obscure Akkadian verb root. When the seminar was over, I asked one of the Jewish scholars whom I knew if it was always like this. "Oh yes," he said, looking utterly delighted, "don't you know that wherever there are two Jews there are three opinions?"

Well, the *Bible* is like that also. Wherever there is one opinion, there is likely to be another. Sometimes the "minority voice," as it were, is muted and subtle; at other times, there is an outright contradiction that stares you in the face and demands of you, "OK buddy, which one of us is right?" Was it God who incited King David to conduct a census (2 Sam 24:1) or Satan (1 Chr 21:1)? Shall we beat our swords into plowshares (Isa 2:4) or beat our plowshares into swords (Joel 3:10)? How can a person be "justified by faith apart from works" (Rom 3:28) if it is true that "faith by itself, if it has no works, is dead" (James 2:17)? Did Jesus die in utter despair, feeling abandoned by God (Mark 15:34) or in prayerful devotion to God (Luke 23:46) or satisfied that his mission was accomplished (John 19:30)?[4] All of which brings us back to the book of Joshua, but now to the subsequent story of Gibeon (Josh 9). (To prevent any confusion, note that the story is about Gibeonites, not "Gideonites," the latter sounding like the name of those people who place Bibles in motel rooms.)

The Gibeonites are a people who live inside the land of Canaan but pretend to live outside. Their pretension is rooted in fear. They know about the God of Israel and Israel's policy of genocide. No doubt they have heard about Jericho, although they carefully do not mention that in order not to give away their location. And they are masters at deception. For their little drama of deceit, the Gibeonite representatives dress up in costumes of ragged clothes, and carry props of moldy bread and broken beverage containers, as if they have been on a long journey from their faraway home.

Well, the Israelite officials fall for it and sign a peace treaty. You see, God has told them that it is okay to make peace with people who live outside of Canaan; only those who live inside are to be wiped out. With the latter God has forbidden any peace treaties or any kind of intermingling (especially, God forbid, romantic liaisons!). It's all in The Manual

---

4. Notoriously, the Gospel of Mark has several endings that suggest scribal (and theological) disagreements. See the notes in Meeks, gen. ed., *HarperCollins Study Bible* by C. Clifton Black.

(which is the book of Deuteronomy; 7:1–6; cf. 20:10–18). But here are the Israelites signing a treaty with the Gibeonites—outsiders—and handing out pens as if it's a wonderful day. It is true, of course, in the end, that Joshua discovers the deception, but by then it is too late. An oath sworn in the name of God must stand, even if the oath disobeys what God has said. And it is true that the Gibeonites are treated as second-class citizens, basically servants, but look what else they are—the altar guild! These outsiders, you might say, are "devoted" to the sacristy rather than to destruction; the hexed becomes sextons. Not only do they survive as part of Israel (however subservient); they work at the very heart of Israelite faith.

In the end, the way the author tells the Gibeonite story creates a revisionist opinion over against the orthodox. The orthodox is: follow the rules, looking neither to the left or the right, as God tells Joshua at the outset (1:7). Loyalty to God and country demand obedience. All Canaanites are infidels. Exterminate them. Show no mercy. Onward, Israelite soldiers. United we stand! This is the will of God, which, of course, we know absolutely. We are (now!) the insiders; no outsiders allowed. And don't even think of dating one of "those people." One God, one people, one land!

But then there's the story of the Gibeonites with all its complex irony. They seem to know the book of Deuteronomy better than the Israelites. They are outsiders, but they become insiders. They are deceptive, yet they are rewarded. They are accursed, yet they are blessed with life and citizenship. They are menial laborers, but they work in the Holy of Holies. All of a sudden, things are not neat and tidy. In fact, it looks like there are at least two peoples, and two lands (the Gibeonites having their own cities), and—perish the thought—maybe two gods, the God of Israel and the god of Gibeon with the name El (which looks suspiciously like Allah).[5]

In a word, oneness has become twoness; unity has become multiplicity; sameness, diversity. Now there are two gods, two peoples, and two lands. Outsiders and insiders together inherit the "land of promise." Actually (as I hinted before) it is that way with the Jericho story too, because there is an exception to the annihilation: the prostitute Rahab and her family are spared. Two adolescent Israelite spies had come to her house (we are not told why!) and when the Jericho intelligence finds out and send police to arrest them, she kindly hides them. She also shrewdly makes an agreement with them that in exchange for her kindness, the

---

5. Actually, the divine name Allah is etymologically related to the ancient Palestinian (and Israelite) God El.

conquering Israelite forces will treat her family kindly as well (Josh 2:12). The word for "kindness" is *ḥesed*, often translated "steadfast love," that quality of faithful loyalty which the prophet Micah says is what God most wants *devotion* to mean (Mic 6:8)!

Look what is happening! The outsiders are being included, however grudgingly. And doesn't the Gibeonite deception ring some bells? Why, wasn't it none other than Jacob, the namesake of Israel, whom God blessed despite his deceit of father and brother? And look: the Gibeonites enjoy mercy and grace without meriting it, and isn't that like Israel, of whom God has said, "I do not love you because you are mighty and righteous, but simply because I love you" (Deut 7:7–8)? What then shall we do with the preceding words in which God condemns the Canaanites to death (Deut 7:1–6)? Could it be that we must reinterpret the very nature of God? Could it be that we must accept the God of grace for everyone, and reject the xenophobic God who sanctions holy war? And we must make this distinction within the same chapter of The Manual?

To raise questions like these and to wrestle with them is why we have two or three opinions, not one, and it is why we ought to read these stories, warts and all. I suppose that the biblical editors (the latest ones anyway) could simply have eliminated passages that they didn't like. Later church leaders would do that—one named Marcion suggested getting rid of the entire Old Testament. But that isn't the way that the biblical editors operated. They were really conservative at heart. That is, they thought it important to repeat Israel's spiritual traditions, even when they didn't agree with them. To do otherwise would be to spoil the party, that party being the delight—as well as the solemn duty—of locking heads with someone across the table. Ultimately, to erase the offending traditions would be to give in to the orthodox line, the insistence that there must be one way, and only one way. And in their refusal to bow to that doctrine, the biblical editors were liberal indeed.

And then there is this, specifically with reference to books like Joshua: ancient Israel refused to sanitize their traditions and stories. They refused to show only the good parts and hide the bad parts. They were ruthlessly honest, to the point of hanging out their literary dirty linen for all to see. To use a contemporary word in vogue, their historical narratives were "transparent." They insisted on telling the truth, even when the truth was embarrassing, even shameful. To point to just one glaring example, there's the story of King David and his affair with Bathsheba, whose husband (Uriah) was off fighting battles for David while David was committing adultery with his wife. Uriah was so pious that he refused to have sex with her when he was on leave (it was forbidden by purity customs), so when she got pregnant by David, he would have known that he was not the father. David had Uriah's commanding officer send him into a lethal skirmish and abandon him to the enemy. When David receives the report of Uriah's death, he says, with cold callousness, "the sword devours now one and now another" (2 Sam 11:25). David is the messianic murderer.

The Israelites lived in a world at least as violent as ours, and they did not flinch from portraying that violence, even when they were critical of it. For ancient Israel, there was at heart a spiritual self-criticism that we can only admire. Part of that criticism is due to the prophetic heritage in which (as even The Manual, Deuteronomy, insists) it is sometimes necessary to say "God curse Israel" as well as "God bless Israel" (e.g., Deut 28:15–68). If we cannot imagine a public official in our country ending a speech with the words, "God curse America," then we need to ask ourselves why. If, as the Pledge of Allegiance says, the nation is "under God," does that not include standing under divine judgment?

In 2008, the Reverend Jeremiah Wright raised a storm of criticism when he delivered a sermon in which he suggested that instead of singing "God Bless America," we sing "God Damn America." The phrase sounds blasphemous, heretical, and unpatriotic. But the critics seemed oblivious to the way in which Wright's words echo those of the biblical prophets and the Mosaic covenant. When Wright said that his condemnation is "in the Bible," he was no doubt referring to the covenant tradition expounded most fully in the book of Deuteronomy. Israel is God's special people, but this election was not unconditional. The covenant had stipulations (e.g., the Ten Commandments). Obeying these stipulations would result in God's blessing; disobeying would result in God's curse (Deut 28). Blessings included material prosperity and national security; curses included drought, plague, military defeat, and exile. In short, God's curse is God's damnation.

Amos summarizes the prophetic version: "You only have I known / of all the families of the earth; / therefore I will punish you / for all your iniquities" (3:2). Many English settlers in America adopted the biblical model of a chosen nation—they were "God's new Israel"—and some of them understood that God was capable of both blessing and curse. In 1630, John Winthrop, for example, warned that if they disobeyed the "Articles" of the "Covenant," "the Lord will surely breake out in wrathe against us . . . and make us knowe the price of the breache of such a Covenant." Then the "blessing" that God had bestowed would be turned "into Cursses upon us."[6] As for Wright, he could point to the treatment of his Black ancestors, as well as Native Americans, as reason enough to invoke divine damnation. Our history is full of great accomplishments for which we may be proud; but it is also one of damnable failures for which we should repent. One may question the conditions that warrant saying "God damn America," but one may not question the principle of saying it without descending into moral arrogance and irresponsibility, which, in fact, *invite* damnation. If we want to invoke God's blessing, we must be willing to endure God's curse.

In August 2019, the *New York Times* launched The 1619 Project, with the intention of telling the full truth about the impact of chattel slavery in American history. The project's name recognizes the four-hundredth anniversary of the date on which White colonists first imported African slaves. Then president Trump was not happy, and countered with his 1776 Commission, an attempt to deny historical transparency about the racism that to this day troubles the nation, with George Floyd being only one in a long list of victims. In a parallel expression of disapproval, the politically appointed board of governors of the University of North Carolina denied tenure to the scholar who won the Pulitzer Prize for her journalism on the 1619 Project. Moreover, an ideologically motivated political action committee (PAC) was formed to "target local school board elections," prompting the director of the American Historical Association to warn that the move constituted an attempt "'to eliminate essential aspects of American history from the curriculum.'"[7] President Biden wisely abandoned the 1776 Commission. Next to the genocide of Native Americans, chattel slavery is another example of the dirty linen in our history. The 1619 Project resembles the chronological coincidence of the Indigenous Peoples' Day in that the recognition of Indigenous Peoples' Day began on the five-hundredth anniversary of 1492. (Compare Juneteenth, the

---

6. Winthrop, "Model."

7. Schuessler, "Support for Teachings on Race." The denial of the pernicious effects of racism—and particularly slavery and the Civil War—contrasts dramatically with the way Germany has acknowledged the evils of Nazism, on which see Wilkerson, *Caste*, 348: "They do not run from it. It has become a part of who they are because it is a part of what they have been. They incorporate it into their identity because it is, in fact, them."

anniversary of the declaration of the end of slavery in Texas in 1865, finally authorized as a national holiday in June 2021.)

We need the book of Joshua precisely because of its diversity and its competing voices and conflicting opinions, for the way it models transparency in historical ethos. We need Joshua because it forces us to ask painful and difficult questions about our own history, about who we are, and who God is, and who we think our enemy may or may not be. One of the lessons that it teaches us is that we are not as right as we like to think, that God is far bigger than we like to believe, and that the enemy often is more human than we want to admit. Strangely enough, in its presentation of Rahab, the kindhearted harlot, the Jericho story foreshadows a saying of Jesus: "Truly I tell you, the tax collectors and the prostitutes are going into the kingdom of God ahead of you" (Matt 21:31). Moreover, although there's certainly no indication that Jesus was aware of it, according to Matthew, Rahab was also a member of his family tree—his great-great-grandmother way back—so preserving the life of this Canaanite prostitute is an ironic turn in the path that led to the fulfillment of Jacob's promise, the birth of the Messiah (Matt 1:5).

Epilogue

The Two Books of God, Autobiographically

Scripture

When I entered my freshman year in college as a premed student, there was a meeting early on in an assembly hall at the University of North Carolina at Chapel Hill. I think the speaker was the dean of the medical school. All I remember of his talk was the point at which he told us to turn to our right and to our left, and that neither of those guys (they were all guys) would be in the premed program when they reached their senior year. I didn't understand the logic of this (wouldn't that have meant that *none* of us would make it?), but I also remember looking at my seatmates and thinking, "Tough luck, guys."

Two years later, I changed my major, and for two reasons: I got a D in chemistry and realized that science was not all that interesting to me (although it is now), and, second, I took a course in the introduction to the Old Testament. I had heard that the course was taught by a professor renowned for his spellbinding lectures, Dr. Bernard Boyd. His reputation proved to be well deserved. Increasingly as I listened to him, I became fascinated with a whole new intellectual world, the world of biblical criticism. He lectured without notes, standing on the stage with only the Bible in his hand. He often quoted Romantic poets and had what seemed like an enormous vocabulary. He always snuffed out his cigarette just before the class started, and he always stopped instantly when the dismissal bell rang, even in midsentence. I remember numerous times that the class—which must have been at least a hundred—uttered an audible sigh, because we wanted him to go on. And there were numerous times when somewhere in his lecture he would say something about the Bible that would literally send a chill up my spine. I was reacting phenomenologically! So, I changed my major from premed to religion, to the utter puzzlement of my friends. The world of biblical criticism had captivated me and does to this day. Like many people of liberal persuasion, entering that world saved me in the sense that it made it possible for me to incorporate my relatively conservative Southern Baptist piety into a framework that was intellectually challenging and, above all, inspiring.

The summer of my junior year, I went on an archaeological trip with Dr. Boyd to Israel, where we participated in a dig near the town of Arad. We also traveled to Jordan, Lebanon, Syria, Cyprus, and Greece. By then I was hooked on biblical studies, and little over a year later I entered Yale Divinity School, then went on to earn a PhD in Religious Studies and Hebrew Bible at Yale Graduate School. Eight years of teaching followed, at which point I found myself in a position that I had had no intention of holding before, a parish minister.

Nature

If Scripture is one world that has shaped the preceding sermons, the other, as you might guess, is the other book of God. That I first learned from my parents (along with the Bible). From a very young age, they took me to the beach every summer, where we would play in the water, build sandcastles, catch crabs and shrimp, gig for flounder, and run free in the sand dunes (most of which are now gone). They also took me to Hanging Rock State Park, where we hiked on trails and camped in hammocks, long before they became popular among some backpackers. The Park is part of the foothills of North Carolina (now only forty-five minutes from where I live), but it seemed like mountains to me. And then they did take us farther west to the mountains to stay in rustic motels like Doughton Park and drive along the Blue Ridge Parkway.

And there was another part of the book of nature: gardening. My father had a sizeable vegetable garden in our back yard. We grew all sorts of vegetables, and one summer my father rigged up a wagon that my older brother and I loaded up and took around the neighborhood, selling spring onions and lettuce and tomatoes. But he also had a much larger garden out in the country, loaned to him by a tobacco farmer (my father was a tobacco *buyer*!). If you stood at one end of a row of lima beans and looked down it to try to see the other end, you couldn't because of the curvature of the earth. You can imagine the enthusiasm that an eight-year-old would feel, being awakened at 5:00 a.m. on a Saturday morning, knowing that those endless rows of beans had to be picked. And Saturday afternoon they had to be shelled. My mother often recalled how she went into the kitchen early one morning and found a note from me, saying, "We've gone to work in the garden, unfortunately."

It's funny how things that you simply hated doing when you were a kid, partly because your parents *made* you do them, become things that you wouldn't give up for anything when you're an adult. Now, all three brothers have a little vegetable garden, no matter how small or how unproductive. And now, of course, I realize that my forced labor was *not* unfortunate. In the long run, it was one or the most fortunate experiences in my childhood because it put me in touch with the earth. I learned how things grow from seed to fruit, how important water and sunshine are. I learned how much work it takes to put food on a table. Even in midwinter, when we ate our homegrown and frozen lima beans or corn, eating was directly connected to gardening, and so all of us were directly connected to the earth and its fertility.

In a sense, the two books dovetailed chronologically during two summers before that Middle East trip: I went out to Wyoming and worked in the Grand Teton Lodge, first washing dishes and then promoted to the august position of soda jerk. Those experiences introduced me to a whole new type of mountains, not the rounded, forested Blue Ridge of North Carolina, but the majestic, rocky, snow-capped peaks of the West. Later, when living in Connecticut, I hiked and backpacked in the White Mountains of New Hampshire. Then my wife, Connie, introduced me to the enchanting high desert landscape around Santa Fe, New Mexico, and to the alpine mountains towering above, the Sangre de Cristo range of the Rockies. There I have spent wonderful days hiking and backpacking. Since moving to my church position in Winston-Salem many years later, I have often hiked and backpacked a beautiful ten-mile loop incorporating the Appalachian Trail in Grayson Highlands State Park, Virginia, where there are wild ponies, ridges with vast, open spaces, and vistas all the way over to the Blue Ridge. I have also returned to the West for Sierra Club backpacking trips in the Sierras and Wyoming. I am now in a retirement community, where I can step off my patio and be in the woods, to repeat a line from Oliver, "the door to the temple."

So, I have been steeped in the two books of God, and, in putting together this collection, I have realized how much the two are inseparable, that I cannot read the book of nature without reflecting on what I experience there through the lens of what I read in the book of Scripture; and yet the book of nature opens me to an encounter with the Creator in a unique way that inspires me to say, with Jacob, "how awesome is this place, none other than the gate of heaven."

A single word from, among others, the Psalms and John Muir and Mary Oliver, says it all: Glory!

Bibliography

Abram, David. *The Spell of the Sensuous: Perception and Language in a More-Than-Human World.* New York: Vintage, 1997.

Albanese, Catherine L. *America, Religions, and Religion.* Wadsworth Series in Religious Studies. Belmont, CA: Wadsworth, 1999.

Albee, Edward. Interview with Edward Albee by Jeffrey Brown. "Focus: A Life in Drama." *The News Hour with Jim Lehrer.* Aired June 5, 2003. Transcript and video. *American Archive of Public Broadcasting* (website). https://americanarchive.org/catalog/cpb-aacip_507-th8bg2j54c/.

Albright, W. F. "A Letter from the Time of Josiah," In *Ancient Near Eastern Texts Relating to the Old Testament,* edited by James B. Pritchard, 568. 3rd ed. with Supplement. Princeton: Princeton University Press, 1969.

Alter, Robert. *The Art of Biblical Narrative.* New York: Basic Books, 1981.

———. *Genesis: Translation and Commentary.* New York: Norton, 1996.

American Heritage College Dictionary. 4th ed. Boston: Houghton Mifflin, 2002.

Austin, Richard Cartwright. *Baptized into Wilderness: A Christian Perspective on John Muir.* Environmental Theology 1. Atlanta: John Knox, 1987.

———. *Beauty of the Lord: Awakening the Senses.* Environmental Theology 2. Atlanta: John Knox, 1988.

Bainton, Roland, trans. *The Martin Luther Christmas Book.* Philadelphia: Westminster, 1948.

Barbery, Muriel. *The Elegance of the Hedgehog.* Translated by Alison Anderson. New York: Europa, 2008.

Barbour, Ian G. *Religion in an Age of Science.* The Gifford Lectures 1 (1989–1991). San Francisco: Harper & Row, 1990.

Barr, Nevada. *Track of the Cat.* An Anna Pigeon Novel. New York: Putnam, 1993.

Barth, Karl. *Church Dogmatics* II/1, *The Doctrine of God, Part 1.* Edited by G. W. Bromiley and T. F. Torrance. Translated by T. H. L. Parker et al. Edinburgh: T. & T. Clark, 1957.

———. *Church Dogmatics* IV/1, *The Doctrine of Reconciliation, Part 1.* Edited by G. W. Bromiley and T. F. Torrance. Translated by G. W. Bromiley. Edinburgh: T. & T. Clark, 1956.

Bartlett, David L. *The Shape of Scriptural Authority.* Philadelphia: Fortress, 1983.

Bellah, Robert N. "Religious Pluralism & Religious Truth." *Reflections: Yale Divinity School.* (Summer/Fall 1995) 9–17.

———, et al. *Habits of the Heart: Individualism and Commitment in American Life.* 1st Perennial Library ed. New York: Harper & Row, 1986.

Benchley, Peter. *The Deep*. Garden City, NY: Doubleday, 1976.
———. *Jaws*. Garden City, NY: Doubleday, 1974.
Berlin, Adele, and Marc Zvi Brettler, eds. *The Jewish Study Bible*. Oxford: Oxford University Press, 2004.
Bernstein, Ellen. *The Splendor of Creation: A Biblical Ecology*. Cleveland: Pilgrim, 2005.
Berry, Wendell. *The Art of the Commonplace: Agrarian Essays of Wendell Berry*. Washington, DC: Counterpoint, 2002.
———. *Collected Poems: 1957–1982*. New York: North Point, 1984.
———. *Hannah Coulter: A Novel*. Washington, DC: Shoemaker & Hoard, 2004.
———. *Jayber Crow*. Berkeley, CA: Counterpoint, 2001.
———. *Remembering: A Novel*. San Francisco: North Point, 1988
———. *A Timbered Choir: The Sabbath Poems, 1979–1997*. Washington, DC: Counterpoint, 1998.
Biro, Adam. *Two Jews on a Train : Stories from the Old Country and the New*. Translated by Catherine Tihanyi. Chicago: University of Chicago Press, 2001.
Borg, Marcus. *The Heart of Christianity*. San Francisco: HarperSanFrancisco, 2003.
Borg, Marcus, and John Dominic Crossan. "Jesus' Final Week: Collision Course." *Christian Century*, March 20, 2007, 27–31.
Bovon, François. *Luke*. Vol. 1, *A Commentary on the Gospel of Luke 1:1—9:50*. Translated by Christine M. Thomas. 3 vols. Hermeneia. Minneapolis: Fortress, 2002.
Bronstein, Herbert, et al. *A Passover Haggadah: The New Union Haggadah*. Rev. ed. Harmondsworth, UK: Penguin, 1978.
Brock, Rita Nakashima, and Rebecca Ann Parker. *Proverbs of Ashes: Violence, Redemptive Suffering, and the Search for What Saves Us*. Boston: Beacon, 2002.
Brown, Francis, et al., *A Hebrew and English Lexicon of the Old Testament*. Oxford: Clarendon, 1966.
Brown, H. Jackson, Jr., comp. *A Father's Book of Wisdom*. Nashville: Rutledge Hill, 1989.
———, comp. *Life's Little Instruction Book: 511 Suggestions, Observations, and Reminders on How to Live a Happy and Rewarding Life*. Nashville: Rutledge Hill, 1991.
Brown, Raymond E. *The Birth of the Messiah: A Commentary on the Birth Narratives in Matthew and Luke*. Garden City, NY: Doubleday, 1977.
———. *The Death of the Messiah: From Gethsemane to the Grave: A Commentary on the Passion Narratives in the Four Gospels*. Anchor Bible Reference Library. New York: Doubleday, 1994.
Brown, William P. *The Ethos of the Cosmos: The Genesis of Moral Imagination in the Bible*. Grand Rapids: Eerdmans, 1999.
———. *The Seven Pillars of Creation: The Bible, Science, and the Ecology of Wonder*. Oxford: Oxford University Press, 2010.
Brueggemann, Walter. *In Man We Trust: The Neglected Side of Biblical Faith*. Atlanta: John Knox, 1972.
———. *The Prophetic Imagination*. Philadelphia: Fortress, 1978.
Brussat, Frederic, and Mary Ann Brussat. *Spiritual Literacy: Reading the Sacred in Everyday Life*. New York: Scribner, 1996.
Buber, Martin. *I and Thou*. Translated by Ronald Gregor Smith. New York: Scribner, 1958.
———. *To Hallow This Life: An Anthology*. Edited with an introduction by Jacob Trapp. 1958. Reprint, Westport, CT: Greenwood, 1974.

Burns, Ken, dir. *The National Parks: America's Best Idea*. Episode 1: "The Scripture of Nature." Aired September 27, 2009, on PBS. 6-episode miniseries. https://www.pbs.org/kenburns/the-national-parks/.
Capps, Donald. *The Child's Song: The Religious Abuse of Children*. Louisville: Westminster John Knox, 1995.
Clyde, Arthur G. "Keep Awake, Be Always Ready." In *The New Century Hymnal*, hymn no. 112. Cleveland: Pilgrim, 1995.
Cohen, Michael P. *The Pathless Way: John Muir and American Wilderness*. Madison: University of Wisconsin Press, 1984.
Cone, James H. *The Spirituals and the Blues*. Maryknoll, NY: Orbis, 1972.
Crites, Stephen. "The Narrative Quality of Experience." *Journal of the American Academy of Religion* 39 (1971) 291–311.
Crossan, John Dominic. *The Historical Jesus: The Life of a Mediterranean Jewish Peasant*. San Francisco: Harper, 1991.
Crowley, Michael, and Elizabeth Dias. "Trump's Visits to Church and Shrine Draw Fierce Rebukes from DC's Clergy." Politics. *New York Times*, June 3, 2020, A20. https://www.nytimes.com/2020/06/02/us/politics/trump-church.html/.
Crum, John M. C. "Now the Green Blade Rises." In *The New Century Hymnal*, hymn no. 238. Cleveland: Pilgrim, 1995.
Cummings, E. E. *100 Selected Poems*. An Evergreen Book. New York: Grove, 1954.
Curry, Andrew. "Who Were the First Europeans?" *National Geographic* 236 (2019) 94–113.
Davies, Paul. *God and the New Physics*. New York: Simon & Schuster, 1983.
Dickinson, Emily. "XLVI: A death-blow is a life-blow to some." In *The Complete Poems of Emily Dickinson*, with an introduction by her niece, Martha Dickinson Bianchi, 204. Boston: Little, Brown, 1926.
Dillard, Annie. *Pilgrim at Tinker Creek*. New York: Harper & Row, 1974.
Dupré, Louis. "Seeking Christian Interiority." *Christian Century*, July 16–23, 1997, 654–60.
Edwards, Jonathan. *A Personal Narrative*. https://www.apuritansmind.com/puritan-favorites/jonathan-edwards/biographical-writings/edwards-personal-narrative/.
Eliade, Mircea. *The Sacred and the Profane: The Nature of Religion*. New York: Harcourt, Brace & World, 1959.
Everson, William. "Annul in Me My Manhood." In *The Crooked Lines of God : Poems 1949–1954*. By Brother Antoninus. 3rd ed. Contemporary Poets Series. Detroit: University of Detroit Press, 1959.
Fackenheim, Emil L. *God's Presence in History*. The Deems Lectures 1968. New York: New York University Press, 1970.
Farmer, Paul. *Pathologies of Power: Health, Human Rights, and the New War on the Poor*. California Series in Public Anthropology 4. Berkeley: University of California Press, 2003.
Fideler, David. *Breakfast with Seneca: A Stoic Guide to the Art of Living*. New York: Norton, 2022.
Fox, Matthew. *Original Blessing: A Primer in Creation Spirituality; Presented in Four Parts, Twenty-Six Themes, and Two Questions*. Santa Fe, NM: Bear, 1983.
Frank, Adam. "The Truth May Yet Be Out There." Opinion. Guest Essay. *New York Times*, June 2, 2021, A19. https://www.nytimes.com/2021/05/30/opinion/ufo-sightings-report.html/.

Frankl, Victor E. *Man's Search for Meaning.* 1962. Reprint, New York: Washington Square, 1985.
Friedman, Richard Elliott. *Commentary on the Torah: With a New English Translation.* San Francisco: HarperSanFrancisco, 2001.
Gerhart, Mary, and Allan Russell. *Metaphoric Process: The Creation of Scientific and Religious Understanding.* Fort Worth: Texas Christian University Press, 1984.
Gilkey, Langdon. *Nature, Reality, and the Sacred: The Nexus of Science and Religion.* Theology and the Sciences. Minneapolis: Fortress, 1993.
Glassman, Gary, et al., dirs. *Native America.* Episode 2: "Cities of the Sky." Aired November 13, 2018 on PBS. 4-episode miniseries. https://www.pbs.org/video/cities-of-the-sky-smcd2a/.
Goldberg, Nathan. *Passover Haggadah.* New York: Ktav, 1966.
"Good Question." *Christian Century,* May 17, 2003, 6–7.
Godwin, Gail. *The Finishing School.* New York: Viking, 1984.
Gottwald, Norman K. *The Tribes of Yahweh: A Sociology of the Religion of Liberated Israel.* Maryknoll, NY: Orbis, 1979.
Greenberg, Moshe. *Understanding Exodus.* Heritage of Biblical Israel Series 2. New York: Behrman House, 1969.
———. *Understanding Exodus: A Holistic Commentary on Exodus 1–11.* 2nd ed. Edited and with a foreword by Jeffrey H. Tigay. Eugene, OR: Cascade Books, 2013.
Greene, Brian. *The Elegant Universe: Superstrings, Hidden Dimensions, and the Quest for the Ultimate Theory.* 2nd ed. New York: Norton, 2003.
Hamid, Mohsin. "We Are All Migrants." *National Geographic* 236.2 (2019) 18–20. https://www.nationalgeographic.com/magazine/article/we-all-are-migrants-in-the-21st-century/.
Hamill, Susan as quoted in "Unjustly Taxed: The Bible and Politics in Alabama." *Christian Century* 121/19 (September 2004) 28–33.
Hansen, Ron. *Atticus.* New York: HarperCollins, 1996.
Haruf, Kent. *Benediction.* New York: Vintage.
Hauerwas, Stanley. *A Community of Character: Toward a Constructive Christian Social Ethic.* Notre Dame, IN: University of Notre Dame Press, 1981.
Hays, Richard B. *The Faith of Jesus Christ: The Narrative Substructure of Galatians 3:1— 4:11.* Biblical Resource Series. 2nd ed. Grand Rapids: Eerdmans, 2002.
Heschel, Abraham Joshua. *God in Search of Man.* New York: Farrar, Straus & Giroux, 1955.
———. *The Prophets: An Introduction.* Harper Torchbooks. New York: Harper, 1962.
———. *The Sabbath: Its Meaning for Modern Man.* New York: Wolff, 1951.
Hiebert, Theodore. *The Yahwist's Landscape: Nature and Religion in Early Israel.* New York: Oxford University Press, 1996.
Hinton, Lynne, and Jan Hensley. *Friendship Cake.* San Francisco: HarperSanFrancisco, 2000.
Hopkins, Gerard Manley. "God's Grandeur." https://www.poetryfoundation.org/poems/44395/gods-grandeur.
———. "Pied Beauty." https://www.poetryfoundation.org/poems/44399/pied-beauty.
Hosick, David. "After a Child Dies." *Christian Century* 120, June 2003, 45.
Hubler, Shawn. "The Year Summer Came with Dread." *New York Times,* July 30, 2021, A10. https://www.nytimes.com/2021/07/28/us/the-end-of-summer.html/.

Issa, Kobayashi. "Napped Half the Day." https://mypoeticside.com/show-classic-poem-13891/.
Jabr, Ferris. "The Social Life of Forests." *New York Times Magazine*, December 6, 2020, 32–41. https://www.nytimes.com/interactive/2020/12/02/magazine/tree-communication-mycorrhiza.html/.
Jenkins, Philip. *Climate, Catastrophe, and Faith : How Changes in Climate Drive Religious Upheaval*. New York : Oxford University Press, 2021.
Jensen, Robin M. *The Substance of Things Seen: Art, Faith, and the Christian Community*. The Calvin Institute of Christian Worship Liturgical Studies Series. Grand Rapids: Eerdmans, 2004.
Jesus Mafa (community), painters. *Jesus among the Teachers*. Painting. From Art in the Christian Tradition, a project of the Vanderbilt Divinity Library, Nashville, Tennessee. https://diglib.library.vanderbilt.edu/act-imagelink.pl?RC=48280. Original source: http://www.librairie-emmanuel.fr.
John of Damascus. "Come You Faithful, Raise the Strain." In *The New Century Hymnal*, hymn no. 230. Cleveland: Pilgrim, 1995.
Kalmanofsky, Jeremy. "Parents at Prayer." *Tikkun* 18 (2003) 56–62.
Kaufman, Gordon D. *In Face of Mystery: A Constructive Theology*. Cambridge: Harvard University Press, 1993.
Kelsey, David H. *Human Anguish and God's Power*. Current Issues in Theology. Cambridge: Cambridge University, 2021.
Klein, Allen. *The Healing Power of Humor*. Los Angeles: Tarcher, 1989.
Ko, Genevieve. "Baking That Rises to Meet the Moment." Food. *New York Times*, September 22, 2021, D2. https://www.nytimes.com/2021/09/21/dining/easy-delicious-desserts-no-mixer.html/.
Küng, Hans. *Eternal Life? Life after Death as a Medical, Philosophical, and Theological Problem*. Translated by Edward Quinn. 1985. Reprint, Eugene, OR: Wipf & Stock, 2003.
Kushner, Lawrence. *Honey from the Rock—Ten Gates of Jewish Mysticism*, 15–16, quoted in *The Daybook: A Contemplative Journal* (Autumn, 1992), 12.
Lanchester, Alex, and Matthew Wright, dirs. *Kingdoms of the Sky*. Episode 1: "Rockies." Aired on PBS on July 11, 2018. 3-episode miniseries. https://www.pbs.org/show/kingdoms-sky/.
Lane, Belden C. *The Solace of Fierce Landscapes: Exploring Mountain and Desert Spirituality*. New York: Oxford University Press, 1998.
———. "Stalking the Snow Leopard: A Reflection on Work." *Christian Century*, January 4–11, 1984, 13–16.
Laozi. *Tao Te Ching: A New English Version*. With a foreword and notes by Stephen Mitchell. New York: Harper & Row, 1988.
Las Vegas Sun. "Where I Stand: Will 105th Congress Be More Kind to Our Environment?" News. *Las Vegas Sun*, November 29, 1996. https://lasvegassun.com/news/1996/nov/29/where-i-stand-will-105th-congress-be-more-kind-to-/.
Lawrence, D. H. *Phoenix: The Posthumous Papers*. Edited and with an introduction by Edward D. McDonald. New York: Viking, as quoted in *The Daybook: A Contemplative Journal* (Summer 1996) 11–12.
Lerner, Michael. *The Left Hand of God : Taking Back Our Country from the Religious Right*. San Francisco: HarperSanFrancisco, 2006.
Lewis, C. S. *The Lion, the Witch, and the Wardrobe*. London: Bles, 1950.

Lindbeck, George A. *The Nature of Doctrine: Religion and Theology in a Postliberal Age.* Philadelphia: Westminster, 1984.

Lobel, Arnold. *Owl at Home.* New York: Harper, 1975.

Luisi, Pier Luigi. *The Emergence of Life: From Chemical Origins to Synthetic Biology.* Cambridge: Cambridge University Press, 2006.

Luoma, Jon R. *The Hidden Forest: The Biography of an Ecosystem.* New York: Holt, 1999.

Lustbader, Wendy. *Counting on Kindness: The Dilemmas of Dependency.* Quoted in *The Daybook: A Contemplative Journal.* (Winter, 1999) 26.

Mann, Charles C. *1491: New Revelations of the Americas before Columbus.* New York: Knopf, 2005.

Mann, Mark H. "Wesley and the Two Books: John Wesley, Natural Philosophy, and Christian Faith." In *Connecting Faith and Science: Philosophical and Theological Inquiries*, edited by Matthew Nelson Hill and Wm. Curtis Holtzen, 1:11–30. Claremont Studies in Science and Religion 1. Claremont: Claremont Press, 2017.

Mann, Thomas W. *The Book of the Former Prophets.* Eugene, OR: Cascade Books, 2011.

———. *The Book of the Torah: The Narrative Integrity of the Pentateuch.* Atlanta: John Knox, 1988.

———. *The Book of the Torah.* 2nd ed. Eugene, OR: Cascade Books, 2013.

———. *God of Dirt: Mary Oliver and the Other Book of God.* Cambridge, MA: Cowley, 2004.

———. "Guest Editorial." *Interpretation* 65 (2011) 337–39.

———. "Job and *The Color Purple.*" *Prism: A Theological Forum for the United Church of Christ* 5 (1990) 69–79.

———. "Passover: The Time of Our Lives." *Interpretation* 50 (1996) 240–50.

Marcuse, Herbert. *An Essay on Liberation.* Boston: Beacon, 1969.

Margulis, Lynn. "Talking on the Water." *Sierra* 79 (1994) 72.

Margulis, Lynn, and Dorion Sagan. *What Is Life?* Berkeley: University of California Press, 1995.

Mathews, Donald G. *Religion in the Old South.* Chicago History of American Religion. Chicago: University of Chicago Press, 1977.

Matthiessen, Peter. *The Snow Leopard.* New York: Penguin, 1987.

McBride, S. Dean Jr. "Polity of the Covenant People: The Book of Deuteronomy." In *Constituting the Community: Studies on the Polity of Ancient Israel in Honor of S. Dean McBride Jr.*, edited by John T. Strong and Steven S. Tuell, 17–33. Winona Lake, IN: Eisenbrauns, 2005.

———. "Polity of the Covenant People: The Book of Deuteronomy." *Interpretation* 41 (1987) 229–44.

McCarthy, Cormac. *All the Pretty Horses.* In *The Border Trilogy.* New York: Everyman's Library, 1999.

McConnell, Frank. "Introduction." In *The Bible and the Narrative Tradition*, 3–18. New York: Oxford University Press, 1986.

———, ed. *The Bible and the Narrative Tradition.* New York: Oxford University Press, 1986.

McCutcheon, John. "Immigrant" (song) and interview on *David Holt's State of Music*, PBS, Season 5, Episode 3. Aired May 15, 2021. Song available on YouTube and other media.

McFague, Sallie. *Speaking in Parables: A Study in Metaphor and Theology.* Philadelphia: Fortress, 1975.

Meeks, M. Douglas. *God the Economist: The Doctrine of God and Political Economy.* Minneapolis: Fortress, 1989.

Meeks, Wayne A., gen. ed. *The HarperCollins Study Bible: New Revised Standard Version, with the Apocryphal/Deuterocanonical Books.* New York: HarperCollins, 1993.

Meyers, Carol L. *The Tabernacle Menorah: A Synthetic Study of a Symbol from the Biblical Cult.* American Schools of Oriental Research Dissertation Series 2. Missoula, MT: Scholars, 1976.

Miller, David L. "Playing the Game to Lose." In *Theology of Play*, by Jürgen Moltmann, 99–110. Translated by Reinhard Ulrich. New York: Harper & Row, 1972.

Miller, Patrick D. *Interpreting the Psalms.* Philadelphia: Fortress, 1986.

———. *The Religion of Ancient Israel.* Library of Ancient Israel. Louisville: Westminster John Knox, 2000.

Mitchell, Kenneth R., and Herbert Anderson. *All Our Losses, All Our Griefs: Resources for Pastoral Care.* Louisville: Westminster John Knox, 1983.

Moltmann, Jürgen. *Theology of Hope: On the Ground and the Implications of a Christian Eschatology.* New York: Harper & Row, 1967.

Montgomery, James. "Journey to Gethsemane." In *The New Century Hymnal*, hymn no. 219. Cleveland: Pilgrim, 1995.

Moore, Michael, dir. *Fahrenheit 9/11.* 2004. Written by Michael Moore. Starring Michael Moore et al. Produced by Jim Czarnecki et al. DVD. N.p.: Sony Pictures Home Entertainment, 2004. Available to stream on Tubitv.com/.

Morreall, John. *Taking Laughter Seriously.* Albany: State University of New York Press, 1983.

Motsinger, Kathryn. "Disease Taught Lessons about Medicine, about Life." *Winston-Salem Journal*, April 4, 2001, A1.

Muir, John. *Nature Writings.* Selected and with notes by William Cronon. Library of America 92. New York: Library of America, 1997.

Murphy, Roland E. *The Tree of Life: An Exploration of Biblical Wisdom Literature.* 3rd ed. Grand Rapids: Eerdmans, 2002.

Neale, J. M., and Henry Sloane Coffin, trans. "O Come, O Come Emmanuel." In *The New Century Hymnal*, hymn no. 116. Cleveland: Pilgrim, 1995.

Nelson, Gertrud Mueller. *To Dance with God: Family Ritual and Community Celebration.* New York: Paulist, 1986.

Nhat Hanh, Thich. *Peace Is Every Step: The Path of Mindfulness in Everyday Life.* Edited by Arnold Kotler. New York: Bantam, 1991.

Obama, Barack. Interview with Barack Obama by Scott Pelley. *60 Minutes.* Aired November 15, 2020. https://www.youtube.com/watch?v=mAFv55o47ok/.

O'Connor, Flannery. *The Habit of Being: Letters.* Edited and with an introduction by Sally Fitzgerald. New York: Vintage, 1980.

Oliver, Mary. *American Primitive.* Boston: Little, Brown, 1978.

———. *Blue Pastures.* New York: Harcourt Brace, 1991.

———. *The Leaf and the Cloud.* Boston: Da Capo, 2000.

———. *New and Selected Poems.* Boston: Beacon, 1992.

———. *Twelve Moons.* Boston: Little, Brown, 1979.

———. *Upstream: Select Essays.* New York: Penguin, 2016.

———. *Winter Hours: Prose, Prose Poems, and Poems.* New York: Houghton Mifflin, 1999.

Olson, Duane. *The Depths of Life: Paul Tillich's Understanding of God*. Macon, GA: Mercer University Press, 2019.

Otto, Rudolf. *The Idea of the Holy: An Inquiry into the Non-Rational Factor in the Idea of the Divine and Its Relation to the Rational*. 2nd ed. Translated by John Harvey. New York: Oxford University Press, 1950.

Patrick, Dale. *The Rhetoric of Revelation in the Hebrew Bible*. Overtures to Biblical Theology. Minneapolis: Fortress, 1999.

Pilgrim, Richard B. "Ritual." In *Introduction to the Study of Religion*, edited by T. William Hall, 508–75. New York: Harper & Row, 1978.

Powers, Richard. *The Overstory*. New York: Norton, 2018.

Public Broadcasting Service (PBS). *PBS News Hour*. "Peru's Indigenous People Call for Protections against Environmental Threats." Transcript of a report by Geoffrey Brown, which aired on December 11, 2014. https://www.pbs.org/newshour/show/perus-indigenous-people-call-environmental-protections/.

———. *PBS News Hour*. "The Race to Develop Quantum Technology." Report by Christopher Booker, featuring an interview of David Alshalom, June 23, 2019. https://www.pbs.org/video/the-race-to-develop-quantum-technology-is-getting-crowded-1561313128/.

Rasmussen, Larry L. *Earth Community, Earth Ethics*. Ecology and Justice. Maryknoll, NY: Orbis, 1996.

Reid, John, and Thomas E. Lovejoy. "We Can Still Save Earth's Forests." Opinion. Guest Essay. *New York Times*, November 3, 2021, A23. https://www.nytimes.com/2021/11/02/opinion/climate-change-glasgow-deforestation.html/.

Reith, Adrian, and Martin Wroe. *101 Things to Do With a Dull Church*. Downers Grove, IL: InterVarsity, 1994.

Renkl, Margaret. "Looking for Light on the Longest Night of the Year." *New York Times*, December 21, 2020, A19. https://www.nytimes.com/2020/12/20/opinion/winter-solstice.html/.

Rohr, Richard. *The Universal Christ: How a Forgotten Reality Can Change Everything We See, Hope For, and Believe*. New York: Convergent, 2019.

Roosevelt, Theodore, as quoted in Century Marks. *Christian Century* 122/12, June 14, 2005, 6.

Rosenblum, Cassady. "Work Is a False Idol." Opinion. Guest Essay. *New York Times*, August 25, 2021, A23. https://www.nytimes.com/2021/08/22/opinion/lying-flat-work-rest.html/.

Rowe, Jonathan. "The Common Good." *Sierra* 90/4, July/August 2005, 54–63. https://vault.sierraclub.org/sierra/200507/commongood.asp/.

Rowling, J. K. *Harry Potter and the Sorcerer's Stone*. New York: Levine, 1998.

Sarton, May. "AIDS." In *Confronting AIDS through Literature: The Responsibilities of Representation*, edited Judith Laurence Pastore, 147–48. Urbana: University of Illinois Press, 1993.

Sanders, Scott Russell. *Staying Put: Making a Home in a Restless World*. Concord Library. Boston: Beacon, 1993.

Schlosser, Eric. "A Grief Like No Other." *Atlantic Monthly* 280.3, September 1, 1997, 37–76. https://www.theatlantic.com/magazine/archive/1997/09/a-grief-like-no-other/376944/.

Schuessler, Jennifer. "Support for Teachings on Race." *New York Times*, June 17, 2021, D1, 5. https://www.nytimes.com/2021/06/16/arts/critical-race-theory-scholars.html/.

Scott, Bernard Brandon. *Hear Then the Parable: A Commentary on the Parables of Jesus*. Minneapolis: Fortress, 1989.

Sears, Edmund H. "It Came upon the Midnight Clear." In *The New Century Hymnal*, hymn no. 131. Cleveland: Pilgrim, 1995.

Seed, John, et al. *Thinking Like a Mountain: Towards a Council of All Beings*. Philadelphia: New Society, 1988.

Segal, Alan F. *Life after Death: A History of the Afterlife in the Religions of the West*. New York: Doubleday, 2004.

Simard, Suzanne. *Finding the Mother Tree: Discovering the Wisdom of the Forest*. New York: Knopf, 2021.

Sinclair, Donna. *The Spirituality of Gardening*. Kelowna, BC: Northstone, 2005.

Soelle, Dorothee. *Suffering*. Translated by Everett R. Kalin. Philadelphia: Fortress, 1975.

Spielberg, Steven, dir. *Jaws*. 1975. Based on the novel by Peter Benchley. Screenplay by Peter Benchley and Carl Gottlieb. Starring Roy Scheider et al. DVD. Universal City, CA: Universal, 2000. Available to rent/buy on Amazon Prime Video.

Stendl-Rast, David. *Gratefulness, the Heart of Prayer*, as quoted in *The Daybook: A Contemplative Journal*. (Spring, 1993) 11.

———. "Learning to Die," as quoted in *The Daybook: A Contemplative Journal* (Winter, 1996) 36.

Smith, Huston. *The World's Religions*. 2nd ed. San Francisco: HarperSanFrancisco, 1991.

Spring, David, and Eileen Spring, eds. *Ecology and Religion in History*. New York: Harper & Row, 1974.

Spurlock, Morgan, dir. *Super Size Me*. Written by Morgan Spurlock. Starring Morgan Spurlock et al. DVD. New York: Hart Sharp Video, 2004. Available on Freevee (streaming service).

Stroup, George W. *The Promise of Narrative Theology: Recovering the Gospel in the Church*. Atlanta: John Knox, 1981.

Swimme, Brian, and Thomas Berry. *The Universe Story: From the Primordial Flaring Forth to the Ecozoic Era—A Celebration of the Unfolding of the Cosmos*. San Francisco: HarperSanFrancisco, 1994.

Tanikawa, Suntaro. "River." Quoted in *The Daybook: A Contemplative Journal* (Summer, 1997) 30.

Tillich, Paul. *The Shaking of the Foundations*. New York: Scribner, 1948.

Tournier, Michel. *The Wind Spirit: An Autobiography*. Translated by Arthur Goldhammer. Boston: Beacon, 1988. As quoted in *The Daybook: A Contemplative Journal* (Summer, 1995) 29.

Trepp, Leo. *Judaism: Development and Life*. Belmont, CA: Wadsworth, 1982.

Trible, Phyllis. *God and the Rhetoric of Sexuality*. Overtures to Biblical Theology 2. Philadelphia: Fortress, 1978.

United Church of Christ. *Book of Worship*. New York: United Church of Christ Office for Church Life and Leadership, 1986.

———. *The New Century Hymnal*. Cleveland: Pilgrim, 1995.

United States Conference of Catholic Bishops. "Renewing the Earth: An Invitation to Reflection and Action on Environment in Light of Catholic Social Teaching.

A Pastoral Statement of the United States Catholic Conference." (November 14, 1991) https://www.usccb.org/resources/renewing-earth/.

United Jewish Appeal. *United Jewish Appeal Israel Independence Day Haggadah*. Based on a text composed by Shlomo Goren, with foreword by Joseph H. Lookstein. New York: United Jewish Appeal, 1979.

Wahlleben, Peter. *The Hidden Life of Trees: What They Feel, How They Communicate: Discoveries from a Secret World*. Translated by Jane Billinghurst. Vancouver, BC: David Suzuki Institute, 2016.

Wallis, Jim. *God's Politics: Why the Right Gets It Wrong and the Left Doesn't Get It*. 1st HarperCollins Paperback ed. San Francisco: HarperSanFrancisico, 2006.

Westermann, Claus. *Genesis 1–11: A Commentary*. Minneapoilis: Augsburg, 1984.

———. *Genesis 12–26: A Commentary*. Minneapolis: Augsburg, 1985.

Wikipedia (website) "Pelikan, Jaroslav." https://en.wikipedia.org/wiki/Jaroslav_Pelikan/.

Wilkerson, Isabel. *Caste: The Origins of Our Discontents*. New York: Random House, 2020.

Williams, John. "Life's a Leaky Boat: Just Plug the Biggest Holes." Review of *Four Thousand Weeks: Time Management for Mortals*, by Oliver Burkeman. *New York Times*. (Aug. 12, 2021) C4. https://www.nytimes.com/2021/08/11/books/review-four-thousand-weeks-time-management-oliver-burkeman.html/.

Wink, Walter. *The Human Being: Jesus and the Enigma of the Son of Man*. Minneapolis: Fortress, 2002.

Winter, Miriam Therese, and Katharine Lee Bates. "How Beautiful, Our Spacious Skies." In *The New Century Hymnal*, hymn no. 594. Cleveland: Pilgrim, 1995.

Winthrop, John. "A Model of Christian Charity." Teaching American History (website). https://teachingamericanhistory.org/document/a-model-of-christian-charity/.

Wolff, Hans Walter. *Joel and Amos*. Translated by Waldemar Janzen et al. Hermeneia. Philadelphia: Fortress, 1977.

Wolterstorff, Nicholas. *Lament for a Son*. Grand Rapids: Eerdmans, 1987.

World Book Encyclopedia. Vol. 19, s.v. "Time." 24 vols. Chicago: World Book, 1988.

Worster, Donald. *A Passion for Nature: The Life of John Muir*. Oxford: Oxford University Press, 2008.

Wright, Robert. *Why Buddhism Is True: The Science and Philosophy of Meditation and Enlightenment*. New York: Simon & Schuster, 2017.

Wuthnow, Robert. *Creative Spirituality: The Way of the Artist*. Berkeley: University of California Press, 2001.

Wyatt, Nick. *The Mythic Mind: Essays on Cosmology and Religion in Ugaritic and Old Testament Literature*. BibleWorld. London: Equinox, 2005.

Yates, Peter, dir. *The Deep*. 1977. Based on the novel by Peter Benchley Screenplay by Tracy Keenan Wynn. Starring Jacqueline Bisset et al. DVD. Culver City, CA: Columbia Tristar Home Entertainment, 2004. Available to rent/buy on Amazon Prime Video.

www.ingramcontent.com/pod-product-compliance
Lightning Source LLC
Chambersburg PA
CBHW021649230426
43668CB00008B/563